I0820050

THE ROAD TO CISTERNA

THE ROAD TO CISTERNA

DARBY'S RANGERS AND THEIR MOST CONSEQUENTIAL BATTLE IN WORLD WAR II

As Told by the U.S. Army Rangers in the Mediterranean Theater, 1942–1945

DAVID LYLE WILLIAMS

LOUISIANA STATE UNIVERSITY PRESS
BATON ROUGE

Published by Louisiana State University Press
lsupress.org

Manufactured in the United States of America
First printing

DESIGNER: Michelle A. Neustrom
TYPEFACES: Minion Pro, text; Abolition, display
PRINTER AND BINDER: Sheridan Books, Inc.

JACKET PHOTOGRAPH: Soldiers of the 1st Ranger Battalion march across the hills of Algeria in early 1943. (U.S. Army Signal Corps photo)

All maps created to scale by Arthur White and designed by Kimberly Morse.

Cataloging-in-Publication Data are available from the Library of Congress.
ISBN 978-0-8071-8503-2 (cloth: alk. paper) — ISBN 978-0-8071-8562-9 (pdf) — ISBN 978-0-8071-8561-2 (epub)

To Col. James B. Lyle
and the men of Darby's Rangers

Col. James B. Lyle, World War II Ranger
U.S. Army Infantry OCS Hall of Fame, 1959
U.S. Army Ranger Hall of Fame, 2003

. . . Send me.

(Isaiah 6:8)

CONTENTS

ILLUSTRATIONS

MAPS

FIGURES

---- ILLUSTRATIONS ----

FOREWORD

Ranger Warren Evans (deceased) agreed to write this foreword, but advanced age caught him before he could do it. Over numerous telephone calls, Mr. Evans told me what he would have written, and I penned the foreword for Mr. Evans, who signed the original draft on 30 April 2015. What follows is an abbreviated version of the original draft.

There are days when I wonder how in the world I made it back alive, when so many others didn't. . . . I ask, "Why me, God?" . . . Not a day goes by that I don't remember. . . .

As the first sergeant major for the 1st Ranger Battalion, known as Darby's Rangers, I received the first battlefield commission in the American army in North Africa. If you count Dieppe, we invaded enemy-held beaches five times. After a while, you think that you won't make it through the next one.

What do I remember? Close combat is personal. You see the faces of those you are fighting—especially their eyes. You remember the look on the face of someone you just killed, the smells and the sounds of killing. You remember the men you lost—you carry survivor guilt. And perhaps worst of all, you keep it bottled up inside you because you know that no one else would understand unless they had experienced the same things. Mentally, you are alone, and you remember. . . .

Our last combat came near Cisterna di Littoria, Italy, where 767* Rangers went on a mission deep behind enemy lines, only to find themselves outnumbered almost eighty to one. During this battle, I remember an explosion. Suffering a concussion, I have little memory of anything else until I came to in a German prison camp weeks later. They told me what happened next.

* For many years, 767 was the stated number of Rangers from the 1st and 3rd Ranger Battalions on the Cisterna mission.

Warren "Bing" Evans, Honorary Sergeant Major of the U.S. Army 75th Ranger Regiment. Photograph taken at 2nd Ranger Battalion, Fort Lewis, Washington, 2005. Courtesy Mark Evans.

We ran out of ammunition, and the Germans began tightening the noose around us. They force-marched a group of Rangers who had surrendered toward my company's position. We old timers could not imagine surrendering, so I ordered my men to shoot the German guards. As we fired, the Germans bayoneted several Rangers in the back. We fired again and more Rangers were bayoneted in the back. Someone called for a ceasefire, but some Ranger fired anyway. With that the German guards dropped to the ground and began spraying the prisoners with automatic weapons fire. Unable to imagine causing the deaths of their own comrades, many of the younger Rangers threw down their weapons and raised their hands. I don't remember any of this; my mind blocked it out, but I do remember being a prisoner of the Germans.

Before being transported to a German POW camp, I was trucked into Rome and paraded around the Colosseum with other prisoners, much like the Romans did in ancient times. I escaped and was recaptured three times. After the third attempt, I was forced to watch the Germans execute an entire Polish family for having fed me, because feeding a starving escapee was a crime punishable by death in war-torn Germany. The brutality I witnessed over fifteen months as a POW is something no one would want to remember, but which I could never forget.

Because I was the first sergeant major in the original 1st Ranger Battalion, I was asked to serve as the Honorary Sergeant Major for the U.S. Army 75th Ranger Regiment, headquartered at Fort Benning, Georgia. Our legacy from World War II has passed down to today's active duty Army Rangers, and since 1999 it is being preserved by a group of Ranger family members, led by David Lyle Williams, the nephew of Ranger James B. Lyle.

A number of authors have written books about us. I've come to believe that writing about history is akin to being in combat. Two men can be in a foxhole together during a firefight. Afterward you ask each to relate what happened, and you might think they were in different battles. Writing is like that; no two people will say the same thing the same way. But it is important to tell the stories, so we keep on telling them. Some are new, some are old and told in a different way, and our future is now in the hands of those who choose to remember us.

Warren "Bing" Evans (deceased)
Honorary Sergeant Major of the Regiment, 1992–2008
U.S. Army, 75th Ranger Regiment

PREFACE

World War II, the deadliest, most destructive war in history, with millions of lives lost, is almost certainly the most written about war. Much of the writing hovers above the blood and gore of the battlefield, concentrating on strategy, troop movements, the doings of generals and politicians. In contrast to that, this book deals with the actual experience of "being there" in the thick of the fighting. Wherever possible, Darby's Rangers tell their stories in their own words. They were America's toughest soldiers, the ones with the most intensive training and the ones sent into the most difficult and dangerous situations, culminating in the Battle of Cisterna in 1944. The reader will get to know the individual stories of more than 160 World War II Rangers, who tell in their own words about their sacrifices and their accomplishments both in combat and off the battlefield.

The story of the World War II American Ranger has its roots in Britain. After France surrendered to Germany in June of 1940, Britain, left to fight alone against the Axis powers of Germany and Italy, soon saw its cities subjected to a merciless bombardment called the Battle of Britain. To respond to this crisis and to mount an offensive of its own, Great Britain formed the Combined Operations Command, whose soldiers were known as Commandos.[1] Proficient in amphibious warfare and in planning and executing raids of all kinds, Commandos could strike the enemy with maximum effect at a time and point of their own choosing.

When America entered the war after Pearl Harbor, the U.S. Army sought to create a force similar to the British Commandos whose mission would be to spearhead landings when America invaded enemy territory and to conduct raids and missions deep behind enemy lines. This force, the 1st Ranger Battalion, was recruited from the 34th Infantry Division and the 1st Armored Division, the two American divisions that had arrived in Northern Ireland in early

1942.[2] Initially trained by the British Commandos, fifty Rangers saw their first action in the Allied raid at Dieppe, on the coast of France. This is where Ranger 2nd Lt. Edward Loustalot, a Louisiana native and LSU graduate, is believed to be the first American killed in ground combat in Europe.[3] The 1st Ranger Battalion went on to spearhead the American invasion of Algeria in November 1942. After the Rangers had helped to drive Axis forces out of North Africa, the 3rd and 4th Battalions of Rangers were formed and joined the 1st Battalion in the invasions of Sicily and Italy.

This book deals only with the 1st, 3rd, and 4th Ranger Battalions,* known as "Darby's Rangers" after their commander, Maj. William Orlando Darby (later lieutenant colonel and colonel, posthumously promoted to brigadier general†). As volunteers, Darby's men had the heart to do the job. Only physically strong men were chosen, and intense training gave these Rangers the legs and lungs to move fast and far when called upon to perform.

Many of Darby's Rangers were in frequent, prolonged combat for almost two years. Five times they assaulted enemy-held beaches at night. They fought in rugged mountains and pitiless deserts. Combat for months on end imposed a huge stress on the mind and body, and at times even these brave men were terrified. The question, "Will I live to see tomorrow?" haunted their minds.

By the end of their service, most Rangers carried mental as well as physical scars as the consequence for their harrowing experiences. The physical and mental trauma these Rangers faced brought on serious health issues, depression, and early aging for many of the survivors. Previously strong, healthy men, they died early, in what should have been the prime of life. After the war, some of them hardly slept through the night without horrible dreams and flashbacks of combat. A few were never able to resume a normal life.

After returning home, the surviving Rangers rarely spoke of their wartime experiences, even with family members. Doing so only brought back painful memories that Ranger veterans would rather forget. Family members were often bewildered and hurt by not knowing what their Ranger had experienced, either because he wouldn't talk about it or because he didn't come home.

* The 2nd and 5th Ranger Battalions were activated in 1943 and later fought with distinction in Normandy and throughout Europe. The 6th Ranger Battalion was famous for the daring rescue of over five hundred POWs from the notorious Japanese prison camp at Cabanatuan.

† Darby is the only American soldier in the nation's history to be posthumously promoted to flag rank.

Despite their silence, Rangers didn't forget their memories of war; in fact, those memories constantly preyed upon their minds. They sometimes found it easier to speak about them with a total stranger than with their family. Often, as I interviewed Rangers, trying to learn about their experiences, I found them reluctant to talk. But if I said, "I bet a day never passes that you don't remember," they would open up because it was the truth.

I have spent twenty-five years compiling the material presented here. Some of it comes from official records and previously published sources, but the bulk of what follows comes from letters, personal interviews, and unpublished accounts gleaned from the Rangers themselves or preserved by their family members. I am indebted to those Rangers who spent time with me, as well as to those who kept notes and wrote memoirs, and to those family members who shared personal information about their World War II Ranger. I have avoided military jargon. The few military terms in this book are footnoted or explained in the glossary for clarity and to give context to action stories.

While telling these personal stories, I will also correct a number of errors and misconceptions that have been repeated over the years, including the commonly repeated error that only six Rangers returned from the Battle of Cisterna, all the others being reported either killed or captured. I have confirmed the inaccuracy of this report and told the stories of twelve other men who returned from the battle who have been previously omitted from the record.

The story of the Cisterna battle has many moving parts and complexities, with events happening at different places on the battlefield at the same time. This is the first time that the story of this battle, told by many different Rangers in bits and pieces as they witnessed it, has ever been tied to the calendar and the clock, giving the story a coherent, understandable structure. Few of these experiences have previously been revealed, and no one has ever attempted to compile and organize these fragmented narratives into a coordinated view of the whole.

This book is full of quotations from different Rangers. In some cases, I did slight editing to make the quotation understandable. Any errors are mine and mine alone. I have endeavored to present an intimate and immediate picture of the actual experience of America's best warriors as they spearheaded repeated invasions on both the African and European continents. These men have earned the right to be heard, so I have let them speak.

MILITARY RANK ABBREVIATIONS

Gen.	General
Lt. Gen.	Lieutenant General
Maj. Gen.	Major General
Brig. Gen.	Brigadier General
Col.	Colonel
Lt. Col.	Lieutenant Colonel
Maj.	Major
Capt.	Captain
1st Lt.	1st Lieutenant
2nd Lt.	2nd Lieutenant
CSM	Command Sergeant Major
SGM	Sergeant Major
1st Sgt.	1st Sergeant
M/Sgt.	Master Sergeant
SFC	Sergeant 1st Class
S/Sgt.	Staff Sergeant
Sgt.	Sergeant
Tech/Sgt.*	Technical Sergeant
Tech/4	Technical Sergeant, 4th Class
Tech/5	Technical Sergeant, 5th Class
Cpl.	Corporal
Pfc.	Private First Class
Pvt.	Private

* Tech sergeants are usually addressed as "Sergeant."

Many men were promoted in rank during and after the war, and the text gives ranks as they were at the time being mentioned. There are various ranks entitled "sergeant," all of which may be called by their full rank but generally are just called "sergeant" (Sgt. in the text). Some men who where in fact technical sergeant 4th class or 5th class are sometimes just called "Tech/Sgt." Men got battlefield promotions, and sometimes the paperwork never caught up with the clerks. One soldier joined the Rangers as a private, was then promoted to private first class, then to corporal, and finally he became a sergeant. However, because of the problems at Cisterna, records sometimes were not complete. At the end of the war, when that soldier got off the ship back in the United States, he found out he was still a private. Such is war.

THE ROAD TO CISTERNA

1

NEWS FILTERS BACK

30 JANUARY 1944: NEAR CISTERNA DI LITTORIA, ITALY

All day long Col. William Orlando Darby had been listening to the noise of battle coming from the direction of Cisterna.* At 0100 hours, Darby had sent the 1st and 3rd Battalions of U.S. Army Rangers to secure the town of Cisterna thirty-five miles southeast of Rome, a town that controlled highways the Allied forces needed to use if they were to advance on Rome and whose use must be denied to the enemy. The 4th Ranger Battalion, operating in support of its sister battalions, had jumped off from its line of departure at 0200 hours, moving north on the Conca-Cisterna road toward Cisterna.[1]

The 1st and 3rd Ranger Battalions had been ordered to infiltrate with stealth through the German lines and capture Cisterna before the Germans knew what was happening. That kind of operation was the Rangers' specialty, something they'd carried out successfully again and again. Successful stealth operations don't produce much noise.[2] But as dawn approached, Darby found himself listening to the sounds of battle rather than the radio communications that he relied on to understand and direct his battalions because the 1st and 3rd Battalions were operating under radio silence. Darby, in a command trailer far from the battlefield, was unable to help.

From the time he had received his orders, Darby had had doubts about the Cisterna mission—doubts shared by his corps commander, Maj. Gen. John Lucas. Darby and Lucas knew that just three days earlier two battalions of the 3rd Infantry Division had been repulsed by overwhelming enemy forces while trying to capture Cisterna. Darby had asked for an extra day to reconnoiter the situation at Cisterna before he sent in his men. Such reconnaissance had been

* Cisterna is a common name for many towns in Italy. For this book, Cisterna refers to Cisterna di Littoria. After the war the name changed to Cisterna di Latina.

the key to Ranger successes in the past; yet Darby's request had been denied. When some of his own subordinates had timidly echoed Darby's misgivings, he had said simply, "These are my orders, those are your orders." That is what soldiers did.

Darby was wired into the telephone system of the 3rd Infantry Division, to which the Rangers were attached. The Ranger Force Journal reflects that at 0615 hours there was no news from the 1st and 3rd Ranger Battalions and that the 4th Ranger Battalion, held up by a roadblock, was taking fire from houses along the Conca-Cisterna road.

In the pre-dawn hours, the 769 enlisted men and officers of the 1st and 3rd Ranger Battalions neared Cisterna. At 0645 hours, with daylight breaking through, there still was no news from the 1st and 3rd Battalions. At 0700 hours, Darby spoke with the commanding officer of the 1st Ranger Battalion, Maj. John Dobson, on the SCR-610 radio and learned that the Rangers were located in an open field about eight hundred yards south of Cisterna. Dobson told Darby that he had been wounded, but not seriously.[3] At about 0800 hours, when radio contact was again established with the 1st Battalion, Darby learned that the Rangers were fighting to gain a foothold on the outskirts of Cisterna near the railroad station and that they were receiving enemy artillery fire.

During two years of grueling combat Darby had come to know the officers and enlisted men of the 1st Ranger Battalion personally. He was more than their commander: he had recruited, organized, and trained these men in 1942 and led them into battle in Algeria and Tunisia. These men, now called the "Originals," were Darby's brothers as only men who share combat can be. The 1st Ranger Battalion would receive the Presidential Unit Citation for its spectacular successes in North Africa, beginning with its amphibious landing at Arzew in Algeria, and on through raids and fights in Tunisia at Sened Station, Djebel Ank, and El Guettar.[4]

Because of these successes, the army had wanted two more battalions, the 3rd and 4th.[5] Darby knew many of those men, too. But the campaigns that followed in Sicily and Italy had extracted a heavy toll in killed and wounded Rangers. There hadn't been time to give their replacements training equivalent to that received by the Originals. After heavy casualties at Chiunzi Pass and in the mountains around Venafro and San Pietro, the ranks of experienced men had been so depleted that almost half the men on this mission had little to no combat experience. To fill the ranks, dozens of men had joined the Rangers only two months earlier and even more just a few weeks before, and almost all of them were complete strangers to Darby.

Much against their will, a handful of the Originals were not in the Cisterna battle but were stuck at headquarters with Darby. Because of a point system the army had put in place based on months overseas, but not enforced until the day before the battle, the army had decided that some of the Originals had experienced enough combat and had to be sent home to the United States.

31 JANUARY 1944: RANGER FORCE HEADQUARTERS

The next morning, Darby had no further news from the 1st and 3rd Battalions, and German artillery shells began landing around Darby's command trailer. One of them hit the trailer, killing two men. Darby and Capt. Axel Anderson were wounded but not seriously. That narrow escape underlined Darby's growing fears about the fate of his men. We don't know his actual thoughts that day, but we may be sure they were somber ones.

2

FORMATION AND TRAINING

In the spring of 1942, Hitler's Third Reich controlled most of Europe and North Africa. The British wanted to get the Americans involved in the fight against Germany as soon as possible, but the demands of the war against Japan kept most of America's war effort directed to the Pacific. Although many of Hitler's troops and much of his war materiel was tied up on the Russian front, Germany's military capacity still exceeded that of Britain and America combined, and the United States was not ready for deployment of an army for full-scale war in Europe.[1]

The future of freedom in the world hinged on Britain and America standing together in a combined effort, whatever form that might take, but the United States could barely handle the commitments already made for the delivery of military equipment to Britain. Yet, in early 1942, the United States began sending American army divisions to Northern Ireland to build up forces for some future action. These included the 34th Infantry Division, which began moving on 15 January, and the 1st Armored Division, which began to arrive in Northern Ireland in May. These units were the only ground forces available for several months.[2]

Gen. George C. Marshall, Chief of Staff for the U.S. Army, was eager for the Americans to have a first-strike force similar to the British Commandos—men drawn from all branches of the service who were trained to execute raids of all kinds, small and large. Not all of Marshall's commanders agreed. Marshall overcame the opposition by proposing that these special units be organized on a provisional basis. Once their jobs were done, the men would return to their parent units. This provisional status, requiring that the new organization would be attached to a larger regular army unit for services such as weapons and ammunition resupply, artillery support, food, medical treatment, and personal equipment replacement, would become a handicap in some of their operations. Maj. Gen. Dwight Eisenhower, Marshall's Assistant Chief of Staff, assigned Col. Lucien Truscott Jr. to be attached to the Commander of Combined Operations, British Army, to study ways to get as much battle experience as possible for American troops.[3]

Vice-Admiral Lord Louis Mountbatten founded the British Combined Operations Command to produce Commandos, officers and enlisted men who could execute landing operations designed to strike the enemy with the maximum effect, at the chosen point and at the chosen moment.[4] Commandos were among the bravest and toughest fighters in any army. In March 1942, British Commandos performed a hit-and-run raid to destroy the U-boat dry docks at Saint-Nazaire, France. A former American destroyer, the USS *Buchanan,* disguised as a German ship, was put back into service as the HMS *Campbeltown* and used by the Commandos in an operation that the British hoped would set back German submarine operations for months.[5] Packing high explosives in the *Campbeltown,* the Commandos entered the harbor and rammed the destroyer into the German dry docks. The explosives were set to go off by time-delay fuses, and the blast, happening several hours after the Commandos were gone, killed over four hundred German soldiers and at least forty high-ranking German officers who were inspecting the damage to the dry docks. The highly successful action caught the eye of the Americans, who wanted similar capabilities.[6]

Truscott visited the Commando training base in Scotland, and after observing their training and learning about their successes, he submitted a proposal on 26 May to Gen. Marshall that the United States "immediately undertake the formation of an American unit along Commando lines." This was approved by the War Department on 28 May. Truscott hand-delivered the proposal to Maj. Gen. Russell P. Hartle, the commanding general of American forces in Northern Ireland, who was cooperative. To name this new force, Truscott reached back to the French and Indian War, in which Rogers' Rangers fought like native Americans on behalf of the British, ambushing their enemies with hit-and-run raids. Since this was the kind of fighting Truscott wanted the new forces to do, he decided that they would be called "Rangers."[7]

Chief of Staff Marshall then authorized Hartle to staff the new unit. A thirty-two-year-old army captain named William Orlando Darby, serving as aide-de-camp to Hartle, was happy to be offered the command of the new unit.

Officers of the original 1st Ranger Battalion, activated in Northern Ireland on 19 June 1942: *Top row, left to right:* Lt. Joseph H. Randall, Lt. Walter F. Nye, Lt. Robert Flanagan, Capt. William E. Martin, Lt. James B. Lyle, Lt. Dean H. Knudson. *Next row, coming down:* Capt. Stephen J. Meade, Lt. Frederic F. Ahlgren, Lt. Axel W. Anderson, Lt. Leonard F. Dirks, Capt. Alvah M. Miller, Lt. Leilyn Young. *Second row:* Lt. Charles Shunstrom, Lt. Gordon L. Klefman, Lt. William L. Jarrett, Lt. William B. Lanning, Lt. Alfred H. Nelson, Lt. Robert L. Johnston. *First row:* Capt. Roy A. Murray, Lt. Edward V. Loustalot, Lt. Frederick J. Saam, Maj. William O. Darby, Lt. George P. Sunshine, Lt. Max Schneider, Capt. Herman W. Dammer, Lt. Earl L. Carran. From Altieri, *Darby's Rangers,* 1977.

Darby made an impressive appearance. He was intelligent, had an attractive personality, and was filled with enthusiasm. A native of Fort Smith, Arkansas, Darby entered West Point with the class of 1933. Upon graduation, he was commissioned a 2nd lieutenant and assigned to the 82nd Field Artillery of the 1st Cavalry, the only remaining mounted artillery unit in the army.[8]

A 1979 letter, written by Col. William S. Hutchinson Jr., commander of the 83rd Chemical Mortar Battalion, which fought alongside the Rangers in 1943–1944, confirms Darby's special qualities: "Darby . . . believed completely in the justice of his cause. His faith persuaded others. Darby's military tactics emphasized surprise by stealth, movement through impassable barriers, climbing forbidding cliffs . . . and most important, explaining the aim of the operation to every man so as to enlist his whole initiative in the inevitable, spontaneously improvised tactics on which the operation will always depend. . . . Darby's vision was contagious. It infected the commanders and the units with which his Rangers served."[9]

VOLUNTEERING AND RECRUITING OF THE 1ST RANGER BATTALION

At Carrickfergus, Northern Ireland, Darby was promoted to major on 1 June 1942, just prior to the 19 June activation date of the 1st Ranger Battalion. Darby chose Capt. Herman Dammer as his executive officer. While Darby was always quick to make a decision, Dammer was more reflective, weighing all options before giving orders. Dammer complemented Darby, earning respect from Rangers who would follow him through three campaigns.[10]

Darby conducted interviews to select his officers, choosing Capt. Alvah Miller, a muscular former church deacon, to command Company D. Capt. Max Schneider, chosen to command 1/E, was good-natured and well-liked by all the Rangers but demanding during training. Capt. Stephen J. Meade, who spoke several languages, would command Company 1/A. First Lt. Alfred H. Nelson commanded Company B for a short time, Capt. William E. Martin briefly commanded Company C until he was named Intelligence Officer, and Capt. Roy A. Murray commanded Company F. After hand-picking his officers, Darby immediately began searching for the right men. They had to be well-built and muscular, with 20/20 eyesight, no eyeglasses, and no dentures. Darby believed that it was your legs and your lungs that carried you to victory. Physical strength, combined with realistic training and having a heart to win, were to be the factors that separated Rangers from other soldiers.[11]

Notices on the bulletin boards of the 34th Infantry Division and the 1st Armored Division invited men to join the Rangers. At the 1st Armored, a 1st sergeant called his men to attention and defied anyone to volunteer for the Rangers. Nevertheless, several men with armored experience wanted the promised action. One of the first to volunteer from the 34th was S/Sgt. Warren "Bing" Evans. When Evans saw a bulletin board notice, he signed up, and a few days later he was interviewed by Darby. Few of the twenty-four hundred volunteers made the cut. Evans was one of them. Intelligent, tall, and strong, he was a natural leader, playing football and basketball in college. He was also a good singer, thus the nickname "Bing," for Bing Crosby.[12]

First Lt. James B. Lyle was another of the first volunteers. Prior to attending Officer Candidate School at Fort Benning, Georgia, Lyle was a staff sergeant with five years' experience in the army. He was from Louisiana and had worked in a shipyard before enlisting. One of his first assignments was to tour British Commando installations with three other volunteers and report back to Maj. Gen. James E. Chaney, the commander of U.S. Army Europe. Along with Lyle, 1st Lt. Alfred H. Nelson, S/Sgt. William Musegades, and S/Sgt. Hubert Wodarczak toured Commando bases, where they were bombed by German aircraft. Lyle actually gave lessons in marksmanship to the Commandos, and when he returned with his report the general blurted out, "I asked for a Lt. Colonel, not a damn Lieutenant." In typing the general's order, an aide had mistakenly left off the word "Colonel."[13]

The men selected as officers weeded out the other applicants: "Why do you want to join? Ever played sports? Have you ever been in bar-room fights, brawls, or gang fights where people have been hurt bad? Have you ever killed anyone? Do you think you have the guts to stick a knife in a man's back and twist it?" Of those who applied, 575 survived the endurance and other contests to be interviewed and were accepted on a temporary basis. After two weeks of Commando training, eighty-seven more men were eliminated, leaving 488 enlisted men and twenty-six officers who became members of the 1st Ranger Battalion.[14]

The 1st Ranger Battalion was organized into seven companies: a Headquarters Company and six line companies, labeled A through F. The designation of these companies in World War II was Able, Baker, Charlie, Dog, Easy, and Fox Companies. For simplicity and brevity, I use the number of the battalion followed by the letter of the company, such as 1/A, meaning the 1st Ranger Battalion, Able Company, or 1/F, meaning Fox Company of the 1st Ranger Battalion.[15]

The youngest Rangers were Sgt. Martin "Junior" Frank, 1/F, and Pfc. Lenuel Harris, 1/E, both just eighteen years old. Sgt. James Mahoney wanted to join because he was tired of close-order drill, and he wanted to kill someone. Pete Preston was a coal miner from West Virginia. Ray Rodriguez, a Mexican, was

SECRET

S E C R E T

HEADQUARTERS
EUROPEAN THEATER OF OPERATIONS
UNITED STATES ARMY

9 June 1942

SPECIAL ORDERS)
:
NUMBER 2)

E X T R A C T

7. The following named officers and EM, 135th Inf, WP on or about this date to Southampton, England, reporting upon arrival to the CO, HMS Tormeto, for temporary duty to carry out the instructions of the CG, and upon completion of this duty will proceed to Lurgan, NI, reporting upon arrival to the CG, Fifth Army Corps:

1st Lt ALFRED H. NELSON, 0385118
1st Lt JAMES B. LYLE, 0452005
S Sgt HUBERT WODARCZAK, 20708480
S Sgt WILLIAM MUSEGADES, 20708273

QMNT. A flat per diem of $6.00 is authorized for Lieutenants NELSON and LYLE while on this duty. FD will pay the above named EM the monetary alws in lieu of qrs and rations prescribed in AR 35-4520, as amended, at the rate of $1.50 for qrs for four (4) days, and at the rate of $2.50 for rations for four (4) days. TDN. FD 34 P -02 A 0425-23

By command of Major General CHANEY:

CHARLES L. BOLTE,
Brigadier General, General Staff Corps,
Chief of Staff

OFFICIAL:

I. B. SUMMERS,
Colonel, A.G.D.,
Adjutant General.

S E C R E T

SECRET

Special Order No. 2. U.S. Army photo.

the fastest runner in Company F. Robert Dunn quoted poetry and made up verses to entertain his tentmates. Sgt. Walter Sieg, an ex-merchant mariner, had been all over the world. His canteen was always full, but not of water. Vernon Lodge, 1/F, played the clarinet and had arranged music for Benny Strong's big band.[16]

S/Sgt. Russell "Bill" Hunt, 1/D, wrote home to let his parents know he had joined the Rangers: "A call was made for men to be in the 1st Ranger Battalion, and twelve from our battalion were chosen to go. Many were sent back, and a few dropped out. The men were all hand-picked but there will be many who won't be able to keep up. As long as they feed me enough, I think I can make it."[17]

Paul Hermsen, 1/C, was a corporal in charge of a machine gun squad in the 34th Division when he spotted a notice asking for volunteers for the Rangers:

> The notice said there would be somebody at a nearby château to give interviews. I went down to the château and found I could not get in the front door as it was locked, so I went around the back and found lattice work going up to a window. I climbed up to the second floor, went in the window and then went down to the main floor. I was told to be back at the château at 5:00 that afternoon, where trucks transported us to Carrickfergus, Northern Ireland, about ten miles outside of Belfast. That's how I became a Ranger.[18]

Cpl. Wilbur R. Gallup, from Iowa, was the quietest and most conservative of the group, always showing off his girlfriend's picture. Pvt. Robert K. Chester, a rugged a man even by Ranger standards, had the loudest voice, and Pvt. John B. Woodall, who was short and stocky, would fight anyone no matter their size.

Pfc. Robert J. Reed, a medic assigned to the 5th General Hospital near Carrickfergus, had never had training in weapons. He volunteered for the Rangers because he was disgruntled and unhappy with his outfit.[19] When passing Darby's tent one evening, Reed overheard Darby, Maj. Dammer, and Capt. Murray discussing rejecting applicants who had not been through basic training. Reed got worried: "I was so afraid that this meant I would be sent back to my unit. But no, as each round of eliminations was posted I looked for my name. It wasn't there. I was still a Ranger." The Rangers' medical officer, 1st Lt. William A. Jarrett, 1/Hq., kept Reed on as a medic.

ACHNACARRY, SCOTLAND: COMMANDO TRAINING

On 1 July 1942, when the newly recruited Rangers arrived at Achnacarry, Scotland, for training by British Commandos, they were addressed in pouring rain by Maj. Gen. Sir Robert Laycock, commandant of the depot. "I know that you have heard all sorts of rumors about the high risk in Commando training: that some men are killed and wounded, the result of using live ammunition in our training. Unfortunately, we have had a few accidents, some through carelessness and some through circumstances which are the fault of no one. . . . Every accident we do have is more than compensated for on the field of battle."[20]

The days began with a run, then another run to the mess station for a light breakfast of foul-smelling kipper, followed by a "speed march" at double the infantry paçe. Then came another run to a field for PT and squad exercises. In between physical workouts came classes in field-craft, survival, weapons, rock climbing, marksmanship, infantry tactics, map reading, armed and unarmed combat, night fighting, amphibious landings, and combat problems. Men learned how to fire, strip, and reassemble all weapons, American, British, and German. To make the cut, the chosen volunteers had to assault positions with live fire zinging overhead, climb cliffs, swim in ice-cold rivers with full equipment, and perform heartbreaking speed marches. In addition to physical training, they practiced beach landings, survival courses, and night raiding techniques.[21]

On the first morning, Rangers got acquainted with the speed march. The length of a Ranger's step had to be thirty-six inches, regardless of his height. Rangers speed marched everywhere they went, covering ten miles in only eighty-seven minutes. Legs and lungs ached. Rangers never walked anywhere; they either ran or speed marched, building up their legs and lungs and toughening their feet.[22] Lt. Edward Loustalot, a native of Louisiana who became a platoon leader in 1/F, explained the rules to his platoon: "Men I want to welcome you all to Company F. . . . Any man who can't keep up with us will be sent back to his old outfit immediately. . . . Discipline in this outfit rests with the individual himself . . . and remember, you are free to request return to your old outfit at any time."[23]

Sgt. James Altieri, in Loustalot's platoon, remembered, "Then I would look at the small lieutenant who was also having a hard time, more so than the rest of us because of his shorter legs. 'Dammit!' I would say half aloud, 'If they can do it, then so can I!' And I would dig in."[24] Due to frequent shin splints from speed marches, Darby ordered that two and a half inches be cut off the top of the required leggings, which completely eliminated this difficulty. Rangers were the only American soldiers to wear cut-down leggings throughout the war.

There were numerous obstacle courses, some of which could be deadly, as explained by Pfc. Charles H. Kazura, 1/A: "The double-time two and one-half-mile runs, the 16½ mile cross country hikes, castle climbing with ropes, mountain climbing (one of which was the highest in Scotland at 4800 feet) with temperatures of 35 degrees at the top. . . . Also there were those 12-mile forced marches, the deadly assault landings under fire. . . . And the log throwing for fun?"[25]

Their Commando trainers were a match even for the high-spirited Rangers. First Lt. Walter Nye, 1/F:

> We were trained by the most astute and tough instructors that I have ever run into. One of them was named Lieutenant Cowieson, and he was a bear. . . . he almost got us to the point where we hated him. One night we went into Oban, about fifteen miles from where we were training . . . for a night of relaxation. We were supposed to leave early, about ten o'clock. The next morning, we were to get up and go on a fifteen-mile speed march. So, we were all in one truck, and we thought, 'Okay, We'll get even with this guy.' . . . We stayed up until about midnight. All of the Rangers went in the truck and got home. We left him there. . . . Well, he ran all the way back . . . fifteen to eighteen miles. He picked us up at 5:00 am and put us through hell. He could have gone another hundred miles![26]

First Lt. Robert Flanagan, 1/E, found the training varied and intense: "Instruction was given in unarmed combat, mountain climbing, demolition work, swimming, handling of small boats, and general physical development courses which involved mainly speed marches over 5-, 7-, and 12-mile distances which had to be accomplished in 45, 72, and 112 minutes respectively. Emphasis was laid on fieldcraft, assault courses under fire, and weapons training. . . . [Training with the Royal Navy] consisted mainly in becoming familiar with the operations and usage of all types of landing craft, beaches of all types and their peculiarities, and landing craft discipline."[27] When one company would make a seven-mile speed march in under an hour, the Commando instructors would order another company to beat their time. The obstacle course was a grind through slushy mud, over dangerous cliffs and high log walls rimmed with barbed wire. When a company made the obstacle course in ten minutes, the company was forced to do it again in eight. If someone straggled, a Commando would taunt him mercilessly. If a man fell out a second time, the Commando would pick him up by the seat of his pants and throw him back in line. If someone fell out from fatigue, unable to keep up the maddening pace, he was ordered to make a speed march after hours. The trainees cursed the instructors and spoke of them as inhuman monsters who had no regard for flesh and blood. But when Rangers complained, they were ordered to do things they thought were impossible. One instructor told them, "Nothing is impossible. It is all in the heart and in the mind."[28] If there was a way to work the Rangers to death, the Commandos knew about it. Tech/5 Clyde Thompson, 1/F, of Ashland, Kentucky, said: "Those bastards tried to kill us, or we thought they did. We maneuvered with live ammunition. There were accidents, too. . . . [One] guy fell off a cliff and broke practically every bone in his body."[29]

The Commandos' favorite training was the amphibious landing. Rangers would go out in boats and assault the shore only to find themselves fired upon with live ammunition. Machine gun bullets would knock the paddles right out of the Rangers' hands, and when Rangers hit the beach, charges of dynamite would explode in their faces. Commandos might throw a live hand grenade into a boatload of Rangers. The first time that happened, the Rangers hit the water. The Commando in charge had them row back out to the middle of the lake and learn the correct thing to do, which was to throw the grenade into the water, where it would explode harmlessly.[30]

To cross rivers, Rangers learned the death slide, a rope stretched across a river at a steep angle. Using their toggle rope, a length of rope four feet long with a wooden handle on one end and a loop on the other, Rangers would throw one end of the toggle over the slide rope, put the handle through the loop, and, grabbing the handle, slide down.[31]

Ranger officers acted as instructors, some in the art of personal combat. Cpl. Larry Schenkel, 1/Hq., got to know Lt. Charles "Chuck" Shunstrom during training:

> I had always admired Chuck Shunstrom*. . . . he had risen through the ranks. He was tough and daring. I mean, when there was something dangerous and difficult that had to be done, you can bet they'd give the job to Shunstrom. A real daredevil. And he demanded the same of his men.
>
> One time when we were in training. . . . There was a bunch of guys standing around, and Chuck, who always had to show off his strength and skill, handed me a knife. "Come on, Schenkel," he says, with this weird, cold look in his eyes, "come at me with that knife." . . . I don't know if he thought I was crazy or what, but there was no way in hell I was going to put myself in that position. At the very least, I knew I'd be humiliated, and at worst I could have been hurt pretty bad or maybe even killed. But . . . I'd rather be in combat with a guy who had that kind of street-smart survival instinct in him than any other kind of soldier.[32]

Rangers were trained to be good swimmers. Pfc. Charles Leighton, 1/E, witnessed the accidental drowning of Pvt. Lamont Hoctel, 1/E: "We were on a speed march in Scotland and had to ford this river. . . . Suddenly I saw this guy Halsted† go down. I dived after him and got a hold of the pack strap on his shoulder and I got him just to the surface. . . . Then I lost my grip, I went down again and couldn't find him."[33]

DORLIN HOUSE: TRAINING WITH THE ROYAL NAVY

On 1 August, the battalion (less fifty Rangers going to another assignment) moved by rail to the vicinity of Dorlin House, Argyle, Scotland, for instruction under the control of the Royal Navy. Rangers were introduced to the British LCA (Landing Craft Assault), the ship that would deliver them to several enemy beaches. They learned amphibious landing operations and practiced getting to shore in a variety of boats and rough water conditions and in all kinds of weather.[34]

* The author of the *Secret of Anzio Bay* referred to Lt. Charles Shunstrom as Schuster. I have restored the correct name when quoting this source.

† The correct name of the Ranger who drowned was Pvt. Lamont Hoctel, 1/E.

DUNDEE, SCOTLAND

On 3 September, Rangers transferred to Dundee, Scotland, for their final training with No. 1 Commando and were assigned to live with Scottish families. Rangers learned how to attack and destroy pillboxes, antiaircraft sites, and seacoast defense batteries. The harbor area, like all coastal areas, was heavily mined against a possible German invasion. Pfc. James Ruscheweiz, 1/C, not seeing the sign that the adjacent field was mined, jumped from a platform over a fence of concertina wire. He landed on an antitank mine, which blew him to pieces and severely wounded and blinded Tech/5 Aaron Salkin, 1/C, who was right behind him.[35] It was on that day that Tech/4 Robert Reed, 1/Hq., learned what it meant to be a medic. Reed and S/Sgt. Wendell E. Buringrud, 1/Hq., were sent to recover Ruscheweiz's body. Reed later recalled, "Slowly and carefully we picked up the pieces and exited the mine field. One piece was a hand, another the side of the skull with hair. It brings you down to earth starkly and you quiver."[36]

Father Albert Basil, a Roman Catholic British Commando chaplain, was in the operating room as a team of surgeons struggled to save Ranger Salkin's life. One of the surgeons suggested that if they succeeded in saving his life, that life would not be worth living, and that Salkin would be better off dying in the operating room. Others approved this sentiment. But Father Basil said, "If that boy dies, I shall repeat your words to the proper authority."[37] Salkin survived.

Deciding that the Rangers needed their own insignia, there was a contest for its design, won by M/Sgt. Anthony Rada, 1/Hq., a former autoworker from Michigan. Unknown to the others, Rada moonlighted in artwork. His prize was the grand sum of $25. The black scroll, trimmed in red and emblazoned with 1st Ranger Battalion in white, would be worn by all the men who went into combat with the 1st Rangers.[38]

Prior to shipping out from Dundee, Darby asked that Father Basil be allowed to join the Rangers for their invasion of North Africa. Father Basil was glad to escape Northern Ireland. The majority of the Rangers were Roman Catholic, compared to 2 percent Catholic for the Commandos he had been serving. Nevertheless, he looked after Catholic, Jew, and Protestant alike.[39]

Following time spent at Corkerhill Camp, where they were assigned to the U.S. Army II Corps and attached to the 1st Infantry Division for administration and supply, the Rangers made one final move, to Gourock, Scotland, where on 26 October 1942 they embarked for their first combat in North Africa.[40]

3

DIEPPE

CODE NAME JUBILEE

For months into 1942, the United States, Britain, and Russia considered when and where to attack German-occupied France. The Russians believed that an American invasion of the French coast would take pressure off Russia's Eastern Front. Gen. George C. Marshall wanted to make this assault as soon as possible, before Germany had time to further fortify the French coast. Marshall pressed Winston Churchill, the British prime minister, and the British chiefs of staff to invade Europe, but the British, knowing that the Allies were unprepared for such a task, were unwilling to take such a risk.[1] Scaling down their plans, the Allies decided to conduct a large-scale raid, called a "Reconnaissance in Force," on the French coast. The results of that mission would give the decision-makers a feel for what an invasion entailed but with limited risk. They chose Dieppe, a French resort city on the English Channel, to be the target of this "Reconnaissance."[2]

PURPOSE OF THE DIEPPE RAID

The raid on Dieppe would test the German claim that their coastal defenses were impregnable and provide the Allied staffs with information about the vulnerabilities of those defenses. Dieppe contained large concentrations of German war materiel, and its destruction would be a costly blow to the German supply system. American planners asked for fifty Rangers to join the raid, in order to give them an introduction to battle.[3] Darby: "There were a number of vital reasons for Dieppe: to test the newly developed LCT [landing craft tank], to determine whether a port could be taken by direct frontal assault, and to see whether the Navy could manage a landing fleet of 253 ships and other craft.

Royal Hamilton Infantry
Essex Scottish Fusiliers
Mont Royal
Royal Marine Commandos
14th Canadian Army Tank Regiment
(Calgary Tank Regiment)
No. 3
Commando
Yellow I
Beach
Yellow II
Beach
Berneval
Royal Regiment
of Canada
Blue
Beach
Red
Beach
White
Beach
South Saskatchewan
Regiment
Cameron Highlands
of Canada
Green
Beach
No. 4
Commando
Orange I
Beach
Orange II
Beach
Cliffs
German
Batteries
Vasterival
Pourville
DIEPPE
Varengeville
Sur Mar
German
Batteries
N
W
E
S
Rangers Killed
1 2nd Lt. Edward Loustalot
2 T/4 Howard Henry
3 2nd Lt. Joseph Randall
0
1
2
3
Miles
Dieppe

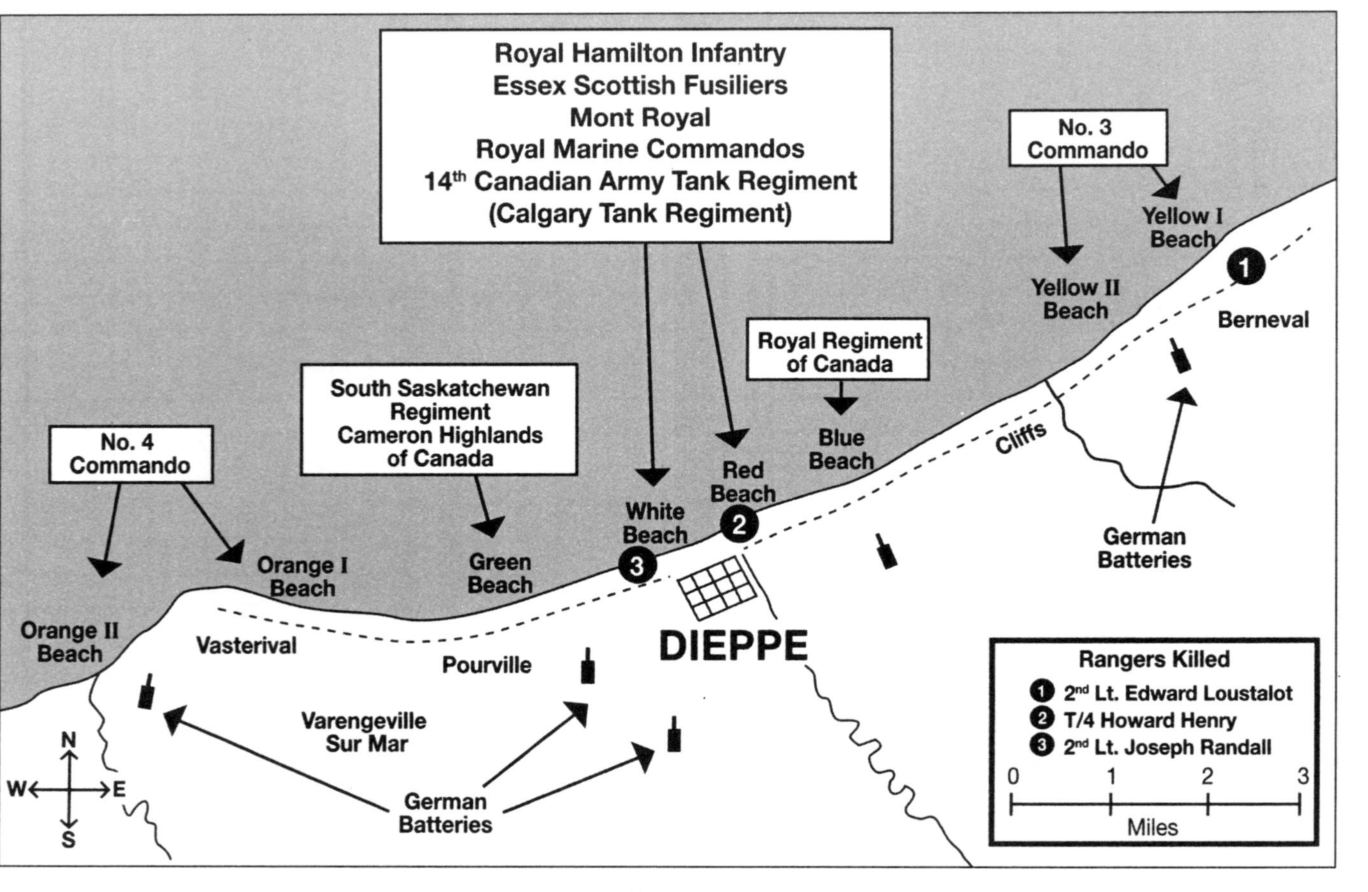

Also to be determined was whether the air organization could gain supremacy over a landing area while providing support for ground troops."[4]

The chief obstacle confronting the landing forces was the massive, almost unscalable cliffs on both flanks of Dieppe, broken only by narrow clefts at the mouths of the rivers. At these breaks in the cliffs the Nazis had doubled their defenses, adding large coastal batteries that had to be destroyed before ships could approach the shore. The beaches were rocky and narrow, dropping steeply into the sea, difficult for landing boats and easily swept by fire from hidden positions.[5] The plan for the assault on Dieppe, called Operation Jubilee, called for a simultaneous assault at eight places along the coast, with the main thrust at the town of Dieppe itself. Canadian infantry were to attack the main beach at Dieppe, to be followed by tanks. British No. 3 Commando, accompanied by American Rangers, was to land in Berneval, about four miles east of Dieppe, and No. 4 Commando, also with Rangers, would attack at Vasterival, about four miles to the west of Dieppe.[6]

Darby, promoted to lieutenant colonel on 6 August, was concerned that the objectives of the raid were vague, its benefits seemingly minimal, and the risks to his Rangers dangerously large. Despite these reservations, Darby selected fifty Rangers to be assigned to British Commandos and Canadian infantry participating in the Dieppe raid. It was a chance for the Rangers to get "bloodied," as Darby once said, to learn what combat was really like and to bring that experience back to the rest of the battalion.[7]

Far from sharing Lt. Col. Darby's reservations about the raid, Lord Louis Mountbatten looked forward to the raid with enthusiasm. He felt that it was impossible to overestimate the value of the Dieppe raid, thinking that it would be a decisive step toward the real invasion.[8]

Darby assigned Capt. Roy Murray, commanding 1/F, to lead the thirty-nine Rangers assigned to No. 3 Commando. Four Rangers were to land with No. 4 Commando, and six Rangers were to land with the Canadian infantry.[9]

OPERATION JUBILEE: THE DIEPPE RAID

Under a clear sky and with the sea unusually calm, the forces loaded ships and landing craft on the night of 18 August. Aboard ship the night before the raid, Mountbatten addressed the men of No. 4 Commando, declaring that the raid must succeed at all costs: "We expect sixty percent casualties and for those of you who will die tomorrow, may God have mercy on your souls."[10] Ranger Alex Szima, 1/Hq., was disturbed by the speech. In case they all died, he wanted the Rangers to be identified as Americans: "When Mountbatten finished speaking I went to convince three fellow Rangers to wear American uniforms."[11]

Escorted by gunboats and destroyers, the flotilla, following in the wake of minesweepers, steamed swiftly toward the French coast. At 0347 hours, seven miles off the coast, a small force of armed Nazi trawlers, escorting a convoy, spotted the approaching ships and sent up a star flare that revealed the invasion force. Surprise was now lost. German E-boats, larger and more heavily armed than U.S. PT boats, with a top speed of forty-five to forty-eight knots, opened fire on the Allied ships, causing the group to become scattered and several vessels to sink. British gunboats returned fire, and a pitched battle ensued, with the remaining Commando boats eluding the E-boats and continuing to their objective at Berneval. But by then the entire coast was alerted and dawn was fast approaching. As planned, the main invasion force landed on a steep, rocky beach in the middle of the town of Dieppe. The landings, already behind schedule, occurred under withering machine gun, mortar, and artillery fire.[12] With surprise lost, the Germans almost wiped out the British and Canadians.[13]

THE LANDINGS OF NO. 3 COMMANDO, TROOP 6, AT BERNEVAL

The other two landings, east and west of Dieppe, were intended to destroy enemy coastal guns before they could fire on the boats of the invasion force. The mission for Troop 6[*] was to land on Yellow Beach, located four and one-half miles east of Dieppe, and capture and destroy an enemy shore battery of four 6-inch guns at Berneval. The landing was delayed by the German E-boats, with most of the No. 3 Commando's boats scattered and with only one boat landing successfully on the tiny beach at Berneval. It delivered parts of Troop 6, with thirty-eight enlisted Commandos and Rangers, plus their officers, including 2nd Lt. Edward Loustalot[†] of 1/F.[14]

[*] Several numbered troops made up each numbered Commando unit. This organization was similar to companies and platoons in the American army.

[†] The name of Ranger 2nd Lt. Edward Loustalot, 1/F, was chiseled incorrectly as "Edwin" into the granite World War II Ranger monument at Fort Benning, Georgia, in 1977.

Men leaped into the surf and ran up the beach. Facing an almost vertical cliff, topped with many rolls of barbed wire, the men worked their way to the top while being showered by grenades and subjected to blistering machine gun fire, exacting a heavy toll from the grim Commandos. At the top of the cliff, German machine gun fire halted the troop's advance.

What was left of the troop, unable to move forward, was pinned down by crisscross machine gun fire. When the British senior officer, Capt. R. L. Wills, was shot through the throat, Lt. Loustalot took command.[15] He pulled the pin on a fragmentation grenade, but as he rose to throw it at one of the enemy machine guns, he was hit multiple times in the stomach.[16] Lt. Edward Loustalot is believed to be "the first American serviceman of World War II to die in land warfare on the European mainland."[17] He was an architecture graduate of Louisiana State University and a native of Franklin, Louisiana, and is incorrectly referred to as "Edwin" in numerous military documents as well as books and articles about World War II Rangers.

Second Lt. Edward V. Loustalot, killed in action in the Dieppe raid, and Pfc. Donald Frederick. Loustalot is believed to be the first American soldier killed in ground combat in Europe. Courtesy Jane Slavin.

Three Rangers who landed with Loustalot, Sgt. Albert T. Jacobsen, 1/B, Pfc. Walter A. Bresnahan, 1/B, and Pfc. Edward Furru, 1/Hq., were taken prisoner by the Germans and sat out the war in a German POW camp.[18] Loustalot's family learned how he died when the Rangers in his troop, released from German captivity at the end of the war, told the story of his death and their capture. One of them, Pfc. Furru, gave this account:

> I don't know what time we landed, but my eyes were on the cliffs because that's where the enemy fire was coming from. We were told to expect very little barbed wire, but there was a lot. I estimate it took about ten minutes to get through the wire. I carried one end of a bangalore torpedo with a Commando on the other. As we got close to a house, the first shots were fired, and I believe that's when Capt. R. L. Wills got hit. Lt. William Wright, the other Commando, was there, and I got my first shot at a Jerry.
>
> We began to receive enemy fire, and that's when Lt. Loustalot and the two Commandos were hit. One of the wounded yelled, to warn me where the Jerries were. I saw a body and knelt. He had a pair of field glasses. I took out my bayonet and cut the strap, taking them with me. It was Lt. Loustalot. One of the eye pieces was shot away, about chest high, so I figured that's about where he was hit.
>
> The Germans opened on us with a heavy gun, like a 75 mm. I saw the shell pass about ten feet over my head. We raced back down the path we had come up. There were some dead Commandos on the beach, and a German sniper on the cliff above was trying to pick us off. Our boat was nowhere to be seen, so we ran up the beach a bit and found a cave where we could get out of the German line of fire. In a few minutes a squad of Jerries came by and there were so many of them and so few of us that we gave up. If you're dead, you're no good to anybody but the enemy.
>
> Eventually they loaded us up in a truck, and once on the highway we were strafed by an American pilot. The truck crashed into a ditch and began burning. I was thrown out the back with another guy who had both legs cut off above the knee. He did not live long. I was alone with a blazing truck and about eight dead men that didn't get out. Blood was dripping from my head, and I had a bullet hole in my knee. I hailed the next truck that passed, and some German officers took me to a hospital. Lt. Wills was there. He had lost

over half his blood from the bullet he took. I wound up in Stalag VIIIB until I was liberated at war's end.[19]

NO. 4 COMMANDO AT VASTERIVAL

The four Rangers, Cpl. William R. Brady, 1/C, Cpl. Franklin M. Koons, 1/D, Sgt. Kenneth D. Stempson, 1/Hq., and Sgt. Alex J. Szima, 1/Hq., who accompanied No. 4 Commando landed and all saw action.[20] Szima told how the Rangers fought their way up a narrow gulley and succeeded in flanking a large caliber, four-gun coastal battery manned by over two hundred Germans: "We had to take out a gun battery on top of a cliff. You get a knot in your stomach until you get into action; then it gets untied and from then on, you're fine. We drove so far up on the beach we did not even get our feet wet. We raced across the beach about fifty yards. Then we crawled to the top of a cliff that had barbed wire strung all along the edge parallel to the beach. . . . We cut and smashed our way through three sets of wire."[21] The raiders took a position surrounding the gun crews, laying down deadly fire as the Germans attempted to man their guns. This action prevented the Germans from accessing the big guns, which, as far as the raid was concerned, was as effective as destroying them. Szima: "The worst was on the way home when we had to run through an orchard with snipers and a machine gun firing at us. That's where I got this bullet hole in my hat. I laid down and another bullet passed close by my ear."[22]

Cpl. Franklin M. Koons, 1/D, was on the far-right flank of the attack, which lasted about four hours. British Commandos led this part of the raid since they were experienced, and the Rangers moved along with them. By 0900 hours the radar installation had been immobilized, and they were headed back to the boats. After the raid, the four Rangers who fought at Vasterival were honored by being driven in an army staff car to London to Gen. Truscott's headquarters. The Rangers asked for a drink, which they were given, prior to meeting Gen. Dwight Eisenhower and Lord Louis Mountbatten. Maj. Gen. Russell P. Hartle called them "Darby's Boys," the handle given them for this trip, which they much preferred to the title of "Yank" given by the British.[23] Cpl. Koons was hailed by the news media as the first American soldier to kill a German, and to celebrate, he was later awarded a British Military Medal in ceremonies at Casablanca in the presence of President Franklin Roosevelt, Prime

Minister Winston Churchill, Gen. Charles de Gaulle, and Gen. George C. Marshall.[24]

CASUALTIES

Three Rangers were killed, and four others were listed as missing in action, presumed captured. Six other Rangers were wounded, all of whom survived.[25] The Canadians and the six Rangers who landed with them in the center of Dieppe took the brunt of the casualties. One Ranger, Sgt. Lloyd N. Church, 1/A, was captured, and two Rangers, 2nd Lt. Joseph H. Randall, 1/D, and Tech/4 Howard M. Henry, 1/E, were killed in the assault on the main beach. Years later Lt. Col. Marcell G. Swank, who was a sergeant in 1/Hq. at the time of the raid, arranged for a plaque to honor the Rangers. In a presentation to a large crowd at Dieppe on the fortieth anniversary, 19 August 1982, Swank remembered Randall and Henry with these words:

> Second Lt. Joseph H. Randall, 1/D, was killed close-by to where we now stand while with the Royal Hamilton Light Infantry. He died on landing, a few short steps from the water's edge, charging head-on into the holocaust. He was twenty-three years old, from Washington, D.C., and the only child of a military family. Lt. Randall is buried in Arlington National Cemetery in proximity to his parents' grave.
>
> T/4 Howard M. Henry, 1/E, died while with the Essex Scottish Regiment, also a Canadian unit, and like 2nd Lt. Joseph Randall, he landed on the Dieppe Beach. He was one of the few men who succeeded in fighting his way into Dieppe, where he was killed. From Science Hill, Kentucky, Henry wanted to be an electrical engineer and had worked his way through one year of college. He was only twenty-two years old, and he is interred in the Normandy American Cemetery in Colleville-sur-Mer, the only soldier from the 1st Ranger Battalion buried at this cemetery, which overlooks Omaha Beach.[26]

JACK NISSENTHALL'S SECRET MISSION

Another mission for the raid, kept secret for thirty years, was to capture the newest and most technologically advanced radar component of the time, the cavity magnetron. It was believed to be located on the coast near Dieppe. Jack Nissenthall, a radar expert, volunteered for what could have been a suicide mission: penetrating a key German radar site near the landing area. For the raid, Nissenthall was given a bodyguard of eleven sharpshooters. At that time, radar was vital to the defense of Britain because the Germans were bombing Britain on a regular basis. Because he was privy to the topmost secrets of British and American radar technology, it was imperative that Nissenthall should not fall into German hands, and he carried a cyanide capsule in case that happened. Furthermore, his bodyguards' orders were to protect him first, but if Nissenthall were captured, his bodyguards were to kill him. Caught between friend and foe, Nissenthall had to succeed or die. His orders were to capture the German equipment, but if that could not be done, he was at least to photograph it.[27]

Nissenthall's Commandos got into a heavy firefight with German guards just outside the radar installation. Unable to access the radar site, the Commandos cut the telephone wires leading from the radar site, forcing those inside to use their radios, which allowed British intelligence to pick up transmissions. On the race back to the beach, under heavy fire, all but two of Nissenthall's bodyguards were killed. Finding their boat gone, the three survivors had to swim to a rescue boat. The results of the mission were kept secret for many years after the war.[28]

LESSONS FROM THE RAID

Intended as a test run for an attack on the French coast, what exactly was learned from the Dieppe raid? The largest lesson, which should have been obvious from the beginning, was that neither the United States nor its Allies were ready for a cross-channel invasion of the European continent. Other lessons included:

1. Naval artillery or air power should soften up the landscape and reduce enemy fortified positions.

2. Naval gunfire could have been used to fire on the enemy gunboats before they fired on Allied ships.

3. Beach obstacles and barbed wire must be removed or disabled immediately prior to the debarkation of Allied troops.

4. Planning for the landing of tanks and other vehicles must assume all the worst possibilities that they might face.
5. Control of the air must be achieved if an attack is to be successful.
6. Special assault units need to be formed and trained to make hit-and-run attacks on known enemy installations.

In their After Action Reports (sometimes referred to as Reports of Action), most of the Rangers who participated said they were disappointed that their boats never made it to shore. But upon returning to England and learning of the disasters that occurred both on the beach and inland, most were relieved and glad to be alive.

4

NORTH AFRICA

ALGERIA

After Germany attacked France on 10 May 1940, French resistance rapidly crumbled, ending in France's formal surrender, effective on 25 June. Germany directly ruled northern France and all its Atlantic coast, occupying them with German troops. The southern half of France, nominally independent but allied with Germany and headed by Marshal Philippe Petain, a French hero in the First World War, was headquartered in the town of Vichy. The Vichy regime controlled the troops in France's colonies, including the North African territories of Morocco, Algeria, and Tunisia. East of these, Italy, Germany's Axis ally, held its own colony of Libya. Using a mixture of German, Italian, and French forces, Hitler clung tenaciously to North Africa because of its oil resources. On 14 June 1940, British forces in Egypt invaded Libya, beginning a prolonged struggle in Egypt and Libya. French patriots who refused to accept their country's subordination to Germany formed their own volunteer forces, the Free French, which contested the Vichy government's control of North Africa and other colonies.[1]

After Pearl Harbor, with the United States and Germany now at war with each other, the British and Americans launched a joint effort called Operation Torch to liberate the French North African territories. The 1st Ranger Battalion, attached to the 1st Infantry Division, commanded by Maj. Gen. Terry de la Mesa Allen and part of the U.S. II Corps, commanded by Maj. Gen. Lloyd Fredendall, saw its first combat as part of the Center Task Force. The American invasion force attacked in three places: Casablanca in Morocco, and Oran and Algiers, both in Algeria. The Center Task Force attacking Oran consisted of the 1st Armored Division and the 1st Infantry Division, including the Rangers.[2] Ranger Sgt. Don Frederick, 1/F: "Several days out at sea after leaving Scotland, it was announced that the battalion was headed for Algeria in North Africa.

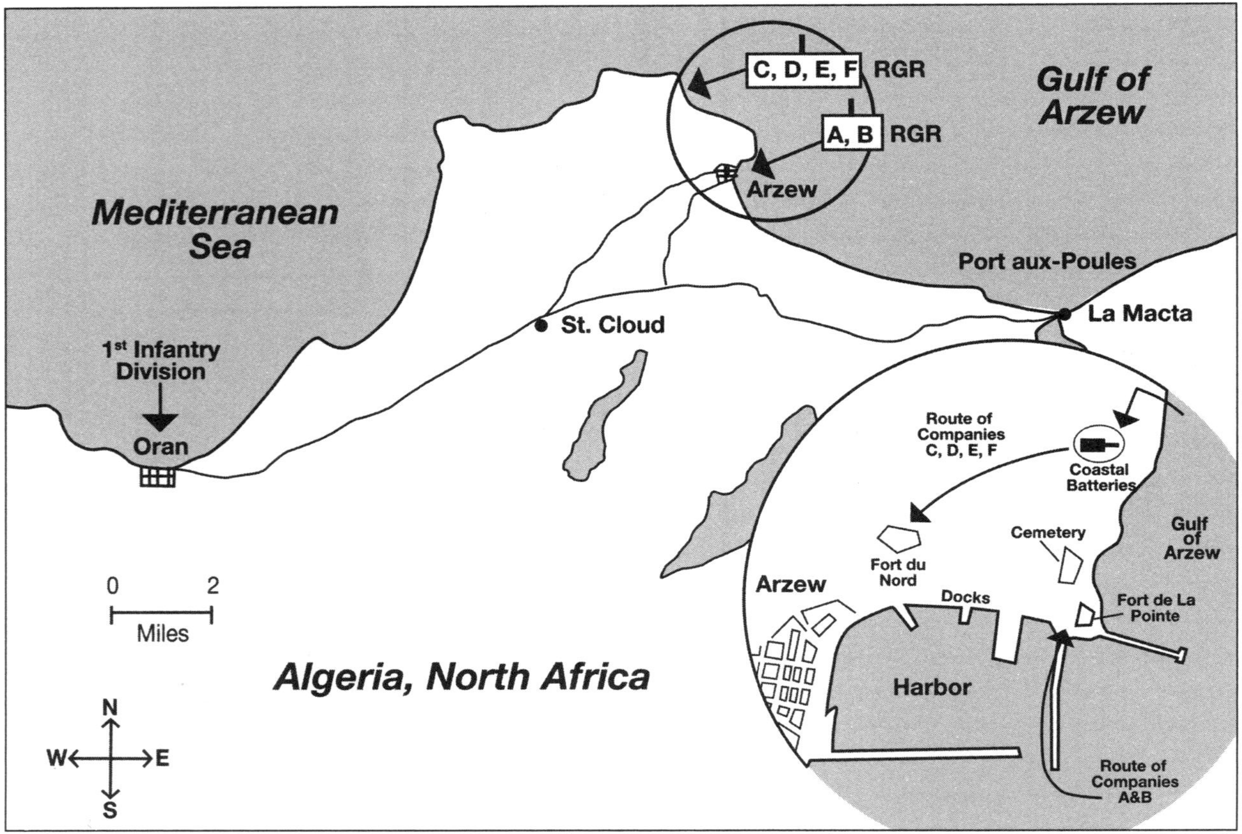

The Rangers in Algeria

We were to be part of the Allied invasion force to land at Arzew, on the Mediterranean, near Oran. A large, precisely defined overlay map with models of our landing beach at Arzew was laid out and studied in great detail."[3]

Just after midnight on 8 November 1942, D-Day* for the American invasion of North Africa, three ships—the HMS *Royal Scotsman* carrying Ranger Companies 1/A and 1/B, the HMS *Ulster Monarch* carrying 1/C and 1/D, and the HMS *Royal Ulsterman* carrying 1/E and 1/F—pulled up and dropped anchor a few miles off the Algerian port of Arzew, thirty miles east of Oran. Before dawn, Rangers loaded into British Landing Craft Assault boats (LCAs) to spearhead the American invasion. The initial objectives were two French forts. One was Fort de la Pointe, a smaller fort that guarded the approaches to the harbor and housed two 75 mm coastal guns. The other, located on high ground beyond the first, was a gun battery armed with four 105 mm guns. These four guns dominated the harbor and were the greatest threat. Behind that was Fort du Nord, a convalescent home for the French Foreign Legion. The objective was to secure and capture or destroy all the coastal guns to prevent them from firing on Allied ships. Both installations were to be attacked at precisely the same time so that neither could warn the other.[4]

FORT DE LA POINTE

The attack began at 0130 hours on 8 November when Companies 1/A and 1/B, under the command of Maj. Herman Dammer, executive officer of the 1st Ranger Battalion, eased into the Arzew harbor, crossing undetected over a protective boom, fortunately lowered at the time of the attack. Capt. Stephen Meade, CO of 1/A, was in the first of four LCAs:

> There was also a local fishing fleet based at that port. . . . The boat in front of me ran into the back end of . . . a French gunboat which nobody knew was there. It was not on the latest aerial photographs. . . . As my boat went under the stern, a French sailor came out and yelled . . . "Qui va?" which in French means "Who goes there?" I yelled back at him in French, "pecheur [fishermen]."

* All Days of Debarkation were called D-Day, not just the famous D-Day in Normandy.

> With that he said "Ca va," and went back into his cabin. So the landing was completed without any general alert being made.[5]

The LCAs rammed the dock, but the noise alarmed no one. Rangers quickly jumped up and ran several hundred yards to the end of the dock, taking up positions around Fort de la Pointe.[6]

Company 1/B established a perimeter around the French fort through which Company 1/A was to pass to directly assault the fort. Lt. James J. Larkin, 1/B:

> I made an inspection of the positions of my men. . . . Their positions were extremely good as the sand table had depicted our sector perfectly. . . . Shortly afterwards, my men were forced to open up on an individual who turned and ran upon being challenged. At about the same time scattered shots were heard from Fort de la Pointe as A Company made its assault at about 0230. Shortly thereafter the Arzew sirens sounded, alerting the entire city. . . . From this time on, French sailors and marines attempted to infiltrate through our lines. However, our men were well concealed and commanded an excellent view of the avenues of approach. They were able in most cases to allow the enemy to approach to a point where retreat was impossible for them. Prisoners were taken whenever possible [and] disarmed.
>
> A group of French marines attempted to pierce our lines by approaching along the road. Frontal fire from our perimeter, plus fire from my runner and myself who were patrolling on their flank, drove them into a quarry . . . they were taken prisoner. . . . During the lulls . . . men were dispatched . . . to the LCA. The four extra L.M.G.s [Light Machine Guns] were set up immediately and manned thus making our position very strong.[7]

Running through Company B, Rangers from Company A assaulted the fort, shooting the only guard. There was little opposition. Rushing inside the fort with bayonets fixed, Rangers slashed ropes holding the soldiers' hammocks, dropping their sleeping occupants to the floor. Tech/5 Donald Hayes Jr., 1/B, described how a surprise attack won victory: "Twenty-five minutes after we landed, we had taken the fort. Very few shots were fired, we took them so much by surprise. The French thought we'd never be able to get them because the fort was on top of a 25-foot cliff. They'd never seen Rangers before."[8]

Tech/5 Murray Katzen, platoon runner for 1/B, armed with a Thompson submachine gun and grenades, cleaned out two barracks single-handedly and captured forty-two men, intimidating them by pulling the pin on a grenade and holding the handle down until he reached the cover of his own men.[9] Capt. Meade fired a red flare to signal the capture of the harbor fort to the main Ranger force. Except for snipers, things were under control by dawn. Lt. Larkin: "Surprise was complete, the guns being captured with speed and with little firing. Approximately fifty prisoners were taken and the guns prepared for demolition and outposts established."[10]

Second Lt. Earl Carran, 1/B, inspected the company's positions about 0330 hours and helped capture eight heavily armed French marines who had snuck under a flatcar to escape capture. Cpl. Anders "Andy" Arnbal told how he and Pfc. Charles Hayes, both of 1/B, took these prisoners:

> I said to Pfc. George Grisamer, 1/B, "I've got to go over there and check what is going on under that trailer. Cover me." With my Colt .45 in my left hand and a grenade in my right, I approached the trailer in a low, crouching stance. Reaching the side of it, I could observe four figures. The odor of foul-smelling tobacco hit me; I knew they were not Rangers. . . . Putting the grenade back in my grenade pouch, I motioned for them to go toward the warehouse front. . . . Leinhas, Musegades, and 1st Sgt. Munro were there. . . . I left them to get back to Grisamer. Lieutenant Larkin, with his high-school French, could interrogate them.
>
> Then it came, indescribably sudden. That sharp splat of lead against the wheels and framework of the trailer, lacing and ricocheting off the dirty brick surface on which we lay. Stunned, with dust particles that blasted into my face and eyes, the acrid odor of hot lead, and the sound of air hissing from the tire punctures all mingled with Grisamer's agonizing, piercing cries, and convulsing movements. Grisamer was the first Ranger to die in North Africa. I not knowing for sure whether I had also been hit . . . by instinct I looked up toward the cemetery wall to our right front, the direction from which the bullets seemed to have come. There were three Legionnaires crouching, ready to run up the trail for more cover than the walls of the cemetery could afford them.
>
> Here the countless hours of machine gun drill automatically took over. My hands spun the traversing and elevation controls, raised the elevation

> sight to 700 yards, sighted the target . . . [and] pressed upward on the trigger. The little, air-cooled, .30-caliber Model M1A 1918 responded fully. . . . My right hand turned the traversing and elevating controls, following the red line of tracer rounds toward the three scrambling figures 700 yards away. . . . I saw the puffs of dust rising at their feet, traversing, and elevating, until the next long burst found its mark. Crumbling, the figures dropped their rifles and rolled, jerkily, a few yards down the slope, coming to rest against some rocks and shrubs. I fired three more short bursts into the bodies in my anger and frustration.[11]

Arnbal was almost sick to his stomach thinking about Grisamer, who was a graduate of Columbia University, but still a country boy at heart. Grisamer had been hospitalized with pneumonia in Scotland but left the hospital early to make the invasion.[12]

Taking several hundred prisoners, Rangers loaded them on 40 and 8 boxcars (railcars designed to carry forty men or eight horses) and escorted them to Oran. First Lt. Manning Jacob, a platoon leader in 1/A, secured a nearby oil refinery: "Immediately after seeing the signal proclaiming the success of Lt. Col. Darby's forces in their attack on Fort du Nord, Captain Meade dispatched my platoon to patrol [an oil refinery that was close to the harbor]. Captain Meade . . . inspected the place, questioning the employees therein, after which he returned to take command of the Fort. My platoon remained in the refinery on patrol until 1630 hours [the next day]."[13]

LARGE COASTAL BATTERIES AND FORT DU NORD

British LCAs carried four companies of Rangers, led by Lt. Col. Darby, to land just after 0130 hours on a beach three miles above the town. Companies 1/C, 1/E, and 1/F were to attack the 105 mm battery that could hit ships five miles out in the bay, and then take out Fort du Nord from the rear.[14] Company 1/D, with its four mortar squads, was to be in a position five hundred yards north of the 105 battery. Cpl. Paul Hermsen, 1/C, led his section in the attack: "Our mission was to capture [the coastal battery] which overlooked the harbor and bay. It was protected by four 105 mm guns and manned by Vichy French. The coastline was rocky and not a good beach to land on. There were about twenty men on each of the landing craft, with almost no resistance on landing."[15]

The gun battery was on a high point, encircled with a double-strand apron of barbed wire and with machine guns covering all possible entrances. To blow up barbed wire entanglements, Rangers carried bangalore torpedoes, long lengths of two-inch pipe filled with dynamite and with connections on the ends so they could be hooked together. Rangers could slide the tubes under the obstacle and detonate them with an electrical fuse.[16]

Sgt. Gino Merçuriali, 1/D, displayed quick thinking and leadership in bringing up the 81 mm mortars that served as the Rangers' artillery. The mortars were heavy, and the Rangers used carts to move them around. Unable to find a path they could negotiate with the carts, Mercuriali unloaded the four 81 mm mortars, and his men hauled them up the cliff on their backs.[17]

To attack the gun battery, Rangers followed a deep ravine that wound its way up to the crest of the hill. They were surprised when, cutting through the barbed wire, two French machine guns opened up. Darby ordered 1/D to lay a concentration of mortar fire on the enemy machine guns.[18] He credited Mercuriali with doing an outstanding job of forcing the French to keep their heads down. The demanding training from the Commandos, teaching Rangers to improvise and think for themselves, was paying off.[19]

As the last mortar shell detonated, Darby, knowing that bayonet charges usually terrified the enemy into surrender, deployed the Rangers in a skirmish line (men abreast with bayonets fixed). Rushing through holes in the barbed wire, the Rangers stormed the gun battery with little opposition, silencing the guns.[20] Racing down the hill toward Fort du Nord, the Rangers broke down the door, taking more than three hundred prisoners, still in their bedclothes. Three hours after the initial landing, Lt. Col. Darby fired success flares, and the Central Task Force of the North African invasion came ashore.

Tech/Sgt. James "Rusty" Rorex, 1/Hq., was in for a pleasant surprise when ordered to secure the mayor's office:

> When we arrived at Arzew we were warmly received by the people, and Darby said that a few of us were to sleep in the town hall for security. We were taken to the area by the mayor's wife who graciously brought us silk sheets, what a luxury! When we left after a few days, the silk sheets went with us, with the mayor's approval. We packed them into our bedrolls, and they . . . were slept on until they were threadbare. I bet we were the only two battlefield soldiers in World War II that slept on silk sheets. Who says Rangers don't go first class?[21]

LA MACTA

Late in the afternoon on 8 November 1942, Darby received orders to send E Company, commanded by Capt. Max Schneider, by train to Port-aux-Poules, a coastal town a few miles east of Arzew, for an assignment with the 16th Infantry Regiment. Arriving before daylight on the 9th, Schneider's men soon located the 16th Regiment, whose commander sent the Rangers on to La Macta, four miles away.[22] One mile from La Macta, the Rangers came under heavy artillery and mortar fire from the French. One platoon, commanded by 1st Lt. Robert Flanagan, laid down suppressing fire on the enemy while the other platoon, commanded by 1st Lt. James B. Lyle, attacked the French flank. Lt. Lyle "borrowed" a half-track with a 75 mm gun from one of the American infantry battalions, taking with him Platoon Sgt. Les Kness, Pfc. Ed Dean, Pfc. Charles Leighton, and Pfc. Joe Dye. After one shot from the 75 mm, the French fled. Rangers then occupied and protected the town of La Macta for a day before rejoining the battalion.[23]

ST. CLOUD

Attempting to capture the port of Oran, the 1st Infantry Division was blocked by the French at the town of St. Cloud. One day after the capture of Arzew, Darby sent C Company, commanded by Capt. Gordon Klefman, to assist the 1st Infantry Division. These Rangers were attached to the 18th Infantry Regiment of the 1st Infantry Division and ordered to make a night march around St. Cloud to prevent the French from escaping.[24] At dawn the next day, 1st Lt. Charles Shunstrom's platoon attacked an enemy convoy that was stopped on the road, but heavy fire from machine guns, mortars, and artillery blocked further progress. Sgt. Robert Bacon, 1/C: "We were caught in the open by a battery of French 75 millimeter artillery. We kept our heads down as much as possible until we could finally get a few men into the enemy gun-position, which we quickly silenced."[25]

When Gen. Allen's men finally captured Oran, the French commander at St. Cloud ordered his men to cease fire. Nevertheless, the Rangers suffered heavy losses when Capt. Klefman, Pfc. Elmer Eskola, 1/C, and Pfc. Alder L. Nystrom, 1/C, were all killed by French artillery fire. Eight other Rangers in 1/C were wounded, including Pfc. Ivan Heid, hit by shrapnel,[26] and Tech/5 Burton Boudreau, shot through the elbow by a sniper round.[27] With Klefman's death, 1st Lt. Manning Jacob was named to command 1/C. With the Rangers now short an officer, SGM Warren "Bing" Evans was promoted to 2nd lieutenant, becoming a platoon leader.[28] This was the first battlefield commission in the American army in the Mediterranean Theater in World War II.

Sgt. Alex Szima, 1/C, with the 1st Armored Division before becoming a Ranger, had experience that helped prevent accidents from friendly fire. Szima:

> During the artillery attack by the French, we saw tanks approaching from the right. Through binoculars I could see that these were from the 1st Armored Division, my former regular army outfit. But the tanks thought we were the enemy and opened fire on us with .50 caliber machine guns. I stood on the shoulders of Pvt. William (Spike) Sandlin, 1/C, giving the old cavalry hand signal fifteen times before they returned the signal, saving a lot more casualties. We put the wounded into a half-track and headed for the closest farmhouse for cover. Pvt. William Sandlin and Pvt. Richard (Monk) Elliott, both of 1/C and from the 1st Armored, were qualified tank drivers and rode with us.[29]

At the end of November all Arzew forts were turned over to the Free French, and the battalion moved to bivouac in some unoccupied beach houses east of Arzew. Here the battalion continued MP duty in the town of Arzew and resumed special training with ten- to fifteen-mile speed marches, weapons drills, exercises by company of fire and movement, and day and night landings.[30]

Rangers got time off in the evening, and some men got passes to go into Arzew for rest and relaxation (R&R). Not everyone got a pass when they wanted it, but most of the enlisted men got to go to town a time or two. Darby put MP arm bands on several of his sergeants to make sure that if any of his Rangers got into trouble, the "Ranger MPs" would get them back to camp before regular MPs could rough them up. When they had the chance, officers also went into town to visit local bars and amuse themselves in "other ways" customary among soldiers in every war.[31]

Lt. Jim Lyle, Sgt. Lester Kness, Cpl. Edwin Dean, and Sgt. Joseph Dye, all from 1/E, called themselves the "Four Musketeers." The four of them would often go on patrol together and became close friends, calling each other at

Christmas for many years. Sgt. Kness recalled how Lt. Lyle handled himself one evening in Arzew when introduced to a fancy drink in off-duty hours: "As platoon sergeant for 1st Lt. Jim Lyle, I knew him pretty well. Lyle was a sergeant before becoming an officer, and we sometimes went to a bar together. Introduced to a Brandy Alexander, Lyle downed a 'few' the first time he tried them. Lyle slipped off the stool at the bar but was hugging it, calling out to the bartender, 'Another Alexander,' as he tried to pull himself back up on the stool."[32]

FATHER ALBERT EDWARD BASIL

After joining the Rangers in Scotland, Father Albert Edward Basil's first official duty in North Africa was to officiate at a mass for the burial of the four Rangers. It was a sad day as the Rangers said a formal goodbye, with full military honors, to the four Rangers killed. Father Basil wore the Commandos' green beret topping off his British uniform. Lt. Gen. George S. Patton Jr., newly arrived in North Africa, was a strict observer of military custom, and when he first saw Father Basil, he demanded that Lt. Col. Darby make the priest dress correctly for an army chaplain. Darby told Patton that Father Basil was the only man in the army over whom Patton had no authority.[33]

Capt. Roy Murray, commanding 1/F, recalled a mass being conducted by Father Basil when they were under enemy shell fire:

> Father Basil said, "You may put on your helmets, if you so desire." Everybody stuffed their helmets on . . . and he calmly proceeded with mass. Sometimes after mass he'd come out on the beach at Arzew and find some of the Catholic boys playing poker instead of going to mass. He would reach down in the pot and grab all the money and stick it in his pocket and tell them, "That's for not going to mass this morning." He wasn't being paid by the British. . . . He was missing from the British Army . . . they didn't know where he was, and he wasn't telling them.[34]

POST ARZEW

After capturing Arzew, the Rangers were "parked" while the American commanders considered where they should next be assigned. Some of the men, bored with the daily training regime and guarding prisoners, left the Rangers. Two months of intensive training in the area around Arzew followed, with emphasis on night operations. The North African terrain was totally different from that of the British Isles, and the men had to become familiar with this new landscape. From 18 to 23 January, Rangers trained for future combat in Tunisia, developing the ability to attack cross-country at night using small unit tactics with contact between adjacent units.[35]

Ranger officers aboard ship in Arzew harbor immediately after the invasion of Algeria, November 1942. Capt. Gordon Klefman is missing, killed in action after the invasion. With his death, Warren "Bing" Evans received a battlefield commission, becoming a 2nd lieutenant. Those actions date the photo. *Standing, left to right:* 1st Lt. Leilyn Young, 1st Lt. Charles Shunstrom, Commando Chaplain Albert Basil, 1st Lt. James Lyle, 1st Lt. Dean Knudson, 2nd Lt. Warren Evans, Capt. Alvah Miller, 1st Lt. Robert Flanagan, 1st Lt. Walter Nye, 1st Lt. Fredric Ahlgren, Capt. Earl Carran, and 1st Lt. Leonard Dirks. *Seated, left to right:* Capt. Max Schneider, Capt. Roy A. Murray, Capt. Stephen Meade, Maj. Herman Dammer, Lt. Col. William O. Darby, Capt. William Martin, 1st Lt. George Sunshine, Capt. Manning Jacob, 1st Lt. James Larkin, and 1st Lt. William Lanning. Courtesy Col. James B. Lyle, photograph by Ranger Phil Stern.

Famed war correspondent Ernie Pyle, called the "soldier's mouthpiece" because he connected with enlisted men and told their side of the war, visited the Rangers. Pyle reported that after their rugged training in Scotland, most of the Rangers thought they were indestructible and deadly executioners. But now they were encamped, running through mock landings, swimming in the Mediterranean on the coldest days, and doing military police duty in a nearby town. They were going nuts waiting to get into action again.[36] Pyle: "I made friends with one Ranger officer, Capt. Manning Jacob who . . . took me on a cross-country walk, following a detachment of Rangers. I had to run to keep up. Finally, I couldn't go on any longer, and had to sit down and pant. I thought to myself, I'm ashamed of being so soft and feeble, but after all I'm past forty. . . . And then it turned out that this lethal athlete called Captain Jacob was forty years old himself."[37]

Maj. Gen. Terry Allen, CO of the 1st Infantry Division, to which the Rangers were attached, was known as the "soldiers' general" because he always put the safety and care of the troops first. He was the favorite general of the Rangers and would often call on them for special operations while in North Africa.[38]

During post-Arzew training, Capt. Jacob, 1st Lt. Dean Knudson, 1/B, and 1st Lt. William Lanning all suffered foot or ankle injuries, which kept them from meeting the Rangers' physical requirements.[39] Consequently, they were relieved of duty and sent back to the United States to train new Rangers. It would not be much longer before the Rangers found out what they were being trained for.

5

TUNISIA

SENED STATION AND KASSERINE PASS

Since 13 September 1940, when Italian troops attacked British positions in Egypt, the British had fought tank and infantry battles against Italian and German forces across the North African desert. Gen. Bernard Montgomery commanded the British Eighth Army, serving under Gen. Sir Harold R. L. Alexander, who headed all the British Middle East forces. Germany's Field Marshal Albert Kesselring named Field Marshal Erwin Rommel to command the Afrika Corps, a force combining infantry and armor. Called the "Desert Fox," Rommel, respected and feared by all Allied commanders, was a genius at catching his enemies off guard, attacking with sturdy, powerful panzers firing the dreaded 88 mm round. The Germans had the most powerful tank, but the British had more of them. Both sides suffered crippling losses as they took turns capturing or losing territory. Overall, the Germans were enjoying tactical success, winning small battles and wearing down the British.

However, on 23 October 1942, Gen. Montgomery launched a major attack on the Germans at the Second Battle of El Alamein in Egypt. Rommel, who had been on medical leave in Germany, returned to the fight at once, but his illness worsened as the weeks passed, including serious digestive issues, insomnia, and boils leading to depression that hampered his judgment.[1] Rommel asked Hitler to evacuate North Africa because he could not see a path to German victory if its army stayed there. But because of North Africa's oil reserves, Hitler refused to let Rommel pull out.[2] Therefore, Rommel no longer respected or trusted Hitler and would later participate in an unsuccessful plot to kill the Nazi leader, which led to Rommel's forced suicide by cyanide poisoning, tantamount to execution.[3]

As the 1st Armored Division, commanded by Maj. Gen. Orlando P. Ward, and the 1st Infantry Division, commanded by Maj. Gen. Terry Allen, began mov-

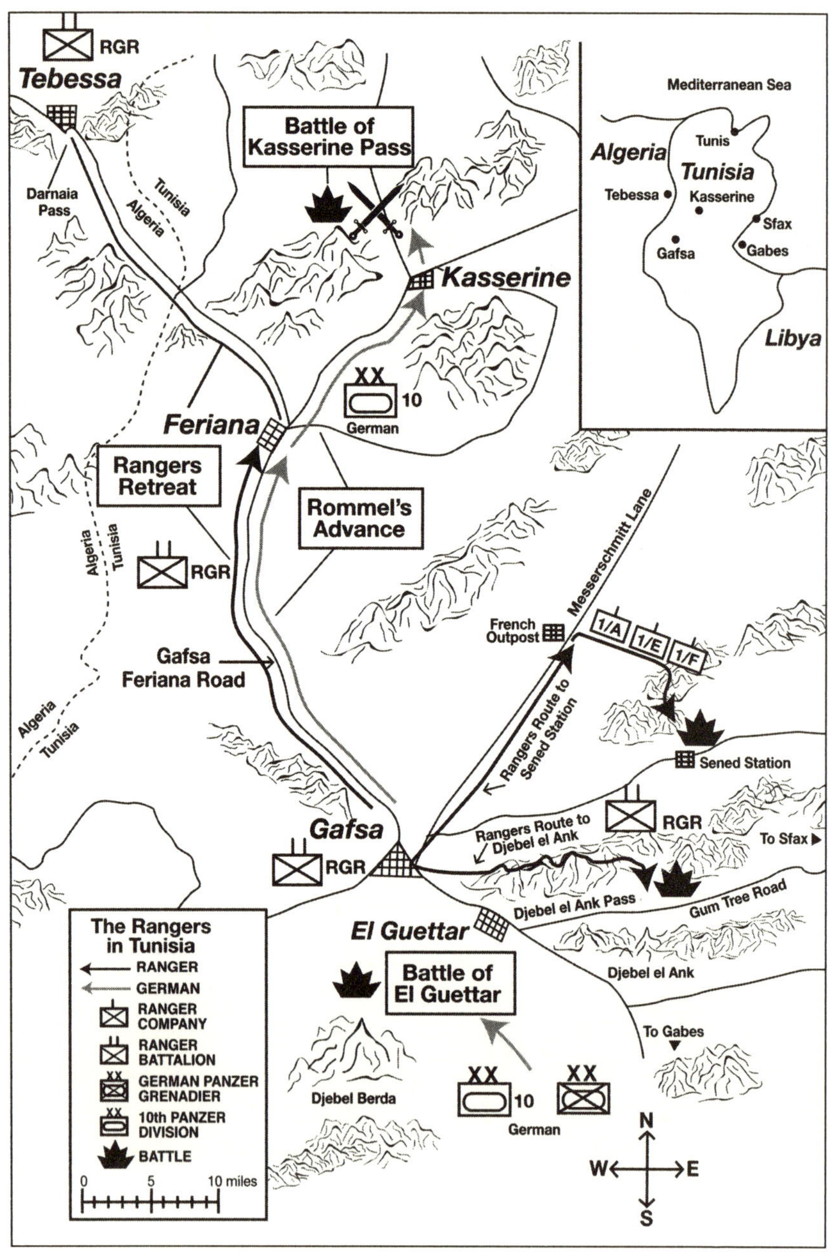

The Rangers in Tunisia

ing into Tunisia, German spies reported massive buildups of men and equipment and an endless supply of ammunition. To counter this, the 10th Panzer Division, commanded by Generaloberst Hans-Jürgen von Arnim, moved into Tunisia to bolster the German forces, with both von Arnim and Rommel reporting directly to Gen. Kesselring in Rome. By early 1943, Axis forces in Tunisia totaled 220,000 men, with 350 German tanks, 90 Italian tanks, 750 field and medium guns, and 900 antitank guns.[4] The German commanders loathed each other. Von Arnim was the son of a Prussian general, whereas Rommel had risen from an obscure background. Eisenhower wanted to get his forces into Tunisia before the two German armies linked up. Had these two enemy armies joined forces, the results in Tunisia might have been very different.[5]

ARRIVAL OF THE RANGERS IN TUNISIA

In early February 1943, the Americans occupied a triangular area with its western point at Tebessa, a city just inside the border of Algeria, roughly a hundred miles south of the Mediterranean coast. Tebessa became the headquarters of the U.S. II Corps. The second point of the triangle, about twenty-five miles southeast of Tebessa, was the Kasserine Pass, a north-south passage through the mountains. About a hundred miles south of Tebessa was the third point of the triangle, the oasis of Gafsa, isolated in the desert and surrounded by mountain ranges.[6] Along the route between Gafsa and Tebessa lay the town of Feriana and the Dernaia Pass, a narrow choke point between mountains that partially protected Tebessa from attack from the south. Within this seven hundred-square-mile triangle, the American armored and infantry forces increased daily.

The 1st Ranger Battalion was ordered into service to fly from Oran to Tunisia with a three-fold mission: harass the enemy, perform reconnaissance, and raid deep behind enemy lines.[7] Transported on thirty-two Douglas C-47s and landing near the headquarters for the U.S. II Corps at Tebessa,[8] the Rangers would soon experience their first sustained combat against a well-armed enemy. Two days after arriving in Tebessa, the Rangers boarded trucks for Gafsa, where they bivouacked outside the town in an olive orchard. Pfc. Austin Miller, 1/F, described Gafsa, which had already changed hands more than once, as "The largest oasis in North Africa, right on the edge of the Sahara Desert, with more strategic importance than Tebessa."[9] In Gafsa, Rangers acquired additional equipment, including toggle ropes and concussion grenades.[10] The thrower of a concussion grenade did not have to take cover as he did with a fragmentation grenade, enabling a Ranger to rapidly follow the grenade to dispatch an enemy who was momentarily stunned by the concussion.

FIRST LT. JAMES B. LYLE PROMOTED TO COMPANY COMMANDER

Having lost Capt. Manning Jacob, CO of 1/C, due to an injury, Darby replaced him with twenty-nine-year-old 1st Lt. James B. Lyle, who was older than most of the other officers. Being a sergeant in the regular army before joining the Rangers gave Lyle a different perspective from that of officers who had never served in the enlisted ranks, experience that would serve the Rangers well. Years later, then Col. Roy A. Murray (retired), who had commanded 1/F in Tunisia, told me that Darby put Lyle in command of Company 1/C because Lyle was able to control young Lt. Charles Shunstrom, who had been a handful for other commanders.[11] In fact, Lyle and Shunstrom had trained together in Officer Candidate School (OCS) Class No. 3 at Fort Benning, Georgia, graduating in December 1941.

PREPARATION FOR THE RAID ON SENED STATION

Two days after entering Gafsa, Maj. Gen. Lloyd Fredendall, commander of the American II Corps, assigned the Rangers the job of capturing Sened Station, an enemy position located in a mountain pass deep behind enemy lines, about thirty miles from Gafsa, off the road to the coastal city of Sfax.[12] Sened Station was manned by Italian soldiers of the Centauro Division and the elite Bersaglieri mountain troops and a handful of German advisors. On the day preceding the raid, Lt. Col. Darby, Maj. Dammer, and the commanders of 1/A, 1/E, and 1/F scouted out the enemy position and selected a safe hideout for use on the mission.[13]

Tech/5 Sherman Legg, 1/Hq., was on the point, riding a motorcycle and armed with a Tommy gun. Legg: "It was my job to find out who was out there and where they were. It could have been Germans in front of us, and it could have been Vichy French. I didn't know what to expect."[14]

When the commanders returned to Gafsa in the early evening, they alerted Companies A, E, and F to prepare for a mission that night, moving out at 2300 hours. Rangers endured a two-hour, eighteen-mile black-out ride to a Free French outpost up a road called "Messerschmitt Lane," so named because the Germans strafed it all the time.[15] Leaving their trucks at the French outpost, the Rangers hiked eight miles over rough desert terrain, arriving just before daylight at the hideout in the saddle of a mountain overlooking the target that their commanders had located the previous day. Each man carried a shelter half, one half of a two-man pup tent that could be buttoned together. Rangers were instructed to hide under their shelter halves the next day so they would not be observed by German aircraft or by roaming nomads. There was also the risk that an enemy patrol might show up. Rangers were told to conserve their food and water because, when that was gone, there was no more.[16]

Through binoculars, the officers and NCOs kept watch on Sened Station, still four miles away, studying the terrain and choosing their points of attack. They estimated enemy strength at a hundred men. First Lt. Leilyn Young, 1/Hq., noted: "Slept but very cold. At 11:15 PM began movement to objective."[17] Sgt. Donald Frederick, 1/F, described the organization for the assault:

> Close to midnight on 11 February 1943, Rangers fixed bayonets and moved out. When we were about six hundred yards from the target, we formed a skirmish line and kept marching, three companies abreast marching side by side in total darkness on a half-mile front. Company 1/A was on the left . . . Company 1/E, held the center . . . while Company 1/F formed the right flank. Tech Sgt. Richard Porter, 1/F, worked out a system of using colored flashlights so that Darby could observe the Ranger formation and use his radio to keep the Rangers in line as they moved forward. Headquarters Company and the mortar sections remained in the rear with Darby. We wanted the Germans to think we had thousands of men at Gafsa waiting to attack.[18]

THE ASSAULT ON SENED STATION

In combat and on patrols, Rangers wore no insignia of rank. However, on the back of each officer's pack was a code letter in silhouette tape that showed his company and platoon. Rangers always removed watches and rings before night combat because anything shiny might give away a soldier's position. To eliminate the possibility of noise from something hitting the steel helmet, Rangers on night patrol wore wool caps instead of helmets.[19] Sgt. James Altieri, 1/F, noting they had marched about a half hour when suddenly the line halted: "We hit the ground, rifles at the ready. Nye whispered back to me, 'Enemy patrol!'. . . . A muffled scream pierced the night, followed by complete silence. . . . Nye again whispered back, 'A Company's scouts got 'em.' I knew what that meant. Ranger knives had had their first taste of enemy blood."[20] When they were within two hundred yards of Sened Station, the enemy must have sensed something was wrong and opened fire with machine guns. Rangers hit the dirt with bullets flying over their heads, but no one was injured.[21]

The Rangers planned for all three companies to assault simultaneously in a straight front, killing most of the enemy, leaving just a few wounded to tell what happened. Unknown to the Rangers, the enemy center was out in advance of the two flanks. When Schneider's E Company was almost on top of the defenders' center, he shouted, "Deploy!"[22] Rangers assaulted suddenly and viciously with bayonets, fighting knives, and concussion grenades before the enemy could muster a defense. The enemy rushed to their guns and began firing wildly and tossed fragmentation grenades. Once their muzzle blasts revealed the Italian positions, the Rangers could destroy them.[23] When the firing started, the Rangers' 60 mm mortars opened up and began dropping shells on the rear of the enemy outpost. Company commanders called in specific targets, which the mortar crews wiped out. Because some of the Rangers slit the throats of their enemies, the Germans branded the Rangers as outlaws, ordering that none of them should be taken alive.[24] Lt. Warren "Bing" Evans, 1/A, was advancing on the far left when he realized an enemy soldier with fixed bayonet was almost upon him: "My mind seized up momentarily except for the quick thought that I was about to die. I froze on the trigger, unable to fire my weapon. The soldier's eyes were as big as saucers, that's how close the enemy soldier was to running me through with his bayonet."[25] Spotting the danger, Pvt. Thomas Sullivan, Evans's runner, shot the enemy soldier, who dropped at Evans's feet. Evans's mind snapped back to reality, and he continued the fight with no more problems.[26] Years later, while Evans was viewing the movie *Saving Private Ryan,* the soundtrack went silent as the video went to slow motion, showing Capt. Miller's mind freezing up. Evans realized that this was what happened to him and blurted out loud, "The vacuum!" He realized that this probably occurs often in combat and is probably when a lot of soldiers become casualties. Sgt. James Altieri, 1/F, was out on the far right:

> For forty yards we crawled under the enemy's searching, scorching fire . . . we moved forward, shutting out the terrible hell around us as though it didn't exist. . . . Another long moment . . . then, "Give 'em hell!" Nye's voice rang out. "Grenade first," I yelled, as I pulled a pin on my grenade and hurled it up toward the stabbing flames of a machine gun. . . . Swiftly we were on our feet, screaming at the top of our lungs, charging up the slopes, firing our rifles and Tommy guns from our hip.[27]

During the action, Darby radioed Capt. Schneider asking how many prisoners he had. Schneider replied that he had two, but the radio crackled, and Darby asked for a repeat. The enemy prisoners bolted, and Schneider fired two quick shots. Schneider radioed back to Darby, "Well, I had two."[28]

In twenty minutes, it was all over. Estimated enemy losses were eighty-five killed, about twenty-five wounded, probably fatally, leaving the Rangers with thirteen prisoners. Twenty Rangers had been wounded, including 2nd Lt. Robert Neal, 2nd Lt. Dennis Matlock, and Pfc. Evan Gannon, 1/E. Stepping in front of an enemy cannon just as it had fired, Ranger Pfc. Elmer Garrison had been instantly decapitated, the Rangers' only fatality in this action.[29] With mopping up completed, the Rangers pulled back to reform for the march back to where trucks would pick them up. It was a race against the clock and coming daylight. After marching less than a quarter of a mile, Darby split them into two groups. The uninjured group speed marched for twelve miles to get to safety before they were caught by daylight. The wounded and enough men to carry them went back to the mountain hideout, where they would await trucks to carry them to an aid station the next night.[30]

One Italian prisoner, who was badly hurt, could not keep up, and there was no one else to carry him. Darby could not turn him loose, lest he might bring help and jeopardize their return. A Ranger was ordered to dispatch the prisoner, but when the Italian began crying and begging for his life, the Ranger could not pull the trigger. Platoon Sgt. Les Kness, 1/E, stepped in and killed the man.[31] Incidents like this gave Rangers nightmares for years after the war. For their valor at Sened Station, five officers and nine enlisted men received the Silver Star, including the officers who personally led the attack.

AFTER SENED STATION: ROMMEL'S RESPONSE

After Sened Station, Rommel asked Field Marshal Kesselring, for permission to launch an offensive to destroy the American army near Kasserine Pass. It was to be a parallel but separate effort between the competing forces of Rommel and von Arnim to split the British and American forces, getting at least as far as Tebessa, where the Americans had a huge store of equipment and ammunition. Rommel must have thought the attack was risky, but it would delay—if not stop—the American move into Tunisia.[32]

THE AMERICAN WITHDRAWAL FROM GAFSA

Rommel began his offensive by sending his panzer divisions on a surprise attack on the Americans at Gafsa. The Americans were not yet ready to face German armor and were ordered to leave Gafsa, for an area near Tebessa.[33] On 14 February 1943, when Rommel's main armor force surged forward from the south and approached Gafsa, the Rangers were the last Americans to leave. Some of Rommel's armored scouting units were already on Gafsa's flanks, and a few were approaching Feriana, where they would be able to cut off the Rangers' retreat. Speed marching learned in training with the Commandos saved the Rangers' lives as they raced to stay ahead of the German armor. Ordered to protect Tebessa, the Rangers were directed to march north from Gafsa through Feriana and then west through Dernaia Pass to reach Tebessa.[34] VanArtsdalen:

> We had to travel on foot as quickly as possible. The battalion had no heavy weapons, only light arms, consisting of rifles, BARs, and 60 mm mortars. Darby told us . . . no one knew what we might encounter while crossing the desolate plain to Dernaia Pass. Lt. Col. Darby told us we had a long way to go. He said, "We don't know what is to the left or the right of us, or what may be in front of us. We know that there are enemy tanks in the vicinity because some of these have been crossing in front of us. We may run into some tanks. If we do, all I can say is God help the tanks."[35]

Cpl. Anders Arnbal, 1/B, described the danger the Rangers faced: "We were told that the Germans were on the offensive, had already routed both the 168th Infantry Regiment and supporting 1st Armored units . . . and had reoccupied Sened, driving toward Feriana and Kasserine. It was very possible that we might even be cut off unless the German drive slowed down."[36] Trucks arrived to carry the Rangers, but not enough trucks to carry them all.

Arnbal's squad hiked the Gafsa-Feriana road until dawn, when they moved off the road into some cover for a brief nap, taking turns standing guard. When they resumed the speed march, Pfc. Leighton badly sprained an ankle. Luckily the squad met some Syrians with a truck. They were cooking breakfast and agreed to take Leighton with them.[37] During the "tactical withdrawal," as Darby described it, the Rangers only defense against tanks were their sticky grenades, which every man carried. Arnbal explained this weapon. "This was a British hand-thrown anti-tank grenade . . . about eight inches in diameter, with a short wooden handle attached. . . . the grenade itself was a glass globe . . . saturated with a very sticky substance. . . . You threw it like you would an overhand baseball or football. Upon striking the tank, the glass globe broke at the point of impact . . . and a large explosive charge was directed against the metal of the tank."[38] Capt. Lyle taught his men another option when sticky grenades were in short supply: "We told Rangers to stuff explosives, with a fuse, in a sock. Covered with axle grease, it usually would stick to a tank when thrown, but we had to be dangerously close to an enemy tank to use it."[39]

The Rangers marched north, moving into the hills near Feriana until enemy tanks arrived. Darby then ordered his men to secure Dernaia Pass, west of Kasserine, where a major attack on Tebessa was anticipated. If the Germans wanted to flank Kasserine Pass, they would have to move along the road going through Dernaia Pass.[40]

Upon arriving at Feriana, Arnbal's squad from 1/B met Capt. Roy Murray, who brought two six-by-six transport trucks to pick up men unable to walk further. Murray had no rations, but he did have water. While Murray waited to see if other Rangers would arrive, the squad from 1/B curled up in the town square for a nap. Early the next morning two German planes, Messerschmitt Bf 109s, strafed Feriana, but no one was injured. The two trucks left with the disabled, and the squad from 1/B was again the last to leave, knowing that they still had twenty-four hours of marching to reach Tebessa.[41]

The Rangers stayed off the roadbed due to the risk of enemy mines, marching on either the left or right side. Arnbal's squad trudged through the dark, even when rain soaked them to the skin. Sticky mud weighed down their boots. Out of food, hard candy, and water, the group used their helmets to catch rainwater. Without the conditioning and the confidence that came from hard training in long-distance marching by the Commandos, they could not have made it.[42] Cpl. Arnbal: "We were challenged by a Ranger outpost well camouflaged behind some shrubs on the left side of the road. [S/Sgt. William] Musegades called out that we didn't have the password, but when we called out our names they recognized us."[43]

It was three days before the entire battalion reassembled to bivouac in the mountains near Tebessa, setting up defensive positions along the Feriana-Tebessa road and sending out patrols both day and night to guard against a potential German attack through Dernaia Pass. One dark night, during a light rain, a patrol from 1/A came upon a German motorized infantry unit with a field kitchen. The Rangers turned up the collars of their field jackets and, hunching over like German soldiers warding off the rain, slipped in the line and got some hot chocolate, sausages, and bread. There was not much these cocky American Rangers wouldn't do.[44] Checking the battalion's positions one night, Darby found the three-man crew of a 37 mm gun asleep and ordered that they be shot at sunrise. Cpl. Arnbal: "The firing squad was to be chosen by lottery from the company that manned the 37s. Daylight came and no execution, as the officers of the battalion had prevailed on Lt. Col. Darby to withhold his wrath and swallow his proclamation in the interest of the battalion's morale. . . . He settled for a court-martial, awarding them loss of one-third of their pay for three months."[45]

On 17 February, Cpl. Paul Hermsen, 1/C, met misfortune on a scouting patrol:

> After a three to four-hour scout, I returned to the assembly point to find the other men and vehicles gone. While searching for the other Rangers, I turned the corner of a mountain trail and encountered a patrol of about twenty Italians led by a German officer. I threw two grenades and opened fire with my rifle, killing three of the enemy, including the German officer.
>
> While reloading my rifle I suddenly felt paralyzed. Another Italian patrol

> had come up behind me, and one of the soldiers thrust a bayonet at my back. It caught on a grommet of my cartridge belt and pinned against my spine. I often wonder why they didn't shoot me, but another Ranger told me years later that often the Italians did not take good care of their equipment, and the enemy rifle probably jammed. I expected death, but American artillery began to land, and the enemy took me prisoner.
>
> I was taken to Feriana and then marched about twenty-five miles to another camp in German-held territory. Eventually, I wound up at Stalag [VIIA], a POW processing facility, at Mooseburg, Germany, about fifteen miles from Munich. From there I was marched to Stalag IIIB which was my home for the next [fifteen] months.[46]

BATTLE OF KASSERINE PASS

Kasserine Pass was less than a mile wide at its narrowest point, making it easy to defend, but American armor and infantry, positioned west and south of the pass, were poorly organized and not well dug in. Men were sleeping instead of installing mines.[47] The inept Maj. Gen. Lloyd Fredendall did not think the Germans would attack since the Americans outnumbered them in tanks and troops.[48] Reaching Kasserine Pass on 19 February, Rommel's forces made a frontal assault, easily overrunning the Americans and knocking out their thin-skinned tanks. Fueled with gasoline, the American tanks, which Capt. Lyle called "rolling coffins," became fiery torches with the first hit. There was no way to defend against the panzers, except with large-bore artillery, and the Allies had very little of it as yet.[49] During 19 to 22 February, Rommel's attack utterly crushed the Americans, inflicting huge losses of men and equipment.[50] Arnbal saw the result: "A formation of forty-one Sherman tanks of the 1st Armored Division had nearly all been wiped out by two German Tiger tanks equipped with the dreaded 88 mm rifle. The Sherman's little 75 mm howitzers were no match at all against the German 88."[51] Maj. Gen. Allen's 1st Infantry Division, known as the "Big Red One" found its back to the wall. With the 1st Ranger Battalion attached, Allen ordered Darby to send in a reinforced company with a "hairy-chested company commander with big nuts."[52] Darby sent Capt. James B. Lyle and his Company C. Unable to find information to the contrary, Col. Robert Black concluded that "the size of Lyle's appendages remained classified."[53]

138

MEMORANDUM TO: Lt. Colonel Darby.

Dear Bill:

This is vital. There is a hell of a mess on our front. Fechet counter-attacks with all he's got, direction north from about 7277. at 2<u>oo</u> PM

Can you send me one reinforced company with a hairy chested company commander with big nuts as Fechet's last reserve? Am sending 3 trucks to move this company unless you are too closely involved to spare the same. Every emergency is needed here from 2 P.M. until dark. Need your help if you can fight in place with what you have and lend me a reinforced company in the interval.

Terry Allen

TERRY ALLEN

3 Trucks are now enroute

Orders to Lt. Col. Darby from Maj. Gen. Terry Allen, Commanding General, 1st Infantry Division, Tunisia, February 1943. Courtesy Col. James B. Lyle, photograph by Ranger Phil Stern, 1943.

Because Rommel was running out of diesel and ammunition, he never made it to Tebessa, and he sustained heavy losses from American bombing of his supply lines. Rommel stopped his forward progress by 22 February had begun retreating back through Kasserine Pass.[54] American generals, who had feared the absolute destruction of their forces, must have been astounded by the German retreat. Lyle's company was not needed and was returned to the Ranger battalion the next day.

---- 6 ----

THE BATTLE OF DJEBEL EL ANK

When Rommel withdrew after the battle at Kasserine Pass, the Rangers were called on to check for German stragglers, spies, and snipers left behind. As they worked east from Tebessa to Kasserine Pass and beyond, they were aghast at the destruction to American forces. Tanks, trucks, jeeps, and destroyed artillery pieces were still smoldering. Burial crews sometimes had to gather up the pieces of bodies blown to bits by German tanks and artillery. Sometimes it was impossible to identify the dead. The Rangers walked through this debris field, feeling fortunate to have missed the slaughter.[1] Pvt. Arnold E. Davis, 1/E: "I was a young man . . . still in my teens. I stood among the cluttered battlefield and looked around and then knew that something big had happened in this place. A few short steps and I picked up a steel helmet, upon which had been fixed, in quieter times, the oak leaf of a [U.S.] major. Where was he now? Was he a prisoner, had he escaped with his life, or was he at this moment in his eternal grave, the helmet, with its emptiness mocking that final disposition?"[2] German patrols still roamed the area, covering their withdrawal. The 1st Infantry Division began to fill the gap left by Rommel, with the Rangers out in front, moving south on the road from Kasserine to reoccupy Gafsa, from which they had just escaped days earlier. Gen. Fredendall had lost contact with the Germans during the enemy's retreat, an unforgivable error in modern combat.[3]

Gen. Allen ordered Darby to advance farther, hoping to find the Germans. With little opposition, the Rangers took El Guettar, fifteen miles southeast of Gafsa on the road to Gabes, a town on the coast fifty miles southeast of Gafsa. So far no Germans! Fredendall ordered Maj. Gen. Allen to find the enemy.[4] Allen sent out several motorcycle riders, one of whom was Pfc. Steve Ketzer, formerly with Ranger company 1/F. Ketzer had left the Rangers because of a foot injury that prevented him from making speed marches. Ketzer found the Germans near Faid Pass, but the Germans shot the bike out from under him,

Drawing by POW S/Sgt. Dennis Bergstrom, 1/Hq., given to POW Pfc. Steve Ketzer at Stalag IIB on 9 March 1944. The drawing shows Ketzer's motorcycle shot out from under him. Ranger Ketzer is captured. He waves "so long" to Ranger Dennis Bergstrom (the artist) and is flown by the Germans to Sicily and then Italy and winds up at Stalag IIB in "Deutschland." All of the Rangers' major battles are shown: El Guettar in Tunisia; Gela in Sicily; Maiori and Monte Chiunzi at Salerno, Italy; Venafro; and finally Anzio, where the Rangers are captured a year later and meet Ketzer in Stalag IIB POW camp. Courtesy Steve Ketzer Jr. and Ranger Dennis Bergstrom.

a piece of the shell puncturing his leg. When captured, Ketzer was whisked off to Berlin to be further interrogated before finally being shipped off Stalag IIB, a notorious German POW camp for enlisted men. He was the first Ranger POW to be held there, but eventually there would be more.[5]

The new Commander in Chief of Allied forces, Gen. Dwight Eisenhower, inspecting the front-line American troops, was horrified at what he found. Commander after commander told him that they had lost all respect for Fredendall. Several area commanders had laid out antitank mines on top of the ground in the event the Germans should attack again, but the mines were never buried so as to be operational. Artillery had not been sited. Furthermore, tanks were poorly placed to defend in the event of another attack. Eisenhower was furious.[6] Fredendall was so afraid of getting killed that he had marshalled all available combat engineers to construct a new headquarters deep in the bowels of a mountain, almost a hundred miles west of Kasserine Pass, further protected by reinforced concrete to keep it safe from bombers and artillery.[7] Eisenhower relieved Fredendall on the spot, replacing him with Lt. Gen. George S. Patton Jr., who arrived at the front on 6 March 1943.[8] Ranger Sgt. Don Frederick, 1/F, remembered seeing Patton arrive to take command of II Corps. He was standing up in an armored half-track with siren blaring, escorted by MPs on motorcycles with sirens and further accompanied by jeeps with machine guns mounted.[9]

Patton insisted on discipline even in small matters. He wanted uniforms to be clean and neat, with neckties worn by officers and shirttails tucked in. Although the Rangers kept their weapons immaculate, they cared nothing about their own appearance. They resented the petty regulations but nevertheless followed them to the letter. Patton was not popular with the Rangers, but he instilled a new confidence in the American army—confidence that would win battles.[10]

Rommel's illness worsened during his withdrawal from Kasserine, forcing him to again fly to Berlin for treatment. Rommel warned Hitler that if he did not pull all German forces out of North Africa they would be defeated. Hitler refused but also refused to allow Rommel to return to North Africa.[11] Gen. Hans-Jürgen von Arnim now took command of all German forces. Rommel and von Arnim approached battle differently. Von Arnim was cautious and led from a position in the rear; Rommel was decisive and led from the front. The change in enemy command would benefit the Americans in the weeks ahead. Patton admired Rommel and was eager to defeat him in battle. Rommel's departure embittered Patton, who said, "I want to fight the champ."[12]

Not knowing why Rommel had withdrawn, some Allied generals thought he was up to some trick. Patton did not yet know that the American Army Air Force, alarmingly absent from the fight at Kasserine Pass, had been pasting Rommel's supply chain behind the lines. Even without knowing the reason for the lull in German advances, Patton sent American motorized patrols down the road from Gafsa to Gabes, where he suspected the Germans might be, but the hidden enemy wiped out all the scouting patrols.[13]

At a gentle curve in the Gafsa-Gabes road, about a mile southeast of El Guettar, a road that the Americans called "Gum Tree Road" veered off to the east toward the coastal town of Sfax. Just past this intersection, Gum Tree Road entered a narrow pass at the foot of a mountain named Djebel el Ank that led into a valley that resembled a funnel with the narrow end at the Djebel el Ank Pass, spreading wider as Gum Tree Road moved east toward Sfax. At its neck the profile of the valley was almost a perfect V, with nearly vertical sides and jagged edges rising on the south side of Djebel el Ank to over sixteen hundred feet, peaking on the north side at thirty-eight hundred feet. At the neck of the funnel the enemy had constructed well-fortified bunkers on both sides of the pass, blasting their entrenchments out of solid rock. From these positions the enemy could hold out for days or even weeks, pouring down deadly fire on troops passing by on the Gafsa-Gabes road. Capt. James B. Lyle (now commanding 1/C): "In this area of Tunisia which was located actually about six miles to the north and west of El Guettar, there were several mountain passes, and one [Djebel el Ank] that was found to be a quite critical pass. It was being held by the enemy at this time. To gain success in this area it had to be in Allied hands. There had been several attempts by various units to move through this pass. Patrols had approached this pass and had been shot all to pieces."[14]

Maj. Gen. Terry Allen assigned the Rangers to capture the enemy positions at Djebel el Ank to open the road from Gafsa to Gabes.[15] Once the Rangers had gotten control of the funnel, the main attack of 1st Infantry Division, supported by armor, would follow. Maj. Jack B. Street, 1/B: "The terrain . . . consisted of bleak, ragged ridges and arid valleys supporting no vegetation other than scrubby desert brush. Cover and concealment in the area was either very effective, in the knife-like jagged ridges . . . or non-existent in the spaces between."[16]

Lt. Col. Darby ordered Lyle to find a path for the Rangers to get above and behind the enemy positions. Lyle: "I [was ordered] to send a squad, led by an officer, to perform a reconnaissance mission. They were to return before darkness that day. The mission was to move along the enemy's front, find his right flank, and return."[17] Newly commissioned platoon leader 2nd Lt. Walter Wojcik, 1/C, led the patrol seeking a path whereby the entire Ranger battalion could move at night, undetected, and make a surprise attack. Wojcik found a local Arab who knew the mountains, and with a squad of Rangers they spent an entire day and night reconnoitering a backdoor approach across rugged mountains and valleys.[18] Upon returning, Lt. Wojcik reported that the enemy defending the valley had well-sited machine guns and artillery plus large stocks of ammunition. Fortunately for the Rangers, the enemy weapons were sited to fire at, and through, the small neck of the funnel, the only logical place for an attack to occur.[19]

The next night, the entire 1st Ranger Battalion of about five hundred men set out on the raid. The Rangers would rely on surprise and shock to force the enemy to a quick surrender. An enemy counterattack would find the Rangers unable to retreat.[20] Armed only with rifles, BARs, Tommy guns, 60 mm mortars, and grenades, the Rangers had to pack them eight miles through the mountains. Ammunition had to be carried on their backs, with grenades and rifle clips stuffed into every pocket. Following the Rangers was a company of combat engineers, experienced in night operations, who brought with them a battery of 81 mm mortars needed to command the valley.[21]

Capt. Lyle's C Company would lead the mission: "We moved out late in the evening, and under the concealment of darkness went through ravines, slid down hills, waded in water up to our neck all night long. No lights, no talking, no smoking, complete silence."[22]

Just after 0100 hours the Rangers began their march over an eight-mile track littered with pebbles and rocks "the size of two or three fists" with little space between, making it difficult to plant a foot on solid ground. It was a cool night for climbing, fresh and clear, dark and still except for the scuffling of Rangers' feet. The moon ticked off the hours: 0200, then 0300. In the rough terrain it did not seem like they had gone very far. Now far behind enemy lines, the slightest slip in discipline could jeopardize the mission.[23] The moon, bright on the plain, disappeared between mountains but appeared again on the ridges. Moonlight bounced off the mountains, making shapes and shadows fluctuate with the moon's movement. At times the light was so bright you could see the whole column of Rangers seven hundred yards ahead winding up the mountain. With a heightened awareness that they were behind enemy lines, perhaps being watched, each man thought that if he could see ahead, the enemy, if he were looking, could see him. Whenever the column halted, the men dropped in place onto one knee as prescribed in their training.[24]

At 0500 hours the Rangers realized they were on the edge of a cliff. Climbing down the cliff one by one required those with rifles and other equipment to pass it down hand over hand because the drop was too steep to climb down safely with one hand. Looking down, you could see a large boulder ten to fifteen feet tall, with a crevice under it on one side. To get down, you twisted onto your stomach and slid into the crevice, supporting yourself with your arms. Sliding down, you bounced from foothold to foothold until your feet hit a stream bed. Then, alone and out of breath, each man disappeared into the darkness, moving rapidly ahead to catch up with the man just in front of him. In this kind of night operation a few Rangers were stationed as guides along the route to give directions: "Climb to that little shelf there, and then curve to the left around the base of the hill and then at the end of the plateau, go down in the valley to the right. And keep closed up."[25]

Near the end of the climb, the Rangers increased their pace so they wouldn't be caught in the mountains at daylight. When the Rangers arrived at their destination, a plateau above a cliff, the first trace of light was just appearing. The sun would be at their backs, blinding enemy troops who might look up at them. The plateau at the top was grassy, almost a mile long and a few hundred feet wide, and littered with boulders large enough for a man to hide behind. At the far end of the plateau the ground rose several hundred feet to a rounded knob of rock from which Lt. Col. Darby would command the assault. Lyle: "We got so close to the enemy that his jamming machines and our radios became so loud, we couldn't use radios for communication. We had to use foot messengers."[26]

The Rangers arrived at the plateau just in the nick of time, as their assault was meant to coincide with the 1st Infantry Division attack that was to begin several miles across the desert at 0600 hours and move toward the Djebel el Ank valley. Ranger company commanders instructed men to pick out targets and to site their weapons. Some of the Rangers were allowed to rest, dozing off immediately.[27]

Advancing forward across the plateau in a crouch so as not to be seen from below, Rangers reached a rock wall about waist high. Peering over this, they could see far down in the valley. The wide end of the funnel-shaped valley was off to the left, and the narrow opening, or neck, was off to the right. From their vantage point, the distance across to the south side of the valley must have been over a mile. The Rangers could see that the enemy was dug-in all along the walls of the pass with heavy weapons concentrated toward the neck in order to block any Allied troop movement along the Gafsa-Gabes road. As the Rangers looked down on Gum Tree Road, running through the bottom of the pass, there was a roadblock of heavy stones to the right, just inside the neck of the pass, so that a vehicle would have to wind in an S curve around and between them in order to pass. Aprons of barbed wire ran off from the sides of each roadblock to block off infantry soldiers.[28]

As the sun rose, the enemy troops, a mix of Germans and Italians, were just waking up. Safely dug in on the sides of Djebel el Ank, so secure that they posted no sentries, they had no thought of the fury about to descend upon them. Capt. Lyle, 1/C, remembered how the action began:

> Knowing I would be the first outfit to reach the assault position, I was told I'd be jumping off first in the assault the next morning and as platoon leaders were preparing their platoons for this assault, I moved along talking to my Rangers. I asked them if they were tired and were they ready to go. They answered, "No sir, we're not tired and you give the word. We'll get em." The order came to assault shortly and we moved off. As we moved through the rocks down into the floor of this pass, there were a great number of rocks and boulders around the area. We could see the enemy hidden by their holes rubbing their eyes, rubbing their heads, and calling to each other very casually. They had no idea that they had early morning callers . . . we did not know their strength, the order was to hit hard and fast. . . . And that is just what every man and officer did.[29]

The Rangers moved fast down the valley in skirmish formation, bayonets fixed. Every few steps, a Ranger would drop behind a boulder or drop flat on his face behind a rock, then, after a few more seconds of running, he would again take cover behind another rock, making it hard for a sniper to get off an accurate shot at any one of them.[30] At 0600 hours the valley came alive as a Ranger bugler sounded "Charge," much like the cavalry in a Western movie. Immediately, the Rangers opened fire, the noise of their guns bouncing off the walls of the pass. Rangers with fixed bayonets began running down the side of the mountain, screaming Indian war whoops, throwing grenades, and taking out any enemy they encountered as they passed. Enemy soldiers began firing back with rifles and machine guns, but as their positions became visible in the early morning light, Rangers at the top of the slope were dropping 60 mm mortar shells on them. Ranger sharpshooters at the top searched out any enemy snipers who dared to open up.[31]

Strongpoints across the valley became visible as the sun rose higher and the enemy began to organize their defense, most refusing to surrender without a fight. The Rangers knew the tremendously demoralizing effects of the bayonet assault ordered by Lt. Col. Darby: "I used the radio to call. 'Darby to C company, Darby to C company. We need a little bayonet work. Report to Lieutenant Shunstrom.' These Rangers had been resting but were on their feet almost in one motion, stretching themselves, pulling the bayonets from their scabbards, and fixing them on their rifles."[32] As they organized for the assault into the valley, a Ranger called out, "Bring 'em back alive," but another Ranger sounded off, "They won't bring no prisoners back."[33]

Most of the Germans in the valley immediately loaded vehicles and escaped down the road toward Sfax, leaving the Italians to stay and fight the attackers. As the Rangers began their assault, they could see small puffs of smoke several miles out on the plain coming from 1st Infantry Division tanks advancing toward them. The Rangers had to eliminate the Axis defense in time for the tanks and infantry to break through the roadblock in the Djebel el Ank pass.[34]

At 0800 hours the attacking Rangers were held up by a fortified machine gun, the strongest point they had encountered so far. The Rangers had expended their mortar ammunition early on when they were keeping the enemy pinned in their dugouts, preventing any organized counterattack. They desperately needed the firepower of the 81 mm mortars being brought up by the engineers. With the heavy loads they carried, combined with a lower standard of training, the engineers had not kept up with the Rangers. Nevertheless, they arrived just in time.[35] Marching with them was Capt. Ralph Ingersoll, a combat reporter:

> [Darby] . . . kept calling for the engineers' mortars, specifying where they should be set up. We came stumbling across the plateau at a trot. We took the mortars to the far end of the plateau and set up one in a hollow where its crew were safe from rifle and machine gun fire.
>
> The first three rounds, to find the range, had been of the small shells. Now . . . the larger charges. . . . The first of the bigger shells hit further away from the target. It's explosion was visibly greater. Whoever was in that machine gun nest now knew that the jig was up.[36]

With Djebel el Ank Pass clear, Lt. Col. Darby radioed Maj. Gen. Allen that his infantry was clear to come on through. Enemy bombers continued to harass the Americans in the pass and beyond, destroying numerous pieces of equipment and inflicting heavy casualties on the infantry advancing out on the plain. The road into the pass had become severely congested with tanks and trucks of the 1st Infantry Division, making an ideal target for enemy bombers.[37]

S/Sgt. Royal H. Wells, 1/D, a BAR gunner, was determined to down one of the German Stuka bombers. Small arms fire from the entire battalion kept the planes high, but finally they dropped bombs, putting a half-track out of action and wounding fifteen soldiers from the 1st Infantry Division. Wells: "Six times the planes passed over, and each time they passed I had my automatic rifle loaded. Six times in less than fifteen minutes I stripped the gun and reassembled it. I never knew you could do that and put it back together so fast."[38]

Capt. Lyle stated that the only casualties for this assault were in his company. They consisted of his 1st sergeant, shot through the left hip because he got a little careless, and one other man wounded but still fighting, with an Italian grenade fragment in his back.[39] Capt. Jack B. Street, 1/B, noted that when the fight was over the Rangers had to recapture about fourteen hundred prisoners who had bolted for the rocks at the first appearance of their own bombers.[40]

The 18th Infantry Regiment of the 1st Infantry Division continued to move forward, now heading down the road toward Gabes. The 26th Infantry Regiment, also of the 1st Infantry Division, moved toward the pass. By the time the lead elements of the 26th Infantry Regiment entered the pass, the Rangers were packing up and preparing to leave on their next mission. The American victory at Djebel el Ank marked the beginning of the Battle of El Guettar.

7

THE BATTLE OF EL GUETTAR

With Djebel el Ank captured and the town of El Guettar in American hands, commanders turned their attention to locating the bulk of the German army. The Rangers, sent by Gen. Allen to search for the Germans, believed that the enemy was somewhere east and south of them. On 22 March, Allen met with Darby and some of his company commanders on a ridge near the town of El Guettar to plan the 1st Infantry Division's attack. South and to the west was the mountain range of Djebel Berda, with nothing but gullies, rocks, and boulders—difficult ground for armor to maneuver. Capt. Jack Street, 1/B, gave his assessment of that ground:

> The terrain in the division zone consisted of bleak, ragged ridges and arid valleys supporting no vegetation other than scrubby desert brush. Cover and concealment in the area was either very ineffective, in the knife-like jagged ridges, boulder-strewn hills and precipitous wadis, or non-existent in the spaces between them. The mountain masses enclosing El Guettar and its road junction on three sides presented formidable obstacles to any forward movement. South of El Guettar was a shallow salt lake, impassable to vehicles.[1]

Alternatively, to the south and east along the Gafsa-Gabes road, the valley was flat and dry with scarcely a blade of grass, making it foolhardy for anyone to attack in that direction. Allen wanted to launch the American attack that night, but Gen. Patton vetoed the idea.[2]

Before daylight on 23 March, noise from that southeastern valley let the Americans know that German armor was coming their way, firing their distinctive green tracers, intending to regain ground they had won, and then lost, in the battle at Kasserine Pass. Soon the Germans' big guns began firing. When daylight broke, the Americans could see the whole valley covered with the enemy, who was launching a swift, massive counterattack, unbelievably attacking from the southeast over the open ground. Maj. Gen. Omar Bradley reported that the first German armor attack began at 0600 hours: "Mark II and Mark IV [German] tanks crawled across the valley floor seeking shelter in the cover of wadies."[3]

Attacking over open ground gave the Germans no place to hide, and any movement by either side over this terrain would be easy to spot. Arnbal described the route of attack: "We could see for miles to our direct front and to our right front as well, where Djebel Berda loomed up across the flat valley, about five miles to the South."[4] Someone made the comment that to attack over that open ground would be suicidal. To Darby this must have seemed almost too good to be true:

> Excitement rippled through the American forces. Six battalions—two each of tanks, infantry, and artillery—of the 10th Panzer Division attacked the sector the Rangers were defending. The German general, thinking to awe the rather green American troops, gambled on a frontal attack. The infantry leading was followed by some sixty tanks in what looked like an attack in the American civil war. The Germans took no cover, seeming not to be aware of the almost certain deathtrap into which they were moving. I was never so wildly excited as when watching this mass of men and vehicles inching toward us.
>
> When the Germans were within 1,550 yards, the Yankee artillery boomed one salvo on top of another. The shells were concentrated dead on the enemy troops . . . a hole would appear in the oncoming carpet of the attack. There was no slowing up by the Germans, but their number was being hacked away by the artillery.[5]

As Ranger companies quickly prepared new defensive positions, the Signal Corps photographer assigned to the Rangers, Sgt. Phil Stern, 1/Hq., nicknamed "Snapdragon," was taking photos of an American armored column when it was hit by Me 109 German fighter planes and dive-bombers. Stern was taking a photo of an American tank and some Rangers when an 88 shell exploded right by him, seriously wounding Stern and his assistant, Tech/4 Harry Launer, 1/Hq. The photograph by Stern of an American tank with infantry was the last picture he took in North Africa. Stern describes what happened just as he took the photograph:

Battle of El Guettar. Photograph by Ranger Phil Stern.

> The explosion knocked me out, shattered my leg and left a big flesh wound. Shrapnel lacerated my neck and tore up my right hand, but I was able to rip open a sulfanilamide pack with my teeth and left hand and pour antibiotic on my wounds. . . . I was . . . flown to the 12th General Hospital in Morocco. My right hand was half ripped off. . . . The surgeons stitched each tendon together again . . . it was my camera hand. . . . They had it working better than before.[6]

Several Rangers said that the massive German armor and infantry attack at El Guettar as portrayed in the movie *Patton* was an accurate depiction of the actual attack. The German attack was ferocious, with the height of the battle occurring just after noon, when American artillery and a few tank destroyers, using direct fire, held off the assault. German Ju 88 bombers continued to harass the American defenses with bombs and strafing. While the Rangers were watching American shells tear through the enemy ranks, the Germans were getting their 88 mm artillery ready to fire. Cpl. Arnbal: "The terror of this gun [the 88], was that one did not hear the shell coming. You only heard it when it already passed by or gone overhead."[7]

Barry Shead, writing about his grandfather, Pvt. Jodie Morris, who told about fighting with the 1st Rangers at El Guettar:

> Pvt. Morris said . . . he was wounded by enemy artillery. The shell explosion knocked him down [and] maybe way up into the air. When he regained consciousness he could not close his eyes or move any part of his body and could see soldiers running and walking past him. He said they would look down at him as they passed by and no one checked on him because they thought he was dead due to his eyes being open. At that moment . . . he thought he might lay there and take days to die.[8]

Tech/5 Thomas Prudhomme, 1/Hq., a medic, saw the worst part of the war at places like El Guettar: "[That's] where I lost my very first best friend. I learned not to get too close to anybody."[9] Once, a bullet ricocheted and cut Prudhomme's nose. An officer thought he had spotted the sniper and shouted at a soldier next to him to hand him his rifle. Prudhomme: "When the man slumped, the officer kept shouting for the rifle, not realizing the other man had been hit."[10]

Pfc. Raymond Costello, 1/E, described the rapid firing of a rocket launcher as the Germans attempted to close on the point manned by the 1st Ranger Battalion: "My four-man bazooka team was firing so fast that when the cease-fire order came, we still had . . . rounds in the air."[11] German losses were enormous, and, unlike the Americans, they had no large reserves of men and equipment in Tunisia. All during that night German recovery crews hooked up and towed disabled German tanks back to their own lines for repair.

That night, Capt. Jim Lyle, commanding 1/C, led a patrol out to the front, where most of the American casualties and destruction of equipment had occurred. Lyle's men returned just before dawn with two American six-by-six trucks, towing two 105 mm howitzers. They spiked the barrels of two more 105s that they could not recover and loaded the trucks with weapons they recovered from the battlefield. A third truck they recovered was loaded with the bodies of American GIs killed earlier that day. Cpl. Arnbal: "They were gone most of the night. . . . They were a discouraged and sad group of Rangers, and we were glad we had not been chosen to go on that detail."[12]

ACTION AT DJEBEL BERDA

On 24 March, the 1st Ranger Battalion was ordered to seize Djebel Berda, a mountain range eight miles south of El Guettar, about ten miles wide and three miles deep, with a peak at 3,041 feet, the highest in the area. From the top of Djebel Berda one could observe activity in any direction for several miles. In the event of another German attack, the Rangers would be able to see it coming.[13] Companies A & B were given the mission of scaling the crest of Djebel Berda, where it was assumed the Germans had an observation post. Capt. Steve Meade's Company 1/A led the way, followed by Capt. Earl Carran's Company 1/B. Going up the mountain with zero visibility was tough, especially with loose, sliding rocks underfoot, the steep sides making it extremely difficult to negotiate. The climb halted when they learned that Company A had captured three Germans, sound asleep, in the observation post.[14]

Cpl. Arnbal, 1/B, and Pfc. Harold Rinard, 1/B, both armed with BARs and paired with their assistant BAR gunners, including Pvt. John Mitchell, 1/B, and another man (unnamed), manned the observation post, keeping an eye out for the enemy.[15] Arnbal described the fight with the Germans when they tried to recapture the top:

> Just as the sun was starting to set behind Djebel Berda, eight Germans came running through the gap. The two in the lead were carrying a base plate and a mortar tube, and the other six were loaded with mortar rounds. . . . Rinard and I zeroed in on them, and our bursts of fire mowed them all down, just as another eight came through the gap with another mortar. . . . Mitchell and I fired on the second crew also. To our disbelief, another six or eight Germans came dashing through the gap. . . . Each group was intent upon getting the mortars set up. . . . Without let up, more groups came dashing through the gap, hoping to overwhelm us. . . . I didn't even try to count them, just fired at them methodically, almost without feeling, cursing them for being so stupid.[16]

As the Rangers put their last magazines into their BARs, the German attack stopped.

Elsewhere on the mountain, ammunition was running low in Capt. Alvah Miller's Company D, and the men were unable to dig in due to the dense rock formations. Lt. Warren "Bing" Evans and 1st Lt. Frederic Ahlgren, platoon leaders in 1/D, positioned their men behind rocks and boulders, arranging their defense as best they could with automatic weapons positioned to fire down the slopes.[17] The entire Ranger battalion was deployed in defensive positions along the northwestern foot of Djebel Berda. Darby: "Two battalions of the 18th Regiment, separated by five miles from the remainder of the 1st Division, were having difficulties in their position on Djebel Berda. . . . Company G of the 18th Infantry was overrun by overwhelming numbers of German paratroopers fighting as infantrymen."[18]

Darby's Rangers, except for the squad manning the observation post at the top, were ordered to come back down to reinforce the infantry, dropping off several men along the descent to defend various ridges they encountered. First Lt. Charles Shunstrom's platoon of C Company, accompanied by soldiers from the 18th Infantry Regiment, armed with six 105 mm howitzers, slipped unseen to flank the enemy.[19] Each cannon fired six shells into the enemy's flank, temporarily halting the German advance. Darby: "Each of the six guns plowed six rounds into the Germans. Shunstrom reported back that they 'really blew hell out of the Germans.' About 1400 the Jerries discovered the Ranger platoon which had been reinforced by the remainder of Captain Jim Lyle's C Company."[20] Arnbal further explained the tight position they were in: "We later learned that the Germans had tried to outflank the Rangers and the 18th Infantry Battalion at the same time, but were thwarted in their efforts by Company C of the Rangers, who in turn were trying a flanking movement on the Germans."[21] Darby summarized the end of the fight at Djebel Berda:

> The German thrust at this far right position grew in strength. C company was drawn from behind the Germans. . . . Our small force held off the Germans from the north slopes of Djebel Berda while the two battered battalions of the 18th Infantry pulled back through the Rangers some two or more miles. The situation was still tight. Nevertheless, we stayed out on this right flank, practically cut off for three days but not giving an inch.
>
> The fighting that the 1st Rangers had done between 16 and 27 March had usually been against overwhelming odds. We had been required to make our long march to Djebel el Ank, a hit-and-run raid, and then a few days later we were asked to stave off a savage counterattack. Through all kinds of combat, my men had fought with skill and cunning, losing only three killed and eighteen wounded.[22]

Capt. Lyle's C company was always at the forefront of the action, and at El Guettar casualties in 1/C were heavy. Killed were Sgt. Leonard Sporman, Sgt.

John Ball, and Pfc. Nelson Trent. Wounded included Sgt. Richard Sellers, Cpl. George Fischer, Pvt. Merritt Palmer, and Cpl. Arthur Spackman.[23]

Fighting in Tunisia continued for another month, but the Rangers' work was done. They loaded into railcars for a seven-day trip back to Algeria.[24] Most of these men had a lot of unwinding to do after the mental and physical strain of the last few weeks. All the officers except Capt. Lyle and the battalion lieutenants went ahead by jeep or truck, not having to endure the dusty, dirty train ride. The lieutenants and Lyle, being the most junior among the captains, rode on the train with the troops. Although they had their own railcar, the wooden seats were uncomfortable.[25] Cpl. Arnbal observed that Rangers did not make docile passengers on this rail journey:

> The two platoons of C Company had some kind of feud going . . . with grenades being tossed back and forth [between cars] . . . all of a sudden we heard grenades going off in the boxcar to our rear . . . the men were trying to get enough curve in the trajectory so that the grenades would go in the doors. At least two grenades made it into the boxcar behind Company C's first platoon, seriously wounding several of the men in the second platoon. Luckily, their company medic was in that car, and the train came to a screeching halt. . . . [At the next stop] the wounded men were offloaded and carried by stretchers . . . to a hospital. . . . In the confusion of the stop, we . . . made a foray on a bar. . . . With a new supply of wine, we made it through the night. . . .
>
> Capt. Lyle and our officers were in a bad mood and rightfully so. . . . Company C . . . had the reputation of being the most aggressive and toughest of the battalion's companies. . . . Lyle ordered that [before the train moved] . . . there would be platoon formations in front of the boxcars with a full-dress inspection of weapons, battle packs, and bedrolls, all laid out in the Ranger manner.[26]

The train stopped by a row of quartermaster food warehouses and stayed there long enough to take on water. Hungry Rangers brandished wire cutters and made a run for the warehouses, cutting through the barbed wire fence in record time. Armed MPs watched helplessly and then called for reinforcements. Rangers grabbed whatever they could carry, from cans of fruit to tomato juice and everything in between.[27] Some Rangers in Lyle's company grabbed unmarked boxes, some with canned condensed milk and others with beer. Arnbal, remembering the inspection, rushed back to the train with his squad: "We ran . . . the rest of the platoon already had their equipment laid out; they had also lined up all the empty wine bottles in a row behind where we would be standing in ranks. In haste the six of us got our display in order . . . every detail was given full attention by the very experienced Captain Lyle. When he finished . . . he addressed us, saying 'It takes good soldiers to stand an inspection after consuming such a quantity of wine.'"[28]

Lyle recalled men in his company downing beer and condensed milk on empty stomachs: "My men were sick for two days after that. It was a good thing they were not called on to fight at that time."[29] The train ride ended at Nemours, in Algeria, but after a few days of R&R the original Rangers began recruiting and training volunteers for the formation of two new battalions, the 3rd and 4th Ranger Battalions. The Rangers' mission was about to expand. Back in Washington, Gen. George Marshall, the Army Chief of Staff, soon would be drafting a Presidential Unit Citation, General Orders No. 56, dated 12 July 1944, for the 1st Ranger Battalion, the highest honor a military unit can receive.[30]

Considering the level of combat in which the Rangers were engaged from Dieppe through El Guettar, casualties were relatively low. Eleven Rangers were killed in action, one died of wounds, fifty-five were wounded, and five had been taken prisoner.[31] German resistance continued until Tunis fell on 7 May. More than 225,000 German and Italian prisoners surrendered to the Allies, including Gen. von Arnim, who reportedly personally put a torch to Rommel's command trailer. Eisenhower refused him an audience, establishing a precedent that no Allied general would personally speak to a surrendering German general until the war was over.[32]

8

SICILY

In preparation for the anticipated invasion of Sicily, Gen. Patton and Gen. Allen were pushing Darby for two more Ranger battalions. Darby wrote Gen. Eisenhower on 14 April 1943 expressing the need for fifty-two more officers and a thousand more men. On 22 April, Eisenhower approved the request, giving Darby the authority to visit "any and all replacement depots in this theater." Armed with this, Darby and some officers and NCOs paid visits to replacement depots to find volunteers. As with the 1st. Battalion, the Rangers continued to be "provisional" units rather than permanent units with their own Table of Organization and Equipment (TO&E). Lacking that, a unit such as the Rangers would have to be attached to a larger unit, such an army division, for administration and support. At this time the 2nd Ranger Battalion was being trained for the Normandy invasion, so the two new battalions became the 3rd and the 4th Ranger Battalions.[1]

RECRUITING THE NEW RANGERS

Once recruitment began for the two new battalions, men poured in from the Replacement Depots (called "Repple Depples"), centers where soldiers were sent upon entering the war zone for assignment to a unit.[2] Much to the dismay of regular army commanders throughout North Africa, many of the best-qualified soldiers were eager to join the now-famous Rangers. Ranger officers would often hop up on the hood of a jeep with a loudspeaker and bark out enticements for men to join. Lt. Shunstrom once offered to fight any of the men he was speaking to, and several volunteered for the Rangers.

Because the 1st Ranger Battalion had suffered losses and because some of its men were now assigned to the new battalions, new volunteers were integrated into the 1st Battalion as well as joining the two new ones. All were turned

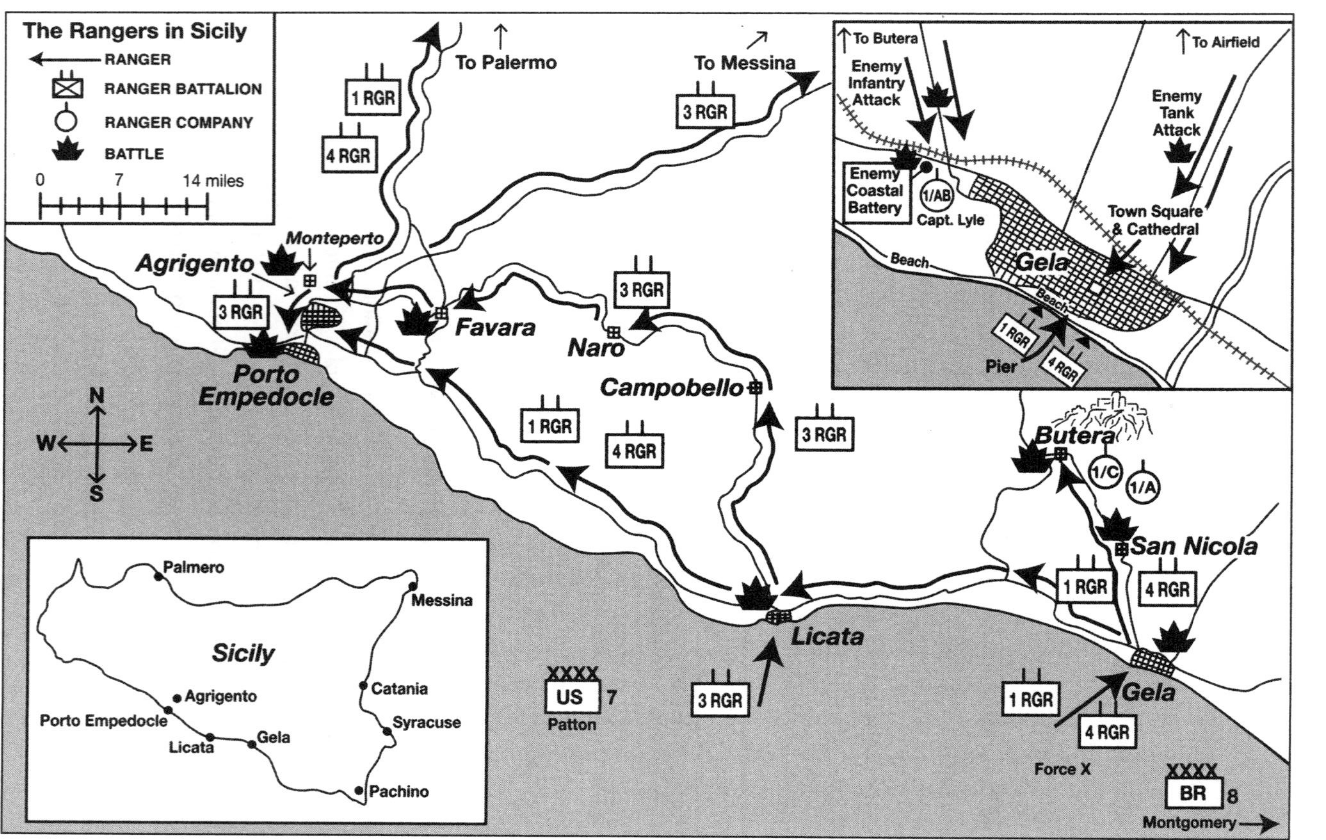

The Rangers in Sicily

over for training to experienced Ranger officers from the 1st Battalion. As in the training of the Original Rangers in Scotland, many washed out or quit as demands grew increasingly severe during the six-week training period.[3]

Men who volunteered for the Rangers were typically rowdy, short-tempered, and eager to fight. Firsthand information about this reorganization and training is relatively scarce, as men naturally had more to say about later combat experiences, but two men who volunteered at this time, Pfc. George W. "Jack" Hall, who wound up in Company D of the new 3rd Battalion, and Pvt. John Hummer, who ended up in 1/C, told how and why they joined the Rangers.

Pfc. Hall had been a fighter from childhood. Orphaned at an early age and raised by a grandparent, four stepbrothers beat him up regularly. In North Africa, Jack and some other soldiers wound up in a "house of joy" and refused to come out when ordered to do so. MPs went in to get them, and a gunfight broke out, killing a prostitute. Jack was court-martialed and fined.[4] While he awaited a possible jail sentence, two Ranger officers roared up in a jeep with a sign reading "Rangers are tough! Can you take it?" That was challenge enough for Jack, who was eager to get on with killing Germans. He was allowed to volunteer for Darby's Rangers in lieu of jail time.[5]

Pvt. John F. Hummer, who was constantly involved in fistfights, was too young to be drafted and had to have his mother's permission to join the army. Landing at Oran, Algeria, in April 1943, he and the other replacements gathered around a platform to hear two Ranger officers advertising the opportunity to join their elite fighting unit. Hummer: "We were promised a 'home' for the duration . . . if in Ranger training we couldn't 'hack' it, or wanted to quit, we'd be returned for reassignment. . . . I volunteered that day."[6]

THE ORGANIZATION OF THE THREE BATTALIONS

The leadership of the new battalions came from 1st Battalion men who had trained with the Commandos in Britain. Now called "Originals," many of them were promoted and given new responsibilities. Companies A and B of the old 1st Battalion formed the cadre of the new 3rd Ranger Battalion, commanded by Maj. Herman Dammer. Likewise, Companies E and F formed the cadre of the 4th Ranger Battalion, commanded by Roy Murray, who had led Company F throughout the North African campaign. Murray, now a major, had first distinguished himself as the leader of the Rangers who had participated in the Dieppe raid. Companies 1/C and 1/D became the cadre for the reorganized 1st Ranger Battalion. Both of the new battalions were officially activated on 19 June 1943, a year to the day from the activation of the original 1st Ranger Battalion.[7]

Among the newly promoted officers was 1st Lt. Charles Shunstrom, one of the most colorful of the Ranger officers, who became commander of 1/C, replacing Capt. James B. Lyle, who was given command of Companies 1/A and 1/B for the coming invasion of Sicily.[8]

Cpl. Kenneth Markham, 1/F, witnessed one of Shunstrom's escapades during training: "Shunstrom was the meanest man in the American army; Shunstrom was demonstrating the [use of] concussion grenades. He looks at the officers and . . . they ain't paying no attention to Shunstrom. He looks at the guys . . . pulls the pin on a grenade and throws it right straight at them, everybody scattered but one guy, he . . . had a busted ear drum."[9] First Lt. Angus McKinnon, 1/F, lost the hearing in his right ear as a result of the blast. None of the officers reported Shunstrom or criticized him for the action, even though any one of them could have been seriously injured.[10]

TRAINING THE NEW RANGERS

On the morning of 2 May, the new volunteers boarded landing craft, which carried them down the coast from Oran to Nemours, Algeria.[11] Trucks took them up to their camp on a steep cliff, high above the Mediterranean, where a single tree provided the only shade. Upon arriving, they were left to their own devices for a time. To amuse themselves they treated their newly issued Springfield rifles as toys, firing them out over the cliff toward the sea. A Ranger NCO soon intervened to stop the shooting, confiscate their ammunition, and put them in formation. Pvt. Hummer recalled, "[We] were presented to Capt. Lyle who, in turn, really chewed on our butts."[12] The next morning the new men were assigned to their battalions and companies, as Tech/5 Lawrence "Red" Gilbert, 1/F, explained: "After about a week and a half of real intensive training day and night, they finally decided to assign us to a battalion . . . so they lined us up [dividing us into three groups by counting off]. I was close enough to the front that I got the 1st Battalion. If I'd been further down the line, I'd have been in the 4th Battalion."[13]

Ranger training was a nightmare for the new guys. They learned to execute the obstacle course and do speed marches while carrying their weapons and field packs. They learned to fire, strip, and reassemble their rifles, the BAR, the Thompson submachine gun, the light machine gun, the .45 pistol, and the 60 mm mortar. Despite intense physical exertion under the merciless summer sun, they were allowed only one canteen of water per day, except at shower time. On 16 June, the new men began amphibious training, making practice beach assaults from landing craft.[14] Sgt. Roy Wade Earnest, 1/C:

> We were shot at with live ammo, hit with gun butts and fists. . . . We double-timed everywhere we went. There were times I thought about giving it up. . . . We took on combat training, mountain climbing, death slide, close-combat night fighting, street fighting, fragmentation, smoke, and concussion grenades. We had more people hit during training than when we were in combat while I was with them.
>
> They gave me eight men to make an assault section. Lt. Kendrick was our platoon leader. We had sixty men in our company including officers. . . . We got passes to go into Algiers. We NCOs were [the] MPs of our company. If any of our men were seen drunk or fighting, we were to get them off the street and into our trucks. . . . [Just as] we went in to the Red Cross building to eat, one of our men came staggering up the street, collar unbuttoned and sleeves turned up. Two MPs were coming up behind him. I . . . took off to get him. I was pulling him toward the RC [Ranger Compound] when the MPs came up and wanted to take him to the MP headquarters. By then three other NCOs from C company were there. The four of us told them we took care of our own.
>
> We went back to the RC and found that Ernie Pyle, a news correspondent, was there. Every GI in MTO [Mediterranean Theatre of Operations] knew Ernie . . . [because] he wrote the GI side of the war. He was always at the front in the mud, blood, cold and heat just like the GI.[15]

Because it gave him a promotion to tech sergeant, 5th class (Tech/5), Pvt. Hummer, now assigned to Company 1/C under Shunstrom's command, volunteered to be a gunner for the newly introduced 2.36-inch rocket launcher, commonly called a bazooka. It was designed to penetrate enemy armor and concrete. Ammunition for the bazooka was in short supply, but Shunstrom sometimes drove Hummer down to the beach to fire the new weapon at metal buoys offshore.[16]

Pvt. Green Kegley, a volunteer in 1/E, fell during training on the death slide and broke his back, which sent him home on a hospital ship to be discharged. After the war, he never told anyone outside the family about hurting himself in Ranger training, but almost fifty years later a friend saw his name on the roster of World War II Rangers. Green Kegley had become a pastor, and even though he was never in combat, his daughters were impressed that their father had volunteered for the Rangers.[17] Tech/5 Donald Hayes, assigned to 3/C after the reorganization, had a poetic take on Ranger training and its consequences for the enemy: "Rangers made friends with the night, borrowing its blackness to creep past wide-awake German troops. They learned to walk like cats, march and fight without food or sleep . . . [and] learned a thousand ways to kill a man silently."[18]

SICILY—OPERATION HUSKY

As the newly trained and reorganized Rangers prepared to board ship for the invasion of Sicily, Lt. Col. Darby reminded every man present that Rangers were made on the training field but must prove themselves on the field of battle.[19] Sgt. Earnest witnessed the dangers, even in the routine process of boarding a ship: "As we loaded boats, one of the men had put two mortar shells in his pack. He took the pack off and threw it on the floor of the LCI; the shell exploded hitting six of my men and two sailors. It killed one man; blinded two and one lost a leg. In all 7 men went to the hospital. It was total confusion on the pier. . . . We got the weapons and gear together in another LCI and went to the ship."[20]

Sicily was a staging base for German troops blocking access to Italy and provided airfields from which the enemy could attack Allied shipping in the Mediterranean. Lt. Col. Darby called the capture of Sicily the first step toward taking Italy out of the war. Darby: "[Operation Husky's] purpose was to secure the Mediterranean line of communications, divert German divisions from Russia, apply pressure on Italy, and create a situation in which Turkey could be enlisted as an active ally. . . . As part of the Husky plan, there was to be an early seizure of ports and rapid capture of airfields, to be used for close support missions of troops. . . . The Allied invasion force numbered 478,000."[21]

Sicily is only ninety miles north of Africa and, at the town of Messina, is separated from mainland Italy by only twelve miles. From Sicily the Allies could leap easily to the European mainland.[22] To maintain surprise, war correspondents were kept in the dark about the impending invasion of Sicily and were unable to report on it in depth. Consequently, the Sicilian invasion is less well known today than other World War II campaigns.

To confuse the Germans about the location of the invasion, the Allies prepared detailed operations orders for a supposed attack on Greece. Plans were locked in a briefcase and handcuffed to a corpse preserved in a cooler. The corpse, dressed as a major in the British Royal Marines, with papers identifying him as "Maj. William Martin," was supposedly killed in a plane crash at sea. A submarine dropped the body into the Mediterranean off the coast of Spain, where it was sure to wash up and be found. Documents in "Maj. Martin's" briefcase indicated that Sicily was a diversion for the real invasion in Greece. Finding the body, an Axis agent sent the briefcase to Berlin, where it successfully deceived Adolf Hitler. As a result, Hitler diverted over sixty thousand troops to Greece, even moving German mine-laying ships from Sicily to Greece, saving countless Allied ships from destruction. Skeptical of this supposed Greek invasion, Gen. Albert Kesselring, overall commander of German troops in Italy, ordered the Hermann Goering Panzer Division and the 15th Panzer Grenadier Division to reinforce the German and Italian forces in Sicily. Before the campaign was over, Kesselring would add the 29th Panzer Grenadier Division and the 1st Parachute Division to bolster his forces.[23]

U.S. Army Intelligence estimated that, at the time of the invasion, there were 200,000 Italian troops and about 50,000 German troops on Sicily, all commanded by Italian general Alfredo Guzzoni. Lt. Col. Darby estimated that Axis forces on Sicily totaled between 300,000 and 365,000 men. The 15th Allied Army Group, commanded by Britain's Gen. Harold R. L. G. Alexander, would lead the assault, which consisted of the American Seventh Army, commanded by Lt. Gen. George S. Patton Jr., which was to land on the southern part of the island, and the British Eighth Army, commanded by Lt. Gen. Bernard Montgomery, which would land on the eastern shores.[24]

Since the war began, Patton had competed fiercely with Montgomery. Patton envied Montgomery for being assigned the landing position in Sicily closest to Messina, the city that Patton called the "Prize." Patton, however, was determined to get to Messina before Montgomery and could not wait to execute his plans to do so. In a letter to Maj. Gen. Troy H. Middleton, Patton wrote: "This is a horse race, in which the prestige of the U.S. Army is at stake. We must take Messina before the British. Please use your best efforts to facilitate the success of our race."[25]

9 JULY 1943: THE LANDING AT GELA—1ST AND 4TH RANGER BATTALIONS

Lt. Col. Darby now commanded "Force X," the name given to it by Gen. Terry Allen of the 1st Infantry Division, to which it was attached. Force X included the 1st and 4th Ranger Battalions, supported by one battalion of the 39th Combat Engineers to clear mines and three companies of the 83rd Chemical Mortar Battalion, which for the first time deployed the new 4.2-inch mortar. It fired high-explosive, white phosphorous, and smoke rounds, giving the Rangers their own mobile artillery.[26]

The 1st Ranger Battalion was loaded on board the USS *Joseph T. Dickman*, a former transatlantic passenger ship converted to a troop ship in 1940. The 4th Ranger Battalion was aboard two British ships, HMS *Prince Leopold* and HMS *Prince Charles*, embedded in the enormous flotilla heading toward Sicily.[27]

Darby's 1st and 4th Battalions were to land at Gela, the largest city on Sicily's southeastern coast, situated on a plateau 150 feet above the sea. Simultaneous with the landing at Gela, the 3rd Ranger Battalion, commanded by Maj. Herman Dammer, was attached to the U.S. 3rd Infantry Division, commanded by Maj. Gen. Lucian Truscott Jr., and would be landing at Licata, fifty miles west of Gela. This was the first time that any of Darby's Rangers were detached from Darby and placed under another command.[28]

The Rangers enjoyed beautiful summer weather before the invasion, with seas as smooth as a carpet. With many Rangers stripped to their undershirts, they gathered on their ship's top deck, one platoon at a time, to study relief models of Gela and Licata.[29] First Lt. Carl R. Hood, 4/E: "On July 1st we boarded boats for Sicily. Our company was on a British Commando Raider—a nifty little job with 8 LCA's aboard. We cruised around the Med. Sea and experienced one air raid from Jerry & saw two of his planes shot down on or about July 9."[30]

To protect secrecy, few men, except for senior officers, knew the destination of the invasion until after the ships were at sea.[31] About noon on 9 July 1943, a storm came out of nowhere, with waves tossing the ships around like toothpicks and almost swallowing the smaller craft. Rangers, until then in a cheerful mood, were suddenly sick and vomiting over the rail or retreating to their bunks, where they got even sicker.[32]

At about 1600 hours on 9 July, German aerial reconnaissance confirmed that a major Allied invasion force was headed toward Sicily but could not determine its exact destination. The Germans notified Gen. Guzzoni, who demanded more information. Naval advisors assured Italy's Lt. Gen. Achille d'Havet, commanding the 206th Coast Division, that this was a false alarm because stormy weather and high seas prohibited a landing. Concluding that Gen. Guzzoni was just nervous, d'Havet went to bed, ignoring the alert. German radar technicians, seeing hundreds of bleeps on their screens, concluded there was no way hundreds of ships could be approaching the coast of Sicily in such bad weather and did not report their findings. However, someone alerted Gen. Kesselring, and by 2000 hours on 9 July the experienced, battle-wise Kesselring put German troops on alert. At 0100 hours on 10 July, Guzzoni declared a state of emergency for all of Sicily, but by then it was too late for the German high command to orchestrate the devastating response of which their panzers and grenadiers were capable.[33]

Col. Jerome Haggerty noted: "All battalions were trained in large-scale landing exercises with the navy in preparation for the invasion of Sicily."[34] Intense training was necessary because the Gela landings were expected to be bitterly contested,[35] and Darby's larger landing force was necessary because Gela, which was located on a high plateau, was expected to be difficult to take. Highway 115, which stretched across the 160-mile-long southern coast of the island, ran through the middle of Gela, where it met roads leading to the interior. Four miles inland was the Ponte Olivo airfield, a strategic target of the 82nd Airborne Division and the 1st Infantry Division. Its quick capture would permit Allied planes to refuel and support the Allied assault.[36]

Even as the weather deteriorated, Gen. Dwight Eisenhower, commander of Allied forces in Europe, launched the invasion with the "Go" signal to 2,700 paratroopers of the 82nd Airborne Division,[37] whose planes lifted off from North Africa at 2010 hours on 9 July. By midnight, gale-force winds were blowing along the southern coast of Sicily.[38] The black night and high winds gave cover for the attackers from the sea but created harrowing conditions for the paratroopers.[39]

As the wall of Allied ships approached Sicily, there was nothing but ships as far as the eye could see. Enemy bombers sank the destroyer *Maddox* as it emerged from the storm, with 211 losing their lives.[40] The Germans dominated the air, bombing and strafing naval vessels, seriously hampering unloading efforts on shore. As ships carrying the 1st and 4th Ranger Battalions converged on the beaches of Gela, Axis pilots flew almost two hundred bombing missions but did not make a dent in the convoy.[41] The navy had poor intelligence about the depth of the water and hidden sandbars. Many LSTs ran aground, so the navy was unable to unload American tanks and artillery fast enough to be of help in the first day of fighting.[42]

Because the army and navy had good radio communications, navy cruisers and destroyers could support the Rangers with thousands of large shells as long as their units were within gun range of the big ships. Cruisers could fire 6-inch shells over ten miles, and destroyers could almost match that distance with slightly smaller shells. The navy served as floating artillery, which, in the coming hours, would help save the invasion from destruction by Kesselring's tanks. Sometime before midnight, the ships anchored and the wind began to drop.[43] The enemy trained huge land-based searchlights across the water, stopping on each ship, signaling that the Rangers had lost the element of surprise. Knowing that the protection of darkness was gone, Rangers who had been touting their bravery were now suddenly quiet. Capt. James Lyle told his men, "If you are not fearful in such a situation you probably are not prepared, and you may not live long." When asked years later if he was ever afraid that night, Lyle responded, "Damn right. You better be afraid if you want to stay alive."[44]

2300 HOURS

About one hour before loading the assault landing boats, Darby called the officers of the 1st Ranger Battalion to the bow of the USS *Dickman* to observe what was happening on shore. The tracers of antiaircraft fire bursting in the sky above the coastline enabled them to see that the enemy was putting up a strong defense against the 82nd Airborne paratroopers, who were landing at that very minute. Darby issued final instructions to his officers, gave a few last words of inspiration, and told the officers to get their units ready to go ashore.[45]

2330 HOURS

The major risk to ships in the invasion force was the enemy's two heavily defended 3-inch coastal guns in concrete bunkers located northwest of Gela. Darby observed, "The sore point of this landing was the gun battery on the west side of [Gela]. Under no circumstances was it to fire. Our taking out the town was incidental to taking out the batteries."[46] Darby had handpicked Lyle to take the combined Companies 1/A and 1/B ashore ahead of the main force to destroy these coastal guns. Lyle remembered Darby saying:

> Jim, I have confidence you will find some method of destroying that gun position. As you well know, we have a great number of officers who have not had any combat experience. I expect you, and the enlisted men who we can class as "old timers" to guide the green officers and enlisted men along. It has been reported that the gun battery will be a hard nut to crack.
>
> During the landing and capture of the gun battery you will probably lose a great number of personnel. . . . Tonight, you must expect to lose from one to seventy-five percent of both companies. But don't forget, that gun battery must be destroyed! If casualties are high, it will not be a reflection on your leadership abilities. . . . May God be with you.[47]

2400 HOURS

To secure the beachhead, the Rangers of the 4th Battalion were to hit the beach on the east side of a hundred-foot-long fishing pier at Gela, while the 1st Rangers were to land on the west side.[48] Lyle's Rangers in 1/A and 1/B were to hit land immediately behind 1st Battalion companies C, D, E, and F, pass through them, and run straight through Gela to destroy the coastal guns northwest of the town. Still on board the *Dickman,* Lyle repeated the warning to his men that the capture of the gun battery was a dangerous mission but essential to the success of the invasion. Lyle: "Until the gun battery is destroyed . . . shoot and shoot to kill everything that moves if you expect to be alive tomorrow."[49]

0030 HOURS, 10 JULY 1943

The lights were dimmed so that everyone could adjust their eyes to the dark. Just after midnight the command came over the loudspeaker, "Rangers, man your boats." The first group to load their assault landing craft stood on the deck of the *Dickman* watching the stormy seas swing the landing craft from side to side, now almost hitting the side of the ship, then swinging away, far out over the water. Eventually, sailors secured the assault boats so the Rangers could load.[50]

High winds and rough seas made it impossible to lower landing boats on the windward side of the ship. The *Dickman* had to lower the boats from the leeward side, then come about in order to lower boats from the other side. This delay kept the boats that were already launched bobbing about in the water for some time. To calm the men's nerves, the captain of the *Dickman* had Glenn Miller's "American Patrol" played over the ship's loudspeaker.[51]

As the landing craft kept circling the mother ship, the Rangers thought that the navy pilots must be lost. Actually, they were only trying to bring all the boats into one formation so they could head to shore together. Darby tells how the landing boats found their way in the dark: "We had a pretty good idea where Gela was . . . we started going in the general direction of the searchlights. We had delayed terribly long to look for our guide boats. [Suddenly, Capt. Leppert showed up in an LCI]. . . . Thank heaven for finding him out in the middle of the ocean. . . . It was just by luck that we ever ran into anybody in the middle of the ocean at night who knew where he was going."[52]

Men who were never seasick on larger ships were now tossing up their breakfast. Eventually, the landing boats, organized into four waves, headed toward the beach. In the high seas the boats could see each other only for a few moments at the crest of a wave before they dropped out of sight in the trough. Tech/5 Theodore "Ted" Fleser, 1/D: "As the boats topped the crest of a wave, enemy searchlights would pick them up, but before the enemy could adjust their fire, they dropped into the next trough and became invisible."[53] During the final run-up to the beach the Rangers could hear the snapping of bullets cracking over their heads.[54]

THE APPROACH: 1ST BATTALION, COMPANIES C, D, E, AND F—THE FIRST WAVE

When their boats were about 1,600 yards out, the enemy pinpointed them with huge searchlights. The cruiser USS *Savannah* opened fire with its 6-inch guns, and the searchlights switched off. But the spotters on shore now had the range on the landing boats.

Among the Rangers in Capt. Alex Worth's Higgins boat was a Canadian, Cpl. Glenn Nantau, 1/F. As the landing boat hit the sand and the ramp dropped, Cpl. Nantau stepped in front of Capt. Worth, yelling out, "Scouts go first," only to be riddled with machine gun fire. The memory of Nantau's sacrifice would plague Worth for many years. One Higgins boat took a direct hit from enemy shells and was sunk.[55] S/Sgt. Albert Kissman, 1/Hq., describes what happened when his boat was hit:

> Our Higgins landing boat was about a mile and a half off Gela when a hit from a shore battery severed the craft's landing cable and I was hurled into the sea. As I went down I began to get rid of my equipment, which included a mortar sack containing 8 rounds of ammunition, a .45 caliber pistol with 21 rounds, my M-1 rifle with six clips, a block of TNT, a canteen of water, a mess kit . . . a half dozen hand grenades, and other odds and ends. I got rid of everything except the [Mae West] life preserver and the grenades. When I reached bottom, I managed to inflate the Mae West and succeeded in kicking my way to the surface where a British landing craft picked me up.[56]

Other 1st Battalion boats, meant to be the first wave, stopped to pick up survivors, which delayed the attack. Lyle's men wound up landing first on the heavily defended beach.[57]

THE APPROACH: THE 4TH RANGER BATTALION

Maj. Roy Murray, 4/Hq., described their mission and getting to shore alive: "At exactly 0310 hours . . . under heavy concentrated machine gun and heavy enemy mortar fire, Rangers of the 4th Battalion began landing on the mine-laden beaches of Gela. . . . The element of surprise had been lost when powerful searchlights had been turned on by the enemy to reveal the whereabouts of the invading Rangers. Even before landing, the Rangers suffered many casualties by direct mortar hits on their assault crafts."[58]

First Lt. Carl R. Hood, 4/E:

> We boarded our landing craft, or LCA, at 0130 hours [about five miles from shore], and we could hardly see the boat next to us as we were lowered into

> the [rough] water. I remembered thinking, "How would we ever get across the beach if it is mined?"
>
> About one hour out from landing we saw huge fires [on] shore resulting from our planes' bombing. . . . Search lights were playing around over the sea, and we were afraid we had been discovered. One of them settled on our ship . . . but the enemy couldn't see us for the rough weather.
>
> At 0315 . . . My boat was to land alongside a big pier & along with 10 men I was to go to the end of the pier & remove all resistance & set up some guide lights for other troops coming in. We were sweating out machine guns at the end of the pier.
>
> Shells were landing within 10 feet of our boat and spraying us with water, one went across our bow and from then on we stayed low and watched through the slits of the armored slotted doors . . . all of a sudden our boat stopped & we had hit a sandbar. . . . The doors went down and over the front of the boat we went into the water . . . it turned out to be about 3 ft. deep. We headed for shore.[59]

S/Sgt. Carold Folsom, 4/Hq., was in a landing craft headed for the Gela beach when an enemy searchlight fell on his boat:

> The German 20 mm guns cut loose, driving shells into the front of the craft, and filled the boat with a huge wave. Thirty-three men struggled for [our] lives in the chill water. [We were] two or three miles from shore, too far to swim for it.
>
> The water was paralyzingly cold after two or three hours, and though the men all wore life preservers, a number had been wounded . . . or killed by the bullets. . . . It [seemed like] hours before . . . [someone] . . . was able to reach us in a support boat. He saved 17 men; the other 16 were killed or had drowned by then. We survivors were taken back to the mothership, refitted with equipment and went on into shore.[60]

COMPANIES 1/A AND 1/B: THE LANDING

Because the first-wave attack by Companies C, D, E, and F had stopped to pick up survivors, Lyle's two companies were all alone in hostile territory. As Lyle's boats sped toward the beach, Lyle feared that he was lost and that his command was being put down on the wrong beach. A submarine that was supposed to lead his boats to the beach was nowhere in sight. Searchlights spotted the boats, and enemy mortars and machine guns opened fire.[61] Darby: "If you have any luck at all, the first wave gets across the beach all right. Then with the second wave, the enemy begins aiming at them . . . by the time the 3rd wave gets in, they are getting good."[62]

When Lyle's men were about seven hundred yards from shore, a rocket barrage from American naval support craft took out the enemy searchlights. Nevertheless, at about five hundred yards, enemy machine guns became more accurate, with bullets pinging off the sides of the boats. Lyle spotted a large red light ahead and realized it was the guide light on the rear of the American submarine that was supposed to lead his boats to the beach. Relieved, Lyle adjusted his boat's direction, but at seventy-five yards out the boats ground to a halt on a sandbar. Unable to get closer, the navy ensign shouted, "Lower the ramp." Trained for this in North Africa, the men rushed off the boat and headed for the beach in water varying from knee-deep to neck-high, firing as they went.[63]

The searchlights that were still operable suddenly came on again, but within seconds naval gunfire knocked them out. Lyle recalled: "Enemy searchlights were turned up to the sky looking for our planes that were flying over, and we could see the big red-hot shells going in on the beach. We hit the beach at 0315 hours, landing to the left of the mines on the beach where we were supposed to. Navy frogmen had set up markers, so we had no trouble."[64]

Lyle recalled, "Upon reaching the beach, there was no evidence that the first wave had landed and the enemy beach positions were still intact."[65] Two Italian machine guns were firing directly into Lyle's men, but the well-trained Rangers jumped in among the startled Italians and destroyed the machine gun positions almost immediately. After trying unsuccessfully to reach the first wave by radio, Lyle's Rangers began moving up a drainage ditch toward the town of Gela.[66]

LANDING OF THE 4TH RANGER BATTALION AT GELA

On 10 July 1943, at about 0310 hours, Rangers of the 4th Battalion began landing under fire. The beach was heavily mined with both antipersonnel and antitank mines. The second wave encountered the dreaded "Bouncing Betty" mines, which, when stepped on, sprang three or four feet into the air before exploding, sending hot metal into anybody within a twenty-foot range. First Sgt. Randall Harris, 4/F, saw his company commander, 1st Lt. Walter Wojcik, 4/F, who had earned a battlefield commission in Tunisia, step on such a mine as his feet hit the beach. Harris suppressed this memory for many years, always hoping it was a dream: "The mines started going off; we were right in the middle of a minefield. Men were being hit all around me. . . . The company commander, Walter Wojcik, was in front of me. He got hit in the chest, and he turned around, looked at me and said, 'Harry, I've had it.' (He called me Harry.) I could see his heart hanging outside his shirt as he crumpled to the ground."[67]

Almost at once, Harris stepped on a mine himself and was struck at waist level, "My stomach opened up. It felt like I got hit with a baseball bat. I didn't feel much pain of any kind; I must have been in some form of shock. A handful of my intestines actually came out."[68] Stuffing his intestines back inside his belly and tightening his web pistol belt to hold them in, Harris fought on. He refused medical treatment until the last of his wounded men were treated, leading his company for two hours more until they captured their objectives.[69] Harris was later commissioned a 2nd lieutenant and became the first Ranger in World War II to be decorated with the coveted Distinguished Service Cross.[70]

Lt. Carl R. Hood, 4/E, in a letter to his father, described his beach landing:

> Heavy guns were only firing occasionally & the machine guns sputtered every now & then. I finally made out the 1st building my platoon was to take. . . . We finally were within two steps of the beach, was it mined, or wasn't it? There were 3 explosions to my right where one of the companies hit a mine field . . . but we had to cross it so we sorta said a prayer & started out. . . . It seemed as if we would never get across the beach, but our section wasn't mined. We were across the beach . . . I checked & we had no one killed. The "Ityes" had mined [the pier] & blew it just as we came in. It was lucky . . . because we would have been blown up with it if [we] had went down the pier.[71]

COMPANIES 1/A AND 1/B:
THE ATTACK ON THE ITALIAN SHORE BATTERY

On hitting the beach, Lyle's men ran straight through the streets toward the northwest. When they saw other figures moving about in the dark, they called out the password. Not getting the correct reply, they made short work of those men, leaving the bodies of Italian soldiers scattered all along the streets. Company 1/A's 1st sergeant, James Dew, encountered four Italians making a hasty dash for the door of a bunker. Dew raced to the bunker, kicked open the door, and fired a few bursts from a Tommy gun followed by a hand grenade. Later inspection revealed two heavy machine guns and a 47 mm antitank gun in the bunker. Dew's actions prevented many potential casualties.[72]

Near the junction of the Butera and Licata roads northwest of Gela, Lyle's men spotted their target, an Italian coastal gun battery protected by barbed wire and sandbags. The Rangers fired 60 mm mortars, while Lyle tried unsuccessfully to contact the 83rd Chemical Mortar Battalion for fire support from their new 4.2-inch mortars. This would have been the first time the 4.2s were used in combat. Not to lose the element of surprise, Lyle attacked without them.[73]

To avoid risking his men in an attack across open ground, Lyle sent a section of twelve Rangers along a ditch leading toward the enemy's rear while the rest of the men waited to attack from the front. At the agreed-upon signal, each of the men attacking from the rear threw two grenades and then jumped into the gun position, fighting in close combat. An Italian machine gun killed one of these Rangers before two hand grenades took it out.[74]

Simultaneously, the main body of Rangers blew the barbed wire with bangalore torpedoes and rushed the gun position from the front. Attacking from the front and rear, the Rangers quickly eliminated the battery. Italian soldiers on a nearby knoll fired mortars, but the Rangers eliminated them with grenades. Not knowing how long they would be able to hold Gela, Lyle's men spiked the coastal guns with explosives lest they fall back into enemy hands.[75] At 0630 hours, Capt. Lyle radioed Ranger Headquarters that the battery position had been captured along with three World War I-vintage 77 mm French field guns and their ammunition.[76]

Suddenly, a large shell exploded only two hundred feet over the Rangers' heads. Lyle assumed it was enemy fire until he heard a second shell being fired from offshore. The cruiser *Savannah,* seeing explosions from the guns being spiked, thought the Italian battery was firing at them and returned fire with 6-inch shells. Lyle radioed Darby's headquarters requesting this fire be lifted, and the cruiser ceased firing.[77]

The Italians had attempted to render the three 77 mm guns inoperable by removing the sights and elevating mechanisms. Capt. Lyle quickly organized three gun crews and trained them to bore-sight the 77 mm field pieces for use against a counterattack that could come at any moment. After two hours of gun drills, Rangers put the guns into a defensive position to cover Highway 115, the main east-west road across the south coast of Sicily. The damaged French guns would be used by Rangers over the next two days to help defeat major counterattacks by Italian infantry and armor.[78] At final count, Lyle reported his success: "Ranger casualties were extremely light . . . they amounted to only one killed and eight walking wounded."[79]

CAPTURE OF GELA

While Companies 1/A and 1/B were eliminating the coastal gun battery, the rest of the 1st and 4th Battalion Rangers were landing. Three companies of the 4th Rangers were fighting their way into the center of Gela, and after a sharp street battle they seized the town square and the cathedral. Two companies pushed out to the eastern edge of town, sending patrols even farther east to connect with elements of the 1st Infantry Division.[80]

Continuing his letter to his father, Lt. Hood said he was excited about his first combat with the Rangers:

> We moved into town just as dawn started to break. . . . It was still dark & you could see about 25 yards ahead of you. All of a sudden a M.G. [machine gun] let loose & we hit the road and a section of Rangers opened fire & stopped it. We finally got to the edge of the square and took it. We were fired on two or 3 times with M.G. but no harm. It was then about 5:30 and you could see quite well.
>
> The Colonel came along & [I] & my platoon went with him down to the fort where quite a little scrap was going on. On the way we ran into a hotel in which the Germans had a command post . . . we tried to break down the door. We finally blew the door with two pounds of TNT and . . . came out with about 50 "Itye" prisoners.[81]

Accompanied by Sgt. James Hildebrandt, 4/F, Sgt. James Altieri, 4/F, who was fluent in Italian, was leading a platoon near the Gela town square. Altieri heard Italian being spoken not far away and yelled out for the enemy soldiers to report to him. Up ran several armed Italian soldiers, only to find themselves captured, Ranger rifles pointed at their bellies.[82]

The Gela cathedral was located on the town square, and snipers were holed up in the tower. Sgt. Altieri: "We were out of the fire line of the snipers . . . and we knew that inside the large cathedral some Italians still held out."[83] First Lt. Walter Nye was on the scene and ordered the cathedral cleaned out. Altieri:

> A few more pings from the tower apertures were convincing reminders that the enemy inside the holy ground was very much alive. . . . From my flattened position on the left side of the stone entranceway, I kicked the door open wide, threw in a grenade, flung myself back as the grenade exploded and, before the debris had cleared, fired eight fast rounds into a corner of the cavernous cathedral. . . . When it was over we had flushed out three diehard Fascists of the Livorno Division; sprawled out grotesquely by the altar were two dead Italians.[84]

Sgt. Roy Wade Earnest, 1/D, witnessed the capture of the Italian barracks:

> Our assault sections were to take the gun positions overlooking the beach. . . . We opened fire on the gun positions and barracks. The men came running out in their underwear. . . . All but one got rid of his weapons. . . . As he ran by me, one of the men fired past my head; the man fell with a bullet hole in his temple.
>
> We searched the barracks . . . and came to the CO office. I looked through his desk and found his papers showing that the Herman Goering division . . . had left the day before to go to Messina.
>
> We had a house-to-house search for firearms . . . I . . . went outside. I heard a voice ask, "how are things in the States?" . . . The man and his wife came out and gave me two bottles of American whiskey. . . . They were from Brooklyn, NY. . . . Lt. Kendrick saw us with the bottles and tried to take them away. We drank so fast the Lt. thought we only had one bottle. The Captain got the other bottle and divided with the rest of the outfit.[85]

The first day of the invasion, Rangers had captured hundreds of Italian soldiers, now prisoners of war. Long lines of them seemed to be marching everywhere. Most of the local people had long since tired of fighting for the Germans. The Germans had taken over their homes, harmed their women, and stolen the few things of value they had, and most of the locals were happy to see the Americans. Everywhere around Gela the men saw beggars, women poorly dressed, and children half-naked, barefoot, and hungry after several years of German domination. Rangers made friends with the locals everywhere they went, passing out candy, chewing gum, and D bars to the children.[86]

TROOPERS OF THE 504TH PARACHUTE INFANTRY REGIMENT, 82ND AIRBORNE DIVISION

Fearing the Americans might not be able to hold their thin strip of beach at Gela, Patton ordered reinforcements with another airborne drop on the evening of 11 July. The Luftwaffe had been active all day, bombing ships and strafing troops on land, flying over seven hundred sorties that day, so the sound of planes made everyone trigger-happy. This resulted in a horrifying "friendly fire" incident. C-47s flying from North Africa to Sicily carrying a combat team from the 504th Parachute Infantry Regiment passed over the Allied ships and the Gela area. Thinking it was more enemy planes, one gunner opened fire, after which every Allied gun joined in.[87] Flying at seven hundred feet, the C-47s were sitting ducks. Rangers saw what they thought were enemy paratroopers landing in their midst, and one Ranger admitted to shooting an American paratrooper out of his harness. Machine gun bullets ripped through the parachute of Lt. John Lynn Watson, whose plane was shot down a few seconds after he jumped. In total, sixty-six planes were lost or damaged, with 229 casualties among the paratroopers.[88] S/Sgt. Shirley C. Jacobs, 1/Hq., was sent to help rescue some of the surviving paratroopers: "The first night . . . we assisted paratroopers who found themselves trapped in a mine field. We got out eight of the paratroopers . . . finding out the next morning that there were fifty-seven booby-traps in the area we had gone through the night before."[89]

10 JULY 1943: ENEMY COUNTERATTACK

The 1st and 4th Ranger Battalion had landed on the most heavily defended beachfront in Sicily. Rear Adm. Samuel Morison, a naval historian, listed the forces now bearing down on the Rangers: "[Directly in front of the Rangers were] the Hermann Goering Panzer Division, the Livorno [Infantry] Division and the Niscemi Combat Group, which included most of the Italian tanks in Sicily [all] poised above the edge of the plain, ready to strike."[90]

The Livorno Infantry Division was the most elite unit in the Italian army, and the Hermann Goering Panzer Division, having fought the Rangers in Tunisia, was the main German panzer defense in Sicily, with at least ninety tanks.[91]

It would take but a few hours for the Italian and German generals to launch major counterattacks, beginning on 10 July and lasting through the next day. At the height of the counterattacks German tanks pushed to within a few hundred yards of American positions, threatening to crush the invasion.[92] Because of shallow sandbars and soft sands, Allied LSTs were unable to unload American tanks and artillery.[93] On the first day, only one 37 mm gun got ashore for the Rangers to use against the enemy tanks.[94]

The enemy's counterattack began about 0900 hours on 10 July, when nine light Italian tanks and enemy infantry attacked Gela but were repulsed by Ranger mortar fire before they made it into town. Three tanks were destroyed by rocket launchers, while the others turned tail and left.[95]

First Sgt. David "Soupy" Campbell, 1/F, was face to face with Italian tanks that came barreling into Gela: "We fought them from the rooftops by dropping TNT and sticky bombs on them. We had a 37 mm [gun] that shuttled to its targets, going from one corner to another, taking pot shots at them as they came in from different directions. Our bazookas were firing point-blank."[96]

In the 4th Battalion sector, Lt. Hood received a message that a counterattack of twenty-five to thirty tanks was on the way: "We rushed upstairs and into a room which turned out to be the living room of the mayor of Gela. We took up positions by the window to see what the tanks looked like. What we saw was only one small 'Itye' tank, and he didn't have enough firepower to do any harm. The tank was knocked out by Rangers in no time. That was about 1300 hours, and nothing else happened that day except for an occasional Jerry plane overhead."[97]

During the morning of 11 July, Tech/5 Sherman Legg, 1/Hq., shot down a German Messerschmitt Bf 110 with a BAR. Legg was on the beach near a wall when the German airplane flew low over the beach, strafing everything in sight. Legg: "He scared me silly . . . the next time he came in, I put the gun on the wall and held it there and he flew right into my fire. I could see the bullets rake him . . . then I saw flames coming out around the gas tanks where I'd hit. He crashed into the sea."[98]

11 JULY 1943: COMPANIES 1/A AND 1/B—NORTHWEST OF GELA

Lyle's two companies, still northwest of Gela near the captured coastal battery, were isolated from the rest of the battalion, but communications had been established with the 83rd Chemical Mortar Battalion. The Rangers were facing terrible odds against an Italian force the size of a regiment. The battle-hardened Livorno Infantry were coming straight toward them in a skirmish line along the Butera-Gela road.[99]

Capt. Lyle radioed Lt. Col. Darby asking for reinforcements. Darby answered, "You will have to fight with the troops and supporting weapons you have at this time. The units in the eastern sector are all engaged in stopping a tank attack."[100]

The 4.2 mortars, now ashore and supporting Lyle's men, were slowing up the enemy but not stopping them.[101] The additional firepower of the captured 77s became crucial. The first shot from one of the 77 mm guns, fired by boresighting, hit Lyle's command post out in front on the gun target line. No one was injured, and the 77's fire was elevated.[102] Capt. Lyle: "As the enemy attacking from the northwest came into artillery and 4.2 mortar range, these weapons commenced firing. Our fire was answered by enemy artillery and mortar fire. The enemy force was deployed with about a battalion in a skirmish line, with the remainder of the unit following in a closed column formation."[103]

The 77s, now called the "Ranger artillery," and the 4.2 mortars were not enough firepower to stop this determined enemy. Lyle wrote:

> While observing the effect of the supporting fires and making corrections for the artillery and mortars from the observation post, the Joint Commander [Lyle] had a visitor. It had been the practice in the past to loosen the chin strap of the helmet when under enemy artillery or mortar fire. The Joint Commander heard this visitor state, "Captain, your chin strap is unbuckled." Without turning around to see who made this remark the answer was "Hell yes, we always unbuckle the chin strap when receiving incoming artillery or mortar fire." A loud clearing of the throat was heard and the Joint Commander turned his head and there stood the commander of the Seventh Army, General Patton! With a quick "Yes Sir," the chin strap was secured.

> The General questioned the Joint Commander about the situation and was informed that it was not too good. Before departing, General Patton remarked, "Kill every one of the God damn Bastards!"[104]

The 4.2 mortar platoon leader reported that his ammunition was running low, and there was no more on the beach. At this point, when things looked very grave, an observer from the cruiser USS *Savannah* appeared at the observation post. His first remark was, "Having trouble, soldier?" After a quick look at the situation on the ground, the naval observer began to radio his fire mission to the *Savannah*.[105] Lyle:

> The [enemy] skirmish line was the first target [of the *Savannah*'s guns]. The barrage, consisting of 6-inch high-explosive time fire which burst just above the ground, hit directly on the enemy line. After moving his fire along the line, the fire was shifted down along the column behind the skirmish line. The whole area was black with smoke and dust. When this curtain lifted enemy troops could be seen staggering around as if thoroughly dazed. [I] ordered "A" and "B" Companies to assault the disorganized enemy units. Without firing another shot, four hundred Italians were taken prisoner, and [my companies] returned to their defensive positions. . . . [When the smoke cleared] there were human bodies hanging from trees and some blown to bits.[106]

Without the initial support from the 77s and the shelling by the navy, the Americans, with their backs to the sea, might have been pushed out of Gela. Fighting was so intense on 11 July that when Gen. Patton returned to the USS *Monrovia* that evening, he penned in his diary that this was the first day he felt like he had earned his pay.[107]

MISSION TO TAKE SAN NICOLA

Once Gela was secure, Gen. Patton sent Darby on his next mission to capture the mountaintop village of Butera. Blocking their way was San Nicola, a fortified hilltop village on the Butera road. A regiment of armored infantry, engineers, and mortar troops had finally landed and were attached to the Rangers for this mission. Outside of Gela the land was flat, but a few miles down the road at San Nicola twin peaks rose abruptly from the plain. Any attack would have to pass through the narrow gap between these peaks. Darby did not know what was out there waiting for him.[108]

In a letter to his parents, Lt. Hood explained his mission on the road to Butera:

> I got the order to report to [Lt. Col. Darby] and it was there I learned I was to go on a reconnaissance about 5 miles out in front of our own lines.
>
> [One] officer, 1 jeep driver & 1 enlisted man was to go with me . . . all 4 of us knew there was something up. You could just feel it & . . . I was plenty worried. So, we got our maps out, found the spot we were to go. . . . We were to find out what was out there. We finally got started at 1:30 and [found the correct road. It] went across a plain of about 2½ miles up a little rise & then down onto another plain of about 1½ miles so we knew we would be under [enemy] observation all of the way but away we went. I was in the front with the driver manning the machine gun and the other 2 in the rear. We had information that the bridges had been mined . . . at each bridge we came to, I got out & looked it over.
>
> We felt fairly safe until we got to the rise in the middle of the plain. . . . We stopped for about 5 minutes & watched through field glasses up ahead where we thought the enemy might be. There were 2 or 3 houses on each side of the road & 3 haystacks on the right side. But no movement could be seen. So, we started out again only this time more cautious because we knew we were being watched by Jerry & there was a house about one and a half [miles] up the road where it went between the two hills & we finally decided to go to that house. There were 3 bridges between us & the house & every time I got out to inspect the bridge, I expected all hell to break loose.
>
> We had just passed the last bridge and were within 400 yards of the house & we saw the trick. Barbed wire entanglements were in a little dip that ran through the valley & we knew it meant enemy positions so there was only one thing to do, make a dash for the house. . . . We drove for the house plenty fast & just as we got to it a head poked out the door. I shot at him with my pistol & jumped out of the car & ran for the door because we had to get in the house. Just as I got to the door a hand grenade dropped from the 2nd story window & I was close enough to it [that it] hit me in the right leg.

> I got in the house and started cleaning out the bottom floor [taking] . . . about thirty prisoners. Then I decided to go to the top floor, & [when] I started up the stairway . . . they threw a grenade down the stairs and it went off in my face . . . about that time they opened up on us from the houses on the hills with machine guns & the haystacks turned out to be pill boxes. Well, I got an "Itye" & put him in front of me & we started up the stairs again . . . & threw a concussion grenade in the door & that stopped them for a while. I still couldn't get out of the house because the windows had iron bars.
>
> I told the driver to turn our car [a jeep] around & they shot him in the head & shot our car. We had to leave in a hurry so I told the other Lt. to start crawling down the edge of the road & I ran out the door & I guess Lady Luck was with me because I didn't get hit. I ran over to the driver, saw I couldn't help him, grabbed his guns, and started crawling for home to [Gela].[109]

The Rangers captured several of the enemy in the house, killing most of the rest. They made their captives crawl ahead of them so they could keep an eye on them. The enemy in the pillboxes fired at the Rangers and their prisoners for about a mile with machine guns and mortars but never hit them. Lt. Hood was awarded a Silver Star and Purple Heart for that action.[110]

ATTACKING THE TWIN PEAKS OF SAN NICOLA, 1ST AND 4TH BATTALIONS

Capt. Alexander Worth Jr., CO of 1/F: "At 4:00 pm I was summoned to battalion headquarters on my radio along with Capt. Jim Lyle . . . and Capt. Colby. . . . We were directed . . . to proceed under cover of darkness across the plains of Gela and make a dawn attack on the enemy at San Nicola."[111]

That night, the 1st and 4th Ranger Battalions attacked the peak on the right, while the attached conventional troops, inexperienced in night fighting, went after the left peak. Climbing the steep sides, cutting through barbed wire, the Rangers captured their peak in a little over an hour. But the conventional troops on the left peak lost their initiative, unable to advance in the dark against a hardened enemy.[112]

Some of the five enemy artillery batteries on the left peak switched to fire on Darby's position on the right peak, giving the Rangers, who had no artillery with them, a pasting for the better part of an hour. Darby was able to turn a possible defeat into victory: "I had [Capt. Ralph A. Colby, an artillery officer commanding 1/D with me, and through field glasses] he could see the gun batteries that were firing on us, some five 149 and 150 mm howitzer batteries that were blazing away. . . . The USS *Savannah* . . . was cruising . . . back and forth south of Gela. [With Colby calling in the shots] we started firing with the *Savannah*. . . . I never realized naval gunfire could be so accurate."[113]

When one of the first shells exploded close to the Italian position, Capt. Colby told the *Savannah* to "fire for effect." The *Savannah* had fifteen guns that could each fire three rounds a minute. Forty-five 6-inch shells were on the way in less than a minute, reducing the enemy position and allowing the Rangers and supporting troops to take the left peak without further trouble.[114]

CAPTURE OF BUTERA

Once past San Nicola, the Rangers advanced to Butera, an ancient walled mountaintop village of about five hundred people, located on the highest peak within fifty miles. With a twenty-five-mile view in all directions, Butera was the perfect observation post for the Axis forces to watch every move made by the Seventh Army, now advancing toward them from Gela.[115] In order for the American advance to move north and west, Butera had to be captured. Darby: "It was a fortress that could have been held against a division."[116]

The mountain on which Butera sat looked like a geometric cone sitting on a flat plain. Three of its sides were sheer rock cliffs. The fourth was a very steep climb, a single narrow lane winding up the mountain, giving cover for defenders to ambush attackers. A sixth-century wall, several feet thick and twelve feet high, had protected the medieval townspeople from thieves and other invaders. Fourteen centuries later it served to keep out Americans.[117]

The only intelligence Darby had was a view of the town from another hill several miles away. Darby assigned the assault to Capt. Shunstrom's Company 1/C. Capt. Jim Lyle's 1/A was to back him up with artillery support if needed. Two batteries of 105 mm guns were in position at 0230 hours, and four self-propelled 75s were to follow the battalion at five hundred yards.[118] Darby picked up a field telephone from his command post for a conversation with Lyle:

"Jim," I said, "We're going to attack. We're going into Butera . . . I'm going to put four self-propelled 75s in your position. So, find a spot for them. I'm sending in one company. If it is fired on we'll blast the hell out of the enemy. I want you to shoot anything that moves while we're getting our stuff up. O.K.?"

"Roger," came Lyle's reply.

I next called Shunstrom. . . . "Chuck, you're the leadoff man. I know your boys are tired. They've fought hard and they need a rest, but they are the best for this job. You understand?"

"Yes, sir."[119]

Once the companies were in position, the supporting artillery opened fire for five minutes. They knew the road up to Butera was mined because three half-tracks had been previously blown to bits. The battalion moved out at 0100 hours. Rangers walked in the middle of the road, hoping that none of the mines were booby-trapped. For the last four miles of the approach to Butera the road wound upward, with the enemy able to observe the Rangers from the wall around the town. There was no smoking and no noise.[120] Sgt. Earnest: "We had our scouts out, one two hundred feet in front, the other 150 feet. We started up the mountain and got about halfway up. We put one man on either side of us as flankers. . . . We came upon a group of Italians putting down mines."[121]

Sgt. Francis P. Padrucco, 1/C, was Shunstrom's bodyguard: "We got to a bend in the road and a machine gunner opened up on us at a range of about 20 feet. He wounded my lieutenant and the radio operator. But our scout [an interpreter named Constantine, or Connie], with a Tommy gun, let go with a whole drum of ammo; he got seven."[122]

Sgt. Earnest described how they collected POWs on the way up: "We gathered the POWs in the middle of the road and went on up to the town. As we passed caves in the mountain along the road, we could hear babies and women crying. Connie would call them out of the caves telling them we were Americans and would not harm them. They came out and would hug and kiss us like we were long lost relatives."[123]

Historian Col. Robert Black explains what happened next at an enemy outpost: "The Rangers encountered an outpost consisting of three Germans and one Italian. Surprised by Shunstrom and Rangers Edward Barbarino, Alvin Buie, and August Passera, the enemy soldiers were captured. According to

Barbarino, Shunstrom said, 'You know the orders. Take no prisoners. What are you waiting for?' Barbarino killed one of the Germans because he felt they were 'the real enemy.' According to Barbarino, each of the other three killed one of the prisoners."[124]

Capt. Alex Worth, commanding 1/F, was also on the scene. In a telephone call, he told me, "I was aghast that this happened, but at the same time I thought, if there were ten thousand more Shunstroms in the army the war would be over soon."[125]

They moved forward up to the city gate. All the way up some of the Italians who had been captured earlier were yelling. Worth did not understand what they were saying, but Constantine said they were yelling, "Don't shoot, crazy man here, will kill all of us if you shoot." Worth later stated, "If it had not been for Shunstrom, we would never have gotten into that town without some Ranger deaths."[126]

Capt. Shunstrom ordered the 1st Platoon to remain outside the wall when they got to the town. Shunstrom set up mortars between the road and the wall near the city gate. The men were instructed to fire eight rounds per mortar, on command, with each to cover about one-third of the town. As the 1st Platoon approached the city gate, a machine gun at an enemy outpost opened fire, catching the platoon leader in the stomach and one of the scouts in the hand. The lead scout tossed a hand grenade to silence the machine gun.[127]

Shunstrom sent the mortar observers and the 2nd Platoon over the wall on the left side of town. The 1st Platoon entered the town through the massive city gate, at what the Americans called "First Street." There they set up a light machine gun and began firing down "First Street," turning it into a killing zone, denying its use to the enemy. At the same time Capt. Shunstrom ordered the mortars to open fire.[128] Capt. Lyle: "After the 2nd Platoon was over the wall, the mortar crews ceased firing, went out of action, climbed the wall and went into position inside it."[129]

The attack split the town into three sectors, so that the Rangers could clean out each sector one by one, going from house to house, entering each one to look for the enemy. Ranger gunners fired down each street, preventing the enemy from mounting a counterattack. This was the first time the Rangers had attacked and cleared a walled village.[130] Of the approximately three hundred Italian soldiers garrisoned in Butera, only one hundred were left alive to be taken prisoner. Sgt. Padrucco: "My platoon killed about 15 and took 60 or 70 prisoners."[131] The Rangers lost only the two men wounded at the start of the attack, once again proving that thorough training, combined with teamwork, yielded success. Both of the wounded Rangers were back on duty within two weeks.[132]

The 1st and 4th Ranger Battalions would fight across the island, capturing several thousand Italian prisoners and a few hundred German soldiers and officers. The final stop in Sicily for these two battalions was near Palermo, where they would be joined by the 3rd Ranger Battalion after its mission was complete.[133]

THE 3RD RANGER BATTALION'S APPROACH TO LICATA

While the 1st and 4th Ranger Battalions landed at Gela, the 3rd Ranger Battalion, commanded by Maj. Herman Dammer, was attached to the U.S. 3rd Infantry Division attacking Licata. Capt. Edward B. Kitchens, commanding 3/C, described the British landing craft that took his company to shore: "The battalion boarded two British Landing Ships Infantry (LSI) the HMS *Princess Astrid* and *Princess Charlotte.* The British LSI is a sleek, fast ship in a class all its own. It mounts seven LCAs, each with a capacity of thirty-five troops, and one Landing Craft Support (LCS) mounting twin 50 caliber machine guns in a turret. Both craft are armored, have a low silhouette, and are capable of high speeds."[134]

The same storm that affected the 1st and 4th Battalions at Gela plagued the 3rd at Licata. Thrashing around in the rough seas, the Rangers quickly lost their breakfast of smoked kipper. The only Ranger not seasick was Pfc. Edward Feigenbaum, 3/D, the son of an army doctor, who advised that it was better to go in on an empty stomach rather than throw up in the landing craft or in their helmets.[135] Arnbal remembered the ride to shore: "There was no room for us all. This was solved by our company medic, as Corporal Prudhomme and I lay in a prone position on the engine cowling at the rear of the LCA. We hung on for dear life."[136]

THE LANDING

As they approached the beach, German searchlights came on and locked on Capt. James Larkin's boat. Enemy artillery opened up, but the shells landed beyond them. Larkin explained:

> We waited, helpless, for them to adjust the range. Before they could succeed, they lost us in heavy seas. The next boat was not so lucky. They found and sank her while looking for us. We got to the beach unharmed. Although dismounting in the heavy surf was wild, we managed. We then encountered miles and miles of heavy barbed wire. . . . Some of it extended right down into the water. . . . We went to work on the wire with "Bangalore Torpedoes," carried to shore just for this purpose. The technique was to shove a pipe-like section of this weapon forward through the wire, attach a second section, and then a third section—as many as necessary to breach the full depth of the wire. . . . [We would then] rig detonators, and blow a nice big hole in the wire. Actually, this was for the main attack elements. Those of us in the lead had to find a faster way to breach the wire. We threw Ranger volunteers onto the wire and ran across their backs, grinding them mercilessly face-down into the barbed wire. It was primitive—but it works. We soon found ourselves inside the wire. Casualties . . . were minimal . . . but . . . my French-Canadian radio operator . . . was killed by small arms fire.[137]

The 3rd Ranger Battalion came ashore, thirty-five heavily armed Rangers in each craft, hitting the beach on 10 July 1944 at 0255 hours.[138] Companies 3/A, 3/B, and 3/C, led by Maj. Dammer, landed abreast on the narrow beach, immediately going to work to knock out pillboxes and machine guns on the left flank of the beach: "It was a beautiful job done by the Navy in finding this place in the first place. We landed . . . and got to our objectives quite easily except that [enemy] weapons . . . opened fire just after we landed. . . . They immobilized two of the landing craft, drilled a hole through them with a 47 mm gun."[139]

Company 3/D, with 3/E and 3/F on its right, got through the wire on the beach and followed straight up the middle. Taking control of the coast road, they stopped at the first building. Cpl. Arnbal: "A patrol [led by 2nd Lt. Norris Teague Jr.] surrounded the house, and kicking in the door, Sergeant Eric Mozzetti, 3/D, shouted out, 'Veni qua, paisan!' Hearing no reply . . . he threw in a smoke grenade. Soon a large family of Sicilian natives piled out with their hands up. Leaflets had been dropped several days previously urging all civilians to evacuate the area, but few had paid any attention to these dire warnings."[140]

The worst danger to the 3rd Ranger Battalion's landing were several German Messerschmitt Bf 109 fighter planes that were coming in low with guns blazing, hitting the port and warehouse areas. As they passed over, offshore gunners on naval vessels opened up with .50-caliber and 20 mm guns. Unintentionally, they seriously wounded nine men of Lt. Teague's platoon, including Sgt. Mozzetti, Sgt. William Arimond, Pfc. Martin Cashner, and Cpl. George Montgomery, all evacuated to army hospitals in North Africa. All these Rangers were back on duty by December 1943.[141]

With the landing under their belt, the Rangers were allowed to take a break. Thirsty and short of water, some helped themselves to green grapes, getting a bad case of heartburn. Others were taking a nap in a cemetery when 1st Lt. Louis Harper, 3/B, and 1st Sgt. Merritt Bertholf, 3/D, showed up with handfuls of German marks they had picked up from locals. The men stashed the money away, hoping to use it for future "entertainment."[142] The Rangers were hungry for real food. To address that pressing issue, a small detail of men from Company D who could not wait on the kitchen to be set up went out on a night patrol, returning at about 0100 hours with what would have been a feast. Arnbal:

> Lt. Preston Hogue, Sgt. George Burnette, Sgt. Ewing Mays, S/Sgt. Richard Hedges, Jr. and a couple of others . . . returned, laden down with a gutted black calf! A fire was started from dead tree limbs . . . and a western-style barbeque soon was in progress. We were stripping off pieces and chunks of meat when [Capt.] Alvah Miller . . . showed up together with some 3rd Division officers. They confiscated all the meat . . . and Lt. Louis Harper [gave] them a lecture about the fact that the U.S. Army did not "live off the land." . . . it did in no way endear us to the brass of the 3rd Infantry Division.[143]

THE 3RD BATTALION'S ROUTE TO PORTO EMPEDOCLE

After the 3rd Battalion had taken Licata, Gen. Patton ordered Gen. Truscott to capture the city of Porto Empedocle, which had a large deep-water port to supply the Allied army in its move across Sicily. On the way to Porto Empedocle the Rangers passed through the villages of Campobello, Naro, and Favara but found the route blocked at the large, ancient city of Agrigento.[144]

On 14 July, about three miles west of the village of Favara, the 3rd Ranger Battalion came under hostile artillery fire, but sustained no casualties. The road passed through a tunnel, and, fearing it was mined, the Rangers climbed over the hill instead. Movement was slow, allowing the scouts the opportunity to reconnoiter the areas adjacent to the road. After they crossed a deep ravine where a bridge was blown, it was apparent that no armored support could reach them beyond that point.[145]

Moving on Montaperto, north of Agrigento, three companies formed a skirmish line with bayonets fixed. Italian soldiers began waving white flags rather than die. Montaperto fell easily to the bayonet charge, yielding over four hundred prisoners. At this point the 3rd Battalion was far behind enemy lines and out of touch with the support units they needed to resupply them with food and ammunition, making the large number of prisoners a burden. Maj. Dammar put the prisoners at the rear of the Ranger column, designating the tail end company to guard them while the Rangers continued their move toward Agrigento.[146]

West of Agrigento, one company of Rangers, noticing a convoy of enemy vehicles approaching rapidly, hid themselves until the unsuspecting Italians were almost right on top of them. Firing 3.5-inch antitank rockets and small arms, the Rangers engaged the front and rear vehicles first, bracketing the convoy so that none of its vehicles could escape. The entire enemy column was either killed or wounded.[147]

Tech/5 Donald Hayes, 3/C, described how the Rangers were pushed to their limit with little rest:

> That first 10 days we didn't have any rest at all. We fought all day and marched all night. Then, [nearing Agrigento,] we came to a big German [position] that the infantry couldn't crack, so we had to go in. Up on top of a big hill was a German observation point. The captain took a bunch of us, and we started up the hill to get them. On top was a bare cliff that went straight up, and they were on top of that. An Italian hollered down and told us to stop or we'd all be killed. But the captain [Kitchens] didn't want to stop. We found a sort of [gully] that looked like it had been carved right into the cliff, so we started up in single file.
>
> When we got near the top, we still couldn't see a soul. Someone told the captain that one of the men ought to climb up the side of the path to the top and look over to see where the Jerries were hiding. There wasn't a man in sight

> when I looked over. I reported to the captain that there was a wall about 200 yards away and probably the garrison was behind that. So, the captain gave the order to charge.[148]

Attacking the gun batteries at Agrigento in a skirmish line with fixed bayonets, Rangers in 3/D could hear "Indian yells" from other companies making first contact with the enemy. Advancing up the hill, the Rangers were fired upon by an enemy machine gun. Lt. Warren Evans, CO of 3/F, was stunned by a stray bullet that penetrated his helmet but not his skull. Lt. Raymond "Slim" Campbell, one of Evans's platoon leaders and new to the Rangers, volunteered to go after the machine gun.[149] Evans: "Campbell's men ran with their rifles and bayonets at port arms, ready to strike. Just as they neared the machine gun position, they'd snap the bayonet down to the ready position and then jump, one to the right and one to the left. Lt. Campbell was killed in the firefight and several Rangers wounded. It was another time that I felt I had been saved by another man's sacrifice."[150]

After the fight for Agrigento, the 3rd Battalion now had over eight hundred POWs, mostly Italian. Because the Rangers could not make the POWs prepare sanitary trenches, the stench was overwhelming, and they were almost out of water in the Sicilian heat.[151] Second Lt. William Musegades, 3/D, began asking if anyone had seen Cpl. Joseph Shuff, 3/D, S/Sgt. William "Larry" Sausen, 3/E, or Pfc. Johnny Stanton, 3/D. Musegades realized that he had not seen them since they had passed through Favara. Cpl. Andy Arnbal answered, "Knowing [these] three, any risk is worth taking if wine is involved." It turned out, the three had taken over the largest bar in Agrigento and swapped rations for wine, then had to sleep it off before catching up with the company.[152] These men were part of a group of the Original Rangers that included Cpl. Arnbal, 3/D, Pvt. Warren "Big Swede" Johnson, 3/E, and Sgt. William "Bill" Jackson, 3/D, who called themselves the "Barrel-Land Dance Hall Rangers." Their motto was "Never let a good bar go to waste." These tough soldiers had shared combat during fighting in Tunisia but frequently sought out "unscheduled" R&R.[153]

After leaving the bar at Agrigento, the three Dance Hall Rangers were moving up the road toward Porto Empedocle in the dark looking for their company when they came upon three enemy tanks in the middle of the road, but there was no sign of enemy soldiers. Assuming that the company had bypassed this roadblock in the dark, and thinking it wise to knock it out, S/Sgt. Sausen jumped on top of each tank and dropped a grenade in its open hatch. Moving on down the road, they ran into 1st Lt. Warren "Bing" Evans, who chastised them for being late and told them where to find their company. After reporting the action with the tanks to Capt. James Larkin and other officers, who verified their story, their misbehavior was forgiven. S/Sgt. Sausen was later awarded a Silver Star for this action even though it was revealed at a later time that a recon unit from the 82nd Airborne had previously destroyed the tanks.[154]

Porto Empedocle, the main target, was a major enemy hub, located on a high bluff overlooking the Mediterranean and heavily defended by German soldiers with large-bore artillery and antiaircraft batteries. Gen. Truscott hoped to capture the port intact so that Allied vessels could immediately begin unloading there.[155]

The 3rd Ranger Battalion circled around to take Porto Empedocle from the north since its coastal guns and defense were sited to the south, facing the sea. Maj. Dammer split the battalion in half, personally leading Companies D, E, and F, while Capt. Alvah Miller, the 3rd Battalion executive officer, led Companies A, B, and C. On 16 July 1943 at 1420 hours, Dammer's men deployed into skirmish lines, supported by their 60 mm mortars, which were set up six hundred yards north of town. Meeting stiff resistance from rooftop snipers, Dammer's Rangers worked their way through the town, down to the port area, cleaning out enemy strongpoints along the way using grenades and bayonets in close-up fighting.[156] Darby: "Captain Miller ran into the crews of a battery of dual-purpose coastal guns. After a short scrap Miller rounded up ninety-one German and 675 Italian prisoners. The battle was over by 1600."[157]

In Porto Empedocle, the Rangers captured an Italian army corps headquarters, where dozens of Italian generals and colonels, plus one German general, were led out at gunpoint by Cpl. Regis McMahon, 3/E. Once the enemy garrison surrendered, the Rangers had 2,500 prisoners. Controlling that many prisoners was a difficult job for a few hundred Rangers.[158]

Maj. Dammer was concerned about the length of time it took to complete the mission, with the result that his men were low on provisions: "We were very close to being out of ammunition. We were out of 60 mm. I considered our situation here rather unfavorable. We consolidated at the port, put out our defenses and sat down to wait for the rest of the troops to come along the coast road. My immediate problem was to get word back as to where I was and what I was doing and how I was doing."[159]

U.S. Navy scout planes, unaware that Porto Empedocle had been captured by the Americans, were dropping leaflets asking the enemy to surrender or be fired upon. The Rangers made a frantic effort to let the U.S. Navy know they had control of the port.[160] Dammer: "[We found] a lot of oil barrels down at the wharf and we spelled out various things as 'Yank' and 'U.S. Troops' and various things to invite [a seaplane] to come down. That took several hours.... Finally . . . he came in, picked me up and took me out to the cruiser. I . . . told them my story . . . as far as being cut off from our other people, being out of food, etc."[161]

Ammunition, water, and food flooded into the 3rd Rangers from the navy stores. The navy contributed greatly to the Rangers' success whenever they operated near the coast.[162]

ON TO MESSINA

Patton, wanting to beat Britain's Gen. Bernard Montgomery to Messina, was enraged at the thought of playing second fiddle to Montgomery, whom he considered a "lesser" commander. Both men had huge egos and heartily disliked each other. Word came down to the Rangers that Patton intended to beat Montgomery to Messina at all costs, and the 3rd Ranger Battalion was ordered to get there first.[163] Tech/5 Donald Hayes, 3/C, could never forget the resulting ordeal: "We were ordered to cut across the island directly to Messina. We marched for two days and one night, exhausted. You'd think you couldn't take another step and then you'd see the guy in front of you still slogging along and you'd think, 'Hell, I'm as good a man as he is,' and you'd go on."[164]

The 3rd Rangers met up with some 1st Battalion Rangers, who gave them mules to carry their heavy gear, including pack howitzers, for the hundred-mile trek across rugged mountains to Messina. The Germans had mastered the technique of setting up one delaying defense after another, dropping back to another hill each time the Allies got in position to overrun them. It was a slow, hot, dirty process that took a toll on the Rangers as their ranks were depleted from wounds and illness. The Rangers marched day and night with few rest breaks. Someone asked Arnbal, "Sarge, when are we going to get a rest break?"

Arnbal answered that a rest break would come when Maj. Dammer gave out, but he'd never known Dammer to give out.[165]

The middle of August found the 3rd Battalion on hilltops overlooking Messina, armed only with light weapons and again out of radio communication. All they could do was watch the Germans blow up their ammunition and move their troops and materiel across the Strait of Messina to safety in Italy. Only 160 men of the battalion were left on duty, not enough to attack Messina. The rest had dropped behind, either ill with malaria or exhausted from fighting and marching.[166] Near the end of the march, Cpl. Arnbal was among those who had fallen out from exhaustion, thus missing the liberation of Messina:

> Day and night passed . . . as in a dream. We had no water and no rations, and we had lived off the fat and water in our own bodies for the last two days! . . . After dark we halted and collapsed wherever there was a bare place. . . . I woke up . . . not quite knowing where I was. . . . The only Ranger I saw was our platoon runner, Pfc. Dean Miller, who was still sleeping nearby. . . . There was no one else to be seen.[167]

Arnbal and Miller heard noise over the next hill and headed in that direction, stumbling into an American artillery battery, where they were fed and refreshed with hot coffee. An NCO pointed the Rangers toward Messina, and the two headed off in that direction, only to find that the Germans had evacuated the city.[168]

The first Allied troops to enter Messina were a reinforced platoon of the U.S. 7th Infantry Regiment entering the town on the evening of 16 August 1943. Patton had beaten Montgomery. On the morning of 17 August, Gen. Truscott was on a ridge above Messina, along with Italian civilian authorities from the city, waiting for Patton to arrive to accept their surrender. Patton's convoy roared in at 1000 hours, and he demanded to know what they were standing around waiting for. Without waiting for an answer, still afraid that Montgomery might beat him into the city, Patton took off, dashing into Messina, dodging enemy artillery fire from the Italian mainland.[169]

It was all worth it to Patton—he had beaten Montgomery. Locals were out on the street welcoming the Americans when suddenly there was gunfire. Arnbal took off at a run toward the sound of trouble and ran into British riflemen, who told him that a German sniper was giving them trouble. The body of one

British soldier was laying in the middle of the street and another was wounded. Arnbal spotted the sniper high up in a building: "'There were a few moments in which [the sniper] ceased firing, and that was all I needed as I leveled my M1 and sighted, all in a second, then squeezed off three rounds in rapid succession. One or more of the rounds hit the German; he fell backward, and his weapon fell in a clatter onto the sidewalk below."[170]

The 3rd Rangers had few encounters with the enemy during their last few days in Messina. When Tech/5 Clarence Eineichner, 3/Hq., was out for a stroll a few blocks from their bivouac in a local cemetery, he spotted some locals, loaded down with large jars, trying to batter down the door of a building. Eineichner approached the locals and told them there would be no more looting and they should leave: "It didn't take us long to remove the door, once we learned it was a brewery. . . . [We] discovered two large tanks with numerous spigots protruding from the sides. I turned on one. The spray hit me in the face, looked like beer, it smelled like beer, it tasted like beer, it was beer! . . . Soaked with beer from head to foot, I headed back to the cemetery dragging a large bell jar filled with beer."[171]

THE ALLIES' LOST OPPORTUNITY

Gen. Hans Valentin Hube, commander of the XIV Panzer Corps, had mounted a brilliant strategic defense of Sicily. With only four divisions, Hube tied down two Allied armies, holding off the invaders for over a month, then escaped with nearly his entire command. Why the Allied navy did not attack the German boats as they shuttled thousands of the enemy and their vehicles across the narrow Strait of Messina is one of the mysteries of the Mediterranean Theater.[172]

PALERMO

Trucks soon arrived to haul the tired 3rd Rangers from Messina to a valley below Corleone, near Palermo, where the 1st and 4th Rangers were resting and refitting, preparing for the attack on Italy. Tech/5 Donald Hayes, 3/C, remembered the long journey from Messina to Palermo:

> Soon after [cleaning up the coastal areas], we pulled out toward Palermo to [the] "bloody ridge." The infantry had tried three times to take it and couldn't,

> so we tried. About halfway up, both American artillery and planes attacked us, so we had to fall back to the bottom and call them off. Next try we made it to the top; there were dead Americans lying all over the place. The men had started to pass out from exhaustion by then. We'd lie down in our five minute breaks each hour and it was awful getting the men up again. One of the boys laid down beside a dead German. When the break ended he rolled over and kept trying to shake the German awake before he realized it wasn't one of his buddies sleeping beside him.[173]

By the end of August, the Battle of Sicily was over, and the three Ranger battalions, soon to be renamed the "Ranger Force," were now reunited under Darby's control. With Sicily under their belt, but with losses from killed, wounded, and non-battle casualties, of which malaria was the worst, the Rangers had only three weeks to recruit and train replacements and get refitted for the next mission. Lt. Col. Darby, Maj. Dammer, and Maj. Murray flew to Algiers to help plan the next action.[174] Destination—the European continent.

9

ITALY

SALERNO TO NAPLES

OPERATION AVALANCHE

With Sicily under control, the Allies had airbases close enough to the continent to counter German fighters and bombers, making it possible to invade mainland Italy, the first Allied invasion of the European continent. The invasion of Italy at Salerno, code-named Avalanche, with Gen. Sir Harold Alexander again in overall command, was scheduled for 9 September 1943. Coming only a month after Sicily was secured, it gave the Allies little time to prepare to combat the forces of Germany's Gen. Kesselring.[1] Three German divisions had successfully withdrawn from Sicily across the Strait of Messina. Pieces of eight more divisions were in the north under Rommel, two more were in Rome, and pieces of six more rushed in from Germany, the Balkans, and elsewhere. Correctly assessing that the Gulf of Salerno, south of Naples, would be the point of attack because the Allies could cover it with fighter protection from Sicily, Kesselring placed his most experienced troops there.[2]

The invasion of Italy would involve multiple units and several separate attacks. The first to land would be the British 5th Infantry Division and the Canadian 1st Division, capturing the Italian naval base at Taranto on the Gulf of Taranto, which forms the "instep" of the Italian boot. From there, they would advance northward along the east coast of Italy.[3] The main landing would come in the Gulf of Salerno on 450 ships under the command of Admiral Henry K. Hewitt. The U.S. Fifth Army, commanded by Lt. Gen. Mark Clark, included two corps, one American and one British, both coming ashore just southeast of Salerno. The American VI Corps, commanded by Maj. Gen. Ernest Dawley, included the 36th Infantry Division and part of the 45th Infantry Division. Landing alongside them on the southeastern part of the Salerno beach was the

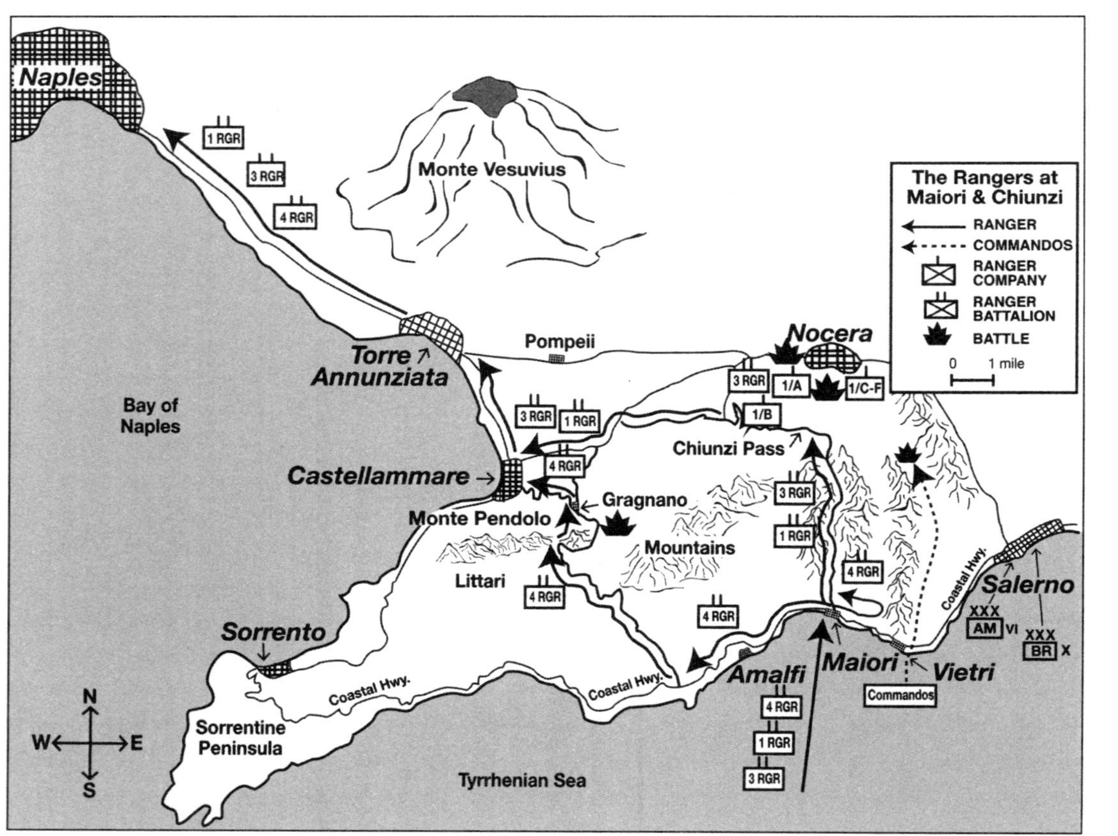

The Rangers in Italy (Salerno) at Maiori and Chiunzi Pass

British X Corps, commanded by Lt. Gen. Richard McCreery, consisting of the 56th Infantry Division and the 46th Infantry Division. After landing, the Fifth Army was to capture Naples, with further landings to come by reserve divisions from both countries.[4]

Late in the afternoon on 8 September, Gen. Eisenhower announced Italy's unconditional surrender to the Allies. Italy gained little from its surrender because the country was already full of Germans who were now occupiers, not allies to the Italians. It was now only Germans, not Italians, whom the Rangers would be fighting for the rest of the war. The news of the surrender was carried over all the ships' loudspeakers, and most of the troops cheered.[5] Men on the ships were celebrating, but Darby must have hoped that the news would not allow his Rangers to let their guard down.

Early on 9 September 1943, the main attack force neared the Italian coast. Against the strong suggestions of Admiral Hewitt, Gen. Clark had ordered that no pre-landing bombardment take place. Clark and his staff were determined to achieve complete surprise. The British were still under Clark's command, but their commanders insisted on a naval bombardment of their landing beaches. In addition to cruisers and destroyers, the British navy had a monitor, a shallow-draught warship that was nothing more than a platform for its two enormous 15-inch guns.[6]

RANGERS AND COMMANDOS

Darby's Ranger Force, under the command of Gen. Clark, consisting of the 1st, 3rd, and 4th Ranger Battalions and two companies of the 83rd Chemical Mortar Battalion, was to land on a one thousand-yard-long beach at Maiori, just west of Salerno on the Sorrento Peninsula. Two battalions of British Commandos, No. 2 Commando, led by "Mad Jack" Churchill, and the Royal Marines of No. 41 Commando, each about the size of a Ranger battalion, would come in at Vietri, just east of Maiori.[7] Together, they would take control of the mountains of the Sorrento Peninsula, thereby protecting the left flank of the Fifth Army, with the Rangers specifically charged with seizing and then defending the passes at Nocera and Chiunzi.[8] In the wee hours on 8 September 1943, the Ranger Force, which was shipping out from Palermo, joined the main convoy cruising toward Salerno. Sgt. Roy Wade Earnest, 1/C:

> We left Palermo about sunrise and headed toward Salerno. About 2 pm the Germans came on us with Fockwolf and Me109s, strafing and dropping bombs at us. The bombs missed us and no one was hit. . . . The L.S.T. had only two machine guns and they wouldn't have stopped the attack. The P38, P40 and Spitfires came to our rescue. They caught the Germans by surprise [and] two of the Me109 went down. We lay on the deck watching the dog fight. The Germans made a run to get away but our planes were on their tails nearly to Naples. We did not see any more planes 'til we were on land.[9]

To ensure a landing at the tiny beach in the dark, the navy assigned a destroyer to lead the landing boats, which would follow the destroyer's taillight. About a half mile offshore, the ship's captain called out to the Rangers, telling them, "You are now on course," and not to change directions. The Rangers hit the beach on the nose.[10]

4TH RANGER BATTALION

The 4th Battalion landed first, at 0230 hours on 9 September 1943, easily scaling the seawall behind the beach, securing the beachhead, and providing flank security for the 1st and 3rd Rangers, which followed in that order.[11] There was no opposition since the Germans were not expecting anyone to land on such a small beach on this dark night. Second Lt. Don Frederick, 4/E: "We made a dry landing at Maiori, a tiny fishing village just west of Salerno. Upon landing, we encountered no opposition on the beach but discovered a cave which contained 1,500 land mines the Germans intended to place along that same beach, a lucky break for the Rangers."[12] Had the Rangers not landed when they did, the mines probably would have been in place on the beach the next morning.[13] Forming a defensive perimeter, the 4th Battalion fanned out toward Salerno to the east and Amalfi to the west to see if the enemy was in the area.

The 4th Rangers captured a German motorcycle bearing an officer and two enlisted men. Farther on, the same Rangers encountered a concrete enemy pillbox at a sharp bend in the road and were fired on with heavy-caliber machine gun fire, raking the entire length of the Ranger company. Rangers returned fire with Tommy guns and BARs, spraying the pillbox apertures. After killing or capturing the enemy in and around the pillbox, the Rangers moved on and encountered a more heavily fortified naval observation post. It took an entire platoon of Rangers almost an hour to reduce this site, killing the entire enemy force, with several Ranger casualties.[14]

Continuing to move west along the coast road toward Amalfi, the men encountered a roadblock, which they promptly reduced, but Amalfi itself was unoccupied. On 11 September, three companies of the 4th Battalion moved north of Sorrento and seized Monte Pendolo overlooking German positions. By 12 September, elements of the 4th Battalion had seized several more heights overlooking Castellammare, a port located northwest of Maiori on the Bay of Naples. After securing the bulk of the Sorrento Peninsula, many of the 4th Rangers were relieved by a battalion of paratroopers of the 504th Parachute Infantry Regiment, 82nd Airborne Division, and were sent to reinforce a British Commando unit nearby. The balance of the 4th climbed up Monte Chiunzi to give additional firepower to the 1st and 3rd Ranger Battalions.[15]

1ST RANGER BATTALION

Sgt. Roy Wade Earnest, 1/C, described the assault landing: "We stayed on the water 'til 2:30 AM and hit the beach above Salerno. Our objective was Chiunzi Pass. We were to hold the pass so the Germans could not come around and get in behind the 36th and 45th divisions."[16]

The 1st Rangers marched inland up the steep, winding road for six miles toward Chiunzi Pass, clearing the road and occupying the 3,700-foot peak of Monte San Angelo di Cava, on the right side of Chiunzi Pass, from which they could observe Route 18, the main German supply route from Naples to Salerno. Killing or capturing an enemy party preparing to lay mines on the road, they reached the high ground just after daylight. That same day, Companies 1/A and 1/B were assigned to support the 3rd Battalion.[17]

3RD RANGER BATTALION

The 3rd Ranger Battalion landed next on the Maiori beach with no resistance and followed the mountain road high up into the Sorrentine Mountains, occupying the 2,800-foot Monte Chiunzi on the left side of the pass. When all the Rangers were in place, occupying the ridges to either side of Chiunzi Pass, they could practically look down the throats of the Germans on Route 18.[18] Sgt.

Carl Lehmann Jr., 3/C, arriving at the pass, stood on a graveled shelf, gasping equally from the ascent and from the startling sight of an immense fire in the sky, pulsing high up and far away in the dark:

> At dawn, the fire dims, and through the mist, a great mountain rises from the plain. It's the massive bulk of *il Vesuvio* erupting fire, smoke, and ash as he's done since long before Etruscans, Greeks, Romans, and Italians peopled his slopes, and whom he's oft entertained with spectacular pyrotechnics. . . . On 9 September 1943 he again has the stage! Brilliant beacon for the Luftwaffe, Allied bombers, and aiming point for the guns of the great fleet of warships accompanying the transports and landing craft riding calm seas off Salerno, and about to deposit 140,000 men upon the continent.[19]

THE FIGHT AT CHIUNZI PASS

Sgt. Earnest, an experienced combat veteran, realized that once the Germans found the pass blocked, they would throw everything they could at the Rangers: "They used troops to draw our fire, then opened up with 88 guns, high-burst mortars, and screaming memees trying to get us off [the pass], but we were dug in and were going to stay."[20]

The Hermann Goering Panzer Division, which the Rangers had previously engaged in North Africa and Sicily, was now directly below the Rangers, moving troops and equipment from Naples toward the main battle at Salerno. To bombard them, along with the warehouses and roads that supplied the German troops at Salerno, Allied ships had to fire a shell with a trajectory high enough to clear the mountain pass but still drop close to the steep backside of the mountain.[21]

To coordinate the naval bombardment, the Rangers had one of their artillery officers aboard a Royal Navy ship called a "Monitor" because it resembled the Civil War ship of that name. Fire direction controllers figured out that if they tilted the ship slightly to one side, away from the mountain, they could lob the large 15-inch shells through the pass, barely clearing it, and drop them on targets on the backside of the mountain. Ranger and naval observers radioed the ship for corrections, and the Ranger aboard the ship made sure the adjustments were correctly interpreted.[22]

Sgt. Carl Harrison Lehmann Jr., 3rd Ranger Battalion, Company C, standing on the edge of Monte Chiunzi looking down at German supply lines below with Monte Vesuvius in the distance. Courtesy Steve Lehmann.

Sgt. Carl Lehmann Jr., 3/C, acknowledging the value of mortars: "With the Rangers was a unit of 4.2 inch chemical mortars and both field artillery and naval artillery observers. With the Plain of Naples . . . in plain view, the Rangers and their observers directed mortar and naval fire upon the roads from the first day."[23]

Capt. Axel Anderson, Ranger Force Supply, was stunned by the size of the rounds fired from British ships:

> Shells were so large you could practically see them when they came over, because they would disturb the air so much that they would almost become vis-

> ible. When the shells would come through the pass, they sounded just like a freight train. Once, I went to the edge of the mountain to see what they could shoot at down in the valley at the base of Monte Chiunzi. There was a quadrangle building, and watching through binoculars, you could see motorcycles and German troops going in and out. We called over this navy observer and told him it looked like some kind of a command center down there. Motorcycled dispatched riders and jeeps were going in and out of this building. So, the forward observer gets his map out and is busy writing and plotting on a chart. He called in the coordinates, and someone on the Monitor replied, "On the way."
>
> The first round hit right on the corner of the building. The second round was inside the building. He adjusted the coordinates, made them repeat them back to him, and said, "fire two more rounds." That was the last of any of the traffic you saw around that building.[24]

It was here for the first time that the Rangers heard German propaganda. Tech/Sgt. Norman Fitzhugh, 1/Hq.: "I knew the Rangers needed a radio man, and I was the man for it. I made my own receiving set over which I heard the German propaganda broadcast."[25] The Germans spread lies over the radio waves that Rangers' wives and girlfriends were cheating on them, sometimes using the names of specific Rangers, probably obtained from their spies in Sicily.

In addition to the naval bombardment, the Ranger Cannon Company, now commanded by Capt. Charles Shunstrom, was pummeling the Hermann Goering Panzer Division. Shunstrom's unit consisted of four half-tracks, each mounting a 75 mm French cannon, a .50-caliber machine gun, a .30-caliber machine gun, and an 81 mm mortar that was too heavy for infantry to carry. When Ranger spotters identified a target, Shunstrom would race forward to the edge of the mountain, fire off several rounds from the 75 mm, and then race back to cover. The Germans responded with their deadly 88s, causing Ranger casualties. Rangers cursed Shunstrom for inviting the enemy fire, but they knew his job was necessary.[26]

Outnumbered ten to one, with little rest or relief day or night, and with limited food and water, the Rangers were thinly spread over a large area, with the larger gaps covered by machine guns. At night, following an artillery or mortar barrage, the Germans could slip up the side of the mountain to attack at close range. In addition to continual enemy patrols trying to break through the Rangers' lines, the Hermann Goering Panzer Division and the 15th Panzer Grenadiers made at least seven major assaults, attempting to drive the Rangers off the mountains.[27] Tech/5 Clinton Westrum, 1/C: "We once endured eighteen straight hours of shelling from German 88s."[28]

The Germans used artillery to try to break the Rangers' stranglehold on the pass. Medic Robert J. Reed, 3/Hq.:

> We were obviously hurting them grievously with our spotting for the air and naval bombardment. . . . Enemy artillery fire was quite severe. . . . There was a pile of 4.2 inch mortar shells just a hundred yards from me. An artillery shell hit the pile and set it on fire. There was a man wounded and I went out to get him. As I passed the burning pile of mortar shells, a second lieutenant was standing there with a little fire extinguisher spraying stuff on the fire. I couldn't get away from there fast enough.[29]

S/Sgt. Jesse F. Yarboro, 4/Hq.: "I was sitting with some other guys in what I thought was a safe place. We were behind a large rock heating some rations when a stray enemy mortar shell was lobbed over the hill which protected us. It was too quick for any of us to duck. Nine of us were wounded by the shell. After a week in the hospital, I rejoined my company."[30]

S/Sgt. Steven Szcesniak, 4/Hq., had to repair jeeps and trucks within a few hundred yards of the enemy: "At Chiunzi Pass, our battalion surgeon, Capt. Richard Hardenbrook, 4/Hq., installed a frame on his jeep which enabled him to carry two litters of wounded on the back and two across the hood, with one person riding beside him. With Capt. Hardenbrook doing his own driving he could evacuate five patients at once from the front line. More than once, I had to repair that jeep within hearing distance of the Germans under blackout conditions."[31]

A couple of men from Ranger Company 4/F went to take drinking water back to their company when trouble found them. First Lt. Lester Kness, 4/A, later recounted what happened:

> Only one man brought his rifle, Sgt. Lloyd Pruitt. They filled the water cans and decided to take a bath inside the "springhouse," the name given to a crude wooden structure built around a spring-fed pool. They stripped off their

> clothing and were enjoying a bath when they heard voices coming towards them. Looking out the door, Sgt. Pruitt saw a German patrol coming straight to the springhouse. He grabbed his rifle. The other Ranger jumped into the cool spring water behind a stone wall. Pruitt opened up, naked as he was, on the Germans. He was a good shot. I don't know how many he hit. When he ran out of ammo, he discovered his rifle belt was on the other side of the doorway. He called for the other man to throw him a clip of ammo and the shootout continued. Men from Pruitt's company heard the shooting and ran down and took care of the rest of the German patrol.[32]

One night the Germans continuously shelled the area occupied by Sgt. Ray Yandell, 3/E, keeping him pinned down all night. With every attack, he scurried for shelter. One time Yandell did not move fast enough and was struck, with wounds bad enough to land him in a hospital in North Africa, his sixth and most serious wound.[33]

By patrolling and fighting in small groups, the Rangers had led the Germans to believe that they were a much larger unit than was the case. Spread thin over a wide area, the Rangers always ran into stiff opposition, with combat so continuous and severe that Darby, being afraid that his men might get pushed out of the mountains, kept an LST parked at Maiori. Another unit wanted to use it, but Darby refused, informing them that: "The LST was being kept handy in case he had to evacuate his troops and suggested they make the best of it by jeep."[34]

Sgt. Roy Earnest, 1/C, in his foxhole, tells of one of the casualties:

> They bombarded us every morning at daybreak and every evening at dusk. . . . At night they would sneak up and fire on us with small arms. Then one night we had six new replacements come in. We helped them dig their foxholes and get settled in. We told them about the artillery and told them to stay in their foxholes while the shells were coming in.
>
> The next morning when it started . . . four or five rounds came in and one of the new men came out of his foxhole running around on top of the mountain hollering that he didn't want to die. . . . We tried to get him down, but he kept running around. The flak from the shells was flying and singing all around us. While we were down a German sniper had slipped in close to

> our position and opened fire on him with a burp gun cutting the kid almost in half. We could not leave our cover to help him. When the shelling stopped one of the men stood up. The sniper fired on him but missed. Our sniper, [Pfc. Ashley Justice], looking through his telescope sight, spotted him and shot the German . . . between his eyes. I got his weapon and kept it.
>
> We came back to the area and checked the kid that got killed. He was only 18 or 19 years old. He may have shaved every 2 or 3 months. We picked up his body and moved it to the rear of our position and covered it with his shelter half. We ate and got the other five new ones and gave them a talk about survival.[35]

Tech/5 Lawrence "Red" Gilbert, 1/Hq., illustrated the moral stresses of war:

> We had a new guy that I took aside and told him what a German paratrooper looked like, the helmet and the uniform. A few hours go by, and this guy sees German helmets off in the distance coming his way. He said, "It was just exactly what you told me they was gonna look like, so we nailed them." Then another Ranger is watching that same area, and a couple of days later sees the bushes moving down off the edge of the mountain. Thinking more Germans are coming up, he opens fire with the mortar. Later he found out that he killed a girl and her family. She was leading her family up over the mountain to safety. Somehow, they must have gotten lost and got off the trail. Earlier, the Ranger had killed Germans in the same place trying to sneak up on him. . . . It's one of those mishaps that happens in war. The guy felt really bad about it, but the Germans were doing everything to get us off the mountain.[36]

Medic Robert J. Reed, 3/Hq.: "One day a shell hit our house and a soldier standing just outside the door was struck by shrapnel. Before he hit the ground I was there with a litter and caught him as he fell."[37] S/Sgt. John Hoffines, 1/B: "I was with a group of British Commandos heating C-Rations behind a hill that we thought would offer some protection, when a German mortar suddenly crashed down in our midst, wounding several. I was hit by three mortar fragments and spent two months in the hospital before being reassigned to Ranger Force Headquarters."[38]

Sgt. Carl Lehmann, 3/C, saw a civilian brave the dangers of war to do an act of kindness: "Italian civilians, living in the mountains, were often grateful and helpful to the Rangers. Crawling slowly from foxhole to foxhole, a cheerful old Italian in ragged dress, greeting us with Mozzarella [di bufala]* from a basketful, despite noisy 88s bursting in the Pass. An odd wicker basket—a yard across—filled with white balls which now, when seen at Nick's Italian grocery I recall them and the basket and the old Italian and his grin—and his bad teeth."[39]

It took the American army at Salerno about three weeks to get a firm foothold, which finally pressured the Germans to slack off their daily attacks on Chiunzi Pass. Eventually the Germans moved north, licking their wounds.

SUPPLYING THE RANGERS IN BATTLE

Something as simple as ammunition resupply was challenging when the Germans had mortars and artillery zeroed in on every bridge and river crossing. Capt. Axel Anderson told this story, accompanied with hand gestures:

> Resupplying the Rangers was difficult, exhausting work because of the terrain. You had to travel to get up to the top of the pass and then down off the mountain. After three days, we were not getting any ammunition, and Darby wanted to know why. With Sgt. Alex Szima as my driver. I took my strength chart and my gun list and said, "We're going to Fifth Army headquarters." When I was going down the mountain, the British stopped me. A bridge we had to cross was three hundred feet high if it was an inch. A good football field high, slung between two cliffs.
>
> The mountains sat back here [gesture], and a river came down here [gesture], going underneath that bridge. But the mountain coming back here had enemy machine guns and mortar set up on it. And they were zeroed in on that bridge. So, when you started across it, you threw the jeep into second gear, gave it hell and you went across. The moment you started across you could hear the "tap, tap, tap" of German machine guns, and then you heard "kaboom, kaboom" of the mortars. When you got through to the other side you realized, "We got to come back this way this afternoon." We got to Fifth Army

* Mozzarella di bufala is a white cheese made from the milk of a water buffalo, an Italian specialty.

headquarters, and I said, "I want two hundred rounds per gun, per day. What can you do for me?" And he says, "I'll give you a company of engineers with a DUKW to unload a ship." So that's how we got the ammunition.

But guess what was on top of that ammunition? Ton after ton of C-rations had to be unloaded before we could get the first bullet off the ship, let alone a shell. Sgt. Szima organized the laborers like a fire brigade and told them to put the ammunition on their shoulders. That's how we got the ammunition, like a bucket brigade.[40]

GETTING INTELLIGENCE: A HEROIC MISSION

On the steep mountains, patrolling was difficult and dangerous. To get intelligence about the Germans' plans, patrols tried to capture prisoners, but they seldom got close enough to the enemy to make a capture. Sgt. William Fox, 3/E, fluent in Italian, decided to make a solo reconnaissance down into the valley to a small town swarming with Germans. If captured, he would have been considered a spy and shot. Capt. James Larkin, 3/E:

> Sgt. William J. Fox came to me to ask permission "to go on patrol." He pouted when I refused, and went anyway. When he returned, 12 hours or so later, I placed him under arrest. He responded, "Yes sir, but what do I do with this guy," pointing to his prisoner, an Italian officer. I soon discovered that Fox had gone all the way down the steep forward slope of the mountain into Nocera, changed into civilian clothing confiscated from a roadside house, and then busied himself counting German tanks going by. Soon bored with this, he entered the Italian garrison and demanded to see the commandant. The Italians . . . had officially surrendered, just days before. . . . [Fox] demanded that the Italian commandant send back with him an Italian officer with knowledge of German troop dispositions, including detailed maps. If the Italians would do so, Sgt. Fox, who claimed to be a US officer, would silence the bombardment of the city. The Italian Colonel accepted the terms. Sgt. Fox now had this Italian 1st Lt. in tow, still armed. I disarmed him, and then rushed him down to Ranger Force Headquarters.
>
> Darby, in turn, immediately took him down further to the Fire Support Coordination Center. They took what time they needed to develop a fire

> plan, which included use of every element of allied firepower within range, including US cruisers offshore. Then they brought it all to bear at the same time. . . . It was devastating. It totally silenced enemy gunfire. It may have saved the Salerno beachhead, which was under extremely heavy attack.[41]

Larkin put Fox under arrest for disobeying a direct order but also began writing up a recommendation for a Silver Star. The award was disapproved. In its place, Darby ordered Fox released from arrest and awarded him the rarely given Distinguished Service Cross, one of the highest awards in the army.[42]

THE MEDICS AT "FORT SCHUSTER"

To serve as their hospital, the Rangers took over the ground floor of a two-story stone house at the top of Chiunzi Pass. Sgt. Carl Lehmann Jr., 3/C, described the house as so solid that shells from German 88s would simply bounce off the building: "The pass included a two-story farmhouse built right into the west wall of the pass, with two of its exterior walls being part of the mountain's solid limestone. It eventually proved impervious to direct hits and sheltered quite effectively the forward HQ of The Force, a principal OP, and the aid station attended by Doc Schuster. Late in this action, Sergeant-Major Kenneth (Scotty) Munro answered the phone, 'Fort Schuster!' It remains so to those of the Third Battalion to this day."[43]

One scary time, there was a call for medics after a firefight, and Robert J. Reed, 3/Hq., carrying the litter, took Tech/4 Frank Ziola, a cook, for an assistant. Reed:

> The man I picked up was only slightly wounded, having a piece of shrapnel go through the palm of his left hand. But it was most poignant. He complained most vigorously and I upbraided him, saying, "Hey, you will be out of this for a while." But he explained, "I'm not even supposed to be here. I'm only a company clerk, but they needed every man, so they gave me a rifle and sent me up here. I haven't even fired the rifle. I've spent five years at the Juilliard School of Music in New York studying the violin, and practicing fingering the strings on the violin with my left hand and now that piece of shrapnel went right through all those muscles destroying my life's work." I thought that this was one of the most serious wounds.

> One day, one of my medics, [Pvt.] Fuqua, 3/Hq., was brought in dead. A German mortar shell had landed on the edge of his foxhole and the concussion had crushed him, no blood, just a mass of flesh held together by his uniform.[44]

Capt. Jim Lyle, commander of 1/A, suffered from malaria contracted in Sicily and was seen by spotters down below crawling among rocks, too weak to stand. Darby ordered Lt. James Steen to get Lyle off the mountain, and Pfc. Jim Harris, 1/B, got the assignment: "Capt. Lyle was very ill. I helped him carry his pack and his rifle down to the hard road where it's a jeep-ride back to the beach area and the aid station. Before he left, he opened his backpack and gave me three boxes of K-rations and said, 'Here boy, I don't think I'll need these rations. You take 'em.'"[45]

THE DANGER OF PATROLLING

Pfc. Harris witnessed a disaster that would kill one Ranger and take 2nd Lt. James Steen and 1st Lt. Donald Anderson out of the war:

> On the night of 27 September, we were given the mission of going down the mountain to take the small village of Salle, Italy. Our platoon leader was 2nd Lt. James Steen, 1/B. We were to follow a platoon of 1/A, commanded by 1st. Lt. Donald O. Anderson. This was after Capt. Lyle was evacuated, or he would have led the patrol. For some reason, the column stopped, and Lt. Steen went forward to learn what the holdup was. Shortly after there was a loud explosion. Company A's scout got into a booby trap and was killed, and Lt. Steen and Lt. Anderson each lost a leg.[46]

Lt. Steen, his leg destroyed, lay helpless through the long night, a "nightmare" he could never forget: "The explosion must have seared the blood vessels so that I did not bleed to death. I was lying next to a low stone wall, and I recall waking up during the night, hearing German voices on the other side of the wall. I was coming and going all night, probably from the morphine someone administered, and I did not dare make a noise."[47]

Pfc. Harris tells how the wounded lieutenants were rescued: "I learned several years later [that] they survived. It seems that Pfc. Herman Junge, 1/B, found the two lieutenants and commandeered a jeep at gunpoint. He loaded the two men aboard, turned around and headed for Chiunzi Pass."[48]

COMBAT FATIGUE AT CHIUNZI PASS

Despite their training, new replacements were often unprepared for the carnage and danger. Seeing bodies blown to bits often left soldiers so emotionally shocked that they could not function. With the Rangers in World War II, PTSD was sometimes called "combat shock" for those new to battle, or "combat fatigue" for men who had been in combat for months. Tech/5 "Red" Gilbert, 1/Hq., remembered an example:

> One new man was armed with a Thompson submachine gun and was busy firing at the enemy almost from the first day. One day he just went berserk, firing everywhere. Luckily, he hit nobody. As soon as the man's clip ran out, a group of Rangers raced over, pounced on him, and held him down while Doc Schuster raced up and jabbed him in the behind with a shot full of morphine. They tied him onto a stretcher and hauled him off, and no one ever saw or heard from him again. The kid had been in combat night and day for about two and a half weeks, and I guess he just couldn't take it anymore—he just went nuts.[49]

ON TO NAPLES: COMING DOWN OFF MONTE CHIUNZI

For a month Darby's forces denied Chiunzi Pass to the enemy, giving the Allies time to break out from their Salerno beachhead. But it was a costly victory. Coming ashore at night and securing the pass was an ideal Ranger mission. But holding the mountain after securing it was the sort of combat that regular infantry soldiers should have been able to do. The result was heavy casualties among these specially trained warriors who could not be easily replaced.

By late September 1943, it was obvious the Germans would not contest Naples but were going to abandon the city once they had reduced it to ruins. From the heights of Chiunzi Pass the Rangers could see fires and dust from German demolition, with the greatest destruction focused on ships at the docks to make the port unusable for the Allies. Naples would be the first major

Axis city to fall into Allied hands.[50] The descent from the mountains was hazardous, as Cpl. Andy Arnbal, 3/D, explained:

> We went down to the Maiori-Chiunzi Pass road, where we scattered out among the trees near the 105 mm howitzer battery and slept through most of the day, despite the artillery battery's firing. After dark, we moved out up through Chiunzi Pass, following the road as it twisted and turned around sharp curves, descending down into the valley. Going downhill was about as bad as going uphill, as it put a lot of stress on the calf and shinbone muscles. The road was also full of potholes and loose gravel; after eighteen days in confining defensive positions, we were not in very good condition for road marching.[51]

The 3rd Ranger Battalion entered an olive grove about halfway down, walking along narrow terraces, when a storm broke with high winds and hard, cold rain. Darkness forced the men to keep one hand on the shoulder of the man in front. The terraces turned to mud, and men sank up to their ankles. As Cpl. Arnbal continued down, the terrace suddenly gave way and he found himself in the air falling into the olive trees below, losing helmet and rifle. He found his rifle but could not locate his helmet. Arnbal continued along that terrace until he met Company D coming down and fell back into line. The Rangers continued the march, eventually bivouacking near Castellammare, but the cold, wet men had no way to heat their C rations.[52] Capt. James Larkin, speaking about the perilous trip to Naples and the conditions they found in the city:

> We jumped off across country from the Salerno beachhead. It was gross. The terrain was impossible . . . Our tanks started down the very steep exposed winding mountainous road on our right. That was perilous too. One tipped over, and went crashing down the steep bank. We took the little village of Sala quickly, and then continued down the mountain. Eventually, we made it all the way in to Naples. The Germans had withdrawn, leaving a lot of "ticking" bombs for us to deal with. We took up positions in the "Botanical Gardens" initially. The people of Naples were half starved by then. The girls were selling themselves for a D-Bar or two. Then, the bombs started to go off, sometimes killing scores of civilians. It was not a very happy "occupation," initially at least. Of course, that's just the way the Germans meant it to be.[53]

SECURING NAPLES

Naples was a place for the Rangers to rest, refit, and recruit replacements for those lost to casualties. The "Barrel-Land Dance Hall Rangers" relieved some of their stress by passing off Monopoly money, stolen in Sicily, as invasion currency to purchase wine and women.[54] The next day the 3rd Rangers had a formal inspection, with the mayor and police chief of Castellammare viewing the troops. The two officials tried to identify the culprits who passed off the Monopoly money but failed because the cleaned-up Rangers all looked alike.[55]

Pvt. Robert Harlow, 1/C, tells how he volunteered for the Rangers from a replacement depot near Naples. At thirty-three, he was the oldest enlisted Ranger:

> After landing in Italy, we went to a staging area north of Naples. It began to rain. We were issued a blanket and a shelter half, which meant we had to double-up to make a shelter for two. It was getting late so Ruffy, my foxhole buddy, and I used our boots as a pillow, one blanket to lay on and the other for a cover. There was no sleeping for us that night. After a short time, the mud began to seep in.
>
> We dug an L-shaped foxhole, by doing this Ruffy could see in one direction and I the other. We dragged two big trees that had been felled by artillery and placed them across the top and then placed sandbags at the entrance. The first morning, Harlow looked up to see they had a visitor, a snake, hanging just above his head. He dispatched it with the butt of his rifle. Morale was low because of the terrible living conditions, plus having nothing to eat but C-rations.
>
> The next night we were shelled very heavily by artillery and mortar. There were quite a few casualties and one of our group was killed. At daybreak I crawled out of my foxhole, grabbed my helmet, and was about to put it on, when I noticed a round hole, dead center, in the front. That was one meant for me, but I wasn't in it. I said a few extra prayers that day.
>
> It was still raining three days later when some high-ranking officers visited our area, seeking volunteers to join the Rangers as replacements. I talked it over with Ruffy and we decided that it would be better than sitting around like dead ducks. . . . We got our gear together and transferred to Ranger Headquarters.[56]

Pvt. Harlow was subsequently transferred to the 4th Ranger Battalion and assigned to a half-track, equipped with a 75 mm cannon and a .50-caliber machine-gun and operated by an experienced crew. He was pleased to be with these men, hoping that he would no longer be living in a foxhole.[57]

With a few days of relaxation, the Barrel-Land Dance Hall Rangers showed themselves again. Cpl. Arnbal:

> There was a shortage of water as the Germans had destroyed the Naples water supply system before they left. . . . [The commander of a U.S. destroyer agreed that] fifty percent of the 3rd Ranger Battalion could march down to the docks and they would be fed and shown around his ship. . . . A couple of our men managed to [steal] a record player and a few records. . . . [As a result], the remaining fifty percent of the battalion would not be allowed to go to the docks, nor would any Rangers ever be welcomed aboard any other U.S. Navy destroyer again.[58]

With many new volunteers, the three battalions resumed training, which, like the training in Scotland and Nemours, was designed to be combat realistic and as dangerous as possible. Arnbal described a tragedy that occurred one foggy, rainy night:

> Company D of the 3rd Battalion was assigned to do a tactical exercise; the second platoon was to defend a bridge that spanned a deep gorge on the road to Castellammare, and the first platoon would try to sneak up on them and assault the defenders. We had blank ammunition and flare guns. Lt. Norris Teague, Jr. was platoon leader of the second platoon, and I was acting platoon leader of the attacking first platoon. Staff Sergeant John Knox was our platoon sergeant. As we approached . . . visibility was almost zero.
>
> Knox was leading the squad, and all of a sudden he let out a yell as he slipped off the side of the gorge. . . . We knew that the gorge was about sixty feet deep, with solid rock sides and a rushing stream at the bottom. We were close enough to the bridge so that the other platoon members heard his scream as he fell to the bottom. . . . medics went down the rope and found Staff Sergeant Knox unconscious at the bottom of the gorge. . . . [Knox was] raced off to the hospital in Naples. Knox was dead on arrival. . . . [and] was buried at the Anzio Cemetery.[59]

S/Sgt. Knox's death was a huge loss for Company D and the Rangers because he was an experienced NCO, popular with his men. With limited time, the Ranger battalions gave their new volunteers a quick review of combat basics, and they were off to the next assignment—the mountains of Venafro and San Pietro.

---- 10 ----

VENAFRO

THE WINTER LINE

After a year of hard fighting, Lt. Col. Darby mused: "What lay ahead, we did not know. The road was long, and it was best to look only to the next bend. We could look forward only to fighting up the boot of Italy."[1] Venafro, sixteen miles east of the heavily contested "Winter Line" at Cassino, in the range of mountains rising up to Monte Sambucaro, would be the scene of some of the toughest battles in the worst terrain and winter weather conditions that the 1st and 4th Rangers ever faced. Nearby, in a valley on the south side of Monte Sambucaro, the tiny village of San Pietro, where the 3rd Rangers would be tested, was home to about fourteen hundred souls who eked out a living growing olives and making baskets. San Pietro overlooked what would soon be known as "Purple Heart Valley."[2]

The Germans defended a line from the Volturno River on the west to Termoli on the east. It was their Bernhard Line, known to the Allies as the Winter Line,[3] a series of heavily reinforced defensive positions in the high mountains south of Rome, one behind the other, that General Hans Valentin Hube had prepared to slow the Allied attack toward Rome. Hube, the one-armed officer who had supervised the escape of the Germans from Sicily, reported to Gen. Heinrich von Vietinghoff, who commanded the German 10th Army. As each line was breached, the Germans fell back from one strongpoint to the next.[4] The army that controlled the high ground would control who passed through the Liri Valley, the access to Rome. On the right side of the valley were eight rugged peaks that had to be reduced, one at a time. To the left were three mountains, equally difficult to capture.[5]

The American attack was led by Gen. Clark's Fifth Army, with the VI Corps, commanded by Maj. Gen. John P. Lucas, assigned to secure the right

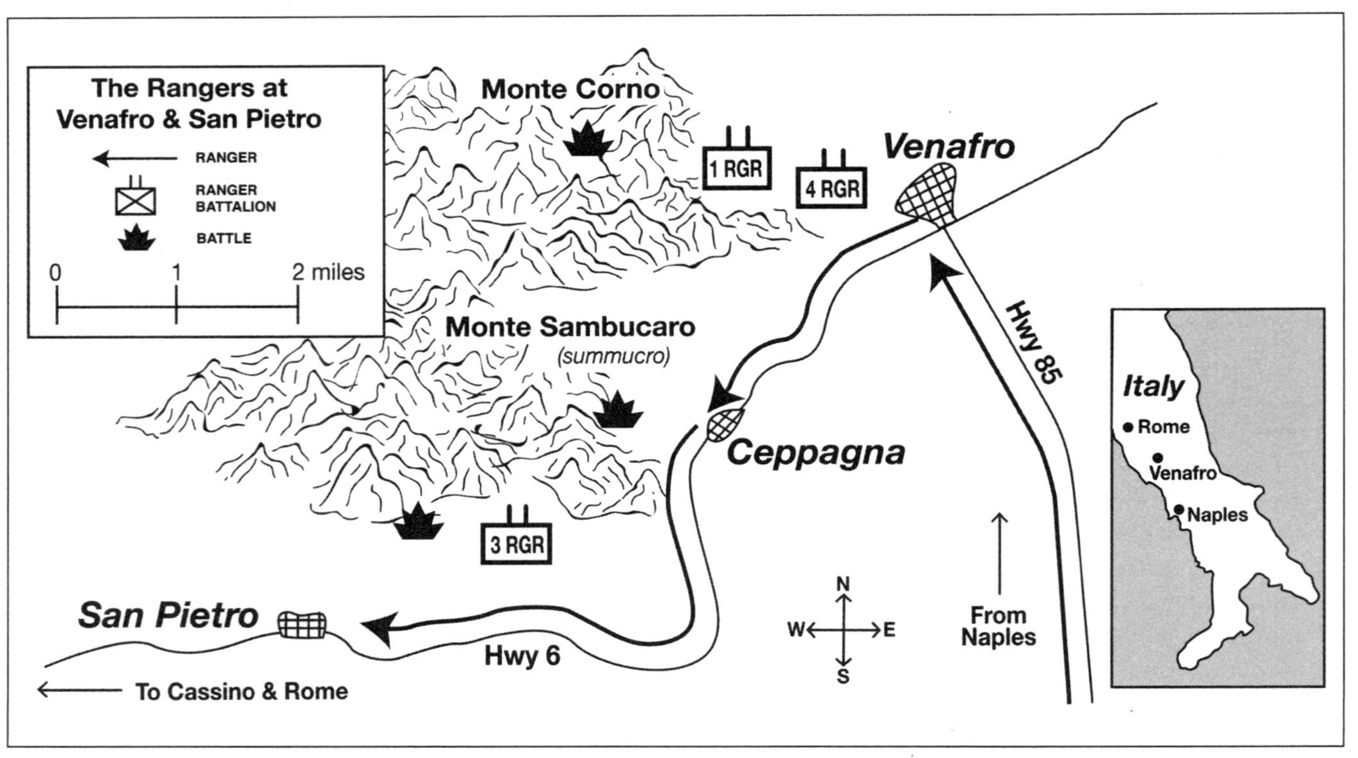

The Rangers in Venafro and San Pietro

side of the gap. The 3rd, 45th, and 34th Infantry Divisions comprised VI Corps, with the 1st and 4th Rangers attached to the 45th Division.[6]

THE 4TH RANGER BATTALION

East of Venafro, American forces were fighting alongside the British Eighth Army, while to the west Gen. Clark's Fifth Army was fighting to gain a foothold along Highway 6, which led to Rome. On 1 November 1943, the 4th Ranger Battalion moved near Venafro, where the enemy was dug in atop mountains overlooking the American positions. The 4th Battalion's mission was to infiltrate through the enemy's position and attack the Germans at dawn.[7] They set out on the night of 3 November, wading across the Volturno River, then followed narrow mountain trails in single file. Hiking all night for twelve miles, the 4th Rangers got above and behind the enemy, who was hidden in the forest on Monte Cavalle. At 0600 hours, the Rangers ambushed a German patrol that was surprised to find Rangers in their backyard.[8] Three Ranger companies under the command of Capt. Walter Nye, 4/Hq., climbed up the summit of Monte Cavalle on a recon mission but were driven off by a strong German attack, with several Rangers captured.[9] Sgt. James Altieri described the enemy fire: "The Germans . . . directed murderous artillery and mortar fire on the three companies [of] Rangers. Completely isolated and without artillery support, the three companies were forced to withdraw. . . . German 88s were even firing point-blank at individuals, so bitter was the battle."[10]

Pvt. Robert M. Harlow, 4th Battalion, described the experience of his patrol:

> One morning after climbing a mountain all night, we took refuge in a small, wooded area. It was raining, and it was daybreak so we could not advance any further because the enemy could see every move we made. Several men were wounded and two killed. . . . [The enemy] . . . just took a few random shots to see if they would get any return fire. We had to wait for nightfall before moving out, and we moved back over the mountain carrying the wounded back down the trail that we had climbed the night before.
>
> Surrounded by so many young men eighteen to their early twenties I often thought, "What am I doing here? I don't want to kill anyone." I was a

> butcher in civilian life, but I could not imagine sticking a knife into a human being, not once, but many times until he was dead.
>
> Every time we made an attack on the enemy in the Venafro mountains, they would counterattack with heavy mortar fire, the most feared and deadliest of all weapons. I saw Rangers blown to bits, many losing an arm or a leg, some both, some lying along the road with their intestines strewn all over, or their eyeballs lying on their cheek bones. Just to think that many of these were my friends who had hardly begun to live.[11]

Pfc. Raymond Boron, 4/A, also new to the Rangers, was impressed by the action: "I can never forget the high, rugged mountains with the Germans looking down our throats, or the cold rain. The front lines were close together. We were bivouacked inside some olive orchards, and anytime we moved, the Germans came at us with their 88s. When we finally captured our objective, we found that the Germans had blown holes out of solid rock for pillboxes and had stacked logs on top for protection."[12]

On the morning of 4 November 1943, the entire 4th Rangers attacked up the slopes of Monte Rotondo, which overlooked Highway 6 and the San Pietro-Venafro road. Maj. Roy A. Murray: "The Germans replied with a terrific barrage of mortar and artillery fire so intense that the Rangers were unable to close in on the enemy entrenched on Mount Rotondo."[13] Some Rangers were killed and many wounded. Out of water and ammunition, the Rangers had to withdraw to their previous position to rest and resupply.[14] Murray: "By 8 November, the American forces had moved forward to the foothills of the mountains overlooking Venafro and Ceppagna, two Italian towns on the so-called 'Winter Line.' An entire valley was now occupied, but the Germans still commanded the heights which had to be taken before the narrow corridor leading to Cassino could be entered. It was imperative that those heights be cleared of stubborn and troublesome Germans who were directing intensive artillery fire on American troop movements."[15]

The Rangers would attack up one ridge, and no sooner than it was taken, the Germans would counterattack, sometimes in waves of infantry. The Rangers held, but with heavy losses to both sides. Sgt. James Altieri, 4/F, describes one German attack:

> Following the shifting of the barrage came the German infantry, advancing from the center and flanks in extended skirmish lines under a curtain of lighter mortar fire. Wave after wave they came, only to be thrown back time and again with terrific losses. . . . Ranger casualties also mounted, but in no proportion to the frustrated enemy. In a mass attack, supported by the dreaded Nebelwerfer rocket mortars, the Germans succeeded in taking back part of the right flank positions. . . . Outflanked, with ammunition running short, the three [4th Battalion] companies holding the center crests clung to their positions with grim determination while losses mounted.[16]

Sgt. Lester Cook, 4/A, was sitting rain-drenched in a foxhole eating cold C rations. Cook had just lit up his pipe when a German shell exploded nearby, burying him, except for his feet, under a heavy layer of dirt. With both feet kicking madly, two Rangers were able to extract him before his pipe went out.[17] Sgt. Cook:

> Capt. Les Kness and myself were on a forward patrol in the Venafro sector. We were scouting out the lay of the land for an advance on the next day. It was quite dark, and all at once we saw a pillbox that was covered with bushes. . . . Kness said, "There is a window there. Cook, you pop a grenade and throw it in when I break the window with my rifle butt." So I pulled the pin and threw it away and Les hit the window in the pillbox with his rifle. Much to our surprise, the window was painted on the concrete of the pillbox. . . . Les shook for five minutes after his rifle butt hit the concrete. I started laughing and almost dropped the grenade. After that, Les [and I began] dropping grenades into all openings. It was just starting to get light when we heard an American voice saying, "Over this way." We knew we had to get out of there, or get shot by our own men.[18]

First Lt. Carl R. "Bob" Hood, commander of 4/E, was out in front of a small patrol in the Venafro area when the Rangers were suddenly caught in an artillery barrage. Writing to his parents, he reported:

> I thought that my time was up. I stayed there all afternoon with Germans not over two hundred yards away, but somehow, they didn't see me. German 88s

were landing within twenty feet of me, sometimes closer. They blew my helmet about twenty feet away, but I didn't go after it. I had to wait about five and a half hours for darkness, about five-thirty. Most of the company had pulled back for the night, and I had to crawl about three hundred yards to get behind a little knoll. I started crawling backwards for about fifty yards when I ran into a small Jerry patrol.

I hollered out, "Are you American?" and no one answered, but the wind was blowing hard. I threw a fragmentation grenade and ran like hell for about a hundred yards. I could see black objects moving to get around me; I threw another grenade and ran over the top of the hill. . . . I saw someone coming over the hill, chasing me. When I fired up all my ammo, I threw my guns away. I had only gone about a half mile farther when I ran into another German patrol coming from the other direction. There were about twelve men in it. I was caught in between them, so I climbed a tree and hid there for about an hour and a half before coming down and getting back to our area.[19]

First Sgt. Edward Haywood, 4/Hq., found the Germans and Rangers intermingled during night patrols with zero visibility:

We and the Germans were both sending out patrols to feel each other out. Fog shrouded the mountains, and the only cover was stunted trees and dense undergrowth. Foxholes were as deep as possible, which was not very deep in the hard rocky ground. On one night patrol I spotted Germans digging into a new position, and we went to inspect. I heard German being spoken, and speaking German myself, I understood the enemy patrol to be saying that they were lost. I let them wander around, keeping track of them all the time.

When the Germans were twenty yards from me, I yelled out "You're surrounded, surrender and save your lives." All was silent. The Germans were debating what to do. Then I began to get nervous because I did not know how many there were, so I yelled, "This is your last warning. We're going to start shooting!" Eight Germans filed out, led by a young German officer, all fresh new troops carrying new equipment. I ordered them to put their weapons in a pile, but they were reluctant because they thought I might be alone. Suddenly, I snatched the officer's pistol, threw it on the ground, and the other Germans added their rifles to the pile. Two other Rangers nearby overheard the German

> language, and thinking they would capture an enemy patrol, slipped up with weapons drawn, only to find me with the prisoners.[20]

Under constant shelling, the 4th Battalion's casualties were heavy. Pvt. Ulysses G. "Blackie" Auger, 4/Hq., and Tech/5 Stephen Mitrick, 4/Hq., dug their foxholes next to a wooden shed. As they eased out of their foxholes for chow call on 18 November 1943, a German mortar landed on them, killing Mitrick outright. Seriously wounded, Auger was trapped under the wreckage of the collapsed shed.[21]

The 4th Rangers, supported by the 83rd Chemical Mortar Battalion, were assigned to capture a German outpost manned by 150 men entrenched on two mountain knobs overlooking the valley where the main body of American forces were moving. The Rangers were to hold the outpost, perhaps for several days, until relieved by a company of the 45th Infantry Division.[22] Maj. Roy Murray, commanding the 4th Battalion, requested that Capt. Lester Kness, commanding 4/A, take out the enemy observation post.[23] Kness gave a full account of the mountaintop combat. "I told [Maj. Murray] that we could take it, but I would not try unless he agreed to my terms. I told him I wanted a direct phone line from the top of the mountain down to the 83rd (They shot the big 4.2-inch mortars that were deadly). . . . We were to move out at midnight. It would be a good four hour climb to get to the top. 'F' Company, already up there, was to send guides down so the two companies wouldn't shoot each other in the darkness."[24]

The night before Kness's company was to attack, they received a severe shelling, wounding two men. Without much sleep, his Rangers were moving up the mountain through brush and rocks on paths mined by the Germans, trying to reach the top before daylight. They arrived late. Their scouts reported that the area in front of them was mined and that the enemy was on the ridges right in front. With only forty-two men, it would have been foolhardy to advance further.[25] Kness:

> There were two knobs on the mountain to our left front that were occupied by the enemy's observation post. Then there was a small knob that protected the large knob. I assumed that it must not be occupied by more than sixty enemy, one platoon of infantry, with maybe two machine guns. The larger knob was

higher and was probably the main observation post with many more infantry surrounding the area to protect it. . . . I committed Sergeant Cook and seven men to take the small knob and Lieutenant [Hubbard] Powell with twenty-one men to take the larger knob. . . . We would drop six rounds of 60 mm on the small knob while the big knob was being hit with the 4.2's. Cook would run for the small knob on the fourth round. Powell would take the big knob by going around to the left, spreading his men out, and, when in position, I would call for a ceasefire with the big mortars and lay in on the 60s.

I got on the phone with the 4.2 mortars. . . . I asked him to throw up a round where I could see it. One came in and I saw it hit about 400 yards beyond the targets. It took about three rounds to find the little knob. Then I swung his fire over to the big knob and told him to mark the two targets to receive fire when I needed it. . . . Sergeant Cook took off for the little knob with his seven men, just as we had planned. I could see where the 60s were hitting the little knob and knew they would cease-fire on about the sixth round. He was to run and take out the enemy holed up there. . . . Powell and his men began to advance as we had planned.

[Powell] screamed into the radio, "Jesus, Les, the frags are right around my neck!" I signaled the mortar sergeant, Zielinski, to ceasefire, and told Powell to hold off and run in on them, which he did. We caught the Germans holed up, waiting for more mortar shells. About eighty-five Germans surrendered at the big knob after Powell and his twenty-one Rangers successfully executed their mission. Sergeant Cook brought in about twenty more from the little knob, and each of Cook's six Rangers brought in several more. Powell and his radio operator chased about twenty down the mountain. The Germans ran into an American Colonel on the roadway below with some of his officers, and they surrendered to him. The Colonel received a medal. . . . To hold the area we had just taken, I left seven men on the big knob and three men on the small knob.[26]

Kness knew that the Germans would soon mount a counterattack:

There were only two logical places for the Germans to make an attack, and that was on either flank. They would probably throw a light attack on one flank, conducting the major assault on the other. Staff Sergeant Jacque Nixson was to take nine men and go on patrol. I had to know which slope the Germans were throwing their major attack, left or right flank. . . . Just after darkness, Jacque moved out with his patrol.

The patrol managed to get down the mountain and into the German area. . . . The German infantry began their move toward the slope leading to our left. Jacque had his men, one at a time, walk out and get into line with the Germans and walk about a half mile to an area where there was a dry culvert under the road. At that point, each man was to step to the side of the road like he was urinating, then slip into the culvert. Every man made it to the culvert. Jacque was the last man to make the trip and slip into the culvert with the other men. He then brought his men around the hill to the rear of our positions. His men had walked the entire night before, had fought all day, and were up all the next night. Jacque moved them to climb the mountain, but ran ahead to tell me that the main body of the attack was to be on our left flank. It was daylight when Jacque got to me. He reported that it looked like about 500 enemy headed our way.

I told him, "Hell, they are here already!" Sgt. Sweazy had called me on a sound power phone and reported he was under heavy assault. My response was "Shoot." He said, "I am!" My reply was, "Well, you can't shoot AND talk to me!" An artillery shell hit about ten feet from Sergeant Nixson. He was blown flat. I ran to him and called out to him. . . . I thought he was dead and tears came into my eyes. I called out "Jacque, Jacque." He moaned and said, "I'm hit." "Whereabouts?" I called. His reply was, "Hell, how would I know?" I called for two men to get him to the medic. That was the last time I saw Jacque for about thirty days. He returned when he was able.

About that time, 1st Sergeant Karboski informed me that the Germans had overrun Sweazy's position on the big knob and that they were coming hard onto us. I called for some volunteers. . . . Five men came running to me. . . . Quickly I told them that we were going over to get Sweazy and his men out of there. I told them, if they did exactly as I told them, they would live. I added, "If you don't, you will die and I will die with you." . . . I put three men to my left and two to the right. As we approached our advance I called their names one by one, to pick out some cover for about twenty feet in front of them and run for it. I told them we would cover them.

. . . On my second run into the enemy, I had only gone about 20 feet when

I ran past a German lying with his head turned the other direction. I assumed he was dead.[27]

Kness remembered something he heard from a Scotsman during training: "Les, never trust a dead German." Kness:

Jim's words came to mind, and I turned back towards the German that I had run past. He turned to shoot me, but I beat him to it. In situations like this, a man does strange things. I jumped upon this man that I had shot and hit him several times in the back of his head with the butt of my rifle. Why, I don't know. I was exposing myself to enemy fire.

. . . On my next run towards the enemy, I did run past a German. . . . He opened fire on me with a burp gun. I heard the sound of his gun and just got a glimpse of him as I hit the ground among some rocks. I had been running low and leaning forward. His shot went across my back and one bullet penetrated my clothing just above my right hip. I felt the blood flow down into my shorts. I hollered, "Get that SOB!" [Sgt. John] Liddell shouted, "I'll get him."

The Germans ran at us in groups of four. . . . I would let them advance to within twenty feet, where I could see them from the waist up, then I would call out to take them, and our guns would bark. . . . I got on the phone to the 4.2's, and asked if he could hit the big knob he had fired at for us the day before [so we could retake it] and he said that he could. "Okay," I said. "Send up four rounds and let me know when they are on the way. Then get ready to do a lot of firing. We have a couple of German units hitting us and need your help." It was just a minute when I heard the four pops from those big guns. He shouted into the phone, "They are on their way."

To all's amazement, a large white flag attached to two poles came up from the Germans. I ordered a ceasefire and the shooting stopped. It looked like about one hundred Germans were coming in to surrender. They had laid down their weapons and were walking toward us. The range was about five hundred yards. There was some shouting in the group of Germans and they dropped the flag and began to run to their rear and down the slope. Rifles, machine guns and mortar were brought back into play. Many enemy fell. I suppose some escaped.

I was moving to the small knob to see if I could spot the German ad-

> vance. Four Germans came out of the rocks and some brush just below the position of Sgt. Cook on the little knob. . . . It was about 100 yards to where they were standing and calling towards Cook for Cook and his men to surrender. Cook stood up with his Tommy gun and walked down towards them, like he was on a Sunday stroll. The Germans placed their guns between their legs and signaled for him to put his hands up. At about 30 yards Sgt. Cook brought up his Tommy gun and killed all four. He then ran back to the small knob. His two men and two artillery officers with the radio operator started to run to the rear. Cook brought up his gun and shouted, "Stop, you yellow bastards, or I will kill you."[28]

As the enemy were gradually worn down, one German company tried to slip away, but the Rangers decimated them with mortar and accurate rifle fire. The Rangers now commanded the heights. The desperate Germans counterattacked in wave after wave, but they could not dislodge the Rangers from their strategic mountain position.[29]

1ST RANGER BATTALION: VENAFRO

While the 4th Battalion fought off German counterattacks, the 1st Battalion assaulted and occupied Monte Corno, another peak near Venafro. Only narrow trails wound their way over the rugged terrain. The Rangers had fought their way upward through minefields under withering fire from enemy machine guns. The 4.2 mortars laid down a screen of high-explosive and white phosphorous shells ahead of the Rangers' advance. After two weeks of fighting, pounded by rain and cold weather, the Rangers held the high ground. Again, ammunition resupply and getting casualties safely down from the four thousand-foot heights was a continual challenge. Patrols from both sides often met in sharp firefights all along the trails.[30] Darby: "The men needed hot food and water. I sent orders back to the Rangers . . . to send up all the 1st Battalion men who were now out of the hospital. . . . Mules were brought to carry ammunition and food up to the men. The kitchens were moved up close, and hot food was cooked for my soldiers."[31]

S/Sgt. Royal H. Wells, 1/E, was leading a section forward to occupy a hill when, unexpectedly, they ran into thirty Germans in reinforced dugout positions. With his platoon sergeant pinned down by enemy fire, Sgt. Wells ordered his men to charge the hill with fixed bayonets. The Germans broke and abandoned the hill, leaving only one man behind with a machine gun. The German fired a whole burst over Wells's head before Wells, already hit by mortar shell fragments, brought him down with two grenades.[32]

S/Sgt. William J Arnold, 1st Battalion, explained that the proximity of German and Allied positions paralyzed both sides: "In the mountains it would have been suicide to move from your foxhole, but the same applied to the Germans who were dug in only twenty yards away."[33]

Tech/5 Theodore "Ted" Fleser, 1/D, witnessed a friend being shot by a sniper. "Snipers were everywhere. . . . At Venafro, Cpl. Robert Lowell, 1/D, was eating some rations with his foxhole buddy when a German sniper shot Bob right through the head. His buddy was so enraged that he lost control of himself, and rising up out of his foxhole, he charged off towards where the shot came from to get the sniper. Three other Rangers chased him down and got him back under cover. We then sent out a patrol that captured the sniper, turning him over to Lowell's buddy, who took care of him."[34]

Darby wanted a prisoner interrogated immediately and sent for Pvt. Erich Scharf, who spoke German: "I would translate Darby's questions for the prisoner, the replies for Darby. . . . The interrogation took place in plain view of the enemy. One day my friend Bill Tryon was ordered to move into a position on a large boulder from which he could direct rifle fire into a bothersome machine gun emplacement on the other side of the ravine. I accompanied him to the rock and suggested extreme care. He agreed and I waved to him and started to return to my post when I heard a rifle shot. Bill had been shot between the eyes."[35]

Pvt. Oral E. Emmons Jr., 1/E, wrote about his fight at Venafro: "On November 21, 1943, six of us Rangers were sent up a hill to rout out fifty Germans in a cave. They seen us before we seen them, and they lobbed potato mashers (hand grenades) on us. I was the lucky one of six that was not killed. I sustained forty pieces of shrapnel. The next day Lt. Col. Darby climbed the back side of the hill and lowered dynamite on a rope, closing the mouth of the cave forever."[36]

Thanksgiving Day, 1943, was one never to be forgotten by 2nd Lt. Russell Tremblay, 1/Hq.: "Our company dug in on top of a hill we had just taken. There was no time for rest as the enemy launched a terrific counterattack that lasted over an hour. Finally, the Germans were repulsed, and we settled back in our foxholes to find that during the battle someone had delivered turkey with all the trimmings right up to our foxholes."[37]

Cpl. William D. Zartman, 1/F, got his first combat experience with the Rangers at Venafro. Zartman was issued a Thompson .45-caliber submachine gun, a pistol, and a knife. While on Monte Corno, they were shelled every day and night with mortar and artillery. In heavy fog, the Germans were often able to get within a hundred yards before opening fire:

> On one of these attacks . . . my friend Danny [Pfc. Daniel S. Smith, 1/F] who was off to my right, became so furious that he stood straight up, raised his BAR as though it were a lightweight rifle, and fired a long burst into the tree line where the Germans had good cover, cursing them for taking our leader. Danny took heavy fire before he fell in a pool of blood. . . . The next day . . . I took Danny down [off the mountain] lying over the back of a mule. . . . One image I will never forget was when Danny's head popped out of the bag as a result of the bouncing around on the mules back. I had to stop, and with help from another Ranger pushed Danny's head back in the bag and secured it shut.[38]

Incoming artillery from the vast German defenses, stretching for miles in each direction, made movements risky both day and night. Of all the weapons, the Nebelwerfer was the most feared, for when one rocket came in there would be several more right behind, wounding and killing many. Having no hearing protection, Rangers' hearing was often irreparably damaged. To worsen a bad situation, heavy ground fog made patrolling especially dangerous, with visibility sometimes only a few hundred feet.

> Capt. Chuck Shunstrom ran patrols at night in the attempt to capture a German officer . . . who could provide useful intelligence. . . . When Chuck went out on a patrol, he carried a piece of piano wire, about eighteen inches long, with a dowel type grip on each end . . . he would sneak up behind a German sentry, throw the wire over his head, and not a sound would emerge as he tightened the wire around the sentry's neck. . . . Our company went up on the mountain with sixty-one men and two officers, and came down with twenty-five men and one officer. We were finally relieved on December 14.[39]

Darby explained the importance of the 4.2-inch mortars, writing that during the thirty-five days in the Venafro sector, the 83rd Chemical Mortar Battalion fired thirty-eight thousand shells, each weighing twenty-five pounds: "By firing all their mortars rapid fire, they could lay down twelve tons a minute—and this they did on many occasions."[40]

11
SAN PIETRO

While the 4th Ranger Battalion held its mountaintop position, and the 1st Ranger Battalion assaulted Monte Corno, the 3rd Ranger Battalion was fighting with the 36th Infantry Division, commanded by Maj. Gen. John E. Dahlquist. The 36th Infantry Division reported to the II Corps, commanded by Maj. Gen. Geoffrey Keyes, the second component of the U.S. Fifth Army. Attempting to take Monte Rotondo and the village of San Pietro, located in a valley below Monte Sambucaro, the 3rd Rangers got to within eight hundred yards of San Pietro before being driven back by mortar and machine gun fire.[1]

TAKING MONTE SAMBUCARO

On 8 December 1943, the 3rd Ranger Battalion entered a valley at the base of Monte Sambucaro. Capt. Leonard Dirks, CO of 3/Hq., led a company through an area that was the "bullseye" for the German artillery on the peak above: "We started out at 7:30 in the evening because we had to enter the village right under the German artillery and couldn't chance being seen. . . . [We] got a special artillery barrage to cover the noise of . . . vehicles entering the valley. . . . It was a dark, foggy night. It was necessary for the whole column to march single file with hands on the shoulders of the man ahead. We crossed the road southwest of Venafro and then doubled back to an enemy-held bridge."[2]

One of Dirks's platoons, led by 2nd Lt. William Musegades, 3/E, got lost in the mountains and stumbled upon Germans.[3] Musegades later told Capt. Dirks:

> That's where we lost you. . . . I tried to send word ahead we couldn't keep up, and then stopped for 15 minutes rest. When we started ahead we heard a noise in the brush and followed it. We thought it was the main body. I now know it was probably a German patrol, which we followed for miles. They must

> have known we were Americans because our platoon never did catch up. The faster we'd go, the faster they went. Just about dawn, we realized we were lost and knew we were following Germans, but never learned how big a force. We heard bells tinkling; we thought they might use them to keep contact with one another.[4]

Tech/5 Joseph Gomez, 3/E: "Yeah, that had an unforgettable result for one party wandering in the hills that morning. . . . We heard a bell in the bushes in front of us and shot a cow."[5] Musegades continued:

> Then came a ravine and a hillside orchard. . . . [I] saw a man standing on a terrace above who looked like our commander, Capt. Edward Kitchens of Mississippi. . . . I called to him, "Capt. Kitchens, where's the rest of our troops?" He didn't answer. . . . The man ducked behind a bush. I saw him crawling out a moment later without a helmet. . . . I yelled, "Answer me now or I'll shoot." Still no answer. So, I nailed him. Two men started over the wall after the body and I found we had stumbled into a German machine gun nest.[6]

Tech/5 Gomez lost a friend there, but he fought back: "They opened up on us as soon as we got over the wall. . . . They killed my buddy, but I got one of them with my rifle. I dropped against the wall for cover and tossed a hand grenade. I'm sure I got at least six more."[7] The noise attracted Germans and Americans alike. Cpl. Jules G. Evans, Pvt. Henry Cordle, and Pvt. Walter Puchinsky hurried to the top of the wall and saw three Germans running across the field toward Gomez and his dead comrade, "It was a cinch. We each picked one; then there were no more Germans."[8] Capt. Dirks said that the patrol brought back valuable information because the Germans were trying to pull a flanking movement between the main body of Rangers and the lost platoon. Musegades was the last to leave the valley, remaining until the end to cover the withdrawal of his men.[9]

Rangers went on countless patrols to find the enemy, to determine how to get through, above, or around them. Heavy German machine gun fire from the heights of Monte Sambucaro forced the Rangers to withdraw in what became a battle of attrition, with both sides suffering heavy casualties. Tech/5 Regis McMahon, 3/Hq.: "The entire battalion had to stay in our foxholes until after dark when we could make a successful withdrawal."[10]

Early on the morning of 9 December, the Rangers assaulted the German positions on Monte Sambucaro with the support of the 4.2 mortars. Rangers of 3/D were the last company going up, occupying a position at the end of a ridge, with Company 3/E on their left. Cpl. Anders Arnbal, 3/D:

> The line of defense overlooked a steep drop-off into the valley, or gorge, between Monte Summacro and Monte Corno. . . . Captain Cannon set up the company command post behind a boulder. He and the company runner scrounged around for rocks to build a low wall around their position. Staff Sergeant [Robert] Keberdle, 3/D, and I had our position behind a large boulder about sixty feet from the company command post. . . . Before dawn the rain let up, and some of the men were eating K rations; of course, there were no fires.
>
> Sure enough at dawn, about 0700 hours, the barrage began. One-fifty and 170 mm rounds came screaming and exploding, most of them [hitting] behind the ridgeline, but many of them hit the defense line of companies holding the ridge. . . . We were also introduced to the fearful screaming of the "Nebelwerfer" rockets. These came in clusters of six rounds and sent boulders rolling down the incline of the mountain. This shelling lasted for an hour, followed by an attack on the positions of the three companies on the far left of the ridge. . . . In this barrage we lost Pfc. [Thomas] Peretich, 3/D, to a direct hit by an artillery round; all we found of him was one boot. Pfc. [Michael] Stella, 3/D, was his buddy. . . . He aided in the search for body parts. After tending to the wounds of T/5 [Walter] Ledford, and Pfc. [Lester] Jackson, medic Tom Prudhomme tied a KIA tag on the boot and had it sent down to Ceppagna with the wounded and shell-shocked. Seven enlisted men and Captain [Charles] Cannon were comatose with shell-shock; the enlisted men [from 3/D] were Staff Sergeant Keberdle, Sgt. [George] Ostlund, Cpl. [Charles] Pestotnick, T/5 [Regis] McMahon, Private first class [Kendrick] Ford, and Privates [Edwin] Sipes and Roberts.
>
> [With the loss of Capt. Cannon], 2nd Lt. Earnest Jensen [took] over as company commander of Company D. . . . I showed him the command post . . . [and suggested that] we go over the roster of present for duty before we made the rounds of our strong point positions. He left his pack, radio, and weapon in the CP foxhole. No sooner had we started eating our K rations than a stray artillery round landed right in the CP foxhole . . . all of Jensen's gear was destroyed . . . a shocking welcome for a new company commander!

> Thus, the first day on Monte Sambucaro was almost a disaster for Company D; we had never had so many casualties in such a short time before. Already under-strength, we were going into the night with only twenty-four enlisted men and again with only one officer. . . . The next morning at dawn we were again greeted with a half-hour barrage of artillery and screaming meemies. Pfc. [Edward] Krusinski and Pvt. [Louis] Varga were wounded, and Pfc. [Carmello] Rossetti went comatose.[11]

Clouds and mists kept Company 3/D from seeing across the gorge to Monte Corno. Cpl. George W. "Jack" Hall, 3/D, described San Pietro as always wet and very cold, and the bloodiest fight they had been in yet. His best friend in the 3rd Battalion, Pfc. Patrick McTeigue, was killed by a sniper on 11 December.[12]

The ingenious cooks down below had found two gas stoves in a partially destroyed church. Stoves and supplies were brought up to the mountains in trailers pulled by jeeps. There was no limit to what hungry Rangers would do to get a hot meal.[13]

Meanwhile, wounded Rangers piled up, like Pfc. Charles H. Kazura, 3/B: "At San Pietro I had nine machine gun bullets rip into my right thigh and knee. Surgery was performed under a tent, and I was flown back to Valley Forge Hospital for more surgery and recovery, with three months in a full body cast."[14]

Capt. Gordon Keppel, the new 3rd Battalion surgeon, was impressed by the Rangers' toughness:

> In medical school we learned about the human body, how much strain it could take. There were limitations. Fatigue could make the body stop functioning, like a run-down motor. Fear could make nerves shake and legs wobble like gelatin. The human body, we learned, could stand only so much. But the Rangers seemed to stand more than this. There was no medical explanation for it, but when you came to a Ranger lying in a hospital cot, you often heard him say, "Send me back to my company. They need me up there and I don't like it back here."[15]

Pvt. Justin Gray, 3/C, followed his own telephone lines to guide him on the right path. The Rangers' bivouac was generally some distance from the front line, but between the bivouac and the front line there usually were several units manning various positions, each connected to their headquarters with telephone lines laid out on the ground. The number of phone lines, lying side by side, indicated how many units there were between the bivouac and the front line. Pvt. Gray:

> The whole battalion was stirring. . . . Everyone was awake. . . . I must have been the last one to start getting ready. . . . We walked down the hillside to where the captain was bending over a map with a dim flashlight. . . . A group of Germans was holding out in a small town way up in the mountains, a tough position to reach. We were to move forward, infiltrate behind the Jerry lines, and attack from the rear.
>
> It was pitch black. We moved in two columns, one on each side of the road, the men about 20 yards apart. You couldn't really see the man in front of you. . . . I started to count the strands of telephone wire, just to keep busy. The wire was a symbol of security and strength. . . . The colonel started off again. . . . My eyes followed only the wires at my feet. . . . The telephone wires were my only contact with time or space. I couldn't tell how far we had gone or what time it was. But the telephone wires told the story. Only a few [strands] were left.
>
> We had to go down into the riverbed and pick our way through a German mine field. There was only one strand of wire left now. And then, that too ended. It led to a telephone in the ditch below us.
>
> A sleepy GI was telling headquarters we were passing his post. This was our good-bye. I wondered when headquarters would hear from us again. We knew our mission had begun.[16]

Lt. Musegades described attacking one hill after the other, taking it, then losing it, then fighting for it again:

> We attacked one hill but were repulsed by the Germans. Two days later my company and another company took the hill. The retreating Germans poured artillery fire on the hill so successfully that we Rangers were forced to withdraw, leaving only a few men to guard the post. The barrage lasted all day, and then the Germans counterattacked. Only thirty-two Rangers were on the hill

> when the Germans counterattacked. We fired rifle grenades at point-blank range to blunt the attack.[17]

Sgt. Julian Cavazos, 3/C: "One night Carl Lehmann almost got us killed asking for directions. Out on patrol, Carl went up to a soldier to ask where Company 3/A was; the soldier was a German. The German ran one way yelling 'Americani,' and Carl ran back yelling 'Jerries.'"[18]

Sgt. Robert Campbell, 3/A, and his men spotted an isolated German: "With our mortars zeroed in, we put out a concentration of mortar fire on an enemy foxhole. [He] must have had some ammo in that hole because the next thing we saw of that Jerry, he was about twenty feet [in the] air, turning end over end as the ammo exploded."[19]

First Lt. Warren "Bing" Evans commanded company 3/F:

> The area we were in was the most rugged mountains we had yet encountered. Jagged peaks soared up and dropped off straight down. When we went out on patrol, which was almost every night, we went in single file keeping the man in front of us close. It was usually so foggy and rainy that footing was sometimes perilous, and we would have to help keep each other from falling down a slope.
>
> One slope, around Monte Sambucaro in particular, was giving the 3rd Rangers a lot of trouble. Several patrols had been sent up this slope at night to reach the top, and all had come down empty handed. They said there was no enemy at the top, but we kept getting enemy mortar dropped on us from the top. My company was ordered to take one platoon to the top and figure out what was happening. I was one of the "old timers," and a job like this required experience.
>
> The night we took off climbing up that slope was a rainy, dreary night, with visibility just a few feet. We got to the top about 0230 hours, and there was no one there. We took up defensive positions behind rocks, and as it began to get light, we could see that there were two peaks on that mountain, separated by a steep drop-off. I figured that the previous patrols had gotten to the top, but being inexperienced, they did not wait for daylight for further inspection. We stayed very quiet and hidden behind rocks. As daylight came, we could hear Germans talking. They were on the other side of the cliff; we estimated about a hundred feet away. In the afternoon, when I was sure they could not easily slip up on us, I called out to them, telling them they were sur-

> rounded by hundreds of Rangers and needed to surrender. A bit later a German speaking excellent English responded, asking how many men we had. We had twenty-five men. I told him over a hundred.
>
> I asked to speak to the one in charge. A German named Hans responded. He said his parents owned a hotel in Leipzig, and he was sent to hotel management school in Michigan. Before the war started, he was drafted and called to return to Germany. I offered to feed Hans and his men each a big steak dinner if they surrendered, and Hans offered us the same thing. Under a truce flag he and I each stood up and looked at each other, each one trying to get the other to surrender. Late on the third day a paratroop commander came up the mountain asking what the holdup was. I explained the situation, but he didn't believe me. He stood up, unarmed, in full view of the other side and yelled across the gap asking if there were any Germans there. Hans stood up in view, with his machine pistol in hand, and yelled back that the other American officer had not been there long enough to die. The colonel almost fainted, falling back off the rock ledge he was standing on. He told me in no uncertain terms that we were to take the other hilltop that night or he would find someone else to do it.[20]

Evans concluded, "That night we slipped down the hill far enough to creep up the other slope and we ambushed the Germans. Later we found Hans dead, killed in the attack."[21]

The Germans used mines armed with trip wires in the mountains, correctly thinking that if they could wound someone it would tie up several more men in getting them to an aid station. Pvt. Donald G. Golde, 3/F: "I was out on patrol when another Ranger tripped a mine, severing both legs. I helped medics carry down the stretcher." Golde never knew if the wounded Ranger survived. Sometimes medics had to tend to the needs of others even when they were wounded themselves.[22]

Tech/5 Mickey Romine, a 3/Hq. medic:

> Our mission was to locate the placement of their gun positions and ammo dumps and direct artillery fire. . . . The Germans spotted us about dawn and pinned us down with mortar and artillery fire. . . . About mid-morning, a large shell exploded about 18 inches from me. The concussion was so great that it literally picked me up and threw me about 20 feet, and I was doubled up in

> a ball. At the same time, I heard someone yell out in pain and holler, "Hey Doc, I'm hit bad." I automatically jumped up and ran over to him. A piece of shell had cut his arm nearly off. I put a tourniquet on his arm and treated the wound with sulfadiazine powder. That night after dark, we radioed for artillery and jeeps to haul out our dead and wounded.[23]

Capt. Gordon Keppel, the battalion surgeon, experienced his first combat with the Rangers at San Pietro:

> In this battle the diagnosis was not difficult. The men lay bleeding from wounds, requiring plasma, sulpha, and compresses. The big problem was with the doctor [Keppel], who was very scared, didn't want to leave his hole but knew he had to go out to the men. . . . In one hour, there were twenty-five wounded, and I went to them with plasma and sulpha and compresses. It's strange, but I didn't notice the shelling at the time, although afterward I remembered it. That night the officers called me by my first name and the men asked me what I thought of the Rangers, now that I was one. It was the most satisfying thing that ever happened to me.[24]

Taken ill at Venafro, Sgt. Roy Wade Earnest, 1/C, was sent to a hospital in North Africa to recuperate. He tells how difficult it was for tough fighting men to deal with life-changing injuries:

> I was out on the hospital's roof garden when a nurse came over and asked if I was from the Rangers. She asked me to come talk to a Ranger she couldn't handle. I went with her and found that the patient was our sniper Pfc. Ashley Justice, 1st Battalion. He had stepped on a mine, and it blew his leg off above the knee. He didn't want his wife or mother to know just how bad it was. I talked to him about the effect it could have if he went home and hadn't told them. He ended up letting a lady from the Red Cross write to his family before he was flown to a rehab center in the states.[25]

THE IMPACT OF THE CASUALTIES

At Venafro and San Pietro, the Rangers suffered extreme casualties during weeks of desperate combat. When they were finally relieved by a battalion of paratroopers, the survivors were withdrawn from battle to Lucrino, a seacoast town several miles north of Naples for rest, training, and recruiting.[26] The kind of fighting done at Venafro and San Pietro was not the specialized missions, such as raids and invasions, for which the Rangers had been trained. These were infantry battles—extreme examples, perhaps—but still within the competence of infantrymen. Nevertheless, commanders at division level wanted the best men they could get in their toughest battles, so they asked for the Rangers when they could get them.

For all three battalions, from Sicily through Venafro and San Pietro, casualties jumped from 13 percent in North Africa to 31 percent. In the Sicily invasion and the protracted battle across the island, thirty-four Rangers were killed, approximately a 3 percent rate. The invasion of Salerno at Maiori was a mission for which the Rangers were trained, but the fighting through the mountains at Chiunzi Pass, which lasted a month, resulted in thirty-eight Rangers being killed. When the Rangers were used for protracted fighting that was equally suited for regular infantry troops, casualties soared. During the six-week period at Venafro and San Pietro, seventy-five Rangers were killed and 229 were wounded, a combined casualty rate for the Ranger Force of 25 percent.[27] During this same time another 286 Rangers were evacuated from those battlefields for illness and noncombat injuries, leaving the Ranger Force having to replace 40 percent of its fighters.[28]

The Rangers would need many new volunteers, with little time to train them, to replace the casualties lost in the mountain fighting. The loss of specially trained and experienced men in the Italian mountains left a deficit in experience and leadership that would have disastrous consequences in the weeks to come.

Concerned by this, on 28 November, Maj. Roy A. Murray wrote directly to the War Department recommending getting replacements from soldiers being trained for the 2nd and 5th Ranger Battalions at Camp Forrest, Tennessee. He further asked that combat experienced junior Ranger officers be promoted into leadership roles with new battalions. He was concerned about the Rangers' "provisional" status and asked that a Force Headquarters be established for administration and planning and also to determine if mission assignments were appropriate. There is no record that Murray's well-intended letter was ever answered.[29]

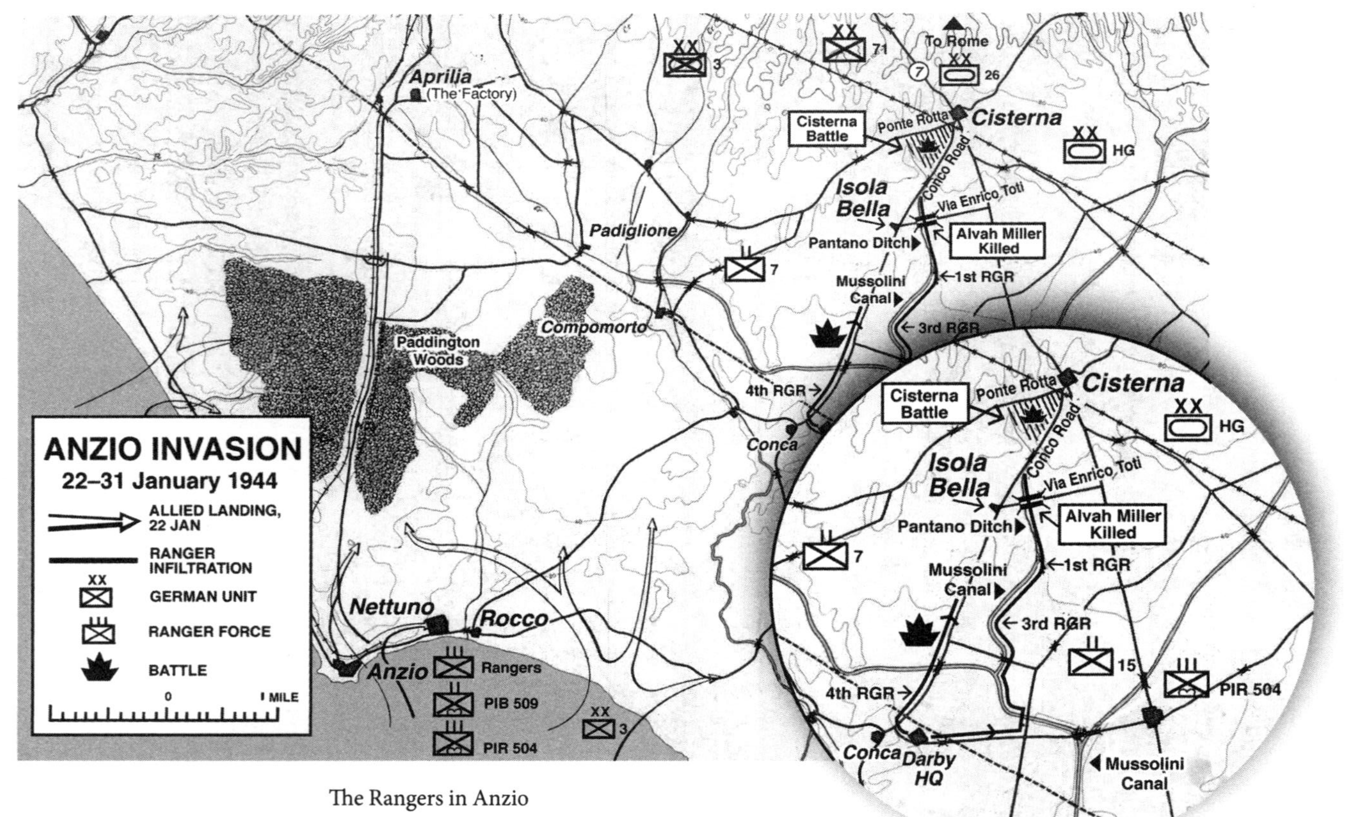

The Rangers in Anzio
(U.S. Army Topographic Command Map VI, "Advances at Anzio," n.d.)

12

ANZIO INVASION

After the fighting around Venafro and San Pietro, the Rangers left the mountains to assemble near Naples. From their assault landings in North Africa, Sicily, and Italy, to combat in the mountainous terrain, the Rangers had seen just about every kind of combat. Nevertheless, they got to celebrate Christmas of 1943 in peace. In Naples, they got hot food instead of C rations, had access to warm sun and blue water, and for the first time got to attend a USO show and enjoy dancing and motion pictures.[1]

Father Basil, the British Commando who had been with them in North Africa, showed up unexpectedly to check on his Rangers. At a mass on Sunday, the Rangers emptied their pockets into the collection plate, knowing that Father Basil would put the money to good use helping orphans and other Italians impoverished by the war ravaging their land.[2] This was a padre whom the Rangers loved, admired, and would sometimes even obey.

Mountain fighting had greatly depleted the Rangers' ranks. Even before leaving the Venafro mountains, Ranger officers were out recruiting and training numerous new volunteers. Once the short holiday break was over, the Rangers resumed training the new men with an intensity not seen since Achnacarry and Nemours. Beach landings went on night after night using live ammunition to teach new recruits what it felt like to be under fire. Original Rangers were now few and far between, and the new volunteers had little time to get adequate training for what lay ahead.[3]

OPERATION SHINGLE

In January 1944, German and Allied forces were deadlocked in the vicinity of Cassino, along the Winter Line, a series of enemy strongpoints constructed of reinforced concrete or blasted out of solid rock that was used to block or

Pfc. Zelly Dineen, 1st Ranger Battalion, Company E, on board a ship en route to the landing at Anzio, Italy, 22 January 1944. Courtesy Joyce Dineen, photographer unknown.

delay the Allied advances toward Rome. As the Allies breached one line, the Germans fell back to occupy another. Because of this, the Rangers were ordered to prepare for yet another beach invasion intended to circumvent the Winter Line.[4]

British intelligence confirmed that the Germans had a corps headquarters and two divisions in addition to a contingent of paratroopers and armored forces near Rome.[5] Britain's Gen. Alexander thought the Germans at Cassino could be cut off by an invasion at Anzio, a small resort and port southwest of Rome, followed by a quick thrust east toward Cisterna di Littoria, only twenty miles away, severing Highway 7, the main north-south highway on the western coast of central Italy. With this action, the Germans would be trapped south of Anzio between two American corps, one at Cassino and one at Anzio, blocking any retreat toward Rome. With the German army divided at Rome and Cassino, the Americans could destroy it. Success at Anzio would allow the capture of Rome and end the war in Italy.[6]

Operation Shingle was set for January 1944. Under the overall command of the experienced Gen. Sir Harold R. L. G. Alexander, the 15th Allied Army Group consisted of the U.S. Fifth Army, commanded by Lt. Gen. Mark Clark, attacking along the western side of Italy at Anzio while the British Eighth Army attacked up the Adriatic coast on the eastern side.[7] Clark was not sure Alexander's plan would work. He surmised that as soon as Allied boots hit the ground at Anzio, it would take the Germans only two days to move two divisions from Rome into the Anzio area. Clark estimated that a third German division from the Adriatic coast could be rushed to Anzio within two weeks. Unless the Americans advanced quickly after landing, Clark feared that his forces might get trapped on the beach because there was insufficient shipping available to bring reinforcements.[8] The strong personalities of Gen. Alexander and Gen. Clark would clash time after time, with Mark Clark wanting to get personal credit for capturing Rome rather than let that trophy fall to the British.[9]

Making the initial landing was the U.S. VI Corps, commanded by Maj. Gen. John Lucas, who was immediately subordinate to Clark. Lucas's forces included the British X Corps, consisting of the 1st Infantry Division, the 46th Royal Tank Regiment, and Commandos. Forces from the United States included the 3rd Infantry Division, the 504th Parachute Infantry Regiment, Darby's 6615th Ranger Force (provisional), and other supporting troops. The Ranger Force encompassed the 1st, 3rd, and 4th Ranger Battalions, the 509th Parachute Infantry Battalion, the 83rd Chemical Mortar Battalion (minus Companies C and D), and Company H of the 36th Combat Engineers. Darby's combined force was almost as large as an army regiment, and upon landing would be attached to the 3rd Infantry Division.[10]

Lucas was unhappy with Clark, both because he considered him too young and also because in the lead-up to Anzio Clark sometimes gave ambiguous orders that led to high casualties. Clark's orders to Lucas were again ambiguous: Lucas was to seize a beachhead in the vicinity of Rome, then advance on the Alban Hills, due north. What Lucas was to do once he was ashore and had troops in the Alban Hills was left vague. A boat shortage would force the invasion to come in two separate landings, three days apart. To direct an amphibious landing requires an energetic, savvy commander, but Lucas was elderly and cautious.[11]

Lucas considered the operation to be risky. Three factors fueled his caution. First was Lucas's low opinion of Clark, second was his concern that the forces he had were inadequate for the mission, and third was the knowledge that additional troops and supplies might not be available.[12] D-Day for the first landing was set for 22 January 1944. A second landing three days later would consist of the U.S. 45th Infantry Division and the U.S. 1st Armored Division.[13] To worsen an already risky mission, U.S. Army Intelligence was totally ignorant of a German troop buildup between Rome and Cisterna di Littoria. Somehow, Fifth Army analysts grossly underestimated the vast numbers of enemy arriving there daily, projecting that four days after landing the Allies would face no more than thirty-one thousand German troops.[14]

As the 6615th Ranger Force prepared for the Anzio invasion, a practice amphibious landing in Pozzuoli Bay just west of Naples on 17 January was dangerously disappointing. Umpires noted that the Rangers' spirit and enthusiasm were exceptional, but because of the many inexperienced replacements, the Rangers violated numerous rules for safe and effective conduct of their missions. If the exercise had been actual combat, the Rangers would have walked into an ambush. Nevertheless, on 20 January 1944, the Rangers were en route to Anzio.[15]

First Sgt. Edward Haywood Jr., 1/C: "We boarded the HMS *Royal Ulsterman* at 1415 Hours on 20 January 1944. British food was very poor. We slept in hammocks, on tables, and on the floor."[16] Cpl. William Zartman, 1/F: "It was considered a sign of good luck to the seasoned Ranger vets that they would be taken to the battle aboard the familiar *Ulsterman*."[17] Sgt. Haywood was thinking about the coming assault:

> We were told that the next day was D-Day, and we had a half-decent meal for supper. About 2000 hours we were given that undrinkable English tea, and at 2330 hours we loaded into the LCA's. At 0030 hours the flotilla started toward shore. Rifles were loaded and bayonets fixed about a mile offshore. It was a cool, clear night. Offshore the rocket ships opened up on the beach to our right. What a sight and such noise! A few minutes later and the beach on our left was also pasted. We fearfully awaited the clatter of machine guns and the glaring of flares, but nothing happened. About thirty yards out we hit a

sandbar, the doors opened and out we went into knee deep, icy water right in front of the casino.[18]

Historian Michael King noted that the mission of the Ranger Force encompassed an array of various tasks: seize the port facilities at Anzio and protect them from sabotage; destroy enemy gun batteries in the vicinity of Anzio; clear the beach area between Anzio and Nettuno, just over three miles east of Anzio, where the U.S. 3rd Infantry Division landed; secure and establish a beachhead; and contact the British 1st Division on the left and the 3rd Infantry Division on the right.[19]

Pvt. Walter P. Krzysztofiak, 1/Hq., claimed to be the first ashore at Anzio, touching down at 0158 hours, two minutes before zero hour.[20] Coming ashore at Anzio in the dark of night on 22 January 1944, the Ranger Force met little opposition. The invasion was an easy one for most of the Rangers. Sgt. Haywood: "We climbed over the beach debris by sections in single file, working our way to the wall just to the right of the casino. The wall was fifteen feet high and impossible to climb. We [turned] left towards the casino, and between it and the wall was an alley with steps leading upward and into the town. Except for running into a few Germans and knocking out two cars there was little action."[21]

Germany's Gen. Kesselring had not expected the Allies to land at Anzio, and few Germans were in the immediate area. Within hours after landing, the Allies had destroyed several armored cars, machine gun nests, and a battery of 100 mm coastal guns, with over forty Germans killed. Any Germans who happened to be in the way were killed or captured, and within three hours the entire port of Anzio was secured in what Ranger Jim Altieri labeled the "most successful landing in Ranger history."[22] By midnight, VI Corps had landed thirty-six thousand men and thirty-two hundred vehicles and had taken 227 prisoners at a cost of only thirteen Allied killed and ninety-seven wounded. The landing was an unqualified success.[23] Cpl. Ken Markham, lead scout for 1/F, wet, cold, and scared as hell, could not believe the lack of resistance at Anzio:

> We formed up in a single file and passed by some buildings. . . . I . . . saw a tunnel which had been dug . . . four or five Russian laborers came up out of the tunnel. They had been used by the Germans [as slave labor]. By daylight, we were ordered to move out through Anzio to the plains beyond. We went out about four miles and dug in. That night I went out on patrol to recon the

front. We pushed out about three miles to the front and about three miles to the right. No contact was made with the enemy.[24]

Pvt. Hollis D. Stabler, 4Hq., a Native American of the Omaha tribe, was a new volunteer. Because he had experience with radios, they put him in the headquarters company, and he had to lay wire everywhere he went. Stabler: "I discovered that there were some other Native Americans in the Rangers. One was Tech/5 Thomas Bearpaw, 3/A, a Cherokee from Oklahoma, and Pvt. Sam Oneskunk, 1/Hq., a Lakota from South Dakota. I was from the Omaha Indian tribe and discovered that my brother Bob's 3rd Infantry Division was located close by, so I got to walk there and visit. It would be the last time I saw Bob alive."[25]

First Lt. Carl "Bob" Hood and Company 4/E, which he commanded, were about a mile inland from the beach when they came under intense fire from several enemy machine guns located next to a railroad bridge. They captured the bridge, but 1st Lt. Hood and 1st Lt. Thomas Bates, who had just recently joined the Rangers as a platoon leader, were both killed, becoming the first Rangers to die on the Anzio beachhead.[26] Lt. Hood was a decorated veteran who had survived combat in Sicily, Chiunzi Pass, and Venafro before his luck ran out on 22 January. First Sgt. Haywood, 1/C, described what they saw when they later reached the railroad, the second phase line, after the initial assault:

> We reached the second phase line where we paused until daybreak, then over the tracks to the third phase [line] a few more miles inland. The houses were all empty and looted. We examined a German recon car, finding books, chocolate, and cookies that I took with me. . . . We paused an hour and then moved to our fourth phase line [about two miles inland]. Here the scattered homes were all occupied by Jerries and "Ites" who left in such a hurry they apparently took only their weapons with them. Large stores of food were left behind, so we spent the rest of the night there with plenty of German food to eat: whole wheat bread, pumpernickel, cheese, margarine, sugar, jam, sauerkraut, potatoes, dried beans, peas, flour, apples, and oranges.[27]

The next morning S/Sgt. Arthur Schrader, 1/F, sent Cpl. Markham back with a detail to get water off a naval supply vessel. While they were gone, German planes strafed and bombed Anzio. Markham: "German bombers made a direct hit on an anti-aircraft gun [close to where I was.] We made it to the ocean and [the navy] filled our water cans. I saw lots of objects floating . . . [one of these] was a sleeping bag of a British soldier. I opened it up and found a bottle of scotch. We had a good day."[28]

Strengthening their coastal defenses daily in preparation for a German counterattack, the Rangers sent out patrols to contact the enemy and determine his strength and location. First Sgt. Haywood, 1/C, was wounded on one of those patrols:

> We moved out in section file across the plains where the civilians gave us bread and eggs. About [another] four miles out we were suddenly fired on by mortars, with the first shell sending a fragment through my right leg. Pfc. Gerald Bortz, 1/Hq., bandaged me up. I gave my records to Staff Sgt. Paul Colbert, 1/A, and showed him how to carry on. I spoke with 2nd Lt. James Dew, 1/A, and Capt. William Bond, 1/A, who had just returned from a patrol, before getting a lift on a British Bren gun carrier to an overpass about two miles away. Col. Darby was there, and I explained the situation to him before walking the remaining two miles to the battalion CP.[29]

The battalion surgeon dressed 1st Sgt. Haywood's wound, which had started to bleed because the bandage had fallen off while walking. After some eggs and a cup of coffee, Haywood turned in his weapons and began waiting for an ambulance:

> I was given a tetanus shot and eight sulphadiazine pills and was considered a stretcher case. After walking four miles to the hospital, they would not let me walk another twenty-six yards to the next ambulance ride to the 95th hospital. . . . About 2010 hours I climbed onto the operating table where my right pant leg was cut completely off . . . felt a jab in my left arm and was told to count to twenty-five. . . . At sixteen my head got heavy, and I don't remember saying seventeen. My thoughts on waking up about 0200 the next morning were vague, but I recall that a German was brought in. The ward was filling up quickly.[30]

With the British X Corps on their left and Gen. Truscott's 3rd Infantry Division on their right flank, the Rangers pushed inland early the next day to expand the beachhead. By early morning of 25 January, they were fourteen miles inland. Nevertheless, the Germans moved in heavy reinforcements to encircle the Anzio beachhead, frustrating one of the main goals of the Anzio invasion, which was to force the Germans to withdraw forces from the Winter Line near Cassino. The Allied plan to link up the Anzio forces with the U.S. Fifth Army in the south of Italy appeared unlikely to succeed.[31] S/Sgt. Shirley C. Jacobs, 1/Hq., was wounded in the continuing battle for the beachhead: "My captain and I looked out the door of my tent to see a German dive bomber heading for our area. We both jumped into a foxhole just as the bomber made a screaming climb after releasing his bomb. A piece of shrapnel got both of us, but we'd have been killed if we had been above ground."[32]

Pvt. Hollis Stabler, 4/Hq., went out laying wire with another Ranger, and they came to a bridge with a low wall. The bridge crossed a small stream, and they decided to go for the bridge rather than chance the stream. The Germans must have had it zeroed in because an enemy shell hit, knocking them into the water. Stabler's injuries were minor, and after he got patched up he decided to go see his brother Bob again. On getting to the 3rd Infantry Division area, he was directed to a lean-to, where bodies were laid out. They had just been hit by German artillery, and Bob was a casualty. Someone directed Stabler to Bob's body, covered by a shelter half, but Hollis saw Bob's ring and would not look at his face:

> After I found Bob, I really wasn't scared, but I thought I'd be more careful. I didn't know what to do. None of the guys in my company knew him, but everyone in the 3rd Division knew him. I walked . . . to a toilet in a big tent. Some guy looked at me like he was really scared. He asked, "Who are you?" . . . "I thought you were Bob," he said.
>
> When I got back to the 4th they were sending out combat patrols. I couldn't tell what it was, but something was moving. It was a long way away, but I had good eyes. . . . I said: "Let me have your gun." . . . I [aimed] about waist high, where I figured a man would be. Sure enough, that guy jumped up. I pulled the trigger, and I hit him. It was a long way. I bet it was in the thousand-yard range! I didn't have a scope or anything, all I had was the leaf scope. No one else could see him but me, but I knew what he was going to do. I knew where I had to aim. He got up and I hit him. That shot was for Bob, you know.[33]

Ranger Joe C. Renfro, 3/C, from Kentucky, who had just joined the Rangers, was killed early in the week. In a 1948 letter to Renfro's mother, Joe's best friend, Pfc. Nelson E. Rice, 3/C, told how Renfro was killed:

> Our lieutenant told us to prepare to go on patrol that night. About half an hour after we left, we ran into a German machine gun nest. They got all of us but Joe and me. We started back to our lines, but a shell landed next to us and a piece of it hit me in the head. Another piece hit me in the hand, and I fell. Joe saw me fall and came back to carry me. I told him to keep running, but he wouldn't. He picked me up and started carrying me back, but a machine gun got him in the back and chest.
>
> I lay there for about half an hour. . . . The Germans that got Joe thought I was dead also, but I got the ones who got Joe. I used a hand grenade and got the whole machine gun nest. I could never have been happy if I hadn't. They sent me to a hospital where I stayed for thirty-five days before returning to the lines. Mrs. Renfro, Joe did not suffer. It was all over in just a few seconds, but I will never forget his loyalty. He could have escaped if he hadn't come back for me.[34]

Pvt. G. W. Guynes, 3/A, was haunted the rest of his life because of an incident at Anzio:

> I was in the front because I was first scout and I noticed a little section of the weeds up in front of me and I looked up there and pinpointed my gun up to the area where the weeds was wiggling. And a little kid stuck his head up. Must have been 12. And he come up with a gun and I could not shoot my gun. I had my gun right on him. And he was just about to kill us. And I knew I had to kill him and it was the hardest thing I ever done in all my born days.[35]

A young Polish private named Stempkofski, serving in the German army, defected to American authorities, reporting that the enemy was waiting to ambush the Americans. He was sent to the rear, and his story only came out after he was interrogated by Fifth Army Intelligence. Army Intelligence was upset with the unit that turned in the private for not finding out his full story when he first defected. However, it was unlikely that a Polish private would have known any more about the Germans' plans than an American private would know about Allied plans; plus, it was doubtful that the private was telling the truth. The German high command was aware that the Americans were building up forces on the Anzio beachhead preparing for an attack. Thus, the Germans were expanding their forces to meet the American attack, which was probably all the private knew. Why he defected is still a mystery.[36]

RANGERS IN THE HOSPITAL—AND OUT AGAIN

Almost every Ranger experienced some kind of wound and passed through the hospital at some point during his service. At Anzio there were two evacuation hospitals (each with four hundred beds), one field hospital, one medical battalion, and several division clearing stations. In these hospitals, medics examined, evaluated, and stabilized the patients. For many, the beachhead hospitals were only a way station before being sent to more permanent hospitals in Naples or North Africa.[37]

The field hospitals were not exempt from attack. German shells from mortars, artillery, and rockets could not see the Red Crosses marking the hospital tents, which were no more than dugouts protected and separated from each other by a wall of sandbags. At Anzio, several tents were wiped out while doctors were operating, killing or injuring patients, nurses, and doctors alike. One German dive bomber, chased by a Spitfire, jettisoned its five antipersonnel bombs on the 95th Evacuation Hospital. Among the twenty-eight dead were three nurses, two medical officers, fourteen enlisted men, one Red Cross worker, and six patients. Sixty-four others were wounded.[38]

Tech/5 Mickey Romine, 3/Hq., bleeding and suffering back spasms after the San Pietro combat, was hospitalized in Naples by Dr. Keppel: "I . . . was on the list to be sent home. A couple of days before [the Anzio landing] the man that took my place as the medic in A Company could not go, so Dr. Keppel asked me to come back to my company. But the doctor at the hospital would not release me as he said I was not fit for combat. Doctor Keppel . . . asked me to go AWOL from the hospital and go on this last job, and he would send me home."[39]

NEXT OBJECTIVE: CISTERNA

On 28 January, under pressure from Clark to be more aggressive, Lucas ordered an attack on the nearby town of Cisterna di Littoria. Holding Cisterna would presumably keep the Germans from moving additional reinforcements to Cassino, and would open the door for Allied moves on Rome. Orders for the attack came down through Truscott, commanding the 3rd Infantry Division, to which the Ranger Force was attached.[40] Col. Darby drafted the Rangers' plan of attack, ordering the 1st and 3rd Battalions to go on a long-range mission the next night, infiltrating under cover to capture Cisterna. The 4th Battalion would attack up the Conca Road, clearing it of enemy, and after reaching Cisterna it would support the 1st and 3rd Battalions.

Battle plans were hastily put together, and on 29 January, at 1800 hours, Darby briefed his officers on the upcoming action. It was to be the last time most of these men would ever see their leader, something Capt. Warren "Bing" Evans, 3/F, never forgot: "My good friend, Capt. Les Kness, 4/Hq., and I had a foreboding sense about the mission and so informed Col. Darby."[41]

Darby respected Evans and Kness, who had access to him almost any time they wanted it. Both were Originals, had received battlefield commissions, and had fought through every engagement since 1942. Approaching Darby, they told him that, despite what 3rd Infantry Division Intelligence reported on the enemy situation, Ranger patrols had picked up a lot of enemy activity in the Cisterna area. They asked Darby to reconsider the mission. Darby, never one to question orders from higher headquarters, said simply, "These are my orders, those are your orders!" There was no more discussion.[42]

Cpl. Anders Arnbal, 3/D, was appalled when Lt. Preston Hogue arrived from Naples with news that Col. Darby had ordered him and several other Rangers back to the United States immediately. The orders also affected Capt. Dirks of Ranger Force Headquarters, three more from the 3rd Ranger Battalion, and five others from the other two battalions. Other Rangers known to have been held back from the Cisterna mission included Tech/5 Evan J. "Tommy" Thompson, 3/F; Pfc. Joseph Schwartz, 3/F; and Pvt. James Simpson, 4/Hq.[43] Their experience and leadership would be missed in the coming hours.

13

THE BATTLE FOR CISTERNA DI LITTORIA

The whole story of this action may never be known.
—COL. WILLIAM ORLANDO DARBY, JUNE/JULY 1944

The plan for the attack on Cisterna di Littoria was predicated on the intelligence report from the 3rd Infantry Division G-2, dated 29 January 1944.[1] The following is a condensed summary of this report.

> The enemy has the Hermann Goering Panzer Division on the Rangers' right flank and front plus a scattering of units on the left front. The enemy has maintained a rather loose and poorly organized line of outposts to the east of the Mussolini Canal and south of the railroad which runs northwest from Cisterna. The enemy does not man strong defensive works west of Highway 6 near Cisterna. The enemy's immediate situation with respect to tanks and artillery is not good, and there is every indication that he is losing equipment faster than the Allies. The enemy situation regarding reserves is hard to assess. It is likely that the mission of these units is to prepare and maintain defenses rather than to be used in a counterattack against the Allies on the beachhead.
>
> Terrain: The heights north of Cisterna dominate the field of battle. The battlefield itself is basically flat, crisscrossed with numerous streams and roads.
>
> Enemy Capabilities: There is evidence that the quality of the enemy's squad and platoon leadership has begun to deteriorate. At present small enemy groups have not shown the excellent discipline that we have come to expect in prior battles. It does not seem probable that the enemy is capable of a major counterattack in this area. He will probably attempt to stage a series of small counterattacks to keep the Allies off guard and to maintain a standstill over the battle area.

This intelligence report was woefully wrong. As soon as the Allies landed at Anzio on 22 January 1944, Field Marshal Albert Kesselring began throwing all available German units into their path. Enemy units reached the Anzio area faster than American intelligence could imagine and included the Hermann Goering Panzer Division and the 3rd and 29th Panzer Grenadier Divisions, along with the 71st Infantry Division, the 26th Panzer Division, the newly formed 4th Parachute Division, plus rear echelons of I Parachute Corps. The local Luftwaffe flak commander rushed his units to the Alban Hills, a group of extinct volcanoes and lakes located twelve miles southeast of Rome and fifteen miles north of Anzio, and finally, Kesselring ordered all other units near Rome to move immediately to the Cisterna area.[2]

Patrols from the U.S. 3rd Infantry Division, collecting intelligence on the enemy, totally missed the German strongpoints strategically placed along likely lanes where the Allies might attack. The major enemy forces, totaling thirty infantry battalions supported by armor and artillery, were being massed just north of Cisterna along the Germans' main line of resistance, from where they could respond to an attack from any direction.[3] Historian Col. Robert Black later estimated that over seventy-one thousand battle-hardened enemy soldiers had slipped into the Anzio area, mostly undetected.[4] Just three days before the Rangers were sent to fight there, an attempt by elements of the U.S. 3rd Infantry Division to take Cisterna from the east had failed miserably. For some reason the intelligence analysts missed the significance of that failure.[5]

On 28 January, with the Ranger Force bivouaced about five miles east of Anzio and attached to the U.S. 3rd Infantry Division, Col. Darby received orders to capture and hold the city of Cisterna di Littoria, about seven miles northeast of the Rangers' current location and about thirty miles south of Rome. The Rangers were ordered to block Highway 7, the main north-south road in western Italy known in ancient times as the Appian Way, which ran through the middle of Cisterna.[6]

To the Rangers' right was the Mussolini canal system, designed to drain the Pontine Marshes that lay between Cisterna and the sea. Ditches and canals built by Mussolini decades before to reclaim swampy land for farming now protected Allied forces from tank attacks from the east. To the northeast of Cisterna were the Colli Laziali mountains, from which the Germans could observe Allied movements.[7]

Lt. Gen. Mark Clark, commander of the U.S. Fifth Army in Italy, was urging Maj. Gen. John P. Lucas, commanding the VI Corps, to make a move inland to secure the Allied position, but Lucas, fearing that he would not be able to secure replacements quickly if an all-out battle began, seemed reluctant to move forward. Clark was impatient, and on 27 January he urged Lucas to attack Cisterna. Lucas agreed, provided he got extensive naval and air support, plus heavy directed artillery fire. On 28 January, Maj. Gen. Truscott, ordered by Lucas to attack, hastily ordered the Rangers to spearhead the 3rd Infantry Division attack toward Cisterna.[8]

ORDERS FROM MAJ. GEN. LUCIEN TRUSCOTT, CO, 3RD INFANTRY DIVISION (CONDENSED)

> Under cover of darkness, all three battalions of Rangers shall spearhead an attack by the 3rd Infantry Division toward Cisterna. The 1st and 3rd Ranger Battalions shall infiltrate at night up the Mussolini canal system to get close enough to Cisterna to viciously assault the city before dawn on 30 January 1944, and block Highway 7. 1st Battalion Rangers are to by-pass any significant enemy resistance. The 3rd Battalion Rangers shall destroy any enemy forces by-passed and provide security for the 1st Battalion. The 4th Battalion is to clear the Conca Road all the way to Cisterna for tanks and infantry to follow, advancing before daylight on 30 January, to link up with the 1st and 3rd Battalions. All units are to hold Cisterna until relieved. The 7th Infantry Regiment [of the 3rd Division] is to attack from the left [the southwest] and the 15th Infantry Regiment [of the 3rd Division] from the right [the east] to cut Highway 7 above and below Cisterna.[9]

28 JANUARY 1944

After receiving orders for the new mission, the Rangers of the 1st, 3rd, and 4th Battalions moved out about midnight, marching seven miles from their staging area northwest of Anzio to an assembly area just east of the town of Conca along the Conca-Sessano road, arriving there just before dawn on the 29th. Darby later recalled: "Our assembly area was about four miles from the coast where the 3rd Division had landed. Due north some eight miles was the town of Cisterna di Littoria, its stone and cement houses spread out along the Appian Way. . . . Due north beyond Cisterna and on the far side of the Appian Way were the first ridges of the mountains. The hill mass was called Colli Laziali."[10] From the Colli Laziali the Germans could watch everything the Allies were doing. Col. Darby: "For that reason, as well as for flank protection, the Allies had to have the Colli, twenty-eight hundred feet high."[11]

29 JANUARY 1944: 1ST AND 3RD BATTALIONS AT THEIR ASSEMBLY AREA

After being told to pack up and be ready to move out in the morning, Cpl. Kenneth Markham, lead scout in 1/F: "The [assembly] area was surrounded by trees. We had our barracks bags there. We were told to rest up and take it easy because we had a busy night coming up. We were instructed to clean our weapons and sharpen our knives."[12] Pfc. Gustav Schunemann, 1/F: "Each man was issued two hand grenades, a bandolier of .30 caliber ammunition and one 60 mm mortar shell. Our light packs carried two days of rations along with clean socks and underwear, toilet articles and cigarettes."[13]

The Rangers spent the day cleaning weapons and stuffing their battle packs with grenades, anticipating the infiltration that would begin just after midnight. Mail from home was delivered to the battalions, but Darby ordered that it be held until the men returned from the mission. Some wrote letters home, some just relaxed, or tried to. For many of the Rangers the Cisterna mission would be their first taste of combat behind enemy lines, and some of the Originals wondered if the new men were ready.[14]

Most Ranger commanders led their units from the front. One such commander was Maj. John Dobson, CO of the 1st Ranger Battalion. An experienced fighter, Dobson was new to the Rangers but was a friend of Darby's from their West Point days. Maj. Alvah Miller, CO of the 3rd Ranger Battalion, chose to march in the center of his battalion for this mission. Because of radio silence and because the 3rd Battalion was strung out in a half-mile-long column, half on each side of the ditch, being in the center of his Rangers provided Miller the most effective command and control.

Maj. Miller, an Original Ranger who had been in continual combat for a year and a half, liked poetry and sometimes wrote it. Late that night Miller, in a pyramid tent, surrounded by young soldiers, perhaps a bit homesick for his wife and son back in the States, took up a pen and wrote a poem on the back of the orders he had received from Col. Darby earlier in the day. Miller's son, James Miller (deceased), confirmed that the date of the orders, 29 January, established that the poem was written that night.[15]

The Men of My Command

'Tis midnight and I stand
Amid the sleeping forms of men—
The men of my command.
And as their troubled murmurs stir
The quiet of the night,
I wonder at the subject of their dreams.
What matter if tomorrow I command again?
Tonight, they are my sons.

This one—the father lying at my feet—
Laughs and plays (in a dream) with the son he's never seen.
(God grant his safe return.)
And over there, a dozen paces to my right,
A boy—a man now, he's just passed twenty-one—
Sobs a name, his brother's.
Today's long-looked-for mail notified him of his
Brother's death.

And on the other side—
But what was that? A child's frightened cry?
No! I see from whence it came,
That youngster there who's writhing in his sleep.
(He's dreaming of that shelling we received the other day,
And who can blame him, 'twas his first.)
"Marilyn!" Whose voice cried out? Oh, yes!
I know the man, and the name he speaks—his wife's.
Spoke in remorse for that last letter, penned in anger's heat.

I censored it, you see, and know its content.
He'll be glad tomorrow when I give it back.
I withheld it from the mail, for I knew his anger'd cool,
And he'd regret the sending of it.

But now my reverie is broken.
Other thoughts and sounds impinge upon my mind
(The distant sentinel's sharp challenge,
The jackal's cry, the scudding clouds that chase the
Moonlight from the sky, to let it reappear again
To form a new kaleidoscope of sight).
And all my present sons lie quiet in their sleep.

I'm thinking now about an absent son—
My own—who sleeps so far away
Beneath the same deep, scintillating canopy
To which I turn my eyes
To ask God's blessing on all my sons,
Both here and there—
Those whose dreams I read, and him
Whose future dreams I'll share (God willing)
And pray that I might be a faithful father, now—
And then.

Did Maj. Alvah Miller have a premonition? Capt. Warren "Bing" Evans, commanding 3/F, thought so. Evans believed that Miller's poem reflected his deep concern about the safety of his men on the upcoming mission.[16]

The remainder of this chapter provides a minute-by-minute narrative of the Battle of Cisterna, pieced together from personal interviews, published and unpublished accounts by Col. William O. Darby, Col. Robert Black, Col. Roy A. Murray, or Pvt. Arnold E. "Pat" Davis, the Ranger Force Log of Action, and the Ranger Force Journal (a record of radio communications during the battle). Time stamps appear throughout the narrative, with the source noted in parentheses. Some of these time stamps, labeled as Estimated, are based on a Ranger's description of the amount of morning daylight as determined by astronomical times identified in the appendix. In some cases, I made estimates of the time based on known times compared to the sequence of events. For more about these methods, see the appendix.

29 JANUARY 1944

1800 HOURS (JOURNAL)

Darby held a meeting of his battalion commanders and several scouts to go over his orders one more time. Weapons for the attack were to be rifles, automatic weapons, sticky grenades, and antitank rocket launchers (bazookas). Radio silence was not to be broken until the troops crossed the road running east through Isola Bella.

1930 HOURS (JOURNAL)

Darby met with Lt. Otis Davey, commander of the Cannon Company, in the Ranger Force command post to coordinate Davey's tank destroyers, which would be needed to support the 4th Battalion as it attacked up the Conca Road to support the 1st and 3rd Battalions.

2300 HOURS (JOURNAL)

Darby's command post was closed and moved to a stone house located adjacent to the Conca Road.[17] The plan called for units of the 3rd Infantry Division to be on the Rangers' right, and American paratroopers and British forces to be advancing from the left. Jumping off at 0100 hours, the 1st and 3rd Rangers would move by stealth, single file, wading all night through the series of canals and ditches that drained the Pontine Marshes. Moving inland, the large Mussolini Canal got increasingly smaller. The Rangers were to move into its upper branch, known as the Pantano Ditch, which was smaller and shallower. Beyond that, near Cisterna, there were only shallow drainage ditches, with dense canebrakes and other vegetation along the banks.[18]

30 JANUARY 1944

0100 HOURS (BLACK): 1ST AND 3RD BATTALIONS CROSS THEIR LINE OF DEPARTURE

Maj. Dobson ordered Capt. William Bond, commanding 1/A, to lead a small patrol to reconnoiter a few hundred yards ahead of the Rangers and to alert Company 1/F if they detected an enemy ambush. There is no record of what they found or when they rejoined the rest of the battalion.[19] Col. Darby: "Men were in good spirits as they swung out for their seven-mile march from the assembly area to the line of departure. At midnight the three battalions . . . had reached a road junction about four miles from Cisterna. . . . My headquarters, accompanying the 4th Battalion, was hooked in by wire and radio with the 3rd Division."[20] At 0100 hours on the morning of 30 January, 396 Rangers of the 1st Battalion led off, with 373 Rangers of the 3rd Battalion following fifteen minutes behind, moving under radio silence in single file, no talking. The order of march was organized by companies, as follows: 1st Battalion, F Company, whose officers and scouts were some of the most battle-tested and experienced, led off, followed by Hq., E, D, C, B, and A Companies. The 3rd Battalion followed fifteen minutes later, with the order of march being Companies A, B, Hq., C, D, E, and F. The two battalions totaled 769 men on the attack.[21]

0201 HOURS (MURRAY): 4TH BATTALION AT ITS ASSEMBLY AREA

The 4th Battalion, commanded by Lt. Col. Roy A. Murray, jumped off from its line of departure at 0201 hours, attacking north up the Conca Road, advancing through the village of Isola Bella (also called Femmina Morta, which means "Dead Woman."). Their mission was to clear the Conca Road of the enemy so that armor could rush forward and reinforce the two Ranger battalions expected to be in Cisterna before daylight. No one suspected that Isola Bella was heavily defended by enemy forces many times stronger than reported by 3rd Infantry Division Intelligence.[22]

Simultaneously, three battalions of the 7th Infantry Regiment attacked from the southwest, and two battalions of the 15th Infantry Regiment of the 3rd Infantry Division attacked from the south toward Cisterna, while the units of the 504th Parachute Infantry Regiment attacked from the southeast. All Allied units were ordered to destroy any enemy in their path and provide all-around security for Cisterna once it was in Allied hands.[23]

Darby was wired in with the 4th Ranger Battalion and 3rd Infantry Division Headquarters, and hooked in by radio with the 1st and 3rd Ranger Battalions. Each company had a handheld radio-telephone, commonly called a "walkie-talkie," for the company commanders to communicate with their battalion commander and with each other.[24] The 1st and 3rd Rangers moved silently north in the west branch of the Mussolini Canal.[25] It was over one hundred feet wide in places, with steep banks topping out at fifteen feet high, effectively hiding the men from the sight of enemies on the surface.[26] At this time of year, the canal held from two to four feet of water, and recent rains had made the sides, over which the Rangers had to march, muddy and slippery.[27]

Tech/5 Thomas Prudhomme and Pfc. Edward Wilkerson, both of 3/D, had contracted high fevers. Capt. Gordon Keppel, 3/Hq., the battalion surgeon, sent them back from the mission, saving them from wounds, capture, or death.[28]

THE INFILTRATION

The Rangers' lead scout on the march was Cpl. Kenneth Markham, 1/F.[29] He had done this before; he was a cool customer who knew that he would be the first one to contact the enemy. Other 1st Battalion scouts from Company F, already well out in front, included Pvt. John See, Pvt. Leo Ferrante, Pvt. Judson Luckhurst, Pfc. Robert E. Jones on the Browning automatic rifle (BAR), Pfc. Osborne Sawyer, Pvt. Wayne Workman, Pfc. James Brennan, and Pvt. William Robertson.[30] Cpl. Kenneth Markham was on the point. Maj. Dobson was next in line, and SGM Bob Ehalt was right in back of him. Next came 1st Sgt. Frank Mattivi and Sgt. John East. Markham:

> I heard German armor moving. I made the statement to Jim Brennan that we were in for a rough night. I was on point on the right and See was on the left side of the ditch. We moved along the ditch for three or four miles when I was instructed to hold up. I heard Major Dobson trying to contact Colonel Darby. We had passed by a battery of 88s on our right flank about 100 yards or so. We

> also had bypassed a machine gun nest. There is no one who can make me believe the Germans let us slip by. We could have killed them at any time. I think we did an excellent job of bypassing the enemy without their knowledge.[31]

Cpl. William Zartman, 1/F: "As scout for . . . the Fox Company Commander, I followed him in the single file line formed by our battalion as we entered the Pantano Ditch. . . . It was just deep enough to make it difficult to see over the top."[32]

On the night infiltration up the Mussolini Canal, Rangers saw German sentries, but the sentries could not see the Rangers. Some Rangers had difficulty keeping quiet, as they occasionally stumbled, tripped, or brushed against the canal walls on this very dark night. The single-file column of the 1st and 3rd Rangers, marching fifteen feet apart, half on each side of the canal, was strung out in a line that was just over a mile long, walking in mud and water. It was foggy with limited visibility. German patrols crossed their path twice but did not detect the Rangers. After moving forward about another mile, the Ranger scouts encountered two groups of sentries.[33] Cpl. Markham, 1/F: "1st Lt. James Fowler had been skilled in personal combat by his company commander Capt. Shunstrom. Accompanied by three members of his company, Fowler crawled forward, and moved to the enemy outpost, where he drew his knife. He silently disposed of the German sentry and signaled for the march to continue. Another enemy outpost was destroyed as Lt. Fowler again silently eliminated the sentry with his knife, a skill that he perfected in combat over many months."[34]

Pfc. Zelly J. Dineen, 1/E, in his first combat: "We were told not to fire as we infiltrated up the canal, that we were going to try to sneak through the German lines that night. We walked right past two groups of Germans, but not one of the Rangers opened fire."[35]

Maj. John Dobson: "I was near the front of the column, no more than seventy-five feet from one enemy gun battery, and we could hear the Germans talking."[36] The Rangers could have wiped them out, but they were under strict orders to maintain silence and remain undetected. An interdicting round from a German shell caught 2nd Lt. Charles M. McBryde, 1/D, in the leg. He was returned to the beachhead on a litter and eventually lost his right leg as a result of the wound.[37]

0215 HOURS (ESTIMATED): 4TH RANGER BATTALION

As planned, the 4th Battalion launched its assault toward Cisterna at 0201 hours, moving in approach-march formation up the enemy-held Conca-Cisterna road. The area seemed unusually quiet and still, without even an occasional burst of fire from German machine pistols.[38] Historian Col. Robert Black explained the company formation: "Charlie 4, Dog 4, Able 4, and Baker 4—in that order—moved 300 yards east of the road and then proceeded north, paralleling the Conca-Femmina Morta Road. . . . Easy 4, Fox 4 and the remainder of headquarters . . . moved in the ditches beside the road. Cannon Company and its four half-track 75 millimeter guns and a platoon from the 601st Tank Destroyer Battalion were prepared to follow the 4th and give support."[39]

The area was flat with little cover except for small drainage ditches about one foot deep. When the Rangers had scarcely moved a mile, one German machine gun opened up, followed almost immediately by many others, some in fields away from the road, and some on both sides of the road, with mortar and small arms firing into the Rangers' ranks. The Germans had the road blocked, with snipers and machine guns placed in houses all along the road. The 4th Battalion Rangers were pinned down, with scouts unable to find holes in the enemy ranks for Rangers to slip through.[40]

0248 HOURS (JOURNAL): RANGER FORCE COMMAND POST

Four radio operators from the 3rd Battalion showed up at Force Headquarters asking for instructions. They seemed to have no idea where they were supposed to report.[41] Darby, who was all too aware of the importance of good communications, thought the lost radiomen were "the god-damndest thing" he had "ever heard of." Darby sent the radio operators over to Maj. William Martin, the Force intelligence officer, with instructions to try to find their unit, but the men never caught up with the 3rd Battalion.[42] Michael King, Darby's biographer, wrote that this was "The first of several events . . . that did not auger well for the success of the mission."[43]

0350 HOURS (ESTIMATED): 4TH BATTALION RANGERS

Capt. George Nunnally, commanding 4/C, led two ferocious assaults that wiped out two German machine gun nests. Murray: "Nunnally next led a charge against a farmhouse held by twelve German paratroopers. In a short but furious battle the house was captured, and its occupants killed. . . . Nunnally again led a Ranger charge . . . a machine gun burst ripped into him as he . . . flung his last grenade . . . the Captain and four other Rangers paid with their lives for that short gain in ground."[44] After these the two Ranger attacks, neither of which penetrated the heavily defended German line, the remaining Rangers in 4/C holed up in a shallow ditch, unable to move due to enemy machine gun fire and mortar explosions over their position. The Report of Action summarizes what the 4th Battalion encountered: "[Enemy] positions were in depth, and were well camouflaged and dug in. MGs [machine guns] were firing about one foot above the ground with very effective cross fire. . . . Sniping and MG fire from the enemy was received when personnel exposed themselves."[45]

0433 HOURS (JOURNAL): 4TH RANGER BATTALION

Murray, breaking radio silence, encountered the enemy after moving just over a mile from the Ranger Force command post and was catching a lot of small arms fire from houses.[46]

0450 HOURS (JOURNAL): 4TH RANGER BATTALION

Col. Darby ordered Lt. Otis Davey to move his tank destroyers up the Conca Road to help the 4th Battalion break through.[47]

0500 HOURS (ESTIMATED): 1ST AND 3RD BATTALIONS

As men moved along the sloping bank of the deep canal, enemy flares lit up the sky from time to time, causing men to freeze in place or drop to one knee, trying to avoid detection. Suddenly, nerves were on edge. Many of the Rangers were in combat for the first time.

George C. Kopanda, 1st sergeant for 3/F, the rear company in the assault:

> As we advanced in the night (seemingly unnoticed), to our left rear we saw and heard every describable type of machine gun crossfire (tracer) and mortar bursts fired by Germans; we assumed that our 4th Battalion had encountered that barrage. . . . To our right rear I saw bursts of heavy artillery and mortar fire. Flares that appeared to be behind this intense machine gun fire were be-

> ing fired to our direct left flank. . . . I saw the silhouettes of troops moving between the flares and us and passed word to the front. These troops did not hamper our advance. We did not stop or send a patrol to encounter them. We met with no resistance until dawn broke.[48]

The firing that Kopanda heard coming from the left rear was the 4th Battalion trying to crack the German defenses along the Conca Road. Only a few hours into their advance and hearing unexpected shooting and explosions off to the left, indicating that the 4th Battalion was already engaged, concern mounted among the 1st and 3rd Rangers, who had been quite confident of success when they initially jumped off. Still dark and about two miles from Cisterna, there was a break in contact between the 1st and 3rd Battalions. The three trailing companies in the 1st Battalion discovered the break and stopped, creating a break in the 1st Battalion as the three forward companies continued on.

Capt. Charles M. Shunstrom, 1/Hq., who was marching in the middle of the 1st Battalion: "About half way to the town of Cisterna . . . the First Ranger Battalion lost contact with the Third Ranger Battalion in its rear. About one-half mile further on the First Ranger Battalion became split, three companies proceeding forward, and three companies halting because of loss of contact. Shunstrom [writing about himself] . . . sent a runner to the rear to contact the 3rd Ranger Battalion."[49]

It is not known exactly when these breaks happened, or how. But under radio silence, runners from the 1st Battalion were working frantically to halt the front half of the column to wait for the others to catch up. The delay ate up precious time when every minute counted. With the battalion halted until the marching units were reconnected, it must have been obvious to Maj. Dobson that they would not reach Cisterna before first light, estimated to be 0554 hours. Dawn was approaching on this cold, damp, and foggy morning.[50]

THE CISTERNA BATTLEFIELD

The shape of the battlefield was a triangle with a long tail (see map, page 176). The northern apex of the triangle was at the town of Cisterna. The Conca Road marked the east side and the Ponte Rotta Road was the northern boundary. Closing the triangle on the southwest was the Matta Creek and a portion of the

Pantano Ditch. Another ditch, the Anima Sante Creek, roughly paralleled the Conca Road about five hundred feet farther west. Cisterna marked the point at which the drained Pontine Marshes met higher ground. Although most of the battlefield was low-lying and crisscrossed by drainage ditches, the Rangers also mentioned ridges and hills generally in the northern part of the area toward Cisterna. The area was dotted with stone farmhouses and barns. Only one of these, the Calcabrini house, can be located today. This triangle is where most of the fighting by the 1st and 3rd Battalions took place.

The "tail" of the battlefield ran southwest of the triangle along the Conca Road and the Pantano Ditch, through which the Rangers approached Cisterna. Parts of the 3rd Battalion did their fighting in this "tail" almost down to the village of Isola Bella (or Femmina Morta). At Isola Bella, a road that today is called Via Enrico Toti runs east from the Conca Road. A dirt road (not shown on military maps in 1944) running from Isola Bella toward the northwest, perpendicular to the Conca Road and connecting with the Ponte Rotta Road, is now named "Via del Rangers."[51]

Darby gave a verbal order that radio silence should not be broken until the troops had crossed the line running east through Isola Bella,[52] meaning the 1st Battalion should have been able to break radio silence when it crossed the Via Enrico Toti. It seems that either Dobson did not recognize the road when he passed under it or his radios failed. Below Isola Bella the Germans blocked the Conca Road. South of that, the 4th Battalion, approaching up the Conca Road, was trying to break through impregnable German resistance to reach the 1st and 3rd Battalions. The map does not show the extension of the "tail," where the 4th Battalion fought.

0515 HOURS (ESTIMATED): DOBSON'S FIRST ATTEMPT TO CONTACT DARBY BY RADIO

The only sounds Dobson was hearing came from the 4th Battalion's fight, too far away to support him. Unknown to Dobson, the two battalions of the 15th Infantry Regiment on his right had fought to a standstill, and on his left the three battalions from the 7th Infantry were stopped by heavy enemy fire. The more than seventy thousand German troops, whose presence army intelligence had missed, had little difficulty blocking the planned advances of the 3rd

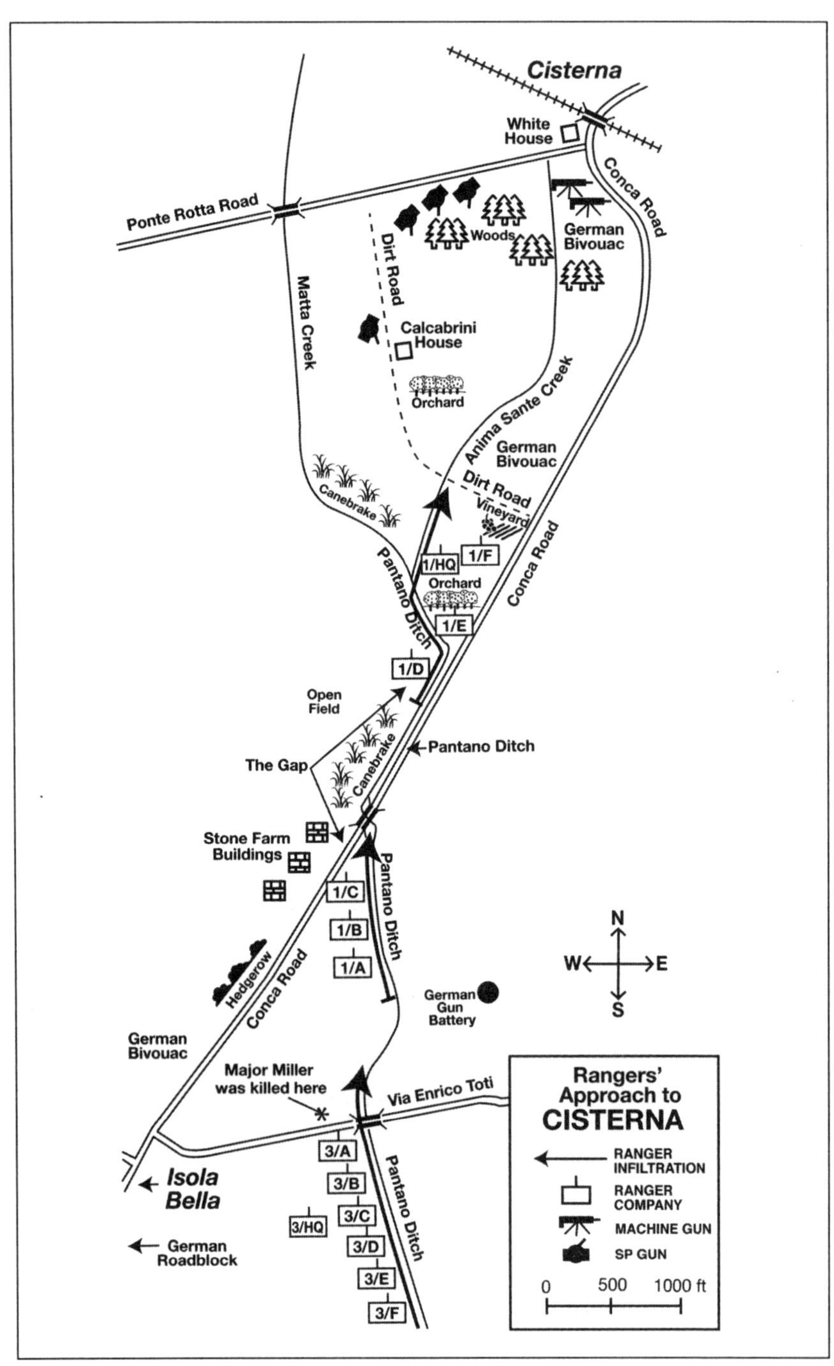

The Rangers' Approach to Cisterna

Division Infantry and the 504th paratroopers. Dobson realized that he was on his own.[53] Dobson tried unsuccessfully to establish radio contact with Ranger Force Headquarters. He wanted to seek permission to either race for Cisterna or dig in and hold in place. The radio transmission failed, probably because the equipment had gotten wet during the infiltration, slogging through the muddy ditches. A heavy fog did not help.[54]

Enemy vehicle traffic was building up on the Conca Road as the Germans moved troops and equipment south to reinforce their position below Isola Bella, now under siege by the 4th Ranger Battalion.[55] Now in the Pantano Ditch, the lead companies of the 1st Battalion, F, E, and D, just under two hundred men, were in a line a quarter mile long. Pvt. Arnold "Pat" Davis, 1/E: "We went under the bridge over the Pantano Ditch and were discovered lying very still in the ditch by some German soldiers crossing the bridge above, very near dawn on the 30th."[56]

It would be about twenty minutes before the first of these Rangers would reach the Conca Road and slip across it. When they did, they crossed in sections, covering each other, able to cross only when there was a gap between south-bound German vehicles whose occupants still had no idea there were Rangers in their backyard. Once across the road, they slipped back into the Pantano Ditch and continued moving toward Cisterna. Following the ditch on the west side of the Conca Road until it ran out, the Rangers found themselves in an open field, with only a few trees and scattered houses dotting the landscape, offering almost no cover except for spotty canebrakes along some of the drainage ditches. Dobson believed they were observed in the road crossing. SGM Robert Ehalt, 1st Battalion, was also certain that he saw Germans watching the Rangers cross the Conca Road because at the same time he saw a German vehicle pull out of a barn and head north along a farm road.[57] Ranger Cpl. Ken Markham, 1/F, lead scout:

> It was just breaking day when the action started. As we were coming out of that large ditch [the Pantano] . . . you could see something in the distance, but [due to darkness and fog] you could not make out what it was. You could see movement, like a vehicle or a person, but you couldn't identify what you were looking at. That's the way it was when we hit that road, coming out of the ditch.

> You had to be careful crossing the road. You're standing there in the dark, and here comes a convoy of German trucks; this German truck goes by from here to that wall over there [gesturing], the German paratroopers in the back smoking and whatever. Laughing and kidding each other, having a good time, they went on by. When the truck got far enough away for a section of Rangers to get across the road, here comes the next truck. That slowed us down considerably.[58]

Cpl. William Zartman had joined the Rangers just before the mountain fighting at Venafro, but Shunstrom had trained him to fight aggressively. Zartman:

> At one point, we came to a dirt road that ran across the ditch we were in, and we were able to hear the sound of a motor vehicle coming in our direction. Dobson motioned for everyone to be quiet and to stay low in the ditch. . . . A short time later, a lone German soldier on a motorcycle with a sidecar passed by and disappeared in the darkness to our right. . . . We [slipped] across the Conca Road and went back into the ditch on the northwest side of the road. We knew then that we had crossed the German frontline and were now in an uncharted area where we had no idea of what we might expect.[59]

0530 HOURS (ESTIMATED): 1ST BATTALION

The point men of company 1/F came upon a lone sentry sitting under an olive tree. Pvt. Judson B. Luckhurst, 1/F, attempted to silence the sentry, who broke loose and let out a scream that awakened the Germans.[60] Maj. Dobson was afraid of getting cut off behind enemy lines with no way to escape and quickly assessed his options: "It was quite clear at that time that the attacks on our flanks were at least two miles behind us from the tracer firings plainly visible. Obviously we had run into a much greater enemy force than G-2 had predicted. My object was to turn at that point, take out the enemy artillery, and sweep what enemy lay between us and our line of departure in the process. Unfortunately, I could not establish communications with Darby, so we had no alternative but to go into our objective—Cisterna."[61]

Cpl. Markham, 1/F, cleared the ditch and crossed the Conca Road just as it was breaking day: "I got to a paved road and made it across with bullets all around me sounding like angry hornets. I hit an olive orchard . . . and it was loaded with Germans in foxholes."[62]

0540 HOURS (JOURNAL): RANGER FORCE COMMAND POST

"Heavy shelling close to [Ranger Force] CP."[63]

0554 HOURS (ESTIMATED): THE 1ST BATTALION ASSAULT

Cpl. William D. Zartman, 1/F: "When the first light of dawn appeared in the eastern sky we realized that time was running out on us. . . . As we climbed out of the ditch and moved forward, we suddenly realized that this . . . was in fact a German bivouac . . . and German soldiers were sleeping in foxholes all around us."[64] Dobson's worst fears were realized. He could not make radio contact; he had no artillery support and no machine guns. He had no one he could contact on his left or his right. His companies were all alone on relatively flat ground with little to no cover, deep behind enemy lines, mostly still in single-file, which made control very difficult, and the protection of darkness was gone. Maj. Dobson made the most important decision of his life. On his order the infiltration was about to change into an assault. Rangers from Company F recalled hearing Maj. Dobson say, "Men, get your knives out, there's work to be done." Zartman: "The major drew his combat knife, and motioned for others to do the same."[65] Maj. Dobson ordered 1st Lt. James G. Fowler, commander of 1/F, to race for Cisterna, wanting to get there quickly before full daylight. Maj. Dobson: "Approximately six hundred yards from the outskirts of Cisterna, we passed what appeared to be a German bivouac area. At this point things begin to pop. A German got up from a foxhole and began to scream when he saw us. In the ensuing melee, using only knives and bayonets, forward elements of the First Battalion killed approximately one hundred Germans as they tried to get out of their foxholes."[66] Company 1/F led the assault toward Cisterna, running up trails, skirting the home where the Calcabrini family lived.* It was a two-story, defensible stone farmhouse, about two thousand feet southwest south of

* The name of the family is "Calcabrini," but the Rangers, and subsequently numerous authors, called it the "Calcaprini House." When quoting Rangers, I use the name "Calcaprini," as they did. Otherwise, I use the correct name, "Calcabrini." It was an aid station and became the forward headquarters of the 1st Ranger Battalion.

Cisterna, a key landmark. Pfc. Raymond Sadoski realized he was in the midst of foxholes occupied by a German unit that was bivouacked there. But he noticed something unusual; heavy wooden boxes were scattered across the field. Wondering what the boxes were for, he lifted one only to see a sleeping German underneath, and realized the boxes were covering German foxholes. Sadoski knifed the German, but not before the enemy soldier pulled a Luger and fired off a round, arousing the rest of his neighbors.[67] The bivouac area that 1/F raced through had a self-propelled gun with four guards posted. These were taken out by the point men of Company F. Dobson: "We continued for about 400 yards more and tried to reach a small ridge along the edge of town. At this point, Sgt. [Robert] Heiser of A Company crawled forward and knocked out three successive machine gun posts by creeping up, tossing a grenade, then going in with a bayonet."[68]

First Lt. James G. Fowler, CO of 1/F, led the point of the attack. When the battalion proceeded through the enemy bivouac area, the enemy opened intense fire. During the ensuing gunfight Fowler personally killed ten enemy soldiers while leading his company into a firing position. Tech/5 Leon S. Paxton, Pfc. Robert E. Jones, and 1st Lt. Harry Van Schriver were right behind Fowler racing toward Cisterna, trying to reach a building that they later named the "White House," on the southern edge of Cisterna, near the intersection of the Conca and Ponte Rotta roads. In the course of this action, Lt. Fowler was struck in the legs by a burst of enemy machine gun fire and dropped his radio. Attempting to recover it by crawling from a depression where he had found cover, he was struck by a second burst of enemy machine gun fire and killed instantly.[69] Just short of the White House, the other three Rangers were also shot down. Pfc. Jones was setting up his BAR to fire when he was killed. Paxton's body was never found.[70]

S/Sgt. Arthur Schrader, 1/F, made it across the Ponte Rotta Road and occupied a shed near the White House. This offered a good firing position for several Rangers until German automatic weapon fire raked the shed, and the Rangers had to scramble for cover, digging in for a long day. Intense fire from the White House stopped the 1st Battalion's advance for good. This was as close as the Rangers got to Cisterna.[71] Zartman, 1/F, described the race:

> [Maj. Dobson] pointed to a German half-track off to the side of the vineyard and motioned for his scout and me to take care of it. . . . I tossed white phos-

> phorous grenades under the half-track . . . then ran a short distance to the small two-story building ahead of us. Daylight was coming fast, and it was light enough for us to make out houses ahead. The volume of small arms fire increased rapidly behind us . . . in a matter of minutes mortar fire was exploding very close to our position behind the house.[72]

Suddenly Zartman and a Ranger, whom Zartman identified as a lieutenant, began taking fire from a tree line behind them, and they threw themselves into a shallow drainage ditch next to where they had been standing. The Germans fired a few more shots, and Zartman, whose head was right next to the lieutenant's boot, thought, "What am I going to do next?" Zartman tapped on the boot and asked if the lieutenant was okay. He then pulled on the boot, asking if he was okay, but he got no answer. The lieutenant was dead. Zartman didn't want to die in that ditch (probably the Anima Sante), so he made a mad dash for the corner of a house and found a number of wounded.[73]

First Sgt. Frank Mattivi, 1/F, and other noncommissioned officers took command of the company and continued the fight. Capt. Frederick Saam, 1/Hq., joined them at some point and stayed with them for part of the fight. Rangers from 1/E and 1/D moved toward Cisterna and formed a rough line to the west of 1/F, just south of the Ponte Rotta Road.[74] By now, the rest of the 1st Battalion had crossed the Conca Road and was hiding in the Pantano Ditch on the west side of the road. The sound of gunfire traveled a long way in the early morning dampness, alerting the enemy that they were under a major attack. Coming out of the ditch, Company 1/C moved forward, following 1/D, while 1/B eliminated enemy snipers in the Calcabrini house. Company 1/A then swung to the left of 1/B and 1/C, and all three companies lined up just short of the Ponte Rotta Road and west of 1/D and 1/E to form a defensive line for the 1st Battalion.[75]

0540 HOURS (ESTIMATED): THE 3RD RANGER BATTALION

When firing broke out in the early dawn, the entire 3rd Battalion was still strung out down the Pantano Ditch behind the 1st Battalion and east of the Conca Road. Company commanders, trained to run toward the fire, led their men quickly toward the front. Sgt. Carl Lehmann, 3/C, confirmed that the 3rd Rangers were still in the Pantano Ditch when the firing began. He thought Maj. Miller was ahead of him in the ditch but he did not know how far.[76] The 3rd Battalion's march up the Pantano Ditch was led by Company 3/A, followed by Companies 3/B and 3/C. Maj. Alvah Miller, commanding 3/Hq., was marching with 3/C, about midway in his battalion, and roughly a half mile short of the Conca Road, when the first shots were fired. Deep in the ditch and unable to contact anyone by radio, Miller and his 3/Hq. company began moving quickly up the Pantano Ditch toward the sound of the gunfire, passing the other 3rd Battalion Rangers.[77] It probably took Maj. Miller and his 3rd Headquarters detachment at least fifteen minutes to cover that distance, running in the ditch on wet, uneven ground, made slippery by the boots of hundreds of Rangers who had already passed.

Miller ordered his two lead companies to go forward and cross the Conca Road, and for the time being he held the other four companies in reserve to guard the rear. Miller ordered Lt. William L. Newnan, commanding company 3/B, to attack stone farm buildings on the west side of the Conca Road from which enemy snipers were firing on the Rangers. A platoon from 3/A commanded by 2nd Lt. Paul W. Johnston was attached to Lt. Newnan's small task force.[78]

The mortar section and part of 2nd Lt. Clarence Meltesen's platoon were put on hold well back in the Pantano Ditch near the rest of 3/Hq. In the same action, Capt. Miller sent part of 3/Hq. to proceed up the Pantano with orders to cross over the Conca Road.[79] Meltesen explained what happened as the patrol reached the Conca Road: "Still in the right ditch, [the Rangers] ambushed a Volkswagen scout car, with three staff officers . . . they stopped, acting as if to check and verify something. The driver dismounted, pretending to check his tires, while he checked the ditches . . . a fusillade took out the driver and the officers with the motor still running. Then the platoon moved across the road into the left ditch and the canebrake [on the west side of the Conca Road]."[80]

Tech/Sgt. Robert H. Halliday, 3/Hq., was then detailed to take a small headquarters group and monitor the Germans seen mounting an attack on the left rear (southwest) of the battalion area.[81]

0600 HOURS (ESTIMATED): 3RD BATTALION COMMANDER, MAJ. ALVAH MILLER, KILLED

The sound of nearby gunfire told Miller it was critical that he make radio contact with Ranger Force Headquarters. He was located near the bridge where the Via Enrico Toti crosses the Pantano Ditch,* accompanied by 1st Sgt. John S. Rembecki, Tech/Sgt. Robert Halliday, Communication Sgt. Clarence W. Eineichner, and Tech/5 Dominick Poliseno, all from 3rd Battalion Headquarters. Also on the scene were 1st Sgt. Arlo Fox, 3/C, Capt. James Larkin, 3/E, and 2nd Lt. Earnest R. Jensen, 3/D. Sgt. Clarence Eineichner, 3/Hq., an eyewitness, describes what happened next:

> Just prior to the break of dawn, Major Miller, 1st Sergeant John Rembecki, Tech Sergeant Robert Halliday, Tech/5 Dominick Poliseno, Major Miller's bodyguard and me, ascended from the drainage ditch onto a farm access road [Via Enrico Toti] that was perpendicular to a highway, I assumed was highway 7.† [Eineichner was mistaken; it was the Conca Road.] The deadly silence, fog and haze that was affecting our vision, gave us a false impression that the enemy was not in our immediate area. Thereby, caution was not foremost in our minds as we walked five abreast down the access road. As we broke out of the fog, we observed a self-propelled artillery vehicle less than a hundred feet in front of us, at the road junction of the highway [the Conca Road] and the access road [we were on]. The barrel . . . began to traverse down on us.[82]

Meltesen was on the scene within a few minutes: "Major Miller, standing on the shoulder of the road, was trying to raise Ranger Force Headquarters on his radio, but the call was never completed. Moving along the ditch to higher ground, Tech/5 Dominick Poliseno spotted a German tank parked on the side of the road and shouted, 'Hit the dirt.' Maj. Miller, totally wrapped up trying to make radio contact, missed the alert and was instantly decapitated by a direct shot from the tank's main gun."[83]

The shell exploded not far past where Miller had been standing, its shrapnel mortally wounding Lt. Jensen, who died later that morning. Some Rangers stated that the shell did not explode, but a tank round, fired at point-blank range and traveling at 1,800 to 2,600 feet per second, depending on the size of the shell, would have detonated less than seven one hundredths of a second af-

* Col. Darby authorized his commanders to use their radios if necessary once they crossed a road that ran east from Isola Bella, and I believe this was Via Enrico Toti.

† Highway 7 and the Conca Road are roughly parallel, so from Eineichner's description of where Miller was killed, it could not have been on either of those roads but on a road perpendicular to them. That would have had to have been the farm road that is now named Via Enrico Toti.

ter it was fired. Hearing the gun fire and the shell explode would have sounded like one explosion to the human ear.

Germans in the armored vehicle crossing the bridge on the Via Enrico Toti had probably spotted the Rangers in the ditch, and after clearing the bridge, they probably stopped and reversed the gun turret to be able to fire on the Rangers when they exposed themselves. Further evidence that Miller was killed on the Via Enrico Toti is the fact that Rangers reported heavy enemy traffic headed south on the Conca Road, eliminating the possibility that Maj. Miller's group could have been walking along the edge of that road. There would have been no road signs to identify the road, and the first glimpse of the morning sun was just beginning to show on the horizon. Capt. Jim Larkin, executive officer of the 3rd Battalion, was standing close to Maj. Miller: "[Miller] and I were . . . suddenly confronted at very close range by a German tank. The tank had pulled out onto a small bridge, and then swung its turret around. . . . There was an ear splitting detonation. I survived. Al was not so quick. His head was blown off."[84]

Larkin broke radio silence, telling Capt. Warren Evans, 3/F, to come forward with his company.[85] Half of 3/E was already forward and near the Conca Road. Larkin then sent out a squad that knocked out the tank with a "sticky bomb."[86] Tech/5 Clarence Eineichner, 3/Hq., described the aftermath of Miller's death: "Immediately after Major Miller was killed, the self-propelled [tank] was disabled. It seemed like the shot that killed Miller woke up the entire German army. All hell broke loose. Simultaneously and in unison, weapons all around us began firing. While the men in a large vacant field across the highway from our location were running for cover, the enemy was firing everything they had at them. Tracers were bouncing all over the place."[87] Larkin realized he had to get men forward and across the Conca Road, so they would not be trapped in the ditches. Tech/4 Edward Krise, 3/F, a medic (later a lieutenant colonel): "When Maj. Miller got killed, Capt. James Larkin, commanding 3/E, took over command of the 3rd Battalion. He sent for Capt. Bing Evans, commanding 3/F, to move up through the column and to join him immediately. No sooner than we got the company moved up, 1st Sergeant Ronald Kunkle, 3/F, was shot by a sniper and killed."[88]

Eineichner: "Realizing we couldn't do anything for Major Miller, his bodyguard removed his map case and some personal items. We moved him to the side of the road to prevent additional mutilation to his body."[89]

0615 HOURS (JOURNAL): DARBY TO 3RD DIVISION

Darby, obviously having no knowledge of what was happening near Cisterna: "Murray is having a hell of a time. There isn't any contact with my 1st and 3rd Battalions. I've got to get this road block out [that is holding up the 4th Battalion]."[90]

0622 HOURS (JOURNAL): DARBY

Col. Darby tried unsuccessfully to reach the 1st Battalion.[91]

0635 HOURS (JOURNAL): 4TH RANGER BATTALION

Someone reported American tanks moving up the road to Cisterna. Murray ordered companies 4/E and 4/F to make flanking attacks to try to break through the German strongpoints, but after advancing only a few hundred yards, both companies were pinned down. Historian Col. Robert Black: "Lt. Orin Taylor, CO of 4/E was killed along with Lt. Lewis B. Case, Jr., 4/F, who had just joined the battalion."[92] Altieri: "The 4th Battalion . . . suffered heavy casualties as it strove to breach the strong enemy walls of fire to link up with the 1st and 3rd battalions."[93] With every new assault, the Rangers' casualties mounted. Murray personally led one last assault on the right flank with Companies A and B. This too was repulsed, with heavy losses to the Rangers.

0635 HOURS (ESTIMATED): 3RD RANGER BATTALION RESPONDS

As the rest of the 3rd Battalion came up out of the ditch, they found themselves with little cover except for a canebrake to the west. There were small ditches and occasional stone farmhouses, most of which were hiding places for German snipers. Now with just enough light to see the landscape, Larkin rushed forward to attempt to locate Maj. Dobson, with no idea where he was.[94]

With Maj. Miller dead, 2nd Lt. Newnan's company, 3/B, took off west and north through a canebrake while 3/Hq. and one platoon of 3/C continued up the right side of the ditch.[95] Lt. Meltesen, 2nd Platoon leader of 3/C:

> I followed my company moving into the canebrake . . . and headed toward the line of contact. Another shower of mortar rounds came in and the mortar section ahead began to break up, moving out of the ditch trail to the right and

left. Before I made my move a round landed in the muck next to my left shoe and did not detonate. . . . T/4 Irvin I. Lingenfelter, 3/C, mortar squad leader, was killed in this action, probably by stray . . . artillery fire. That's when I took a sniper's round in the neck and returned to the platoon spitting blood. 1st. Lt. Wilbur Fulkerson, 3/F, took over the hunt for the sniper and medics field-dressed the wound, giving me a shot of morphine from a syrette in the aid package. I then passed out in a shallow ditch for a couple of hours.[96]

Tech/5 Mickey Romine, a medic in 3/Hq., recalled: "[We crossed a road] and entered a ditch [the Anima Sante] that had about two feet of mud and water in it. . . . When it started getting light, we were still about a mile from [Cisterna] . . . so, we left the canal and ran for the woods. . . . For almost two hours, it was like we were in a shooting gallery—they were totally surprised. . . . But then they got organized and the slaughter changed sides."[97]

Tech/5 Clarence Eineichner, 3/Hq., probably still in shock from Miller's killing and still not realizing exactly where he was:

Sergeant Rembecki, Sgt. Halliday, and I saw a beige two-story building on the other side of the highway. We headed for it, hoping it would provide us some protection which we did not have standing in the middle of the road. We discovered it was occupied by the enemy. . . . We relieved them of their weapons, and some other items we felt they did not need. We then ordered them to lay down in a depression in the yard at the front of the house.

In a distance to the northeast, I could see silhouettes of building roofs extending above the trees. Assuming the buildings were part of Cisterna under the control of the 1st Battalion, I left the beige house and headed toward those other buildings. Sergeants Rembecki and Halliday did not go with me. I entered a water-filled ditch [the Anima Sante] paralleling the left side of the highway and proceeded slowly up the ditch. Disabled vehicles, Ranger and enemy casualties were scattered along the road. I moved two Rangers from the water-filled ditch and placed them on the berm. . . . Across the road were five Rangers; lying motionless in a shallow ditch. I decided to join them, and then to continue on towards Cisterna.

Immediately after hitting the dirt, the area was sprayed with machine gun fire. I lay motionless for a few moments, took inventory of my extremities, everything seemed OK. I yelled to the others "Let's get out of here," then took

> off for a much larger ditch about fifty feet from our present location. When I reached the ditch, I looked back. The others had not moved. . . . Looking to a ditch adjacent to my new location, I discovered it was occupied by S/Sgt. Joseph Phillips, [3/C], plus an officer and an enlisted man. . . . To the west of my location was an old two-story building. Through the openings on the second floor that once were windows, I could see figures moving about. . . . Except for an occasional confrontation with the individuals in that old building, I was restricted to the ditch. Continued movement toward Cisterna was restricted by enemy action.[98]

In the 1st Battalion area, Dobson had no idea of the 3rd Battalion's location. To Dobson's immediate front and a few hundred yards away were heavy woods, in which were hidden three German self-propelled guns. To his left front German paratroopers were trying to infiltrate into the Ranger group and were taken under fire by the Rangers. Maj. Dobson instructed Cpl. Markham to go back and contact Maj. Alvah Miller to bring up the 3rd Battalion while Dobson set up his command post in the Calcabrini house.[99] Markham: "I came to a hedgerow, and I jumped over it and onto a dirt trail or road. There were five Germans right there. I reacted first and shot them with my Tommy gun and at the same time jumped into the bushes. Combat is like anything else, the first to react is the one who survives."[100] Markham made his way back, almost a mile, and met up with Sgt. Donald Burke, 3/D. Markham asked, "Where's Major Miller?" Burke pointed to a hole where an artillery shell made a direct hit, killing Maj. Alvah Miller.[101] Markham: "All I could see was arms and legs, and I headed back to my battalion. When I got back, they were just being slaughtered. I got into the ditch along the Conca Road, and I guess there might have been ten dead Rangers in there with me. . . . I had only one clip of ammunition left, but I needed to get back to Major Dobson to let him know that Major Miller had been killed."[102] German tanks were now running up and down the Ponte Rotta Road and the Conca Road, firing at anyone who moved. Trying to get back to Maj. Dobson, Markham dove into some cover and found himself next to Capt. Saam and Capt. Shunstrom.

Capt. Shunstrom: "The runner [Cpl. Markham] returned with the information that the 3rd Ranger Battalion had lost its . . . commander . . . killed by a shell from an enemy tank, but the 3rd Battalion was on its way up to establish contact with the First Ranger Battalion."[103]

0700 HOURS (DARBY): 1ST BATTALION, RADIO SILENCE BROKEN

Months later, Darby wrote: "About 0700 the 1st Battalion, following orders, broke radio silence. The commanding officer, Maj. Jack Dobson, reported that he was located in an open field about 800 yards south of Cisterna where three German self-propelled guns were giving him a good deal of trouble. The 3rd Battalion was strung out just east and to the rear of him. Daylight caught them in this exposed area immediately outside the town. . . . Dobson was slightly wounded; the commanding officer of the 3rd Battalion had been killed."[104]

0720 HOURS (JOURNAL): 4TH RANGER BATTALION

Darby ordered 2nd Lt. Otis Davey, commander of Cannon Company, to move up his half-tracks to attack the roadblock.[105] However, one of the half-tracks and an M10 tank destroyer ran over mines and were destroyed, while others bogged down in the wet fields.[106] Artillery could not be used due to the close-in fighting because it would have caused additional casualties among the Rangers. Not even the 83rd Chemical Mortar Battalion could support the 4th Rangers because the heavy base plates that supported the 4.2 inch mortars sank into the mud.[107] Pfc. Robert Harlow, 4/Cannon Company:

> We ran as fast as we could, firing our weapons, landing in the muddy ditches as . . . bullets whistled over our heads. Moving our half-track forward, we tried to get close enough to bring fire on the farmhouses and machine gun nests which were giving us so much trouble. Men were crawling on their knees and stomachs over and between dead bodies trying to keep as low as possible. We finally got the half-track in close enough to hit the farmhouse and the machine gun nests. Shortly thereafter, the men moved in throwing hand grenades and rapidly firing Tommy guns.[108]

Pvt. Louis Cashen, 4/C: "I was wounded that day and handed my rifle off to someone who had lost theirs. I figured since I was wounded, the other guy had a better chance. I still get choked up when I try to tell how hard we fought to rescue the 1st and 3rd Battalions."[109]

Second Lt. Max O. Fordham, 4/Hq., was storming a stone building under machine gun fire when he hit the deck for cover. His rifle went off, and he realized that he had shot himself in the leg. He would not accept a purple heart for his injuries.[110] Pfc. Raymond Boron, 4/A: "I was a BAR gunner in a company commanded by 1st Lt. Hubbard Powell. The Germans had fields of crisscross machine gun fire set up, so it was almost impossible to get through without getting hit."[111]

0720 HOURS (ESTIMATED): 1ST BATTALION COMMANDER, MAJ. JOHN DOBSON, SERIOUSLY WOUNDED

Back near Cisterna, Dobson and his runner came upon a German tank that was not running. Jumping up onto the rear of the tank, Dobson dropped a white phosphorus grenade down the hatch. The explosion detonated the tank's ammunition and sent a large chunk of armor plate into Maj. Dobson's behind, his second wound of the morning. Dobson, "I was thrown off the rear deck of the tank, severely wounded."[112] Lt. Norman Alloway, 1/A: "The tank blew into a million pieces. A piece of it hit Major Dobson."[113] The runner dressed Dobson's wounds, and the major was laid next to another burned-out German tank in a shallow ditch for cover before being carried to the battalion command post in the Calcabrini house.[114]

According to Shunstrom, after Dobson was seriously wounded, Dobson immediately turned over command of the 1st Battalion to him. From Shunstrom's Report of Action,* it appears that he then devised a plan of action, sending companies 1/C and 1/D on an enveloping movement to the right flank and holding 1/E in reserve. Companies 1/A, 1/B, and 1/F were given the mission of holding their position just south of the Ponte Rotta Road, with the 3rd Battalion in reserve. Shunstrom's stated plan was to use 1/C and 1/D to knock out the enemy machine guns holding up the advance, and then use the 3rd Battalion to attack through the 1st Battalion toward Cisterna. Shunstrom noted that there was heavy machine gun fire pouring into the Rangers' ranks all along the front.[115]

Events that happened next indicated there was confusion about who was in command of the 1st Battalion. Before 1/C and 1/D could deploy to the front, Capt. Frederick J. Saam, 1/Hq., returned from a patrol and changed Shunstrom's orders. Shunstrom:

* Shunstrom wrote the Report of Action. He was the first officer who returned to American lines after escaping from a brief captivity as a POW.

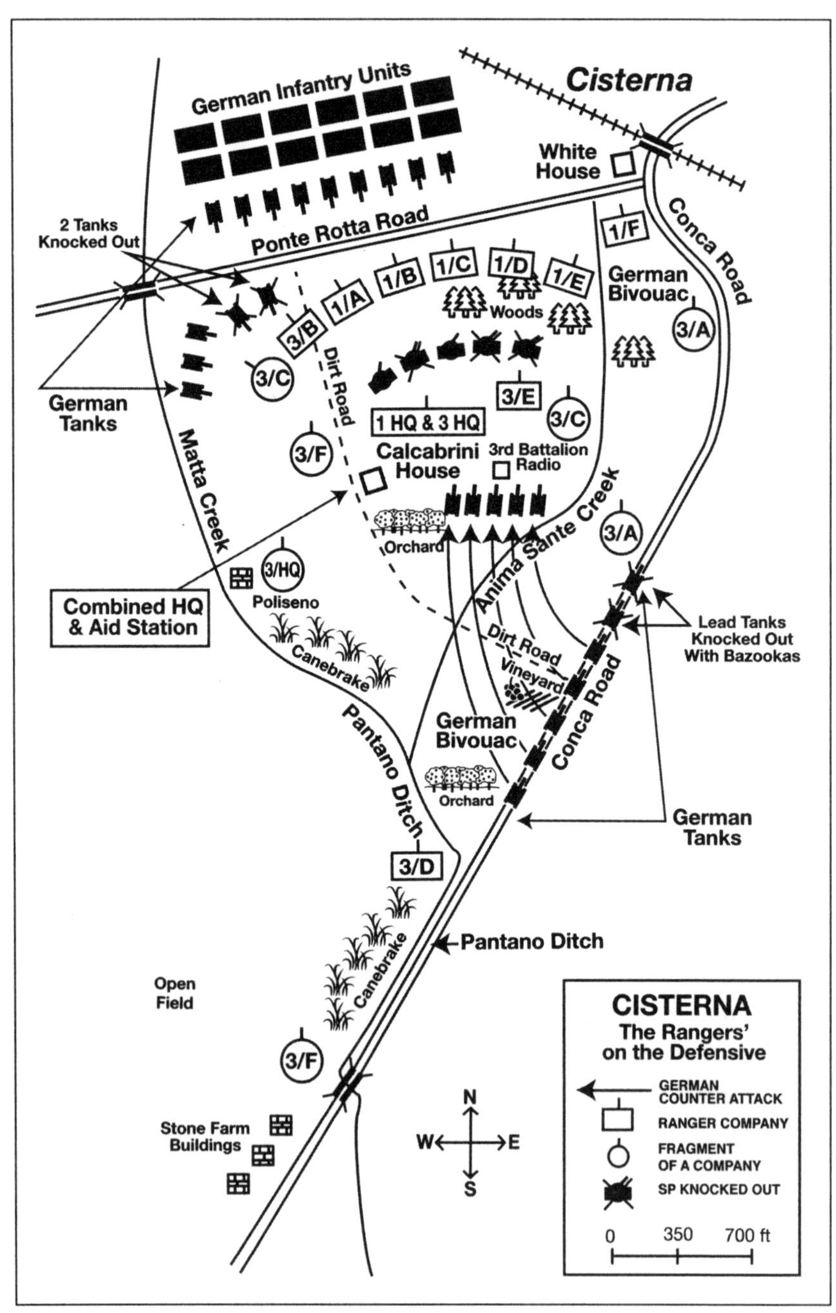

The Rangers on the Defensive

> Captain Saam . . . immediately took charge of both battalions. Saam took two companies of the Third Ranger Battalion and sent them to a position about three-hundred yards in our rear with a mission of closing the gap in the circle that we had formed and to dig in and hold at all costs. He informed Captain Shunstrom that C and D companies [of the 1st Battalion] had been unsuccessful in their enveloping movement to the right flank, and that he had ordered them to dig in and hold the ground that they had. This left four companies of the Third Ranger Battalion in the immediate vicinity of the command post in reserve. He then gave orders that the radio operator call back for reinforcements. A battalion aid station was set up in a building where the radio was kept about 25 yards from the command post position.[116]

0730 HOURS (ESTIMATED): THE GERMAN COUNTERATTACK

It was now daylight. German commanders, originally taken by surprise, were trying to figure out who was attacking them and the size of the attacking force. A few panzers began to move about. Within the next hour, more panzers, panzer grenadiers, and self-propelled guns were racing across the area trying to locate and exterminate the invading Rangers.[117]

First Lt. Gerald Simon, 1/B, and 1st Lt. Tom Magee, 1/D, ordered their men to dig in along a barbed wire fence south of the Ponte Rotta Road, though it offered little to no cover. Lt. Magee was wounded in this action. S/Sgt. Robert S. Hendrickson, 1/D, was shot through the chest and evacuated to the principal aid station in the Calcabrini house, where he died. Magee recovered and eventually wound up in Oflag 64, the German POW camp for officers.[118]

0740 HOURS (ESTIMATED): RANGERS GO ON DEFENSE

By now the Rangers realized that they had unknowingly walked into the midst of a massive German buildup and that they were surrounded and heavily outnumbered.[119] Companies 1/D and 1/E soon found themselves being attacked by German armor and tank-infantry units coming across the Ponte Rotta Road. These companies dug in, pinned down for the rest of the morning by small arms and mortar. Pfc. Zelly Dineen, 1/E: "When the firing started, I spotted a trench about twenty feet long and about three feet deep. Next to it was a

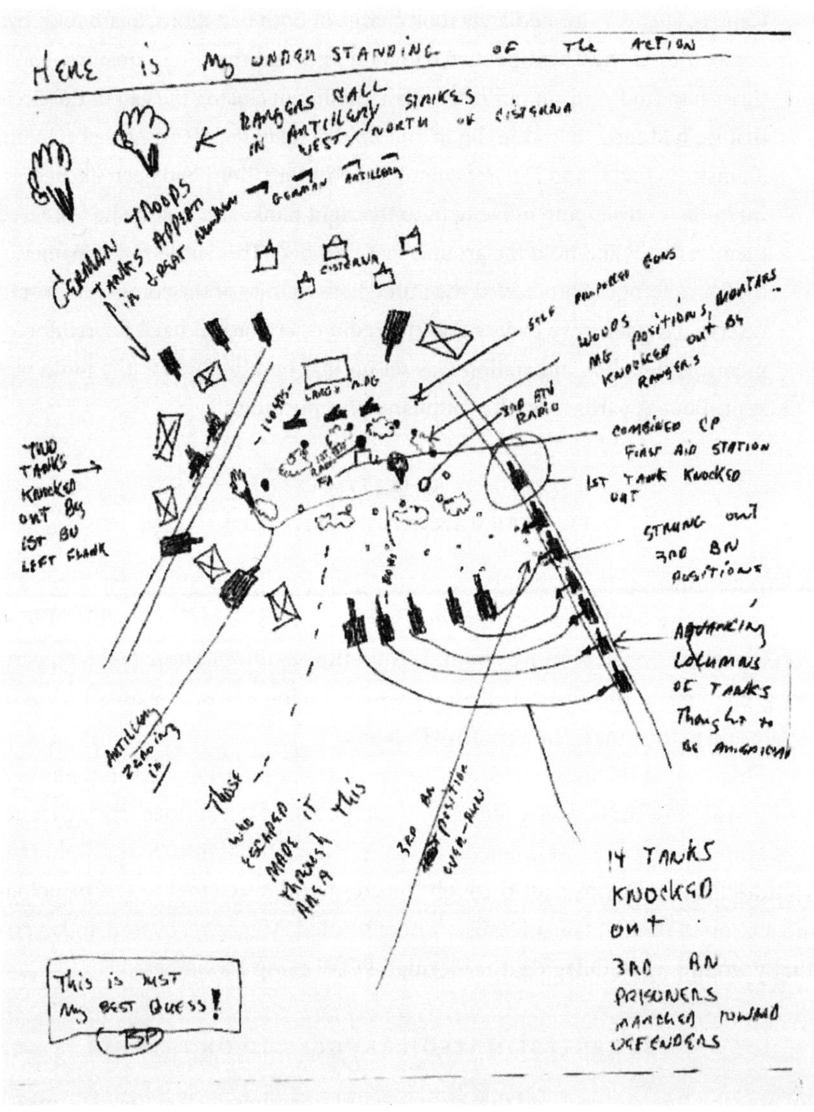

Cpl. John Giannopoulos's hand-drawn sketch of the Rangers on the defensive at Cisterna. The six rectangles with an "X" (for Infantry) represent the six companies of the 1st Ranger Battalion. The two roads aimed at Cisterna represent the Ponte Rotta Road and the Conca Road. The sketch is a close approximation of Ranger positions on the battlefield and confirms that the Rangers destroyed at least fourteen German tanks and other armored vehicles.

Cpl. John Giannopoulos, 1st Ranger Battalion, Company C.
Courtesy Jerry Giannopoulos.

shell hole with three Rangers in it huddled and hugging each other, but they wouldn't look up. They were scared to death. I figured they were some of the new men we had just gotten a few days before."[120] Things were happening fast and, with little command and control, the Ranger organization quickly unraveled. Rangers units were scattered and most men were no longer operating in organized units, but rather in squads or small groups of a few. There was no "front line," and the heavily outnumbered Rangers found themselves mixed up with German troops. Capt. Edward B. Kitchens Jr., CO of 3/C, reported that C Company ceased to exist as a coordinated unit soon after initial contact.[121]

Pfc. Raymond Sadoski, 1/F, rounded the corner of a stone farmhouse and saw stairs going down into a cellar. He investigated and found a lot of ammunition down below. He threw in a grenade and ran. Before he got far, he heard a huge explosion. He later said, "The whole world blew up, Holy Moly! I didn't know what the hell happened." Large shells were cooking off. Sadoski dove onto the ground with pieces of casing and shells falling all around:

> So, I'm lying there face down with my arms close to my body and a damn shell came down and hit me right in the back. I couldn't move my legs. I was paralyzed. So, I'm layin' there with bullets flying all around, and this guy walked up near me yelling, "Hey Sadoski, start shootin." It was 1st Battalion SGM Robert Ehalt. Ehalt: "You got hit in the back by an empty shell." I thought I got hit by shrapnel. Ehalt: "Crawl over to that house over there. We're going to set up headquarters in there."[122]

Sadoski, probably embarrassed by Ehalt's bravery when he realized that he was not really hurt, crawled into the Calcabrini house and spotted a wounded Ranger laying there with an M1 Garand. "Gimmie your gun," yelled Sadoski, who then charged upstairs to see what he could see from a second-floor window. The aiming sight had been shot off the rifle, but even so, Sadoski dispatched a German soldier who was shooting at him.[123]

0800 HOURS (DARBY): DARBY CONTACTS 1ST BATTALION

After an hour of disrupted communications, Darby made radio contact with the 1st Battalion, but does not say who he spoke with. He was told that the men were fighting to gain a foothold in the outskirts of the town near the railroad embankment and were receiving heavy fire from enemy artillery.[124] Snipers kept the Rangers pinned down, preventing them from occupying the stone farmhouses that dotted the area. Pvt. Arthur F. Wilson, 1/D: "My outfit, D Company of the 1st Battalion, was right in the middle of the action. German tanks were hiding in buildings, and the buildings seemed to come apart as the tanks moved forward to attack us. The self-propelled 88s and tanks came out firing. Also, a lot of machine guns opened up on us."[125]

First Sgt. Frank Mattivi, 1/F, performed an act of heroism by climbing aboard the back of a tank and dropping an incendiary grenade (probably white phosphorous) into the open turret just as the tank was hit on the opposite side by a bazooka round fired by another Ranger. Mattivi was blown off the tank. Flipping head over heels, he hit the ground running, unhurt.[126]

Pfc. Sadoski, 1/F, was a witness to Mattivi's feat: "Pretty soon I saw this tank. And I said, geez, American tanks broke through; this is great. And so, I'm looking at that tank gun, and that tanker is bringing that 88 gun up to point right at me. And boy, I can't move. I thought I was like in a dream, sometimes you can't run or nothin'. And he's going to blow me right to pieces, you know. And this Ranger jumped on it and dropped a hand grenade down the hatch. Saved my ass, man."[127]

Cpl. Ben W. Mosier, 1/C: "When it got light, we saw a building with trees around it. Behind it was one tank, and when we saw it, we cheered. We thought it was ours. We were not seeing very well, and then it opened up on us."[128]

0815 HOURS (ESTIMATED): 1ST BATTALION

Second Lt. Norman Alloway, 1/A: "Most of my platoon stayed together. We moved to the left of the Calcaprini House and . . . hastily digging slit trenches, we got cover just in time. Using a bazooka and grenades we fought off another German tank that rolled through our area."[129]

Pfc. Dineen, 1/E:

> I was very close to a brick and stone wall about six feet tall and was watching a farmhouse where some Rangers were holed up and appeared to be surrounded. Minutes later a huge tank came slowly around the wall toward us. A guy next to me ran towards the tank and stuck an explosive against the side. The tank passed within three feet of me, went about another thirty feet, and then exploded. Pieces of the tank were coming down all over and one of the Rangers got hit with a piece of it. It looked like one guy was trying to crawl out of the tank, but there was so much smoke I couldn't see well enough to shoot, so I took off back towards Cisterna and passed that same shell hole with those three Rangers still sitting there hugging each other. They had not moved during all this time.[130]

0900 HOURS (ESTIMATED): GERMAN TANKS AND INFANTRY WORK TOGETHER

Even this late in the morning visibility was limited by fog due to the wet ground. German infantry began to get organized. Armed with automatic weapons, the Germans were coming up the Conca Road and began encircling the Rangers using fire and movement. This blocked any attempt for the Rangers to withdraw or link up with the 4th Battalion, which the Rangers still expected to arrive. Many of the Rangers, new to combat, were paralyzed with fear and didn't know what to do.

By this time Meltesen had awakened from his morphine nap and had rejoined elements of 3/C that were clearing buildings when they spotted two German armored vehicles, probably self-propelled guns, coming at them from around one of the buildings. Rangers hugged the dirt while trying to see what the self-propelled guns were doing. Lt. Paul Johnston, 3/A, tossed a grenade into the open rear of a self-propelled gun, destroying it.[131] Two German flak wagons now approached the Rangers' positions from the left rear. Lt. Newnan called on his mortar section, which dropped a shell into the crew area of one of them, knocking it out. As the other flak wagon changed directions, Tech/5 James O'Reilly, 3/B, ambushed it with two grenades, killing the crew.[132]

Companies A, B, and part of C of the 3rd Battalion were fully engaged but operating in small groups. Reacting from training, S/Sgt. Wayne Ruona, 3/C, climbed onto the deck of another tank that was stopped on the Conca Road just south of the bridge over the Pantano Ditch. He dropped a white phosphorous grenade into the turret, taking that tank out of action. Other tanks were firing into the stream beds and ditches as they passed along the road.[133] Dozens of fights were in progress all over the area as Rangers engaged the Germans, singly and in small groups. Rangers from 3/B were clearing nearby farm buildings of snipers and machine gunners. Lt. Meltesen:

> Lt. Newnan, now commanding 3/B, had worked out with Lt. Paul Johnston a method of joint operation. Lt. Johnston had pulled his unit back to the [Conca] road to reorganize. . . . A portion of the company had moved forward with 1st Sergeant Donald McCollam. . . . McCollam kept on with assembling 3/B men and sending them on missions of support and attack. He led one group to seize a building in the nick of time and gunned down the German platoon arriving to do the same thing. . . .
>
> T/Sgt. Robert H. Halliday and six 3/Hq. personnel found a German infantry attack forming to the south beyond the nearby outbuildings. The Germans were armed with automatic weapons, showing considerable skill in fire and movement, and blocking any orderly withdrawal or linkup via Isola Bella with the 4th Ranger Battalion.[134]

Lt. Earnest Jensen, 3/D, wounded when Maj. Miller was killed, would die from his wounds. Meltesen: "The death of Lt. Jensen left the company in charge of 2nd Lt. David L. Bennett who was now seriously wounded. 1st Sergeant Burke had understood the mission given to Lt. Jensen, that 3/D would handle security of the right rear sector."[135] Cpl. George W. "Jack" Hall, 3/D: "There was water in the ditch where we took cover. The sides of the ditch had slippery slopes and we had trouble keeping our footing. I got shot in the right knee, and to survive I stayed in the ditch, firing and moving. We began taking ammunition from casualties, but I had a hard time finding ammo for my Tommy gun."[136]

Capt. Jim Larkin and a few Rangers seized a farmhouse to seal off a critical gap between 3/B and 3/F. One section of Rangers headed toward the house for protection. Germans, seeing them moving, fired on them with artillery, killing two Rangers. The others raced toward the Calcabrini house.[137] Lt. Meltesen ran into Capt. Beverly Miller, commanding 1/E, who directed him to use what was left of his platoon to cover the right open flank of the 1st Battalion. Meltesen: "Within ten minutes after our talk, Miller was severely wounded by a burst of machine gun fire that practically sheared off his left arm. He was in extreme pain."[138] Pvt. Arnold E. Davis, 1/E, was standing by Beverly Miller when he was hit. As Miller was being carried off the field he passed the word, without being too explicit, that Rangers should start looking for a way to withdraw. Davis:

> Our company was near the point of this offensive to capture Cisterna. . . . Just then, [Capt. Beverly Miller] my company commander . . . took a couple of machine gun bullets in his arm. Carrying his arm in the other hand, we made it to the [Calcabrini] house.
>
> Bev Miller went into the house to lay down. He was losing a lot of blood. . . . My company commander was out of action, as were other company commanders. Radio communication with Darby, who was located near a stone farmhouse several miles away, failed early in the operation. The 3rd Division artillery fire was nowhere to be seen, nor were our tanks or tank-destroyers anywhere about. We were all alone on that fatal field, with dead and wounded lying about.[139]

First Lt. William Cool took the lead of Company 1/E after Capt. Miller was wounded. Realizing the end was near, Cool decided to lead a withdrawal of

1/E from the field if it was still possible. Meltesen promised Cool's platoon ten minutes of covering fire for an escape attempt. Meltesen: "All I could think to say to them was, whatever happens, stick together."[140] When the Rangers ran out of ammunition, some men tried to escape, but with the flat ground and no cover it was nearly impossible. Dobson: "The Germans had already shot the wounded men left in the ditch."[141] When there was a lull in the fighting, Pvt. Davis moved around the area and along the route the company had followed coming into the position. He was the only Ranger to report a slackening in the enemy fire. Davis eventually escaped around noon and returned to Ranger Force Headquarters via the ditches.[142]

1045 HOURS (LOG OF ACTION): DARBY TALKS TO KITCHENS BY RADIO

By radio, Darby assured Kitchens, who was in the Calcabrini house, that friendly tanks would soon be moving up the Conca Road.[143] At about this time Lt. Meltesen, 3/C, observed a German flak wagon firing all four guns in his direction from the southwest. Enemy shells were streaming overhead fifteen feet off the ground. The Calcabrini house was taking a pasting. Meltesen dove for cover behind a slight rise in the ground and ran into 1st Sgt. McCollam from 3/B.[144] Meltesen, 3/C: "Sergeant Major Kenneth C. Munro, 3/Hq., arrived on the scene but was unable to tell me where [the other platoon of company 3/C] was located. . . . I then went back on the dirt trail to isolate the sniper that was pegging away at our backs from the orchard below the Calcaprini House. I met 1st Lt. Frank H. Corbin, 3/C, and sent him to join my platoon."[145]

Tech/5 Red Gilbert, 1/F, handled the mortar for his company and directed fire at the Conca/Ponte Rotta Road junction until they ran out of ammunition. The mortar men then became riflemen and helped hold the company position. Gilbert noticed a Volkswagen scout car arriving in the area, with the Germans taking note of the Ranger locations. Gilbert next checked out a deserted German command post, answering the ringing phone in his best German. From the other end came, "Who is this?" Gilbert left the phone dangling and took off.[146]

Second Lt. William L. Newnan, commanding 3/B, replacing Lt. William Musegades, 3/B, who had been wounded by shrapnel the day before the mission, returned the fire of a German flak wagon. Tech/5 James P. O'Reilly, 3/B, destroyed it with a sticky grenade: "I threw a sticky grenade but it rolled off. I threw another and it landed inside the gun platform. . . . It was an awful mess."[147]

One platoon of 3/F, pulling right-rear security, protecting against an enemy attack from the south, set up a roadblock on the Conca Road, but they were getting hit with German mortar shells.[148] They held back the Germans advancing from the south for several hours until they were captured. Meltesen:

> S/Sgt. Wayne Ruona, 3/C, reassembled his platoon of 3/C between the dirt road and the [Conca] Road. He came forward to speak with 1st Sgt. McCollam, 3/B. They met 2nd Lt. Paul Johnston, 3/A, who told them that the 1st Battalion was pinned down and that he could not advance until they did. Ruona returned to his unit. He observed the 3/D platoon moving forward in the right side [of the] Anima Sante ditch and come under enfilade fire from a German machine gun positioned on the rooftop of a farm building. The artillery observer from 3/C dropped his radio battery pack as he dodged incoming artillery and mortars as the Rangers first came under fire, and he had no way to call in protective artillery fire against the enemy machine gun.[149]

With so much enemy fire coming from all directions, the Rangers tried to consolidate along the south side of the Ponte Rotta Road. German tanks and armored vehicles counterattacked the Rangers from the rear, sometimes overrunning the Rangers' positions. Despite that, the Rangers continued to knock the tanks out with bazookas and sticky grenades. Dobson, speaking years after the Rangers' daring tank battles: "During the ensuing melee we knocked out twenty German tanks and self-propelled guns with bazookas and sticky grenades."[150]

Company 3/B moved a hundred yards farther forward toward Cisterna, until three tanks, at first thought to be American, came up the Conca Road firing into the ditch they were in. Gunner Tech/5 Richard Glasscock, 3/A, with the group, manned a rocket launcher. He and his loader, a Native American named Tech/5 Thomas Bearpaw, 3/A, waited until the tanks passed. When they saw an opportunity for a good shot, they blew up one with a bazooka rocket to the rear end. First Lt. Charles Palumbo and 2nd Lt. Johnston, both 3/A, knocked out another vehicle, and Tech/5 O'Reilly, 3/B, blew up another flak wagon with sticky grenades.[151] Sgt. Thomas B. Fergen, 1/D, also observed the tanks, spaced about a hundred feet apart, coming up the Conca Road and swinging into the field where the Rangers were scattered: "The tanks caused most of the trouble. I was in a field with the rest of my men when the tanks moved in. They came from Highway No. 7 [actually the Conca Road], swinging into the field, racing after us. You could run about twenty yards and then hit the ground. If you waited longer, they got you. They got three next to me with a direct hit."[152]

First Sgt. George Kopanda, with company 3/F at the far south end of the Ranger column, still in the Pantano Ditch:

> Our companies . . . held our positions as best as possible, firing our bazookas and mortars at tanks and Germans attacking our rear. They zeroed in on the canal proper with their artillery and machine guns. In the meantime, our medics placed the wounded men that they recovered into the canal [canal bank] approximately 100 yards from the last man; this was the only place the wounded men could be attended to, and they were also being shelled.
>
> Our communications between companies was almost nil. Most of the radios got wet in the canal . . . our Company was doing fine holding the enemy back, but we were slowly running out of ammunition as our mortars and bazookas were already expended. The German machine gunners were firing at a professional pace from two to five hundred yards away. Their bullets came into the canal proper, which was anywhere from ten to twelve feet from ground level. Their fire was very effective at killing a few men, which hampered our travel in the canal.[153]

As the Rangers began to arrange positions on the south side of the Ponte Rotta Road, the Germans set up their main line north of the Ponte Rotta Road all the way to the railroad embankment in Cisterna. German infantry with machine guns and mortars were attacking Ranger positions all along the road, keeping the Rangers pinned down on the south side with nowhere to go or hide.[154]

Pfc. Dineen, 1/E, crawling along and firing, trying to get back to his company:

> I ran into another 2nd Lieutenant, can't remember who, and I saw one dead German. The Jerry had a P-38 pistol still in his hand. I took the P-38 in my right hand, had my M-1 in my left hand, and went back towards one of the buildings. The town was across some tracks, but I could not get across. I looked

> up the road and saw one of our medics shot in both legs and both arms. Then I ran into another 2nd Lieutenant and we crawled down into some bushes. The lieutenant gave me a cigarette, but I didn't smoke, I chewed. Bullets were snapping all around and I took a bullet through both cheeks, so I just stayed down.[155]

S/Sgt. Arthur Schrader, 1/F, a crack shot among the Rangers: "I . . . located the M/G [machine gun]; I waited for the pop-up target. I shot and heard the bullet hit a helmet. Another M/G opened up;—same thing. After several more targets, the first gun opened up again with the same result. . . . All told that day I am sure of 11 head shots."[156]

1115 HOURS (LOG OF ACTION): DARBY TO KITCHENS

Darby: "We [4th Ranger Battalion] are working our way up slowly but surely. Hold on give them everything you've got . . . hold on."[157]

MEDICS ARE SWAMPED

Ranger medics were the heroes of the wounded Rangers on 30 January, as most of the Rangers who were not killed were wounded. Meltesen: "When the Germans came, [we] thought all the wounded would be shot, as was reported to be the German practice on the eastern front."[158] The 3rd Battalion aid station was located approximately twenty-five meters east of the Calcabrini house. Tech/5 Mickey Romine, 3/Hq.: "[Tech/5 Alvin D. Ezzell (nick-named Easy), 3/Hq., and another medic and I] set up in an aid station in a rock building, and it was full of wounded. I looked through a window and saw a German slipping up toward the window with a hand grenade. I took my .45 and shot him in the face. I have shot that man a thousand times in my dreams."[159]

Capt. Gordon Keppel, 3rd Battalion surgeon, had an organization of thirty litter bearers who braved bullets and shells to give aid, mostly in the form of morphine. The biggest killer among the wounded was shock, resulting from blood loss. Morphine, which helped with the pain and fear, came in the form of small syrettes that were jabbed into a person through the clothing. Battlefield wounds were nasty, and about all the medics could do was stop the bleeding and give pain medication.[160] Pvt. Clifford J. Kimbler, a green recruit and medic, was unable to cope with the horrors of the day until Dr. Keppel gave him courage. Kimbler: "I guess I was shell shocked and half crazy. I was told to go out and pick up one of the wounded boys, and he was so badly chewed up I couldn't stand to look at him. When I told the captain, he said to me, 'I hate to use the word, but the job you are doing is sacred.' He talked a little more, and then I went out and brought in that boy."[161]

As Capt. Keppel was moving about the battlefield tending wounded, he turned the corner of a building where medics were directing him toward the most severely hurt. Making a wrong turn, he and his assistant were captured by the Germans. A rumor later spread that Capt. Keppel had been executed, shot in the face by a German officer for failing to leave his patients after he was captured. The rumor was the result of a story, "Rangers Died Fighting at Dawn," published in *Stars and Stripes Weekly* on 18 March 1944, that was repeated by numerous published authors who all worked from the same material. The story circulated for years until Dr. Keppel surfaced at a Ranger reunion.[162]

Ranger medics took Capt. Beverly Miller, 1/E, to an aid station and laid him next to Maj. Dobson. When the Germans captured the aid station and discovered that Miller was an officer, he was hoisted onto a door mounted on two sawhorses. After a quick whiff of chloroform, a German surgeon began cutting on his shoulder, and Miller passed out.[163] When the doctor finished with him, Miller was shoved into an over-full German ambulance, which jerked as it started off, dumping Miller out the back door.

1144 HOURS (LOG OF ACTION): DARBY TO KITCHENS, DARBY CLEARLY NOT UNDERSTANDING THE FULL EXTENT OF THE RANGERS' PLIGHT

"The tanks [4th Battalion] are proceeding good . . . there is still a lot of mopping up to do. The tanks went across laterally . . . how are things with you. Hold on, we will be there soon."[164]

LATE MORNING (ESTIMATED): RANGERS RUN OUT OF AMMUNITION—CAPTURE BEGINS

German counterattacks continued all morning, with fire coming from all sides. The 1st and 3rd Ranger Battalions were surrounded and practically out of ammunition.[165] Shunstrom later reported on how the Rangers responded to this: "The order was given for all four companies remaining in reserve to give one half of the ammunition they were carrying to . . . companies on the line. All this time help was being asked for on the radio. Our plan now was to hold what we had until help came. To advance any further than where we were now would be suicide."[166]

Second Lt. Norman Alloway, 1/A: "German tanks were everywhere. Mortar and artillery rounds were crashing all around us, but for some reason my platoon's casualties were lighter than most others in the 1st Battalion. Near the end of the action a German Tiger tank came at our position, and a Ranger from another platoon knocked it out with a bazooka. I was only a Ranger for a few weeks, and at the decisive battle I wound up a prisoner of the Germans with most of my friends dead."[167]

The 1st Battalion and three companies of the 3rd Battalion were in a crescent-shaped defensive line on the south side of the Ponte Rotta Road, with other parts of three 3rd Battalion companies providing security from the west and south. Eventually, the forward elements of the 3rd Battalion came online with the 1st Battalion and manned the left flank of the Ranger force.[168]

Tech/5 James O'Reilly, 3/B: "There was little organization anywhere. . . . It was a section here and there, badly shot up and holding the Jerries off as best they could."[169]

Earlier, when moving up the Pantano Ditch, Capt. Evans, commanding 3/F, and Tech/4 Edward Krise, 3rd Battalion medic, had seen the decapitated body of Maj. Miller. Despite German explosives and shrapnel, Evans had managed to bring over half of his company to link up with Capt. James Larkin's 3/E, strengthening the left flank of the Rangers' main line of defense on the Ponte Rotta Road. When moving forward, Evans and his men were caught in an artillery shoot.[170] Evans: "A shell of some kind hit close to me, but I did not get hit. I don't remember anything except the ground coming up to hit me. It's one of the recurring dreams that I have had since that time: the ground comes up to hit me, but I've never hit it."[171] This near miss produced a concussion, resulting in Evans remembering little of the rest of the battle.[172] Parts of three companies were still in the rear for security and to guard the wounded. First Sgt. George Kopanda, 3/F: "The Germans fanatically overpowered them with grenades, machine gun fire, artillery, and mortars. The Germans took the wounded and

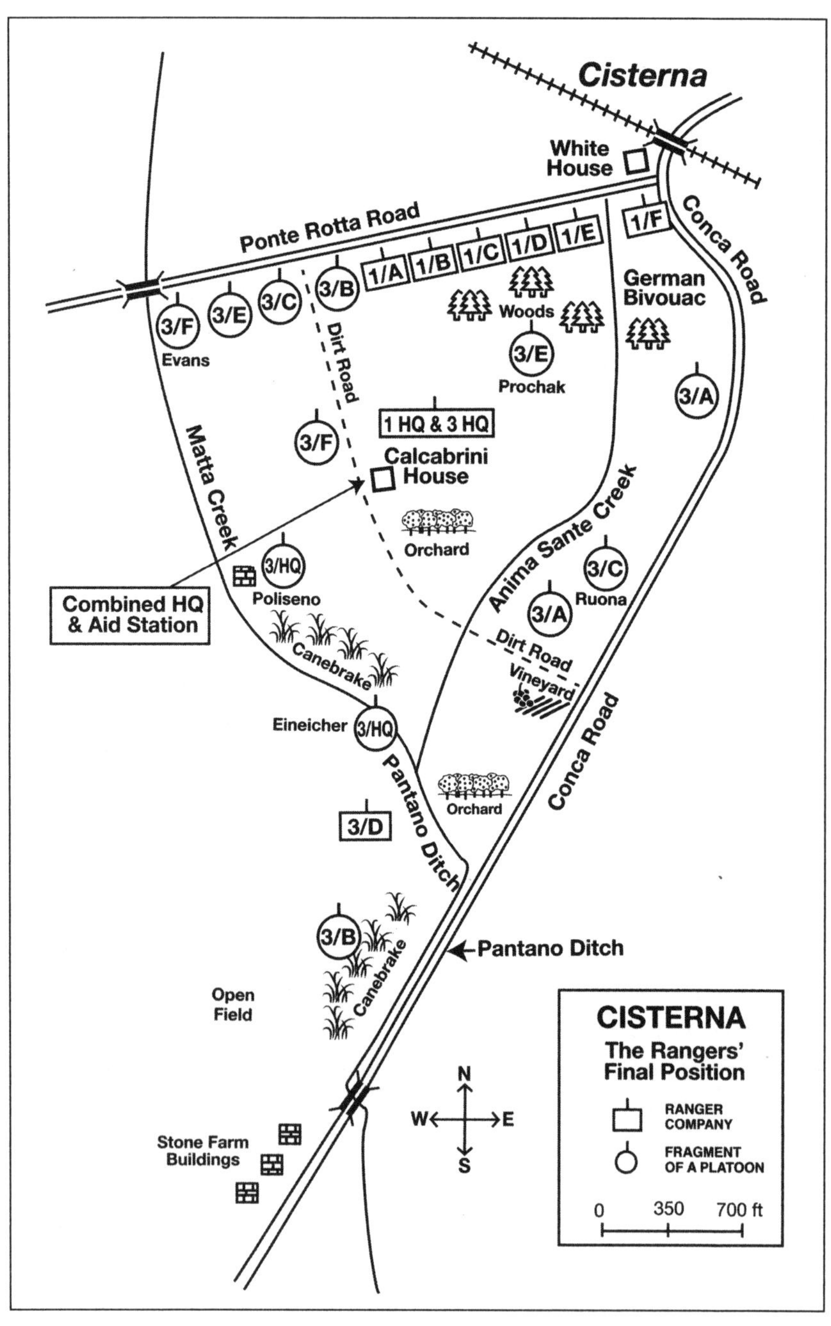

The Rangers' Final Position at Cisterna

other members of the battalion that could walk, surrounded them, and walked towards our front, stating that if we kept shooting they would kill every man they had surrounded. The badly wounded and inexperienced men threw up white flags and cried for mercy, or cried asking us to stop firing. At this time ammunition was even more scarce, no help came, and we had no artillery support whatsoever."[173]

For Pfc. Raymond Sadoski, 1/F, the morning seemed to fly by. After firing at Germans from the second-story window of the Calcabrini house for two hours, he began to see some Rangers coming his way on the Ponte Rotta Road. Sadoski: "The Rangers were giving up. We were wiped out, frankly, and Rangers were being marched up the road. Germans were pushin' em. If you shot one of them Germans, they'd shoot ten Americans. That's how they got us. The Rangers wouldn't shoot their own men. If it had been a German outfit that was captured, they'd mow their own men down and keep fightin'. But we wouldn't kill our own guys."[174]

Second Lt. James D. Cooney, a platoon leader in 1/E, was seriously wounded, and there was nothing to do but hang on until he was captured or rescued: "I was taken unconscious from the battlefield by the Germans. I was a POW for one year of which seven months was spent in the hospital, and I was eventually liberated by Russian troops on 22 January 1945."[175]

Cpl. Zartman, 1/F, began to realize that, with all order lost and with many officers dead or badly wounded, the Rangers had no choice but to surrender:

> Most of us were out of ammo or had few rounds left. It was all too clear we could not advance from our position, nor could we retreat. . . . We were under siege by mortar and small arms fire from all directions when our ammo ran out . . . there was the constant unnerving sound of groans and crying coming from both sides, men who were in the process of dying and could only beg God, or their mother to save them or ease their passage. It was clear to me that our situation was hopeless.[176]

When Capt. Collins Kendrick Jr. was wounded, 1st Lt. Tom Miller, a platoon leader in 1/C, took command of the company. Miller ordered some of the company to provide covering fire so that one section of his platoon could try to escape. Additional covering fire from Company 1/D assisted the section in moving south, away from the Ponte Rotta Road. Cpl. Ben W. Mosier and Tech/5 James J. Holbrooks, both of 1/C, and Pvt. Lonnie E. Johnson, 1/D, with a bullet wound in the arm, made it back to Allied lines the next day.[177] Cpl. Mosier: "There were eight of us together. The lieutenant [Tom Miller] told me that he wouldn't be captured and showed me his two bandoliers of ammunition. He was loaded up and firing to cover us with his carbine as we set off. We headed for the ditch. All this time the tracers were flying close enough to stop them with your hand. Along the ditch there were snipers all the way."[178] Mosier also remembered the wounded Capt. Kendrick saying, "I hate to do this, but it's too late now. That direction is south. Take out and God bless you."[179]

Lt. Newnan's 3/B had been fighting in the canebrake west of the Conca Road all morning, while Germans were attacking from the south and west with tanks and infantry. Casualties were heavy, and due to poor radio transmissions, American artillery fire was ineffective.[180] After the war, Lt. Newnan wrote the following passage to the father of Pfc. John Burke: "John was killed along with two others [Pfc. Phillip Defranco and Pfc. Roy Weinzettel, all of 3/B] while attempting to silence a German machine gun on our left flank. Endeavoring to knock out the same gun, I came upon his body along with that of Weinzettel and another chap I failed to recognize under the stress. Later, in the prison camp at Fara Sabina I checked with my 1st Sgt. McCollam and Platoon Sgt. [Robert] Taylor as to fatalities in the company."[181]

Lt. Meltesen described how Tech/5 Dominick Poliseno, 3/Hq., facing two Mark IV tanks, attacked the lead tank by dropping two grenades on it, causing enough damage for the crew to lose control and veer off the road. Meltesen continued:

> The following tank was taken on by another Ranger, who, from the rear, ran up the tracks to get on the deck and then dropped a grenade in the turret. He was spotted by a half-track . . . but did not get hit by any of the fire thrown his way. [Upon reaching a farm building], Poliseno and the other Ranger found four Rangers in the house with a smaller shed occupied by a German sniper and a machine gunner. One Ranger was wounded in both legs. . . . [All] the others, except Poliseno who stayed with the wounded man, took off to try to infiltrate back to the lines.[182]

A group of captured Rangers, surrounded by German soldiers with a loudspeaker, were being forced to walk up the Ponte Rotta Road. Markham heard the loudspeaker and clearly understood that Ranger prisoners would be shot if the German captors were fired upon. Moving up the road toward Cisterna, the Germans picked up other Rangers from ditches and hiding places. Some gave up willingly; some had to be forced out. Some of the wounded were shot by the Germans. Rangers who were not injured helped carry or support the wounded who could barely walk.[183]

1208 HOURS (LOG OF ACTION): DARBY RADIOS KITCHENS

Col. Darby told Capt. Kitchens, now in the Calcabrini house, some more bad news. Of a 3rd Infantry Division jeep company reconnaissance team of about forty men, coming up the Conca Road north of Isola Bella in the predawn hours, all but one was either killed or captured. Darby asked: "Where do you estimate them to be? Maybe you can break this thing up and rescue them."[184] There was no way Kitchens could mount a rescue. The Rangers were surrounded and practically out of ammunition.

Darby may not have realized (or wanted to realize) what was happening to his Rangers, but Pfc. Gustav Schunemann, 1/F, was experiencing the desperation of the Rangers' situation:

> We were quickly surrounded by enemy troops coming from everywhere. I saw half-tracked vehicles, loaded with enemy troops about five hundred yards away, coming fast in our direction. They had us pinned down in a cabbage patch and the Germans were making sauerkraut out of it with machine gun fire. ... Eventually, that machine gun nest was knocked out by somebody in Charley Company, and the guys in my squad were able to move out of there to a better [firing] position, by a small concrete outbuilding. We weren't there long before the krauts scored a direct [hit] on our building. Cement dust was everywhere.... We were in a hand-to-hand combat situation, too busy to be scared.[185]

Cpl. Markham, 1/F, was still in a depressed firing position along the Ponte Rotta Road near company 1/D along with Capt. Shunstrom and Capt. Saam: "The two [captains] had been arguing dates of rank while being sniped at. Each thought they should be in command at that point. With Major Miller dead and Major Dobson severely wounded, one or the other, Captains Shunstrom or Saam, were in charge of the two battalions."[186]

1225 HOURS (LOG OF ACTION): DARBY, REALIZING THE SCOPE OF THE DISASTER AND THAT RANGERS ARE GIVING UP, RADIOS KITCHENS AGAIN

"Nobody is giving up. Issue some orders and don't let the boys give up God damn it. Who is walking with their hands up. . . . Don't let them do it. . . . Before you give up get the old men together and lam for it. We're coming through. Hang onto this radio until the very last minute. Stick together. Who is with Dobson? Use your head and do what is best. You are there and I am here."[187]

1235 HOURS (LOG OF ACTION): DARBY AGAIN RADIOS KITCHENS

Darby, speaking for the last time before the radio was killed: "Unfortunately . . . [we] can't help you but whatever happens God bless you."[188] Darby, writing on 2 February 1944 about this same conversation: "This was the last communication with the two battalions . . . when I spoke with Sergeant Ehalt, Battalion Sergeant Major. He said that he was alone with a great number of wounded and that he saw a group surrendering and that he could do nothing to prevent it."[189]

In June 1944, Darby wrote again about this final conversation: "The captain [probably either Kitchens or Saam] talking to us from the 1st Battalion was overwrought and weeping, so I called for one of their sergeants whom I knew would be nearby. . . . In an unexcited voice [SGM Robert Ehalt] stated simply: 'Some of the fellows are giving up. Colonel, we are awfully sorry. . . . They can't help it because we're running out of ammunition. But I ain't surrendering. They are coming in the building now. Maybe when it's all over I'll see you again.'"[190]

Darby wrote, "The radio went wham, wham—and was dead."[191]

THE GERMANS OVERRUN THE CALCABRINI HOUSE

In a conversation fifty-three years after the battle, Tech/4 Edward Krise, 3/F, a medic, described the situation at the aid station in the Calcabrini house: "We had an aid station set up in a house . . . full of wounded. You would get some guy patched up and a bullet would come through the wall, killing him. It was a discouraging business. There was a lot of noise and commotion, Germans everywhere. They overran the whole position. I had a sidearm with maybe three rounds in it, and we don't talk about what medics do with sidearms. There are stories that Germans went around shooting wounded who could not walk, and I saw that happen."[192]

SGM Robert Ehalt, 1/Hq., ordered Pfc. Sadoski, 1/F, to stop shooting at Germans because the Germans were taking it out on the captured Rangers. Finally, Ehalt pulled out his .45 and pointed it at Sadoski, "Sadoski, you're gonna give up and you're gonna give up with me." Sadoski: "I never heard of making a guy give up. I don't think there's anything in the American rule books. So, he takes me over to the door, and he kicks open the door and there's a German standin' with a machine pistol. . . . He takes Ehalt's .45 and he shoots, two shots . . . [he says] 'Piece of scheisse' . . . and he throws the gun on the ground."[193]

As Sadoski, Ehalt, and others were being herded out toward the Ponte Rotta Road, an American artillery round found the Calcabrini house and blew part of the roof off. "That [German] kid saved my ass, the bastard," thought Sadoski.[194]

SURRENDERS AND CAPTURES END THE RANGERS' RESISTANCE

Surrendering is one of the hardest things a soldier can do, especially when he's trained to never surrender. But, out of ammunition, there was no alternative. Meltesen:

> As I prepared to surrender, I saw a German three-man patrol heading my way wearing airborne helmets. I waited and tried to surrender at a distance of 50 yards. I pulled out my new Red Cross handkerchief, took my helmet off and wiggled a white flag on a . . . piece of cane. Then I made another appearance and was allowed to surrender. In my school-book German, I tried to tell [them] that there were wounded in the shed. My captors were very happy capturing Rangers. One . . . said he had been . . . in Sicily when the first battalion had shellacked them.[195]

S/Sgt. Arthur Schrader, 1/F, still in his company area watching other Rangers walk out to the road to surrender, dropped his weapons in a hole. As he got to the road to surrender, a German soldier hit him on the shoulder with a rifle butt to stop him, frisked him, and then sent him to join the other prisoners.[196]

1345 HOURS (JOURNAL): REPORT COMES IN THAT THE ENTIRE 1ST BATTALION WAS WIPED OUT

Bits and pieces of three companies were still in the rear area and were being rounded up by German soldiers. In that group was Tech/Sgt. Robert Halliday, 3/D. As he was being marched up the road, the POW group passed a house where Tech/5 Dominick Poliseno was holed up. Moving along in front of a tank with his hands up, Halliday yelled out to Poliseno, "Don't shoot or they will shoot the rest of us." At this point there were about one hundred Rangers in that group of prisoners. POWs were being marched back and forth near a canebrake where Rangers were hiding, being told to surrender or they would be shot. From his position Poliseno could see Rangers of 3/C led by Sgt. Perry Bills coming out the canebrake, which was in an area south and west of the Calcabrini house. Poliseno was torn about what to do.[197] Several Rangers from 3/E, including S/Sgt. Wayne Ruona, 3/C, were opposite the building that Poliseno was defending in the same general area where the canebrake fringes the open field at the head of the Pantano Ditch. Lt. Meltesen: "Ruona and a company medic kept firing at the Germans until 1st Sgt. Arlo Fox, 3/C, came running up and yelling for them to stop, for the Germans were shooting a prisoner every time Ruona fired."[198] When Ruona realized it was useless to continue, he broke up his weapons and stomped the parts into the mud. As he turned, he was face to face with the muzzle of a German machine pistol. Ruona told the German to go ahead and shoot. Two other Rangers in a foxhole close by were gunned down by the same German soldier even as they had their hands held high. The German spared Ruona.[199]

S/Sgt. Ruona discovered that one of his men, Sgt. Phillip Gangnath, 3/C, was critically wounded, and it did not appear that he would survive:

> As we were surrendering . . . all the medics had been killed or wounded, and the survivors were at the aid station. We wanted to try to save Sgt. Gangnath, so we made a makeshift litter with a shelter-half, and four of us carefully lifted him onto it. Just as we lifted him, a German officer appeared with a Luger in

> hand, telling us to put him down. I said, "This man is badly hurt and won't survive unless we get him some help fast." The German officer repeated himself and added, "If you don't put him down, I'll shoot all of you. Put the man down, turn around, and run toward the collection point. Do not look back."[200]

As Ruona and the others headed off to the collection point where the captured Rangers were being assembling under guard, they heard a single shot from a Luger and knew the German officer had executed Gangnath.[201] Ruona: "We had heard stories that Germans fighting on the Russian front had a habit of killing their badly wounded men to keep them from falling into Russian hands. We were a sad bunch as we tried to face up to what was happening, knowing that it would probably only get worse."[202]

Tech/5 James O'Reilly, 3/B: "I had one clip of M-1 rounds left in my belt. I had fired my own two bandoliers and a belt load and also two bandoliers and a belt load I had taken off a dead Ranger. Sgt. Michael Syroid, 3/B, had fired all his Tommy-gun clips and other clips he had taken from some of the dead boys. The rest of our band was as bad off or worse off than we were. The BAR gunners were out completely."[203]

The Germans were rolling up the Ranger lines, trying to get all of them to the collection point, where they could control their captives.

1400 HOURS (ESTIMATED): RANGER PRISONERS FORCE-MARCHED IN FRONT OF A GERMAN TANK

The Germans had overrun the security team on the south end of the battlefield, and several 3rd Battalion Rangers were seen marching with their hands on their heads, followed by a tank.[204] At the other end of the battlefield, another group of captives was force-marched up the Ponte Rotta Road headed east toward Capt. Bing Evans's 3/F position on the far left of the Rangers' defensive line.[205] Lt. Meltesen: "On the far-left flank, 2nd Lt. James F. Ralstin, 3/F, was pinned down in a shallow drainage ditch where he was captured. There was a German tank equipped with loud speakers. In the front was a screen of perhaps a dozen Rangers and a couple of guards. The same announcement [given repeatedly] was, 'Surrender, now, and if Germans are killed we will kill prisoners.'"[206] As the march approached Evans's company, with the German on the loudspeaker still calling for the Rangers to surrender or be killed, Evans refused to surrender and his men fired on the Germans, killing a few.[207] The Germans responded by killing two Rangers, running them through with bayonets.[208] Capt. Evans's company still refused to surrender and again fired on the Germans. Two more Rangers were bayoneted.* Evans's company eventually ran out of ammunition and had to surrender, with Evans being made to lead the prisoners up the road. In a conversation with me years later, Evans said: "I have a vague memory of it. Some say I gave the order to shoot at the German guards, and others disputed that. I don't remember. An artillery or mortar shell burst practically in my face, and I must have had a concussion. Somehow I continued to function as a company commander with no recollection of events over the next two weeks."[209]

At the same time there were Ranger prisoners from the 3rd Battalion being marched four abreast northward up the dirt road toward the Calcabrini house.[210] Tech/5 Larry Kushner, 3/Hq., had rejoined the Rangers at Anzio after being wounded at San Pietro. When capture was imminent, Kushner broke up his Thompson submachine gun and buried his dog tags, which labeled him as Jewish. Kushner had heard what the Germans did to Jews.[211] He remembered the German on a loudspeaker calling out to the Rangers in perfect English to surrender or they would be killed: "I saw one group of about eighty Rangers being herded up a dirt road [probably the road next to the Calcabrini house] with a tank behind. Some Rangers fired on the Germans, and the Germans

* In *We Led the Way* by Darby and Baumer (page 168), the published version of "The First Rangers in Mediterranean Combat," Darby makes no mention of Germans bayoneting Ranger POWs. However, in June/July 1944, when Darby dictated the book, he wrote about Rangers firing on Germans who were force-marching Ranger POWs. Darby: "Two of the German guards began to slump and then collapsed in the dirt. Immediately . . . the Germans bayoneted some of the American soldiers who had their hands in the air." This last line was omitted from the published version of his book, and we do not know why. In the next paragraph, Darby dictated: "Instead, the company is said to have ambushed two more of the guards with the Germans retaliating by again bayoneting prisoners." The sentence in the published version of the book ends with the word "guards," again leaving out any reference to Rangers being bayoneted. No doubt, immediately after the Cisterna battle, Darby heard about the bayoneting. On 10 July 1944, Capt. Shunstrom mailed Darby a copy of his report, "Capture of the First and Third Ranger Battalions," confirming the bayoneting. Perhaps Maj. Gen. Baumer, the coauthor, was not certain the bayoneting happened and deleted it from the book when he published it in 1980, thirty-five years after Darby's death.

gunned down several Rangers. One was wounded and fell, and the tank ran right over him."[212]

Rangers were using the many ditches to hide in or to try to escape. Tanks would run up to the edge of the ditches, lower their guns, and shoot point blank.[213] Casualties were extreme. Cpl. George W. "Jack" Hall, 3/D: "We were some of the first Rangers captured when we ran out of ammunition. I jammed my Tommy gun barrel first into the mud with a hand grenade under it, the pin pulled. Hopefully, my crude booby-trap worked when some enemy soldier picked it up. When the Germans got to my position they yelled out 'hands hock.' We had to take off our helmets, and that was it."[214]

Cpl. William C. Fauber Jr., 1/D, put a grenade under the flap of his pack and rigged a booby trap for the German who found it. He later heard it explode.[215] Shunstrom saw Ranger prisoners being marched under guard toward the depression where he and Saam were holding out. Saam planned an ambush for the oncoming German soldiers.[216] Shunstrom:

> Capt. Evans was made to lead this column up the road. The Germans kept shouting, "Surrender or we will shoot the prisoners." . . . The orders for our ambush were not to fire until given the order, but someone fired a shot into the oncoming column and killed one of our own men. This one shot started everybody else in the ambush firing. . . . The Germans . . . took cover and started to spray [the captured Rangers] with automatic fire from submachine guns. The men that had set up an ambush immediately ceased firing, and a few of them who were evidently new in combat immediately got hysterical and started to leave their positions and surrender. All attempts to stop this disobedience of orders failed. Even an attempt to stop them by shooting them* failed.[217]

Pfc. Zelly Dineen, 1/E, describes his surrender:

> Next time I looked up, here come about fifty Rangers in front of a German tank—coming in my direction. They were prisoners. I could have shot the German guards, but I knew they would begin killing the Rangers. I knew we

* Except for this statement by Shunstrom, there is no evidence that Rangers fired on their comrades to prevent them from surrendering.

had to give up. . . . A German officer came over and took me and the two other guys away from the rest of the group. He put us in line next to Captain Saam and told us we could not talk. A German MP was pointing a pistol at us. I figured he would shoot us. The German officer said, "They put up a good fight, let them live." One of the officers was too badly wounded to walk; I didn't know him because he was too new. I learned later it was probably our battalion commander Major Dobson. As I walked through the underpass I walked by a brand-new tiger tank. It was beautiful and made our tanks look obsolete.[218]

Ranger Ken Markham, 1/F, realized surrender was inevitable:

It was getting late in the afternoon . . . when I looked up the road. I saw the walking wounded the Germans had captured from an aid station of ours. The Germans put them in front of tanks with loud speakers. The Germans said they were going to shoot down these hundred or so wounded soldiers if we did not surrender.[219]

One Ranger, I don't know his name, stood up right in front of those Germans who were marching our guys up the road. He raised his rifle and fired one shot at the Germans, and at least fifteen of them shot him. Captain Saam instructed us to give up. Then I saw Capt. Shunstrom breaking up his Thompson and throwing away the parts. Capt. Shunstrom was the meanest man in the whole American army, and if Shunstrom was giving up, the rest of us had no choice.[220]

1430 HOURS (ESTIMATED): THE END OF RANGER RESISTANCE

Sgt. Eineichner, 3/Hq., experienced hope, then despair:

About 2:30 p.m., January 30th, off in a distance down the highway, I could see US troops and armored vehicles coming toward me. At last, the 3rd [Infantry] Division with tanks had arrived to help us! As they came closer, my jubilance changed to despair . . . I lay face down in the ditch hopeful that the enemy would not see me.

A column of Rangers and a military vehicle loaded with casualties was

> moving slowly along the highway [the Ponte Rotta Road], as enemy soldiers on both sides of the road were flushing out dug-in Rangers. Any hesitation or resistance of capture was met with rifle fire, potato mashers or retaliatory shooting of men already captured. The column of captured Rangers and the vehicle with the wounded had already passed by me before I heard "Rouse, Rouse!" At about 3:00 p.m., I was ordered out of the ditch and forced out onto the road. Not once did the thought of being captured ever enter my mind that hectic day.[221]

Tech/5 Mickey Romine, 3/Hq.: "We noticed more Germans working their way toward [our] building, so we decided to leave the wounded to the mercy of the Germans and the three of us slipped out and tried to work our way back to the canal, but we walked right into a bunch of Germans and they said, 'Hands up!' and we did."[222]

Sniper fire had driven Tech/5 John M. Prochak, 3/E, into cover, where he removed the trigger assembly off his rifle and then smashed the barrel against a rock. He met his section leader, Sgt. Robert Perryman, and S/Sgt. Dancil Mitchell. They were being pursued by fire from German soldiers with machine pistols. Learning the German word for "hands up" and "surrender," they joined the rest of the POW group on the Conca Road.[223] Second Lt. Norman Alloway, 1/A: "I decided to hang on to my .45 pistol and tucked it in my waist band. When I was herded into the ravine area with the other prisoners and saw the German machine guns set up on high ground, I quickly disposed of the pistol, realizing that I would be shot on the spot if it was found."[224]

Cpl. Lawrence "Larry" Schenkel, 1/Hq., witnessed a bloody firefight at an outbuilding that left three of the group dead and five badly wounded. Schenkel decided that he should go for help. "That was probably my first mistake."[225] Cpl. Schenkel had seen gunfire coming from a barn and walked toward it, asking if anyone spoke English. Two Germans came out, and Schenkel let them know that he had wounded men and asked if they would get them medical attention. Schenkel, speaking to the Germans:

> Are you going to give me that? "I'll take care of those men," the German said, "as long as you don't fire at us." I told him, "They won't fire as long as I'm standing here with you." Then he asked me, "What do you got on the side of

your hip there? . . . And what do you use that knife for?" he demanded. "To cut bread, slice open cans," I said. "Look around you," he ordered. But I wouldn't, because I knew what he wanted me to see. He wanted me to see all the Germans lying dead with their throats cut. . . . Then the German motioned to one of his men, saying, "See that soldier out there on the road. . . . He's waiting for you. I'll take care of the wounded in the building."[226]

The Germans ordered the Rangers into a ditch and began talking about killing them. Before the German soldiers could get off a shot, a vehicle roared up and a German officer got out, screaming at his soldiers, telling them to get the Rangers up on the road. Schenkel: "I've often thought that if that officer hadn't come along, I'd have been a dead body in a ditch."[227]

RANGER POW COLLECTION POINT NEAR CISTERNA

Survivors, now POWs, were herded into a ravine, described as a gully by some and as a flat depression about the size of a football field by others. Pfc. Gustave E. Schunemann: "After getting us all into the gully the Germans set up machine guns along the banks on both sides. We thought, for sure, this was it. . . . We fully expected it because they were really mad at us, having suffered the lion's share of casualties. . . . There was [Pvt.] Leroy Kraft, standing there, in complete shock, with half his face blown away."[228]

Pfc. Angelo DiMarco, 1/E, witnessed a Ranger medic trying desperately to save a gravely wounded man. The medic either ignored or did not hear the commands from a German officer to stop working on the wounded man, resulting in the German officer executing first the medic and then the wounded Ranger. DiMarco kept telling himself that he must be dreaming.[229] Pvt. Harry Perlmutter, 1/D: "Because I'm Jewish the first thing I did was destroy my dog tags. I only had time to destroy my weapons and scatter the parts before the Nazis were upon me. Then they herded us into a gully and divided us into groups of thirty in an open field. Italian scavengers with wheelbarrows came out and started picking up anything they could find. They grabbed odds and ends like helmets, entrenching shovels, and the busted stocks of rifles. Half of this junk you wondered what they were going to do with it."[230]

First Sgt. Peter Vetcher, 3/A, who had fought all day on the left flank of the

Ranger line, was bleeding from shrapnel wounds in the hip and chest. He was physically numb. Now a POW, all he could think about was, "God oh mighty, what am I going to do?"

First Lt. Meltesen reached the ravine holding area about 1430 hours. By that time Maj. Dobson and Capt. Beverly Miller had already been moved to the German rear.[231] Meltesen:

> The walking wounded . . . were still in the ravine, and I made a special point to the Germans in my limited German that we all needed medical attention and that I would not go down into the ravine. A feldwebel [a German NCO] in a jeep-like truck equipped with the round boiler tank and chips that were used to generate gas took me back to some medical check point. . . . [There] I met up with Sgt. Rembecki and about seventy of our lightly wounded. When an ambulance arrived, I was sent on with two German litter patients . . . and soon I was in a hospital bed.[232]

Late in the day, the seriously wounded commander of the 1st Battalion, Maj. Dobson, was rolled up in a piece of carpet and loaded onto a door, used as a makeshift litter, and taken in a German ambulance to a German aid station somewhere in Cisterna.[233]

LATE AFTERNOON (ESTIMATED): CAPTIVE 1ST AND 3RD BATTALION RANGERS ARE MOVED FROM THE BATTLEFIELD

The Germans organized a truck shuttle and worked at top speed to clear the field of captured Rangers by dark. Not having a plan for handling such a large group of prisoners, the Germans loaded the Rangers onto trucks and sent them to a variety of places for the night or for the next few days. A few men were able to evade capture, and a few escaped after capture, either this night or soon after.[234] Sgt. Ruona's group was among those marched up the Conca Road and sorted into groups of twenty, then loaded onto trucks and taken to a building described as an old castle, probably Castel Genetti. At dusk the American artillery began registering rounds in the area, hoping to hit Germans, and a few more Rangers were wounded by friendly fire.[235]

Sgt. Eineichner: "It was getting dark by the time we left the canebrake.... A number of us were wounded with varying degrees of severity. Immediately, after the conclusion of the barrage, we were whisked off to a big structure that looked a lot like a castle. I kept my wound concealed from my German captors, not wanting to be placed with the wounded. I was still thinking escape."[236]

First Lt. Lynn Olesen, 1/E: "My right thigh was shattered during the battle, so I couldn't get back with my company. The Germans took me prisoner and sent me to a field hospital. There they set my leg, put a cast on it, and then sent me to a prison hospital. I was then moved to three different camps. After we were finally settled, the Germans allowed us to write letters and receive parcels from our folks and the Red Cross."[237]

RANGERS: ALIVE AND DEAD LEFT ON THE BATTLEFIELD

Rangers always made superhuman efforts to recover their wounded and dead from the battlefield. If a man was wounded, Rangers would risk their own lives to bring him in. The same unwritten rule applied to those killed in action. At Cisterna, however, there was no way to recover the dead. The Germans executed some of the more severely wounded, and some of the American dead were left to rot. It must have been devastating to the Ranger survivors, both POWs and escapees, to know that the families of their fallen friends and comrades might never know what happened to their loved ones.[238]

END OF THE DAY: THE 4TH RANGER BATTALION

The 4th Battalion had fought to a standstill. Altieri: "By nightfall the 4th Battalion had advanced only a mile-and-a-half to within 700 yards of strongly fortified German positions."[239] Many enemy machine guns, sited for effective crisscross fire over open fields that offered little cover for the Rangers, kept the battalion pinned down along the Conca Road all evening and into the night. All avenues of approach were covered with continual deadly enemy fire. Rangers kept down low in icy water-filled ditches. If they raised their head they would be shot. The battalion dug in, holding the ground it had won during the day, while its officers planned their next move. In the coming hours there was no rest for anyone.[240]

31 JANUARY 1944

0200 HOURS (ESTIMATED): RANGER FORCE HEADQUARTERS

Capt. Axel "Andy" Anderson, Ranger Force Supply Officer, recounted being wounded far in the rear of the battlefield:

> Darby called me up to get ammunition. A German Me109 fighter plane shot me off my motorcycle as I was looking for an ammunition truck. A piece of metal went through my leg and ruptured the oil tank, and oil was running down my leg. I went back to camp when some guys came by, picked me up and found the ammo truck I was looking for. Doc treated my wound, and then I reported to Darby to find out what he needed. Darby says, "Sleep here tonight. I want you to be able to move in with your supplies first thing in the morning."[241]

0600 HOURS (ESTIMATED): 4TH BATTALION

Dawn arrived on the Conca-Cisterna road, misty and bleak, and with it came another German artillery barrage, raining down on the 4th Ranger Battalion positions. Darby ordered the Rangers to renew their attack up the fiercely contested road, with the immediate objective being a group of farm houses.[242]

0630 HOURS (ESTIMATED): 4TH BATTALION

Lt. James Altieri, now commanding 4/F after Lt. Randall Harris was again wounded, led the attack. Joining in the attack was 2nd Lt. Ed Dean's Company 4/E. Altieri: "Captain Robert Neal, commanding 4/B, was to give cover and supporting fire. In addition, the 15th Infantry Regiment and the Ranger Cannon Company were to follow and give additional support."[243]

0700 HOURS (ESTIMATED): 4TH BATTALION

The attack moved along slowly, parallel to the Conca Road, with light tanks and half-tracks from the Ranger Cannon Company pouring deadly fire into the buildings along the road, hammering them one by one to kill the enemy snipers. Altieri's attack went forward but at a high cost: "Three noncoms were killed during Fox company's attack; Staff Sergeant Edward Karas, Staff Sergeant James Hildebrandt, and Staff Sergeant Dominick Lamandre, while Sgt. Leroy Buss, T/4 Talmadge Wagstaff, and Sgt. Joe Williams were badly wounded."[244]

All companies in the assault suffered casualties. One Ranger, Pfc. Raymond Boron, 4/A, who had just joined the Rangers a few weeks earlier, got an ugly taste of death: "I was a BAR gunner, and my assistant gunner was a replacement named Pvt. Thomas Bell, from Michigan, who had joined a few days before. For some reason Bell stood up, not three feet from me, and got hit. My close friend and buddy T/5 Paul Arbogast was right next to me."[245]

0800 HOURS (DAVIS): RANGER FORCE HEADQUARTERS

Pvt. Arnold E. "Pat" Davis, 1/E, and Tech/5 Joseph Sitarchyk, who had evaded capture the day before, now met with Col. Darby and Maj. Bill Martin, the Force Intelligence Officer, in Darby's command trailer located well south of Isola Bella. Davis:

> We climbed into this trailer of Darby's. There was a table down the middle, and bench seats on each side of the table. Not much room. Darby pulled out a map, and he asked me to show him how far we got. Finally, we located Cisterna, at least where it should be on that poor map, and after some orientation we pointed to our forward position on the top of the rise, going up from the ditch. Bill Martin asked no questions; and it seemed to me at the time that Darby did not ask any important questions—only curiosity questions.[246]

0957 HOURS (JOURNAL): 4TH RANGER BATTALION, IN THE ATTACK

Lt. Otis Davey, CO of Cannon Company, brought up two more of his half-tracks with their 75 mm guns. As he raised his head to look around, he was shot in the neck by a German sniper. Two more tanks joined the fight in close support of the Rangers, but due to the muddy fields, all tracked vehicles were still restricted to the road, which was mined by the Germans.[247]

1000 HOURS (ESTIMATED): RANGER FORCE HEADQUARTERS

Capt. Anderson spoke briefly with Darby: "I saw Darby; he was practically in tears because the Rangers had to give up, being out of ammunition and water. All the Rangers could do was surrender because the Germans had started killing them if they didn't give up. I had just gotten out of Darby's command vehicle when the Germans began shelling the area."[248]

1154 HOURS (JOURNAL)

A report came in that Lt. Davey died.[249]

1200 HOURS (ESTIMATED)

Near noon, the 4th Rangers fought a pitched battle, sometimes hand-to-hand, as they cleaned out the stone farm buildings. The Rangers again suffered terrible casualties, but many of the enemy were also killed and wounded. As the ac-

Grave registration assistants place the body of a dead Ranger on a litter for carrying to a grave. Unburied bodies form a double line in the background. Note the Ranger scroll on the left arm of the soldier without a helmet. Army Signal Corps photograph, National Archives.

The village of Isola Bella, just south of Cisterna, was as close as the 4th Ranger Battalion got to Cisterna. The gates of the village were shot to pieces by both sides in the assault. Photograph by Stefano Solferini.

tion was about to end, the 15th Infantry Regiment appeared with its tanks. The battle ended shortly thereafter with the surrender of the enemy troops at Isola Bella, including almost an entire battalion of enemy paratroopers. After two days of bitter fighting, the 4th Battalion fight ended in a costly victory. Most important to them was the difficult fact that they had been unable to come to the aid and rescue of their brothers in the 1st and 3rd Battalions.[250] The capture of Isola Bella came at a huge price. Three officers of the 4th Battalion lay dead after two days of bitter fighting: 2nd Lt. Lewis Case Jr., 1st Lt. George Nunnally, and 1st Lt. Orin Taylor.[251] The 4th Ranger Battalion remained in their forward position until 3 February, when they moved to the same bivouac area that they had used immediately before the attack on Cisterna.

1220 HOURS (JOURNAL): DARBY TO CAPT. HOWARD KARBEL

Col. Darby: "Capt. Karbel, I'd like for you to check around to see if you can find any of our men. Check 15th Inf., 7th Inf., 509th Para." Reply: "Yes Sir."[252]

1235 HOURS (JOURNAL): MESSAGE FROM 4TH BATTALION TO DARBY

"1st Bn. of the 15th Inf. is now passing through our troops, with orders to. . . ."[253]

The transmission ended abruptly at 1235 hours. An enemy artillery shell had made a direct hit on Darby's command trailer. The last comment on the radio transcript is a hand-written note that reads, "Shelling of CP resulted in killing of Major [William] Martin & 5 em [enlisted men], demolishing CP truck." Those killed included Cpl. Pressley Stroud, Darby's clerk. Darby and several others were wounded.[254]

3 FEBRUARY (DAVIS): FIFTH ARMY HEADQUARTERS

Pvt. Arnold Davis, who escaped from the battlefield, described an interview at Fifth Army Headquarters:

> I had the same feeling [as I had talking to Darby], when I was interviewed by an intelligence professor-type colonel. We walked together, the colonel and I, down one of the halls of an old castle and found an empty room. He mentioned that he had never himself been in one of those terrible battles but hoped to see one someday before the war was over. . . . Right away, I knew we would not get too far on anything really important. The colonel at the 5th Army seemed to ask the wrong questions about the wrong battle. I assumed he knew his job; though now, I have doubts about that.[255]

THE END OF DARBY'S RANGERS

Historian Col. Robert Black: "February 10, the 4th Rangers were relieved of their assignment to the Ranger Force and attached to the 504th Parachute Infantry Regiment as reserve."[256] On 17 February, Darby was re-assigned as commander of the 179th Infantry Regiment of the 45th Infantry Division.[257] On 25 March, the 4th Rangers were relieved of responsibility to the Fifth Army.[258] On 27 March, the surviving Originals of all three battalions left Anzio, and on the morning of 29 March this group boarded a ship for return to the United States.[259] In April, Darby was relieved of command of the 179th Infantry Regiment and assigned to the Operations Division of the War Department General Staff at the Pentagon in Washington, D.C.[260]

Once back home in the United States, Darby's Rangers would be awarded four more Presidential Unit Citations in recognition of their most difficult battles and greatest accomplishments.

- 3rd Ranger Battalion, dated 28 February 1944, for outstanding service in the area around Monte Sambucaro and San Pietro.
- 1st Ranger Battalion, dated 1 May 1944 (their second PUC), for outstanding service in the mountains around Salerno.
- 3rd Ranger Battalion, dated 1 May 1944 (their second PUC), for outstanding service in the mountains around Salerno.
- 4th Ranger Battalion, dated 25 May 1944, for outstanding service in the area around Venafro and Ceppagna.[261]

The Rangers were further spotlighted with tributes given to them on 12 June as part of the Infantry Day celebration at Camp Butner, North Carolina, with many dignitaries present.[262] This was the end of Darby's Rangers, but not the end for those captured or wounded.

4 JUNE 1944: THE ALLIES CAPTURE ROME

Immediately after the Cisterna battle, many thousands of German troops remained in place south of Rome, within just a few miles of the American and

British positions. The Allies had to fight a protracted battle from February to June before taking Rome.

ANALYSIS OF THE CISTERNA BATTLE

Any analysis of the Battle of Cisterna needs to answer two questions: First, what were the causes of the disaster? And second, were the bravery and sacrifice of the Rangers in vain?

It is seldom mentioned but important to remember that the Rangers' mission was part of a larger operation—namely, the 3rd Infantry Division's attempt to capture Cisterna. It is also important to remember that the 3rd Infantry Division had tried unsuccessfully to take Cisterna three days before. The Rangers' specific role was to slip through the German lines and capture Cisterna by stealth, after which the 3rd Infantry Division would secure the entire area around Cisterna before the Germans could realize what was happening. But that is not what happened.

CAUSES OF THE MISSION'S FAILURE

1. Poor Intelligence Affected All Three Ranger Battalions

Prior to the Ranger attack on Cisterna, elements of the 3rd Infantry Division fought from 25–27 January to force their way into Cisterna but were stopped cold three miles from the town.[263] Incredibly, this went unnoticed in the intelligence report issued just prior to the attack. The enemy strongpoints that the Americans encountered were incorrectly interpreted by 3rd Infantry Division Intelligence as isolated units rather than coordinated enemy positions. The reality was that in preparation for their planned attack on the Anzio beachhead, the Germans had placed crack assault forces in strong positions at several strategic places north of Cisterna, forming an intermittent line almost seven miles long.[264]

Given that strong enemy resistance had halted the 3rd Infantry Division a few miles short of Cisterna just three days before the Rangers' infiltration, Intelligence should have recognized the Germans' strong presence. It is difficult to understand how the intelligence report could have been approved by Division or why no American or British commanders saw or understood the

German buildup and questioned the risk. Michael King, Darby's biographer, summarized it: "Uninspired generalship and poor intelligence on the American side all but guaranteed that the attack on Cisterna would fail."[265]

Had Intelligence recognized the German strength, Gen. Truscott probably would not have sent the 1st and 3rd Rangers on an infiltration mission to Cisterna, against odds that were almost seventy to one, nor sent the 4th Battalion up against hard defenses that only armor could reduce. Intelligence failure at the division level was the primary reason for the catastrophe at Cisterna, and while it is easy to say that lower echelon commanders should have questioned intelligence that they doubted, the chain of command seldom offers that option during combat.

2. Decline in Leadership: 1st and 3rd Ranger Battalions

Many authors have emphasized that recent actions in Italy had so reduced the number of highly trained men that the Cisterna infiltration was destined for failure. Due to losses in Sicily, Chiunzi Pass, Venafro, and San Pietro, the Rangers were almost 20 percent short of a full complement, and approximately half of the Rangers were recent volunteers, untried and untested. Most of the Originals trained by Commandos in 1942 had been either killed or wounded.

Furthermore, the day before the attack, ten of these scarce Originals were pulled from the Cisterna mission and returned to the United States.[266] How critical was this one decision?

No one has previously reported how many Originals were among the 1st and 3rd Rangers sent on the Cisterna mission. Comparing the list of 1st and 3rd Battalion officers present at Cisterna to the list of officers trained by the Commandos reveals that only *four* of the officers at Cisterna were trained by the Commandos in 1942. One of the four, Maj. Alvah Miller, 3rd Battalion commander, was killed when he first contacted the enemy. The others were Capt. James Larkin, 3/E, Capt. Frederick Saam, 1/Hq., and Capt. Charles Shunstrom, 1/Hq.

In addition to these, four other officers, Capt. Warren Evans, 3/F, 2nd Lt. James Cooney, 1/C, 2nd Lt. James Dew, 1/A, and 2nd Lt. Earnest Jensen, 3/B, were Original Ranger NCOs who had received battlefield commissions. Jensen was mortally wounded early in the day, and Evans received a severe concussion before noon. Subtracting those officers killed and disabled leaves only *five* functioning officers who were trained by the Commandos.

Commanders, both at the company and battalion level, need to know each other's strengths and weaknesses and how best to communicate orders. Orders are orders, but how they are interpreted and followed determines their outcome. Maj. John Dobson, commander of the 1st Ranger Battalion, was a tested combat veteran, but Dobson had only joined the Rangers in November, just prior to the Anzio invasion.[267] There is no evidence to indicate that Dobson's men did not trust him, but Dobson and his Rangers had not yet shared the combat experiences that develop the mutual understanding vital in life-and-death situations.

The early morning break in the line of march that forced the Rangers to halt until organization was restored caused the Rangers to arrive later in the morning than planned.[268] An earlier arrival, however, is unlikely to have changed the outcome.

3. Use of Rangers as Conventional Troops: All Three Ranger Battalions

The Rangers sustained only light casualties on the small-scale raids for which they were trained, but casualties soared whenever they fought as conventional infantry in Sicily and Italy. But the Rangers' fighting qualities led battlefield commanders to seek their assistance all too often when well-trained infantry could have handled the mission. For the rest of July, the Rangers fought as infantry, losing an estimated 30 percent of their men from wounds and disease, especially malaria. Although the losses were great at Maiori while repelling numerous German counterattacks, the subsequent holding of the heights at Chiunzi Pass was a proper Ranger mission. However, the protracted engagements in the mountains around Venafro and San Pietro so depleted Ranger ranks that half the Rangers landing at Anzio were recent volunteers.

4. Lack of Support from the 3rd Infantry Division

The Ranger attack on Cisterna on 30 January was supposed to be followed immediately by the arrival of units of the 3rd Infantry Division. But when daylight came, Dobson realized that these reinforcements were not forthcoming.[269] Darby probably informed Dobson at 0700 that the 4th Ranger Battalion was pinned down and could not move. Dobson's only orders were to capture Cisterna. Having no orders to withdraw, with no reinforcements coming, and with Darby not clearly understanding what was happening, Dobson continued to fight, attacking Cisterna with what he had, causing his Rangers to be mowed down by enemy machine guns.

Facing a German counterattack in force, the Rangers, greatly outnumbered and outgunned, with little unit cohesion, took cover. Rangers were used to offensive fighting, hitting hard, moving fast, overpowering their enemies, and never fighting solo or in small groups except on patrol. Unfamiliar with defensive fighting, disaster was inevitable.

5. Loss of Command and Control: 1st and 3rd Rangers

Darby learned at 0700 hours that Maj. Miller had been killed, that Maj. Dobson was wounded (Dobson's first, less serious wound), and that the 1st and 3rd Battalions were surrounded and suffering heavy casualties. In his book, Darby wrote that, "Due to casualties among the officers, a single captain commanded both battalions. This young officer was equal to the situation, immediately closed the gap in the rear of the circle and ordered the men to dig in."[270] Darby does not name the captain, but we learn his identity from the Report of Action written by Shunstrom on 10 July 1944, after Shunstrom escaped from German captivity: "Captain Saam, executive officer of the 1st Ranger Battalion . . . immediately took command of both battalions. . . . Capt. Saam immediately took two companies of the 3rd Ranger Battalion and sent them to a position about three-hundred yards in our rear with a mission of closing the gap in the circle that we had formed and to dig in and hold at all costs."[271]

There is no known order from Darby or Dobson establishing a chain of command that would have put Saam in command of both battalions. Markham tells us that Saam and Shunstrom were arguing over who was in command.[272] Only Shunstrom tells us that Saam was in command, but is it possible that Shunstrom was pointing to Saam because he was afraid that he would be blamed for the disaster? After the Rangers were captured, the Germans considered Shunstrom, not Saam, to be in charge. After Miller was killed and Dobson was incapacitated, Capt. Saam, assuming that he found himself in charge of the two battalions, must have thought, "The mission is blown! I'm thrust into command. Do I attack, defend, or withdraw?"

An orderly withdrawal was probably impossible because men were scattered and disorganized and there was no way that anyone could move from a ditch without being hit by heavy German fire. No officer or NCO could have brought the two battalions back together for an organized attack or withdrawal. Saam was probably waiting for reinforcements from the 3rd Infantry Division that never arrived.

Even if Saam had wanted to withdraw, he may have been reluctant to countermand Darby's orders. Darby told Kitchens on the radio that his tanks were on the way. Saam had no way to know for sure. On the day before the mission, Darby had told Evans and Kness, "These are my orders, those are your orders." Saam may have overheard and remembered that comment.

There is no record that Darby gave withdrawal as an option, so perhaps Saam never considered it. By digging in and waiting for reinforcements, Saam probably thought he was following orders.

Saam and Shunstrom probably had different ideas about what to do. Shunstrom had been a company commander for months, demonstrating aggressive leadership that showed that he was not the kind to seek withdrawal. Saam was a staff officer, and in the absence of a record of his leadership skills, he may not have had the experience to lead two battalions in combat. I believe that since the argument that Markham witnessed happened around midday, there was little Shunstrom could have done had he been in command, but based on Shunstrom's prior record, it seems that had if he thought he had a fighting chance, he would have taken it.

The commander of the 3rd Ranger Battalion, Maj. Alvah Miller, was killed before daylight, and Capt. James Larkin, commanding 3/B and Miller's executive officer, took charge of the battalion. With the death of Miller, Larkin tried to get orders directly from Dobson since Dobson was now the senior commander, but Larkin was unable to reach him. Obviously, there was no plan of how to proceed in such a situation, adding to the confusion.

In 2002, Larkin's widow told me that then Capt. Edward Kitchens, commanding 3/C, "struck her husband" in an argument during the Cisterna battle.[273] We do not know the timing of this, but with two recorded incidents of arguing, tension among the officers must have been incredibly high. Presumably, the argument was over who should be in command of the 3rd Battalion and may have been over dates of rank. We do not know. Larkin was an Original, whereas Kitchens, who later became a brigadier general, had only joined the Rangers in January 1943. In this case, it is probable that Kitchens questioned Larkin's decisions, but we will never know. The argument may have been over whether to attack or withdraw, but with the lack of communications, both options may have been impossible.

Because the mission was put together in a hurry, some matters that turned out to be crucial were not addressed. There is no record of an order placing one battalion commander in charge of both battalions in the event one was killed or incapacitated. I believe that Darby never considered that he would lose one or both battalion commanders, and that he probably believed that if he lost one he would rely on radio communications to direct the fight.

6. Failure of Communications

On this mission, communications were almost nonexistent. Initially the Rangers were under radio silence. When the fight began, Dobson tried to reach Darby but failed, probably due to dampness in the ground and heavy fog affecting the radio. The four radio operators from the 3rd Battalion who got lost and wandered back to headquarters may or may not have made a difference in radio communications, but even if they had been present, they would not have been up front with Dobson and the 1st Battalion, where they were needed most. There had been little time for preparation, and with radio silence being enforced, this critical need for communication redundancy was probably overlooked. Or, with the Rangers stripped down to the bare essentials for this mission, many of the heavy, bulky radios may have been left behind intentionally. The question remains whether Darby, Dammer, or Alvah Miller should have addressed this problem ahead of time.

7. Were the 1st and 3rd Rangers Ambushed?

Numerous writers have stated that the Rangers walked into a German ambush.* Except for Shunstrom, Rangers who were interviewed or who wrote their memoirs deny this to a man, saying that the Germans were ambushed, not the other way around. Shunstrom stated in his report of capture that the Rangers were ambushed. Why would he have said that? Was that cover to explain the disaster? If an ambush had been set, it seems odd that the Germans

* Some of these writers include Martin Blumenson, William Breuer, John Eisenhower, Jerome Haggerty, Michael King, Lt. Col. Chester Starr, and Milton Shapiro. Col. Robert Black personally knew many of these Rangers, as did I, and both of us concluded there was no ambush.

allowed the men of 1/F to kill so many of their men who were still sleeping on the ground and in foxholes.

When the Rangers attacked before dawn on 30 January, the Germans, far from preparing an ambush, were confident they were being protected by security. German sentries who could have sounded the alarm were silenced by the knives of the Ranger scouts. Brig. Gen. John Dobson stated that no commander would ever have allowed an enemy force to enter his bivouac area, confirmation to himself and others that the Germans had not considered the possibility of the Rangers' infiltration.

8. Were the 4th Battalion Rangers Ambushed?

When Lt. Col. Roy Murray's 4th Battalion attacked north up the Conca Road toward Cisterna, he had no idea the Germans were encamped in force in isolated stone and concrete farmhouses all along the road. The Germans probably installed their forces in the farmhouses to stall or stop any Allied attack utilizing the Conca Road. The fact that the 4th Rangers were fired on so soon after leaving their line of departure might give the impression that they were ambushed. However, I believe that the enemy, knowing the importance of Cisterna and having already experienced an attack on it three days before, was simply protecting the Conca Road, which, being the main route from the sea to Cisterna, was the most likely avenue of an Allied advance.

9. Could the Mission Have Succeeded: 1st, 3rd, and 4th Battalions?

In a 1984 letter written to James Altieri, Brig. Gen. Dobson wrote, "The only reason we got to Cisterna is that we attacked along the boundary line between two divisions, the reconstituted Hermann Goering Panzer Division and an [unidentified enemy unit],* always the weakest part of a defense."[274]

However, at the time of the attack, neither Dobson nor other Ranger officers knew the location of any German units, so the fact that the Rangers slipped through the German lines at a weak boundary point was pure luck.

* Dobson referred to the "unidentified enemy unit" as the 92nd German Parachute Division. There is no reliable reference to this unit being at Cisterna at that time. Professional historians have questioned the accuracy of Dobson's comment. Small elements of this unit may have been operating in the Alban Hills, but there is no other known reference to it. Dobson was severely injured early in the fight, and he may have been confused, or he may have been correct.

Had the 4th Battalion had armor with them when they attacked up the Conca Road early on 30 January, they might have broken through the enemy's defenses in time to reach Isola Bella and help the 1st and 3rd Rangers.[275] Dobson thought so: "In my opinion, had we been followed by armor at first light, the operation would have been a tremendous success since our attack had completely disorganized the better part of one German regiment plus supporting armor, which is about three enemy for each one of us."[276]

THE RANGERS' SACRIFICES WERE NOT IN VAIN

The combat at Cisterna was a bitter American loss, but it had two effects that significantly aided the overall American mission at Anzio.

1. It caused enough confusion among the German commanders that Field Marshal Kesselring postponed his attack on the Anzio beachhead by four days.
2. It exposed the rapid German buildup, letting the Allies know they were outmanned and outgunned by the enemy. This gave the Allies a few days to prepare for what would be a protracted battle of attrition lasting four months. Had the Germans not delayed their attack, the entire Anzio invasion might have become a catastrophe for the Allies.

THE ISSUE OF RADIO SECURITY

On the basis of radio logs, Lt. Gen. Clark reprimanded Maj. Gen. Lucas for "complete disregard for radio and cryptographic security" by units of the Rangers on 30 and 31 January 1944:

> Violations consisted of information sent verbally, in the clear, that revealed: (a) Location of troops; (b) Names of units and personnel; (c) Movement of troops and tanks; (d) No contact with friendly troops; (e) Unauthorized code with very insecure mixture of plain text and code; (f) Size and type of units in combat; and (g) Physical condition of men.
>
> Radio operators and all personnel using radio-telephones must be trained so that they will keep radio discipline under the most pressing battle

> conditions. It is needed most during such periods when a unit is helpless or badly battered. If they fail to do this, their training has been worthless and they endanger the success of the operation and invite disaster to their unit.[277]

The reprimand was unjustified. Dobson himself had trouble establishing radio communications, and most of the men, in their first combat and new to the Rangers, probably had little or no radio experience. The younger men must have been frightened beyond belief, watching their comrades being killed and wounded. It would be a far stretch to assume that these young Rangers could remember radio protocol, if in fact they were trained for it, under such dire circumstances.

The morning after the fight, Gen. Clark, in a conversation with Gen. Truscott, stated that the Rangers should not have been sent on the mission because they were not suitable for it. Truscott: "I reminded him that I had been responsible for organizing the original Ranger battalion and that Colonel Darby and I perhaps understood their capabilities better than other American officers."[278] Nevertheless, Clark, known to fear unfavorable publicity, ordered an investigation anyway to fix responsibility for the failure of the mission. Truscott: "This was wholly unnecessary for the responsibility was entirely my own, especially since both Colonel Darby and I considered the mission a proper one, which should have been well within the capabilities of these fine soldiers."[279] Perhaps the reprimand for violations of radio security was simply part of Clark's personal cover for the fiasco.

14

AFTER THE BATTLE

SURVIVORS AND CASUALTIES

THE EIGHTEEN WHO RETURNED (NOT SIX)

Some American newspapers announced in early February 1944 that two Ranger battalions had been wiped out near Anzio, but because of military security and protocols for news coverage, there were no details. Families suffered the agony of not knowing if their son or husband was dead or alive.

Shortly afterward, telegrams from Western Union, such as the following one addressed to the Henry Breuers family, began to arrive at the homes of Rangers' parents: "The Secretary of War desires me to express his deep regret that your son Sergeant Jacob Breuers [3/B] has been reported missing in action since 30 January in Italy. If further details or other information is received you will be promptly notified. [signed] The Adjutant General."[1] A few telegrams told parents their son was killed in action, but for most of the 1st and 3rd Rangers who were killed at Cisterna, the army kept them listed as MIA until the end of the war, when they did not return home.[2]

When the survivors of the 4th Battalion returned to Ranger Force Headquarters on the afternoon of 31 January, 1st Lt. James Altieri, 4/F, sent out 2nd Lt. Edwin Harger, 4/Hq., to lead a patrol to search the Conca Road area for wounded. The patrol returned with seven wounded Rangers whose names have not been recorded.[3] Pfc. Joseph P. Ryan, 1/Hq., a member of Harger's patrol, could never forget helping to recover the wounded and get them back to an aid station. All of the wounded were from the 4th Battalion because the battlefield where the 1st and 3rd Battalion had fought was still crawling with Germans.[4]

EVADERS FROM THE 1ST AND 3RD RANGER BATTALIONS: EIGHTEEN, NOT SIX

Numerous authors have reported that only six Rangers returned from the battle at Cisterna on 30 January, but none have identified them or recorded their names. The six were:

1. Pvt. Arnold Davis, 1/D
2. Richard G. Smith, 1/Hq.
3. Tech/5 Joseph A. Sitarchyk, 1/D
4. Cpl. Ben W. Mosier, 1/C
5. Sgt. Thomas B. Fergen, 1/D
6. Tech/5 James J. Holbrooks, 1/C

These men are called "evaders" because, once the battle was clearly lost, they evaded capture and made it back to Allied lines.[5] Although the number six has been given by almost every author over the past eighty-one years, at least twelve other Rangers evaded the enemy and returned from the Cisterna battlefield. In addition to "the six," the other evaders that I have been able to identify are:

7. 2nd Lt. David Bennett, 3/D
8. Tech/5 John Brady, 3/D
9. Pfc. Edward Kwasek, 3/E
10. Sgt. Carl Key, 3/Hq.
11. Pvt. Clifford Kimbler, 3/Hq.
12. Pfc. James Palmer, 1/E
13. Pvt. William Eger, 1/B
14. Pvt. Lonnie E. Johnson, 1/D
15. Pvt. Donald G. Golde, 3/F
16. Pvt. Thurman Ellis, 1/C
17. Pvt. Charles Facer, 1/D
18. Pvt. Clayton C. Rodgers, 1/C

The stories of these men, told below, put an end to the myth of "the six."

Pvt. Arnold Davis, 1/D, explained how he knew for certain that at least eight men had returned from the Cisterna fight: "After the battle someone put out the number six, and everyone else who wrote a book has repeated that error for almost the past fifty years. On or about 2 or 3 February 1944, Joseph Sitarchyk, 1/D, Ben Mosier, 1/C, [and] I and one or two men from headquarters company . . . sat on the barracks bags in the woods near Col. Darby's headquarters and wrote out the names of eight men who returned from the Cisterna battle. I still have it in my file, in the handwriting of Joseph Sitarchyk."[6]

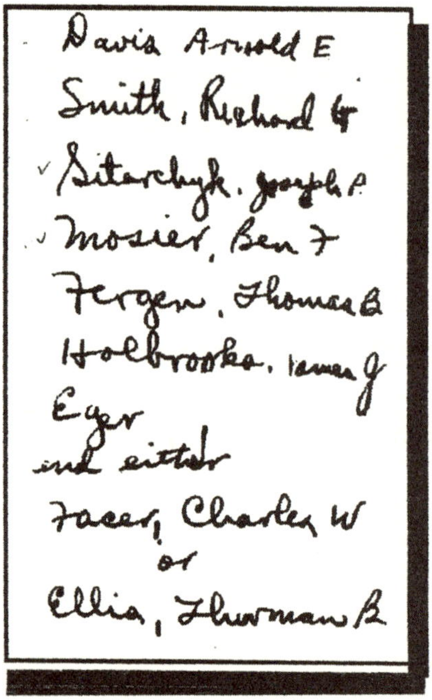

Davis Arnold E
Smith, Richard G
Sitarchyk, Joseph A
Mosier, Ben W
Fergen, Thomas B
Holbrooke, James J
Eger
and either
Facer, Charles W
or
Ellis, Thurman B

Tech/5 Joseph Sitarchyk, 1st Ranger Battalion, wrote the names of nine known, or suspected, Rangers who returned from the Cisterna battlefield on 30 January 1944. Courtesy of Ranger Arnold "Pat" Davis.

Sitarchyk actually wrote nine men's names. At the time he was only certain that eight returned, but in fact all nine men named below made it back from the battlefield.[7]

1. Arnold E. Davis
2. Richard G. Smith
3. Joseph A. Sitarchyk
4 Ben W. Mosier

5. Thomas B. Fergen
6. James J. Holbrooks
7. William Eger
8. Charles W. Facer
9. Thurman B. Ellis

SGT. THOMAS FERGEN, 1/D, AND TECH/5 JOSEPH SITARCHYK, 1/D

With shells and bullets still flying overhead, Joseph Sitarchyk escaped to the American lines. On the way he encountered Sgt. Thomas Fergen, who was tending wounded men who were too badly hurt to be moved. Fergen then led a group of eight Rangers, including Sitarchyk, in an attempt to get back to the Pantano Ditch and on to safety. Only about half of them got as far as the ditch. Continuing south, Sitarchyk was lucky enough to meet a weapons squad from the 3rd Infantry Division who took him back to Ranger Force Headquarters later that night. Of the eight who started out, only Sitarchyk and Fergen made it back to the American lines. The names of the other six, presumably killed or captured, are not recorded.[8]

CPL. BEN MOSIER, 1/C

Col. Darby interviewed Cpl. Ben Mosier after he returned to Ranger Force Headquarters. During Mosier's escape, he checked the edges of canal banks for snipers and flopped into the water whenever an incoming round came too close. Finding a vacant farmhouse, he stayed overnight, and the next morning he made it into 3rd Infantry Division lines.[9]

TECH/5 JOHN BRADY, 3/D, LT. DAVID BENNETT, 3/D, AND PFC. EDWARD KWASEK, 3/E

Lt. Clarence Meltesen, 3/C, tells how these three men managed to survive and evade capture:

> As large-scale surrender began, Pfc. Edward Kwasek, 3/E, began looking for a place to hide until dark, suffering from shrapnel wounds on both legs be-

> low the knees. He spotted a disabled German tank on the edge of a ditch and crawled under it. Already there, he found Tech/5 John Brady, 3/D, whose knee was badly torn up by shrapnel. . . . Brady was in a lot of pain. As dark settled in, Kwasek crawled out to check some bodies of Rangers nearby, looking for morphine syrettes and first aid packets. One of the men, Lt. David Bennett, 3/D, was still alive after losing an ear and part of his jaw, so Kwasek dragged him back to their hideout under the tank.[10]

Despite the danger from a German machine gun operating about thirty feet away, the three exhausted, wounded Rangers fell asleep under the burned-out tank. Brady was almost delirious. The three men used up all their morphine syringes; they still had codeine tablets but no water. Crawling to a stream after dark, Kwasek was filling a canteen when a soldier from the 3rd Infantry Division came along stringing telephone wire. Kwasek convinced the soldier he was a Ranger even though he did not know the current password. Later that night the wire party returned with a heavily armed squad, medics, and litters to rescue the Rangers. They also captured the nearby German machine gun squad. Army doctors told Lt. Bennett that falling into thick mud probably saved his life by sealing off his wounds so that he did not bleed to death.[11]

SGT. CARL KEY, 3/HQ., AND PVT. CLIFFORD KIMBLER, 3/HQ.

Second Lt. Clarence Meltesen, while a POW, made notes of what he remembered of the Cisterna battle, and after the war he spent years tracking down details of the battle and the aftermath:

> When German forces overran their aid station, medics Sgt. Carl Key, wounded in the morning, and Pvt. Clifford Kimbler were being marched to captivity by a German soldier. As they walked, Key spotted a badly wounded Ranger slipping into a ditch. Key treated the wound as best he could and saw that the Ranger was beyond help. About that time a stray artillery or mortar round hit close by, distracting the German, and Key and Kimbler slipped into some bushes, running several miles to American lines, back down the ditch the way they had come earlier that morning.[12]

PFC. JAMES PALMER, 1/E

Pfc. James Palmer was in shock and had no recollection of how he escaped: "The day after the battle, I was found walking down one of the roads, wounded and dazed, not sure of where I was. I knew I had been in a fight the day before but could not recall details at the moment."[13]

OTHER EVADERS

After the battle, Sgt. Milton Lehman, a reporter for *Stars and Stripes* newspaper, interviewed several Rangers, all of whom were later transferred to the First Special Service Force (FSSF) because they had insufficient time overseas to be returned to the United States. They included Sgt. Thomas Fergen and Cpl. Ben Mosier, who were also interviewed by Darby. The others that Lehman interviewed were Tech/5 Joseph Sitarchyk, Pvt. Clifford Kimbler, Sgt. Carl Key, and Pvt. Thurman Ellis, who had just joined the Rangers on 23 December 1944.[14] The names of Richard Smith, 1st Battalion, Tech/5 James Holbrooks, 1/C, Pvt. William Eger, 1/B, and Pvt. Charles Facer, 1/D, appear in Sitarchyk's handwriting on the paper preserved by Pvt. Davis. The details of their evasions are not known.

PVT. LONNIE E. JOHNSON, 1/D

The notice of Pvt. Lonnie Johnson's evasion appeared in the March 2010 edition of the Ranger Battalion Association newsletter. Ranger Johnson brings the total number of evaders to sixteen.[15]

PVT. DONALD G. GOLDE, 3/F

A story in the 14 April 1944 *Jewish News* states that Pvt. Donald Golde was one of the Rangers who evaded capture, bringing the number of evaders to seventeen.[16]

PVT. CLAYTON C. RODGERS, 1/C

The role that Pvt. Clayton Rodgers played in the Cisterna battle is not clear, but he brings the number of evaders to eighteen. Rodgers told his family that during the worst of the combat an officer said, "Every man for himself." He slipped away from the fighting, crawling to keep from getting shot, and perhaps went the wrong way. At first he hid, probably in the canebrake. He only moved at night, keeping out of sight of the roving Germans. It took him more than two weeks to return to Ranger Force Headquarters.[17]

AN ATTEMPTED EVADER WHO WAS CAPTURED

Pfc. Clarence Goad, 3/D: "I hid in a culvert until morning when a German MP patrol found me and whisked me off to join the other Rangers. I wound up in a German POW camp, eventually escaping, and got back to Allied lines in mid-1945."[18]

RANGERS CAPTURED AT THE END OF THE DAY

By mid-afternoon of 30 January, most of the Rangers had given up hope of being rescued. They could have held on for a few more hours had they not run out of ammunition. The captive Rangers were exhausted from having marched all night the night before and then having fought for their lives. They were long since out of water and rations. The Germans counted on the fact that few of them had the energy to attempt an escape.[19]

While the newly captured Rangers were milling around wondering what was coming next, and expecting the worst, German soldiers and officers checked them for weapons and relieved the Rangers of any visible wristwatches. The captors identified the more seriously wounded who needed immediate medical treatment.[20] German officers interrogated some of the captured Rangers on the battlefield and others at holding areas, while some were never interviewed. The POWs got the usual questioning by their German captors and gave the required answers: name, rank, and serial number. Most of the wounded were transported to German military hospitals, and a few seriously wounded were taken to civilian hospitals. For most of the Rangers, if they were fed that night or the next, it was only a thin soup, perhaps with a piece of black bread that tasted like sawdust.[21]

Germans loaded the Rangers onto trucks and took them to various hastily secured facilities to spend the night. Some of the new POWs were taken to a railroad roundhouse in Rome, while others, mainly enlisted men, were herded into open areas secured with barbed wire. Many of those captured did not know the correct name of the place they were held, so there are inconsistencies in their stories.[22] The men often had confused memories of the period immediately after their capture. Most were wounded and scared, now captured by the very enemy they had just been killing. Where were they first taken? A large building. No name. Were they taken to the streetcar barns in Rome before the forced march around Rome or after? How long after capture were they taken to Laterina, where most of them went before being shipped to German POW camps? Stories varied from "the next day" to "a few days." Tech/5 Mickey Romine, 3/Hq.: "When it was almost dark, they put us in trucks and drove us to Rome. They put us in an old streetcar barn and made us stay down in the grease pits. They kept us there for several days without food or water."[23] The Germans kept no records of the hastily arranged places POWs were held before reaching a permanent encampment in Germany or Poland, so there is no way to verify the exact locations of the temporary holding areas except by personal testimony of the captured Rangers.[24]

Several Rangers, mostly officers, along with some prisoners belonging to other Allied units, were taken north on Highway 7 and held in what they described as an old castle, probably Castel Genetti. Later that evening it was fired on by American artillery, wounding several men who were being held in the courtyard; at least one was killed. Capt. James Larkin, 3/Hq.: "Our first imprisonment was in a primitive castle. It had huge walls and towers. I remember spending literally hours staring at a big tree outside the walls."[25] Tech/4 Edward Krise: "There was not enough room for all in the castle; some stayed outside. About ten o'clock that night the Germans brought in some very heavy barley soup. We had no utensils, so we used our helmets as bowls and drank it. It was hot and delicious and the last meal we would get for some time."[26]

Sgt. Clarence Eineichner, 3/Hq., speaking about the building he thought looked like a castle:

> We were taken to a room on the second floor. The room was completely lacking in furniture, but a satisfactory hostel for the night. This would be the first building we had slept in since I can't remember when. [The next day we were] still in enemy hands. Hope to be liberated by friendly troops is [waning]. En-

emy defensive line appears to be impregnable. As the day gets brighter, we discover a veranda outside our second floor room. On the veranda are three beekeepers' beehives. The last time we have eaten was the afternoon of January 29th. It didn't take us long to polish off those beehives honey, honey combs, and most of the dormant bees.

Shortly after our honeybee feast, a German officer in a long black coat entered our room. After a "Good morning" to all the guys, he remarked it was his opinion that we were some of the most outstanding soldiers he ever encountered, the type of courageous men any military leader would like under his command. He also remarked about the marksmanship, stating most of their casualties were hit above the shoulders. Someone blurted out "That was the only part of your men that was visible." The German officer started to leave our room. He hesitated a moment, then turned around and said, "Why aren't you men shaven, like the soldiers I think you are?" To the man in concert we replied, "Your men took our packs which contained our personal items, Sir." He left the room without commenting.[27]

The relative courtesy of this German officer exemplifies the fact that frontline troops treated captives better because they knew that they might be captured themselves at any time. Rear echelon troops with little or no combat experience gave prisoners worse treatment. Sgt. Eineichner continued: "We were told to assemble in the courtyard for roll call, and then herded back into the building. We had just gotten back into the building when a fighter-bomber bombed and strafed our building. One bomb dropped in the courtyard we had just left. The other hit a building that housed German soldiers, killing many of them. Fifty caliber slugs were bouncing all around our room. Fortunately, no one in our room was hurt."[28]

In the confusion of the American bombing, some of the unnamed captives escaped. Because of that escape, the Germans moved all the prisoners into the castle for interrogation. The night was cold, and the Rangers began tearing boards off bunks to make a fire in a giant fireplace. Sitting around the fireplace trying to warm up were Capt. Warren Evans and Capt. Charles Shunstrom.[29] Regardless of who won the argument between Shunstrom and Capt. Saam about who had the oldest date of rank, the Germans apparently considered Shunstrom the senior officer after the loss of Maj. Dobson and Maj. Miller.

ACCOUNTING FOR THE CASUALTIES

Adjutants compiled the first list of men from the 1st Ranger Battalion[30] and the 3rd Ranger Battalion[31] who did not return from the Cisterna battle and listed them as Missing in Action. Maj. Walter Nye compiled the casualty list for the 4th Ranger Battalion.[32] A few of those listed as MIA had actually escaped from the battlefield and made it back to safety. Others managed to escape capture after being transported to makeshift German POW camps. At least seventeen of the Rangers who were wounded on the battlefield were rescued by American units a day or two after the battle. Nevertheless, some of those rescued by other American units were still listed as MIA when the official list was made.

A number of Rangers were wounded too badly to rise up and surrender. At the end of the day on 30 January, these men, still lying on the battlefield, had had little to eat and drink in the last twenty-four hours. They could live without food but not without water. Some were probably afraid the Germans would kill them because of their wounds, as they had Sgt. Gangnath. If they could move, they crawled into some cover, hopefully near one of the ditches that had water in it. Some were no doubt delirious, or close to it. Their only hope was to be rescued, but by whom? They knew their battalions had been wiped out, and with every hour that passed the hope of rescue seemed more remote.

However, by the afternoon of 31 January, the 4th Rangers, with support from tanks from the 3rd Infantry Division, had penetrated Isola Bella and were closing in on the Cisterna battlefield. By the end of that day, these American units had control of the southern sector of the Cisterna battlefield, moving farther north every hour.[33] They found a few wounded Rangers, whom they immediately transported back to safety. We don't know how these Rangers got wounded, much less how they managed to survive for one or more days. But we do have their names, thanks to research done by Julie Anne Foley Belanger of Albion, Maine.

JULIE ANNE FOLEY BELANGER'S RESEARCH

Julie Belanger, webmaster for the Descendants of World War II Rangers, Inc., and the niece of 1st Battalion Ranger S/Sgt. John J. Foley, 1/D, undertook an exhaustive study, the first of its kind, requiring months to complete, to determine the names of the Rangers from the 1st and 3rd Ranger Battalions who were killed, wounded, and captured during Anzio and Cisterna. Her report for the 1st Ranger Battalion is entitled "Report on Ranger Force Casualties during Anzio and Cisterna."[34] The report for the 3rd Battalion is entitled "Third Ranger Battalion Casualties, Anzio/Cisterna."[35] Reconstructing the rosters of the men who fought in the 1st and 3rd Ranger Battalions, she examined Morning Reports, After Action Reports, and reports from the National Archives in the first thorough attempt to correctly count the casualties and also confirm the names of Rangers who returned from POW camps as published by the National Archives. Belanger described her process:

> I used After Action Reports from 22 to 30 January 1944. Based on a Ranger's serial number, I looked up every MIA in the National Archives POW database to confirm whether each soldier was a POW. If I could find no POW and KIA information I checked Robert Black's* database and also Rangerroster.org,† an on-line WW II Ranger database developed by Julie Rankin Fulmer whose father was WW II Ranger Cpl. Richard E. Rankin, 2/A, and J. Ronald Hudnell whose father was WW II Ranger Pfc. James H. Hudnell, 2/D. I searched in Find-a-Grave by name for a death date on headstones or other locations. For the WIA (Wounded in Action) I used Morning Reports to find the dates on which Rangers were wounded and also entered each Ranger's serial number in a Fold3 search to find an Army Hospital admission and discharge record. I made a family tree in Ancestry for every Ranger to find date of birth, date of death, and the state in which he resided, along with photos when available. Finally, I compiled these data into two spreadsheets—one for the 1st Ranger Battalion and one for the 3rd Ranger Battalion. The initial scope of my work did not include casualties for the 4th Ranger Battalion, but subsequently I went through the same process to identify the names of those 4th Rangers killed in action and missing.

Belanger's reports consist of extensive spreadsheets showing, by name, the Rangers who fought from 22 to 31 January. I extracted those Ranger casualties

* Robert Black, author of *Rangers in World War II and Ranger Force.*

† http://www.rangerroster.org, an online database of World War II Rangers.

for the period 30–31 January to arrive at the Ranger casualty statistics for the Cisterna Battle, which are summarized in the included table. A total of 769 Rangers from the two battalions attempted to infiltrate into Cisterna during the night of 30 January. One Ranger was wounded on the infiltration and two litter bearers carried him back, taking three men off the battlefield. A total of fifty-four Rangers were confirmed killed in the battle, and many more were wounded. According to reports, of the 654 Rangers captured that day, at least half were wounded. The data on wounded were not recorded because, except for the eighteen evaders and the seventeen wounded who were later recovered from the battlefield, all of the other wounded were captured.

WOUNDED AND RECOVERED AFTER THE BATTLE

Because they fought in the southern part of the battlefield, wounded Rangers from the 3rd Battalion were the first to be found. The ten found were Charles M. Causey Jr., Dannie Ingram, Charles M. Lindsay, Donald A. Nahodil, James E. Piercey, John M. Aiken, Edward M. Krakowski, Hugo J. Miele, Major S. Reed, and Calvin J. Adams.[36] First Battalion Rangers found wounded but alive on the battlefield included: Delbert E. Brown, Glenn Durham Jr., Van Livingston, James O. McNeely, Elmer T. Rogerson, William A. Searle, and Edward A. Sichler. Nothing has been discovered as to exactly how they were found or how they were processed after being recovered or when they returned to the United States.[37]

CASUALTIES FOR THE 4TH RANGER BATTALION AT THE CISTERNA BATTLE

Belanger compiled a summary of the 4th Rangers' battle casualties for this book and reported that from 30 to 31 January 1944, twenty Rangers were killed in action and forty-three were wounded.[38]

On 3 May 1944, 199 Original Rangers from the three Ranger battalions returned to the United States. They constituted the bulk of the Originals who had survived since their organization in June 1942. A few Originals were hospitalized, and fewer were POWs. Thousands of people turned out at Camp Butner, North Carolina, to welcome and honor the returning Rangers, now treated to an awards ceremony and a pass-in-review parade in front of dozens of digni-

Casualty Report for Cisterna Battle, 30–31 January 1944: 1st and 3rd Ranger Battalions

Ranger Actions	1st Ranger Battalion	3rd Ranger Battalion	Total 1st and 3rd Rangers
Wounded on Infiltration	1	0	1
Litter Bearers to Extract the Wounded	2	0	2
KIA—Killed in Action	24	22	46
DOW—Died of Wounds	0	2	2
FOD—Finding of Death	4	2	6
Evaders	12	6	18
WIA—Wounded in Action and Recovered (found) after the Battle	7	10	17
Escaped from Laterina	6	3	9
Escaped from Boxcars	5	9	14
Total Rangers Not Captured	61	54	115
Total Number of POWs	334	320	654
Total Rangers on the Cisterna Mission	395	374	769
Total Deaths: KIA, DOW, and FOD	28	26	54
Total POW count	6	6	12
POWs Wounded, Captured, Exchanged	1	0	1
Died while a POW	7	3	10
Died in Plane Crash After Escaping from a POW Camp	1	0	1

Note: In this research study, Rangers were not considered POWs until they reached prisoner of war camps in Poland or Germany.

taries. Darby visited the Rangers on 19 June to help them celebrate the second anniversary of their activation, after which most of these men were transferred to Stateside units to serve out their commitment.[39]

RANGERS TRANSFERRED TO THE FIRST SPECIAL SERVICE FORCE

Most of the Rangers who were not on duty on 30 January were either hospitalized or had been transferred to another unit, thereby missing the Cisterna action. With the Originals going home, and upon the dismantling of Darby's Rangers, 970 Rangers who had joined at Nemours in 1943 or later were transferred into the First Special Service Force (FSSF), then in combat near Anzio.[40] The "Force," as it was called, was among the first units into Rome when the city was captured on 4 June 1944. The Germans called them the "Black Devils" because they blackened their faces for camouflage when going on stealth night operations. They were also known as the "Devil's Brigade." Such nicknames show that these were some tough soldiers.[41] The Force served in Italy into August 1944, then played a leading role in Operation Dragoon, the Allied invasion of southern France.

Morale among the former Rangers now in the FSSF was low. The Rangers resented the strict military discipline imposed in the FSSF, because discipline under Darby had been more relaxed. By November 1944, fifty-eight of the Rangers had been killed or wounded and 431 of the 961 had transferred out of the FSSF. Reasons for the transfers are unknown, but during the time the Rangers fought with the FSSF, eighty-four of them were court-martialed for a variety of reasons.[42] The army decided that the need for these special troops had passed, and on 5 December 1944 in southern France, the Force was disbanded and the men reassigned to other units. I was privileged to get to know a number of these FSSF veterans who had first fought under Darby, and the question of morale never came up in our discussions.

WALL OF THE MISSING AND FINDING OF DEATH

The bodies of some Rangers killed in the Cisterna battle lay where they fell for three months while Americans and Germans fought for control of the area. Sometime in late May 1944, just prior to the Americans' capture of Rome, Allied forces secured the area in and around Cisterna, and U.S. Graves Registration units began locating and burying bodies, identifying them whenever possible. At the Sicily-Rome American Cemetery, managed by the American Battle Monuments Commission, the names of several Rangers killed at Cisterna and the date they were confirmed dead are found on the Wall of the Missing, mute testimony to the tragic, lopsided battle.[43]

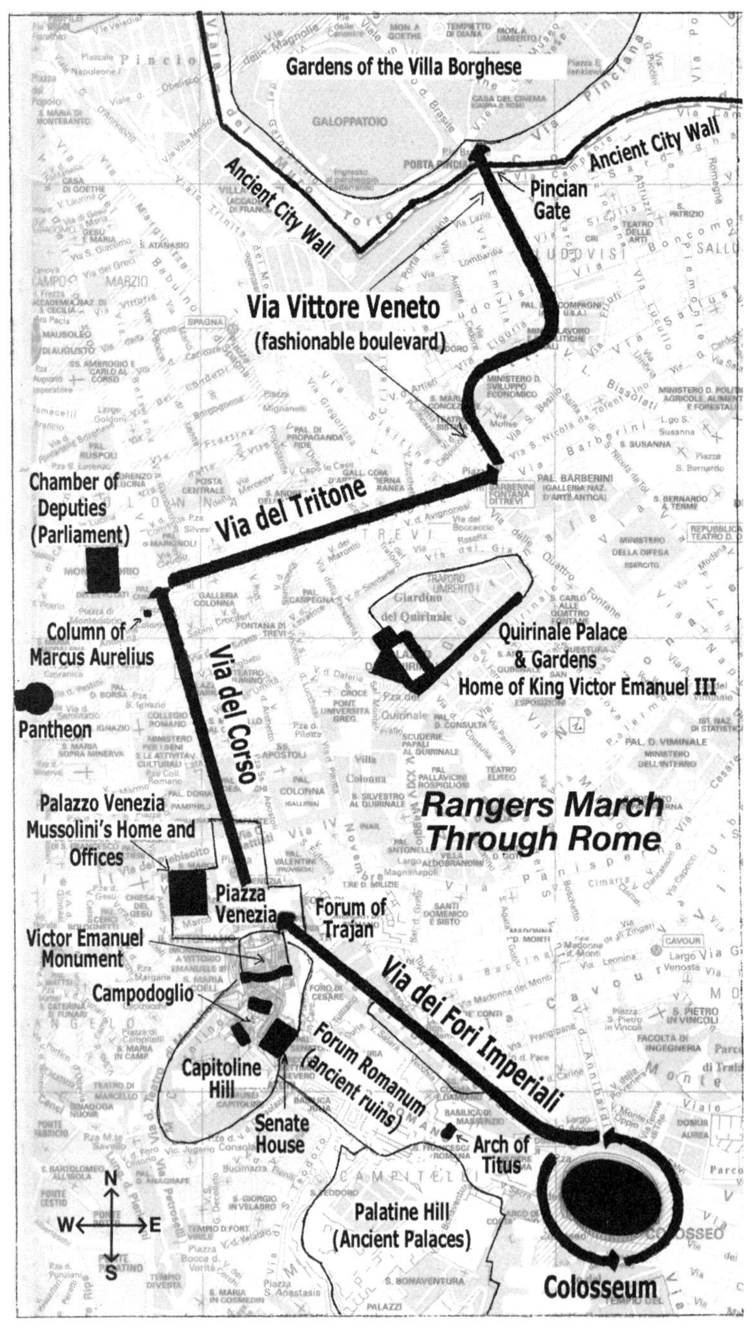

Route of the March through Rome (Background created by Federazione Autotrasportatori Italiani. Italia Centro, 1:200.000, Atlante Stradale, Milano: Touring Editore, 2011. Arthur White, with assistance from personnel at La. Digital in Lafayette, Louisiana, inserted the text and route.)

15

THE MARCH IN ROME

A WAR CRIME

Allied armies had moved farther and farther north into Italy with each passing month. Since the Allies were at Anzio, only thirty-eight miles south of Rome, the Germans, afraid that the Italians, particularly those in Rome, might think the Germans were losing the war, sought to demonstrate that they were in control of the situation. For that reason, and for general propaganda purposes, Gen. Kesselring decided—in violation of the Geneva Convention on the treatment of POWs—to parade his prisoners through Rome on 1 February 1944, film them, and distribute the film as widely as possible.[1] In America, many family members, not yet notified that their Ranger was missing in action, learned that he was a prisoner of war from newsreels showing him being force-marched under German guard near the Colosseum in Rome. Tech/5 Clarence Eineichner, 3/Hq.:

> We were loaded in trucks and transported to Rome. HURRAH! The first American troops in Rome! On arrival in Rome, we were assembled in front of the Colosseum. . . . While waiting for the march to begin, we were given a small ration of bread. Although we had not eaten, except for the honey, since the afternoon of January 29th, we made sure we were not chomping that hunk of bread while the cameras were rolling. The march was a great propaganda play for the Germans. The area was infested with both movie and still photographers. The story of the Rangers' defeat would be in every paper and movie house in Germany and surrounding country. . . . It was the first good news in Germany for quite some time. As we were marching through Rome, the thoughts of escape were foremost in our minds. The route was well fortified with guards, tanks, and Rome's Civilian Police. Therefore, a successful escape was impossible.[2]

Rangers being unloaded from trucks in Rome. This image comes from a captured German newsreel located in the National Archives.

Rangers being assembled by the Colosseum in Rome. This image comes from a captured German newsreel located in the National Archives.

Rangers being force-marched through Rome under heavy German guard. Photograph found in a German bunker at war's end.

Pvt. Arthur F. Wilson's parents learned he was a POW when they received a telegram from the War Department stating that an "unofficial intercepted shortwave broadcast" mentioned his name as a prisoner of war. Wilson, 1/D: "We were lined up and forced to march down Rome's main street—a move by the Germans to brag about their victory—and a clear violation of the rules of war. Italian people threw garbage at us and jeered, and the march was filmed by the Germans for historical documentation."[3]

Pfc. Gustave Schunemann, 1/F: "We were loaded onto trucks, packed like sardines, so tight we couldn't sit or lie down. . . . We rode that way all night long, arriving at the outskirts of Rome early in the morning. . . . At the Colosseum area we dismounted and marched through the streets of the city for one huge propaganda extravaganza. The Germans had movie cameras on every corner. . . . We flashed 'V' signs and other finger gestures that they probably did not understand."[4]

I first met Pfc. Thomas M. Mascari Jr. at the 1997 reunion of the Ranger Battalions Association of World War II, Inc. He was captured at Cisterna and held prisoner for over a year. In 1998, in Baton Rouge, Louisiana, where the American Ex-Prisoners of War next met, I brought along a VCR tape of captured German film showing the Rangers' forced march in Rome. As I played the tape for Pfc. Mascari, a crowd gathered as he explained the march to the group. You could have heard a pin drop except for Mrs. Mascari's tearful remarks, over and over: "Tom, you never told me."

WAR CRIMES TRIAL

After the war, in September 1946, the U.S. Army, Mediterranean Theater of Operations, issued General Order Number 212, convening a military commission to prosecute war crimes committed by individual German soldiers during World War II. The forced march of Allied POWs was on the docket, and Germany's Lt. Gen. Kurt Maelzer was charged under the Geneva Convention for the Treatment of Prisoners, which outlawed using prisoners for propaganda purposes and subjecting them to public humiliation: "Wrongfully and in violation of the Law of War, Maelzer caused to be exposed to acts of violence, insults, and public curiosity . . . soldiers of the United States Army, who were then Prisoners of War under the custody of the said Lieutenant General Kurt Maelzer."[5] Lt. Gen. Maelzer pleaded "Not guilty" to the charge.

The war crimes trial was held in Florence, Italy, 9–14 September 1946. Much material for the prosecution came from attorney Carl Harrison Lehmann Jr. from Baltimore, Maryland, an Original Ranger who served in 1/B and 3/C before his capture at Cisterna. Lehmann never forgot the abuses he suffered at the hands of the Germans as a POW, and he wrote numerous accounts of his capture, imprisonment, and brutal treatment by the Germans. In each writing, his final comment was always, "There was much hate. Much remains."[6] When the war crimes trial began, Lehmann secured the testimony of several Rangers who were captured at Cisterna, and their depositions were offered in as evidence at the trial. These stories, briefly summarized here, have never been seen outside of Lehmann's files. He entrusted me with the files, saying, "David, these need to be published for all to see, and I know you'll get it done." The disparity of information given by different Rangers indicates that, at the time of the forced march, these men were under extreme physical and mental pressure, exhausted, and starving for something to eat. The Germans gave each man a of chunk of bread to chew on during the march, so it would appear that the prisoners were being well cared for, but the Rangers put the bread in their pockets, refusing to eat it in front of the cameras. No doubt they were dehydrated, explaining the uncertain impressions given by some of the captured Rangers.

The first Ranger deposed was Sgt. Martin John Frank, 1/F, who volunteered for the Rangers in May 1943, fought at Gela, Salerno, and Anzio, and was captured at Cisterna:

> We arrived in Rome about 1 February 1944. We were told to get out of the trucks and form a column. It was about 0900 hours when we started to march through the streets of Rome; German guards were on both sides of us. The streets were lined for blocks with Italian civilians. As we marched, the civilians jeered at us, cursed us, spit at us and threw rocks. At times the German guards had to use force to keep the crowds back on the sidewalks. The parade lasted two and one-half hours, during which time we zigzagged back and forth through the business district of Rome. We were finally loaded back onto trucks and taken to a transit camp about twelve miles north of Rome. Witnesses to this that I knew are Pvt. Arthur Wilson, 1/D; Cpl. Claude Robertson, 1/E; and 1st Sgt. Frank Mattivi, 1/F.[7]

Capt. William Ross Bond,* 1/Hq., describes the hostility and humiliation the Rangers encountered:

> At the Colosseum we were made to get out of the trucks in which we had been riding and march down one of the main streets in Rome . . . past St. Peter's Church. Thousands of people lined the streets. The Fascisti and others jeered at us, made thumbs-down gesticulations, spit at us and screamed at us. Photographers took countless pictures of us. . . . Rome was an open city at this time. I recall that we marched past the Spanish consulate where many dignitaries watched the parade. The march lasted an hour and a half, and we finally stopped at a large municipal park, where we were again picked up by the trucks we had ridden in before.[8]

Pfc. Daniel W. McCall, 3/E: "In Rome we were subjected to public ridicule. We were unloaded [from trucks] at the Colosseum and put in columns of four or five and forced to march through the entire city. I think this was a staged parade because German and Italian photographers were taking pictures. We had not had an opportunity to shave or clean-up for days prior to this, so consequently we looked very ragged and dirty."[9]

First Lt. Charles L. Palumbo, 3/A: "I witnessed atrocities and mistreatment of American citizens at this time. They moved us up to the southern outskirts of Rome by truck, unloaded all the prisoners by the Colosseum and put a guard on every three men. There were about 600 in the column of prisoners.† They marched us through the central district of Rome. . . . Italians threw rotten vegetables, fruit, and the usual stuff at us."[10]

Cpl. William Albert Wood, 3/B: "They marched two thousand of us five abreast through Rome on about 2 February 1944. . . . We had no change of clothes since they captured us, and we were dirty, sloppy, and needed shaves. We looked bad. . . . We were dirty as hogs, and my pants were burned off. Everybody was taking pictures, and there were big cars lined up all around. [People] spit down on us from the buildings."[11]

* Bond became a brigadier general and was one of five American flag officers killed in Vietnam, the only one to die in ground combat.

† The prisoners who were force-marched through Rome were not all Rangers. The Germans had captured soldiers from several countries and marched them all together.

When asked about the German guards, Wood replied: "It was a special German escort guard. They looked like Buck Rogers. The commanding officer . . . was just a young punk . . . [he] was right in front of us [and looked to be] about 20. . . . I believe he was a 1st lieutenant."[12]

The defense counsel at the trial were American soldiers who were qualified defense attorneys. The following is a paraphrase of their arguments:

> The political loyalties of the Italian people were largely toward the Allies . . . not the Germans. The Germans engaged in various forms of propaganda, seeking to retain the loyalties of the Italian people, particularly the population of Rome. Some of the defense depositions stated that most people along the route were making a "V" sign with their fingers, indicating a sign of sympathy for the captured. Men testified [that] the Italian people were jeering. Actually, they were cheering, so that the sum and substance of the charge is, according to the extent of the evidence, that General Maelzer made housekeeping arrangements for a parade through the city of Rome when several hundred prisoners of war appeared in public view.
>
> The German quartermaster personnel (the guards) were there to protect the marchers, to make sure they were not injured, to check off the names of men as they offloaded from trucks and when reloaded, to make sure that all were accounted for.

The defense then offered a lengthy argument that Gen. Maelzer only followed orders, to provide security for the marchers. "After all, none were injured or killed."[13]

After a short recess, the attorney for the prosecution, a captain in the U.S. Army, countered the defense's arguments one by one, arguing that there was no evidence to show that the German guards were offering protection. Rather, the German guards were guarding the prisoners to keep them from escaping. The following paraphrase presents the rest of the prosecution's argument:

> At issue is the credibility of the American prisoners of war. Here we have two to three hundred* prisoners of war who had just come through hell at Anzio—

* The exact number of Rangers captured at Cisterna are: 1st Ranger Battalion—334 POWs; 3rd Ranger Battalion—320 POWs. Total Ranger POWs—654. Some of these were seriously wounded and were patients in military or Italian civilian hospitals. There is no record of these totals, but not all of them were on the march in Rome.

> those men had been fighting [from] the 22nd to the 31st of January before they were captured. You can imagine their condition and how they felt at that time. They were brought up to Rome and exhibited like wild animals or . . . people from Mars. They were put on exhibition intentionally and that intent is indisputably criminal under international law. These men had no animosity toward the accused. They didn't even know who ordered the march. They simply told the truth about the hell of Anzio and making the march and the treatment received there. I am not asking for the death penalty in this case, only for a penalty that will deter actions of this kind in the future.[14]

On 14 September 1946, after fifty minutes of deliberation, the commission found Maelzer guilty as charged. He was sentenced to ten years in prison. In December of that year, a review of the sentence headed by Lt. Gen. John C. H. Lee, U.S. Army, remitted seven years of the sentence. The resulting three-year sentence was confirmed and was duly executed.[15]

16

AFTER THE MARCH

PRISON AND ESCAPE

The Italians had set up a POW camp at Laterina in Tuscany, near Arezzo, about 150 miles northwest of Rome, to house British soldiers captured in North Africa. After the Italian surrender, Germany took over the site and used it as a transit camp where POWs were held until they could be shipped off by rail to more permanent prisons, called "Stalags," in Germany, Poland, and Austria.[1]

CONDITIONS AT LATERINA

At Laterina, Rangers were introduced to intense and prolonged hunger. The Germans knew that men who were fed very little lost weight, strength, and perhaps even the will to fight, and that, being in poor physical condition, they would be less likely to try to escape. Pfc. Edward Feigenbaum, 3/D, considered Laterina a starvation camp. He never saw any meat and said that they smoked pine needles.[2] Pfc. Zelly Dineen, 1/E, was starving after the march in Rome and never forgot it:

> After being marched around Rome, we were loaded on trucks and hauled to an Italian camp and given one biscuit to eat and some coffee. That's it. The biscuit was so hard you couldn't eat it, and it had worms in it. We ate it anyway. There I saw Capt. Saam, and his mustache was really drooping. Saam asked me how to keep it straight. I told him to take wax out of his ear and curl up the ends. That's the last time I ever talked to Captain Saam. One to two days later we were again given something to eat, this time some turnips and horse meat. I stood in line waiting to get some bread, but they had so little they ran out. I did get a bone with some gristle on it and thought I had hit the jackpot.[3]

Rangers were held in wooden barracks and told that if they ventured outside at night they would be shot. One evening after dark, when S/Sgt. Wayne Ruona opened the door to take a look outside, a guard fired, splintering the door frame, the bullet narrowly missing his head. He resolved then to escape.[4]

THE FIRST ESCAPE: CAPT. CHARLES SHUNSTROM AND LT. MICHAEL MAURITZ

Capt. Shunstrom's escape was in the planning stage before sunset on the day of the Cisterna battle. Arriving at Laterina on 7 February, he knew he had to escape before he was shipped off to Germany. After the march in Rome, Cpl. Kenneth Markham, 1/F, reported: "Shunstrom told me that he would not be here tomorrow."

When Shunstrom returned to American control, he wrote a report on his escape, which, at the time, was accepted as a truthful account.[5] Years later, Lt. Michael Mauritz, who escaped with Shunstrom, gave a very different account of their escape, months on the run, and return to American lines. In his book, Mauritz gives Shunstrom the pseudonym "Schuster." In quoting Mauritz, I have used the actual name, confirmed by Ranger Lawrence Schenkel, 1/Hq., who was also captured with Shunstrom.

Lt. Mauritz, a fighter pilot, was flying a Curtis P-40 off the coast of Anzio just before the Cisterna battle. The plane's engine failed and the P-40 plunged into the sea in shallow water. Able to swim to land, Mauritz was immediately arrested by Germans and wound up in the castle along with the Ranger officers. During the Cisterna battle, Capt. Saam apparently was in charge of both battalions after Maj. Miller and Maj. Dobson became casualties. There is no record of Saam turning over command to Shunstrom, or of Shunstrom assuming command, but it must have happened after capture. The Germans, who considered Shunstrom to be the senior American officer at the castle, wanted to be able to issue orders to Shunstrom, so when Mauritz, who spoke German, arrived, he was assigned as Shunstrom's interpreter. When Mauritz first met Shunstrom, he found Shunstrom and Bing Evans already discussing escape plans and told them that he also intended to escape.[6]

Laterina had about twelve barracks, all in poor condition. A double fence had gaps in it, which the Germans were repairing. Each corner of the compound had guard towers, manned by soldiers with machine guns. There were several empty barracks next to the fence. Shunstrom and Mauritz planned to escape through these empty buildings, slipping from one building to the next, hoping they could slip through both parts of the double fence. Cpl. Schenkel, 1/Hq., who had served under Shunstrom, discussed their situation with Shunstrom while walking around Laterina. Schenkel:

> Chuck [told me], "Do everything you can, Larry, to make life miserable for them." . . . The next day I looked for him, but he wasn't out walking. I thought maybe something was funny. Then toward late afternoon, or early evening, we were all ordered outside to stand at attention. . . . They told us that two men were missing, and they wanted us to tell them who they were. . . . That's when it dawned on me. . . . [Shunstrom] was casing the place, watching the guards, studying the fences, all that. . . . [They] warned us not to try to escape, saying that they'd shoot two of us for every one that got out.[7]

Bing Evans and Shunstrom had discussed plans to escape together, but when Shunstrom and Mauritz escaped, they left Evans behind.[8] They may have felt that Evans was unfit to travel because of the concussion he had sustained at Cisterna just a few days before. However, Shunstrom needed Mauritz to be his interpreter, and Mauritz needed Shunstrom because of his skills, strength, and savvy.

As planned, on the day of the escape Capt. Shunstrom and Lt. Mauritz ran from one empty building to another until they got close to the two fences. Two Italians, who were making repairs between the fences, realized what the escapers were up to and motioned for them to slip through the two fences and into an empty woodshed, unseen by the German guards.[9] They almost immediately got a big scare. Lt. Mauritz:

> Before we could devise a plan a piercing siren screamed. Shunstrom and I could only look at each other in horror. . . . We were caught! My mind raced, trying to think what to do. . . . Nowhere to run. . . . When we looked out the window, we saw that the guards . . . were calmly lining up the prisoners two abreast and marching them slowly toward the main gate. . . . It was chow call. . . . and we walked out of that prison camp into freedom.[10]

Walking, so as to not attract attention, the two came upon a farmhouse and knocked. Telling an elderly woman they were hungry, she hurriedly handed them a loaf of bread and some sausage wrapped in a towel, the first real food they had eaten since capture. Devouring the food as they walked, the two men tried to put distance between themselves and Laterina before the evening headcount, when their escape would inevitably be discovered.

At the next farm they found someone who spoke broken English who told them to head across the Apennine Mountains to Ancona on the Adriatic coast. Shunstrom had heard that British submarines there would pick up escaped POWs, and the two decided it was better to risk the mountains than to head south, where it would be next to impossible to get through the German lines. Once in the mountains, Lt. Mauritz had a hard time keeping up with the Ranger-fit Shunstrom, who could walk for miles without stopping. As they walked along, Shunstrom shared combat stories with Mauritz: "I could tell [Shunstrom] loved talking about this. . . . I understood how necessary it was that we have men like him who can fight a war on such a personal level and take care of the business that can only be handled in that way."[11]

Once, in a tiny mountain village, where they felt reasonably safe, they were in a tavern eating "hefty" sandwiches of sausage with roasted red and green peppers. Lt. Mauritz:

> Because it was too dangerous for us to speak in public, we were happy to just sit there stuffing our mouths and bellies when two German officers walked in. "Boots!" I whispered to Chuck. . . . By this time the black shoe polish used to camouflage our brown military books had worn off. With every other Italian wearing nothing but black, I knew our boots could give us away. . . . Happily, the Germans . . . didn't look at our feet . . . they were far more interested in downing one of those sausage sandwiches and a good glass of beer than catching two dirty, ragged escapees.[12]

High in the mountains, a few weeks into their escape, they were caught in a blizzard, a total whiteout. Walking along on the edge of a cliff, they were afraid they would fall into the abyss, but they had to keep moving or freeze to death. That night, just as they thought they could go no further, they spotted a light in the distance. Finding themselves at a cabin, they were too weak even to knock on the door. But an old man holding a candle invited them in. A few more minutes and they would have perished. The old man's wife warmed some wine and gave it to them, along with some crusts of bread and a piece of cheese. Then they passed out in front of a roaring fire.

As they approached the Adriatic coast, they encountered an Italian who had been to New York and Chicago. He fed them a fine dinner and introduced them to an Italian partisan who was willing to be their guide on the last leg of their journey. The partisan put them in the back of a stolen canvas-covered truck, carrying armed partisans holding a Fascist prisoner at gunpoint. Mauritz was finishing a cigarette when gunfire tore through the canvas on the truck, with bullets just missing his head. When the truck stopped, its radiator shot through, the partisans rushed out to find a group of their comrades who had mistaken them for Germans. They hiked a long way back into the mountains to the partisan camp, but then found they had to move higher into the mountains because the spot was too dangerous.[13] Shunstrom and Mauritz spent several weeks at this mountain hideout. The partisans then killed their Fascist prisoner and loaded everyone else into the back of a truck, hidden under a tarp. At a checkpoint, a German guard wanted to look under the tarp. The driver dropped a grenade just as the guard walked by, but the other guards opened up with machine guns. Throwing back the tarp, the partisans began firing and the truck began racing down the road, chased by machine gun fire. Shunstrom and Mauritz knew that if they were captured, they would be summarily executed for being caught with the partisans. It was time to make for the Adriatic coast and seek out the British submarines.

Slipping away from the partisans, the escapees found sympathetic Italians as they neared the coast. One day Mauritz awoke to find Shunstrom gone. Shunstrom had contacted the British submarine and, despite all they had endured together, abandoned Mauritz. Mauritz resumed the escape route, one morning finding himself caught at the front line in an artillery duel between German and British forces. Mauritz calculated how much time he had between shells landing and made a dash for the Allied lines. At a debriefing, he told the story of his escape with Capt. Shunstrom. The officer said, "Yes, Captain Charles Shunstrom, a Ranger. He came through here about a month ago . . . he didn't mention you."[14] When Shunstrom wrote a report of his escape, he made no mention of Mauritz.

Fifty-eight years later, Mauritz received a letter from Italy saying that his plane had been recovered. The Italians were able to trace him because the Army Air Corps files identified the plane and the pilot. Mauritz and his family made the trip to Italy, visiting several Italians who had risked their lives to help him and Shunstrom escape.

THE SECOND ESCAPE: 1ST LT. GERALD SIMON, 1/HQ.

No one at Laterina knew how Simon pulled it off, but some suggested that the British escape committee helped. Escapers were supposed to get permission from their commanding officer, which would have been Shunstrom, who had left the day before. It was rumored that Simon simply walked out the front gate with a British tank officer, and there was no one to dispute it.[15] Simon joined a band of Italian partisans but was captured by the Germans and taken to Gestapo headquarters, where he was cut to pieces while alive.[16]

THE THIRD ESCAPE: 2ND LT. WILLIAM NEWNAN, 3/B

Lt. Newnan dictated his memoirs immediately upon returning to the United States after his escape from the Germans, so his account is considered especially reliable: "Being captured was quite a shock to all of us because we had been able to visualize very graphically the idea of being badly hurt, or perhaps even killed, but the idea of being taken prisoner was something that none of us had considered at all. As a result, we were temporarily off balance."[17]

After the parade through Rome, some of the Rangers were trucked about forty miles northeast to Fara Sabina, which, like Laterina, was a temporary holding camp for prisoners awaiting transfer to camps in Germany or Poland. While there, British officers, who had escaped and been recaptured, told Newnan that Italians in the back country were friendly, food was plentiful, and it was probably safe if you stayed away from railroads, highways, and towns.[18] From Fara Sabina the Rangers were moved to Laterina, where they kept warm by busting up cots and burning them. Because Laterina's fences were still under repair when the Rangers arrived, Lt. Newnan knew that he needed to escape quickly.

The morning after Lt. Simon escaped, the Germans held a long roll call (called an *appel* in German), creating a chance for Lt. Newnan to move away from the officer group and make his way in among the enlisted men, where he would be less conspicuous. Spotting a building used for truck repair that was close to the fences, Newman slipped inside. He could see a hole in the outer fence big enough to get through. When the mechanics left for lunch, Newnan climbed over the first fence, dropped in between the fences, and ducked through the hole in the outer one. Walking, not running, to avoid suspicion, he went about twenty-five yards to a group of buildings, where he hid. He remembered: "There was another fence two hundred yards outside the main stockade . . . but since they were short-handed [there was no guard]. . . . I was over that fence in nothing flat and then kept running as fast as I could go."[19]

To his left was the Arno River, and to his right a highway. A place about sixty yards wide where the river was breaking white indicated that there was a ford. The water was about knee-deep but very swift and dangerous. When Newnan neared the opposite bank, he was exhausted from struggling through the rapids. Fortunately, a farmer on the bank held out his pitchfork and pulled Newnan in: "He didn't say anything and I didn't say anything; we just understood each other. And then I took off on the run again, now making for the high ground. . . . [Looking back, I could] see six Germans looking for me . . . the Italian [farmer] across the river didn't tip them off."[20]

Another farmer provided a map, and in training Newnan had learned how to use his pocket watch as a compass. Pointing the hour hand at the sun, he could bisect the smaller of two angles between the hour hand and twelve o'clock to find due south. Lt. Newnan chose to head south, toward Rome, because the Germans would not be looking for him there. Although the Germans would torture and kill anyone who sheltered an escapee, he found farmers willing to risk sheltering him. Lt. Newnan felt somewhat protected because the country was full of men who were streaming home after escaping from German labor camps. Few Italians wore glasses as he did, and he worried that his height, glasses, and army shoes would give him away. As he walked through a town he got lots of stares—he wasn't fooling any Italians. As he got closer to Rome, hospitality dried up, the country was poor, and there were more roads. Good roads meant Jerries, and if there were any Germans nearby the Italians dared not help anyone.[21]

Newnan paid his way by writing chits, a promise to pay scrawled on paper in exchange for helping American runaways. Newnan then stumbled into a

British sailor, who had connections with Italians in Rome. There, the Allies had established an underground to house and feed POWs. But to get there, Newnan had to board a train. Someone brought him civilian clothes and a train ticket, and a woman carried his uniform rolled up in a piece of newspaper. Newnan, "We got on the train, sat down in our seats, the conductor came along and he asked one man for his identification papers, but he didn't ask us, thank goodness, and we rolled into Rome."[22] Lt. Newnan was taken to a large apartment house, where he stayed with an Italian family. An escaped British prisoner, Lt. Simpson, had taken charge of all the escaped POWs in Rome. A shrewd businessman, Simpson knew his way around and had all the contacts needed for POWs to survive. He somehow managed to get paid through the Italian underground, and he would give money to the POWs to cover their rent, food, and other expenses. Newnan: "There we were . . . practically right in the heart of Rome. . . . I was taken [to live with] an Italian family, and oh, were they frightened! They wanted me to stay right in my room every minute . . . It wasn't a bad idea, but it was hard on me. I would pace up and down the room [saying to myself], 'You can't fritter your time away and you'll learn Italian fast.'"[23]

These people had children and were afraid that if the Germans discovered they were hiding a POW they would be killed or worse. Simpson then took him to the home of a widow. Newnan took her to dinner at the Casino delle Rosa, and she pointed out four men sitting at the next table a few feet away. She said, "Those are the head of the Gestapo in Rome." The waiter let them know that all was okay, but Newnan was too nervous to enjoy his dinner.[24]

One afternoon the Fascists and Germans had a May Day parade. Newnan was out for a walk and witnessed Italian Communists throwing bombs into the parade and killing some Jerries: "The Germans immediately threw a cordon of troops around that whole section of town and picked up the first 320 Italian men they could get their hands on. Many of these were prominent lawyers, doctors, and merchants. They took the whole bunch out to a cave outside of Rome and machine-gunned them in the cave and then blew the mouth of the cave shut with dynamite."[25]

Early one morning, after hearing gunfire all night, Newnan heard a lot of commotion and went out to investigate. The German army was pulling out of Rome. Lt. Newnan: "I finally ran into some of the Special Service boys . . . half Canadians and half Americans. They told me that the Rangers had all been sent home except for the men that had been in only a year and under, and that those men had just been automatically put into the Special Service force."[26]

The soldiers took Newnan to meet their commander, Brig. Gen. Robert T. Frederick, who knew all about the Rangers' fight at Cisterna and offered to take Newnan in his armored half-track to meet Gen. Clark. Newnan had saved a bottle of champagne and presented it to Gen. Frederick: "On the way out of Rome I had seen where about seven of our tanks had been knocked out along the road by well-placed anti-tank guns. . . . Truck after truck of German equipment was burning alongside the road. . . . Finally, we got to a place that was just a pile of rubble, and the General said, 'Do you recognize this?' I said, 'No.' He said, 'This is Cisterna.' Just flattened—absolutely nothing left. We went from there to 5th Army Headquarters. And from there on my trip became quite routine."[27]

From Naples, Lt. Newnan was flown to Oran, where he learned that his first scout, Tech/5 James O'Reilly, 3/B, had escaped from a boxcar north of Florence. O'Reilly had stolen a German machine gun and lots of ammunition, and the last the other Rangers saw of him he had it on his back, heading into the hills.[28]

THE FOURTH ESCAPE: TECH/5 PASQUALE D'AMATO, 3/E, AND PFC. JAMES ADAMSON, 3/E

When D'Amato and Adamson heard that anyone caught outside their hut at night would be shot on sight, they decided to escape in broad daylight. After observing Italian civilians and other prisoners on work details coming and going from Laterina, they obtained dirty civilian clothes and, on 12 February 1944, pretending to be on a work detail, simply walked out the back gate. Once clear of the camp, the two ran across an open field at least a mile and a half before looking back. They would not be missed before evening *appel*, gaining a three-hour head start on any pursuers. The first locals they ran into knew they were Americans because they walked too fast. D'Amato spoke fluent Italian, so the two Rangers lived off the land with help from friendly farmers. D'Amato told about their most frightening day:

> On May 29 . . . we walked into a German bivouac area and were immediately spotted by two goose-steppers. For ninety minutes we hid in the bush without

> moving a muscle and again luck was on our side. Next day we were fortunate to meet some people . . . who fed us and begged us to stay until the Americans, who by then had entered Rome, reached the town. . . . Never once during those five long months did we think of giving up. We didn't learn until it was all over that we could have been shot as spies had we been captured in civilian clothes! We believed God was on our side and He was, all the way.[29]

OTHER ESCAPES FROM LATERINA

Four more Rangers are known to have escaped from Laterina, including Pvt. Harry Perlmutter, 1/D, who had been given useful escape information by Lt. Gerald Simon. On 15 February, Perlmutter went out with a work party. When the German guard turned his back, Perlmutter hit him on the head with a piece of iron, knocking him out. He then worked his way through abandoned barracks, found a gap in the wire, and crawled through an irrigation ditch to reach the Arno River. Perlmutter swam the Arno and then began following the directions he'd gotten from Lt. Simon. Perlmutter met no Germans en route, and in three days he met up with Lt. Simon and Pfc. Louis Glass, 1/B, a medic.[30] There is no record of how Glass escaped from Laterina. Pvt. George Nimmo, 1/A, and S/Sgt. Robert Taylor, 3/B, also escaped from Laterina, but nothing is known about how they escaped.

THE BOXCARS

Ranger prisoners of war destined for long-term internment in German prison camps were loaded into boxcars at Laterina. The boxcars, called "40 and 8s," were designed to carry either forty men or eight horses, but were now packed with so many men that often they could hardly move. The doors were nailed shut, and the men were rarely allowed out of the cars before reaching their destination. Pvt. Arthur F. Wilson, 1/D:

> We were loaded aboard a train in small boxcars, about fifty men to a car. There wasn't much room and many had to stand the whole time. Frozen beef and black bread was thrown in the one small window and the GI POWs close to the window got food and did not share, but tried to eat as much of the frozen

> food as fast as they could. Some got to eat, and some did not. The men who ate the frozen food so fast had severe cramps later because . . . it expanded after it was thawed. So they were in severe pain (tough). . . . [The trip to Stalag IIB] took 4 or 5 days in that cramped little boxcar.[31]

First Sgt. George Kopanda, 3/F, found himself in a boxcar headed for Stalag VIIA, located just north of the town of Moosburg in southern Bavaria: "this was a three day trip with one loaf of bread, one bowl of soup, and a cup of coffee for the entire trip. Our defecation buckets were overloaded in the course of the trip. There were fifty men to a boxcar, and some men had to sleep right next to the bucket; most of the men had to urinate out of a small hole by the door."[32]

Enlisted Rangers were usually sent to Stalag IIB in northeastern Germany, while officers were shipped to Oflag 64, about seventy miles farther east in Poland. Either camp was just over a thousand miles by rail from Laterina, but in war-torn Europe travel was often beset with detours and delays. Along the way, American planes strafed the train, unaware it contained POWs. Men arrived dehydrated, weak from lack of food, and sick with dysentery or worse.

ESCAPES FROM THE BOXCARS

On 28 February 1944, Pfc. Gustave E. Schunemann, Cpl. Kenneth Markham, Pfc. Arthur Lyons, and Pfc. Raymond Sadoski, all from 1/F, were in a group that was frisked and loaded into boxcars bound for a German POW camp. As they passed through a gate, Sadoski tossed a knife over the fence to a Ranger who had already been searched. Fortunately, all four men wound up in the same boxcar as the guy with the knife, which had a blade on one end and a screwdriver on the other. The train pulled out at about 1600 hours with the doors locked and the two portholes on each side of the car sealed shut with barbed wire on the outside. The men went to work immediately on their escape.

Pulling out of Florence, Sadoski, and Markham pried an iron bar out of the floor of the boxcar. Using the bar, Markham worked a board out from between the two portholes, making a gap large enough to slip through. A German soldier was on the roof of the car, but road noise prevented him from hearing what the Rangers were doing.[33] By 2000 hours the first man was ready to escape, risking life and limb by jumping from a moving train. Sadoski, a stout man, held one end of a blanket and anchored himself, letting most of the blanket fly out through the gap. Hanging onto the blanket, the men were able to push themselves away from the moving train. Markham and Lyons went first and went off together on their own. Two unnamed Rangers went next, and nothing is known about their escape. Schunemann was fifth in line to go out, sliding out on the blanket anchored on the inside by Sadoski.[34] Sadoski, who had done the most to make the escape possible, remained behind. Soon after Schunemann escaped, the POW train stopped to seal up the escape hole, and under threats from the Germans another Ranger fingered Sadoski as the ringleader of the escapes. He was beaten by the Germans and sat out the war in Stalag IIB, finally escaping on the Westward March in the winter of 1945. Meanwhile, Markham and Lyons stuck together. Markham, about his escape from the boxcar:

> It was cold and dark. I told Arthur Lyons I was going to take a crack at it. We crossed a bridge, and I told him I would work my way back to the bridge and wait for him for about an hour. . . . I let [a] blanket fly out of the port hole, and then I went out headfirst and slid down the blanket. The train was traveling about thirty miles per hour. The real trouble seemed in pushing away from the train and not getting caught under the wheels. I . . . landed on the rocks on the side of the tracks. . . . The guard saw me jump and shot at me three or four times and missed. I cut out for the bridge. I heard some more shots and guessed that Lyons had made a break for it also. About thirty minutes later, Lyons showed up.[35]

Markham and Lyons took off at a run, up a road away from the railroad. After about five miles they came to a house where they took the risk of asking for food, but the woman there, fearing German reprisals, was afraid to help escapees. Farther down the road they were surprised to find an Italian riding a bicycle at three o'clock in the morning. Following him to his home, he agreed to let them sleep in the barn. The next morning the man hooked up a wagon and said he was going into Florence to meet the underground. Markham wondered if he should trust him or kill him, but decided to let him go to Florence. While he was gone, his wife washed their clothes and heated water for them to bathe in an old wooden tub.[36] Markham:

> By nightfall, the Italian man returned from Florence and said he had made contact with the underground and they would be out to pick us up on Sunday. ... The underground came to the house riding bicycles built for two ... they also brought some civilian clothes for us. ... We rode the bicycles into Florence and right through the heart of town ... to an apartment building. A nice old Italian woman and an old man met us at the door. We were introduced to three British soldiers who had been captured in Crete. The British soldiers ... would go out at night. Lyons and I stayed in at all times.[37]

One day the Gestapo followed the British men back from a bar. The Germans surrounded the apartment and set up a machine gun near each corner of the building. Lyons and Markham hid on the roof, lying down flat. The Italian couple also went out on the roof. They walked to the edge and raised their hands in surrender, but the German machine guns cut them down. When a German officer armed with a Luger appeared on the roof, the Rangers surrendered. They and the three British were crammed into a tiny cell for thirty days until they were moved to Stalag VIIA in Moosburg, Germany.[38]

Because Schunemann was the last to exit the car, he emerged just as the train was about to pass through a railroad station ahead. People stared at him, but he hung onto the side of the car, not daring to jump right then:

> The electric train accelerated through the marshalling yards and out into the open countryside ... at a very fast clip. It was so dark I could not tell if I was on a bridge or in an underpass. I had no idea where I was. ... Out of pure desperation, half starved to death, and with the strong will to survive, I kicked away from the boxcar, formed into a ball, and went head over heels down the crushed rock railroad bed. Picking myself up I checked for damage and found only a slightly sprained thumb. Again, thank God.
>
> I headed straight away from the tracks. ... I walked all day long in a westerly direction ... keeping off the main roads most of the time. ... As I continued walking through the woods, I could hear someone chopping wood. ... In broken Italian ... I told him I was an American, I had escaped from the Germans and I was hungry. ... [He] motioned for me to follow him. ... Mrs. Gradi ladled out a bowl of soup, cut off a slab of freshly baked bread and said, "mangiare" (eat). To this day, I haven't tasted anything better than that soup.
>
> I spent the next few days keeping out of sight in an upstairs room and get-

> ting acquainted with the people of the tiny village. . . . It was risky for anyone to harbor an escaped POW, and I did not want to put the Gradis in any danger by my presence. So, after a few days of their hospitality I decided to move on. . . . I fixed myself a real nice pad inside a stack of cornstalks that had been piled up in teepee fashion to dry. . . . I spent most of my nights . . . on the farm, high on a hill, above the village.
>
> . . . In mid-June we learned about a band of partisans operating in the area about ten miles away. . . . [I was] issued an Italian rifle of World War I vintage, and some ammunition. . . . That very night, with a blazing bonfire that could be seen from miles around, they were roasting chickens and rabbits that were either given to them or stolen. I would guess the latter. They had plenty of wine and soon began singing at the top of their voices.
>
> Early the following morning . . . we encountered a few German soldiers on their way up the hill to investigate what was going on with all the noise, bonfire, etc. Our leader . . . shouted, "Run boys." We must have had over a hundred men, all armed. They scattered . . . in all directions. . . . That ended my brief experience with the partisans.[39]

Schunemann made friends with Gerardo, the son of a farmer who had sheltered him. Gerardo was afraid that the Germans would pick him up and put him into a work battalion. The two of them went looking for a hiding place. Finding a deep gully with a brook running through it, they dug a cave behind some bushes. Gerardo and Schunemann narrowly escaped being nabbed by the Germans on two occasions; consequently, they kept out of sight.[40] Schunemann:

> On the morning of 10 August, I crawled out of the cave and . . . there on the hilltop was a jeep with the . . . [British] "bullseye" mark on it. Without a second thought I hobbled up the hill. . . . I identified myself as an American escaped prisoner. . . . [He] drove me to a command post . . . where he introduced me to the battalion commander. . . . With detailed maps of the area, I was able to pinpoint German gun positions, supply and ammo dumps as well as show him where the mines and booby traps were located.[41]

After debriefing at Fifth Army Headquarters, Schunemann was briefly hospitalized to treat a severe foot infection and was soon on a ship to the United States.[42]

Ranger Pfc. Angelo DiMarco, 1/E, never told anyone his story until he was in a hospital, near death. He suddenly told his son to grab some paper and a few pencils. "I have a story to tell you. . . ."[43] DiMarco and two other unnamed Rangers captured at Cisterna were certain that treatment from the Germans would be much worse once they got to a permanent POW camp. Somewhere near Florence the trio slipped through a hole in the bottom of their moving boxcar, narrowly missing the wheels, and headed out, hoping to survive off the land. DiMarco split away from the rest of the group, thinking an individual would have less chance of getting caught by the Germans.[44]

> With his clothing in tatters and seriously weakened from lack of food, he approached a farmhouse, hoping they would take him in. The farmer's daughter spoke some English and encouraged her father to show favor. DiMarco ended up staying with this family, living in an attic bedroom, working to help the farmer and making weekly trips into Florence with the farmer and his daughter. When, after many weeks, he learned that the French would soon be in Florence, the farmer took DiMarco to the Florence market one last time and turned him loose, along with a parting gift from the family of food and water to tide him over. Days later, DiMarco spotted a French convoy and convinced them that he was an American Ranger. A few days later, DiMarco was in Rome where he was cleared by U.S. Army intelligence and on the way home to the USA.[45]

At Laterina, Pfc. Thomas Mascari, 1/A, was marched to the rail station and issued a small can of tuna fish and a small piece of bread, his food ration for the trip, all of which he downed immediately. Mascari's car held twenty-two men, with no guard inside. After sizing up the car and finding one ventilation window that was vulnerable, he pulled out a board and snapped the barbed wire. When the train slowed down, Mascari jumped, followed by Pvt. William McNeilly, 3/D. Finding themselves in an area with small, scattered homes, Mascari, who could speak Italian, decided to trust the locals, who gave them bread and sausage and told them to move on to Monte Morello, where they could hold out with partisans.[46] Pfc. Mascari: "With many Germans in the area, it was unsafe to stay in a home. We lived in a cave and depended on the partisans for food. Each morning women baked bread in outdoor ovens and left some on the side for the partisans, who, from time to time, would in turn donate us a sheep or lamb, probably stolen. Bill and I were a team until Bill disappeared, going out on his own where he was recaptured. When the British broke through into this area, I raced down the hill to meet them, free again."[47]

Other known boxcar escapers included SGM Kenneth Munro, 3/Hq.; Tech/5 James Mahoney, 1/C; 1st Lt. Patrick Teel, 1/D; Cpl. Lawrence Hurst, 3/C; Tech/Sgt. Robert Halliday, 1/Hq.; Pvt. Frank Duffy, 1/B; Pfc. Edward Feigenbaum, 3/D; Sgt. Charles Hodal, 3/D; Pfc. Albert Dzinkowski, 3/F; and Sgt. Dale Greenland, 1/Hq.[48]

GERMAN STALAGS: PRISONER OF WAR CAMPS

Once Rangers had been shipped to permanent POW camps, the German administration would sometimes notify the Rangers' families that they were being held, usually months after their capture. Often the U.S. military intercepted these messages and sent their own telegram to inform the family, such as the one sent to Henry Breuers, updating the status of Sgt. Breuers, 3/B, from missing in action to prisoner of war: "Western Union dated June 6, 1944: Based on information received through the Provost Marshal General, records of the War Department have been amended to show your son Sergeant Jacob Breuers is now a prisoner of war of the German government. Any further information received will be furnished by the Provost Marshal General. [signed] The Adjutant General."[49]

The Germans had underestimated the number of prisoners they would capture, and lacked facilities to accommodate them. When Italy surrendered to the Allies, 600,000 Italian prisoners were sent to POW camps in Germany, where they joined more than 50,000 previously captured British and American POWs. Eventually 134 camps held British and American prisoners.[50] Administering each camp were a German commandant and a staff of officers and NCOs, called *Feldwebels.* The commandants had some flexibility in how they managed their camps, and in some cases, ignoring the Geneva Convention, they inflicted their own forms of punishment for almost anything. Most camps had collaborators who were on the lookout for escape attempts and troublemakers. The ordinary prisoner had little to do with the camp officers, dealing only with the actual guards. As Germany needed ever more men to serve at the front, the quality of the guards decreased, with many being soldiers who had been wounded or crippled, totally unfit for the job.[51]

American prisoners of war were starved, beaten, almost worked to death. They suffered from battle wounds and from illnesses, for which there was scant medical care. They often endured torture and witnessed others suffering the same tortures they had endured. They saw shootings for small infractions and feared the same fate for themselves. Their continual worry was food. Cpl. George W. "Jack" Hall, 3/D, described their starvation diet: "Once a day we got potato soup, without potatoes. It was just flavored water, and once in a blue moon you might get a bone from some horse meat. We were practically starving, but the Germans were actually starving the Russian prisoners. Daily, they would take out wagon-loads of dead Russian POWs. I got gum disease there and a German dentist had me strapped down. He pulled all my teeth without anything for pain."[52]

Each POW camp had its own system of self-government, and the Allied officer in charge at a camp was supposed to maintain order and discourage disruptive actions. Paradoxically, it was also understood by all parties that this leader was also supposed to encourage his men to escape, which was the most disruptive action possible in a POW camp. Most camps had an unofficial "escape committee," whose job it was to approve escape plans, or deny them if the committee thought the plan might risk the lives of other POWs.[53]

Regardless of rank, all POWs called themselves "Kriegies," a shortened version of the German word for a POW.[54] Some of the enlisted men and a few NCOs were put to work on farms. S/Sgt. Wayne Ruona, 3/C, was one of them: "We were always trying to foul up something to keep the guards off balance. We clogged up machinery and did other things to cause problems. They never did catch on to what we were doing."[55]

STALAG IIB: HAMMERSTEIN, GERMANY (NOW CZARNE, POLAND)

Stalag IIB was in a region of extreme cold, where the clothing was never adequate for the climate. The camp, covering twenty-five acres and surrounded by double rows of barbed wire fence, was a mile and a half west of Hammerstein, in northeastern Germany. Internal barbed wire fences kept different nationalities separate. Prisoners lived in barracks where there was no privacy. The wooden bunks were stacked three high, and the few coal-burning stoves gave hardly any heat. When the coal ran out, the Rangers would burn the slats from their bunks to keep warm. The only lighting was a single twenty- to forty-watt naked bulb swinging from the ceiling. At night the men were locked in—anyone seen outside was shot. For night use, there were latrine buckets at each end of the barracks. The smell of unwashed bodies and latrine buckets was overwhelming to new prisoners, but they inevitably adapted.[56]

Regardless of the weather, the POWs were called out daily, sometimes more than once, to stand outside for an *appel*, or head count, so the Germans could determine if anyone had escaped during the night. During an *appel*, prisoners might be forced to stand for hours, regardless of their physical ability. Often, prisoners would have to support other soldiers who were too weak to stand. The penalty for not standing at attention during *appel* could be a beating or death. If the Germans did not get a correct count, they would start the count over. To delay the Germans from discovering an escape, Rangers would duck or move, confusing the count, forcing the Germans to begin again. In some cases, disrupting the count was the Rangers' idea of entertainment—anything to bedevil their captors.[57]

The only source of healthy food was Red Cross parcels, which were seldom distributed. Weighing about eleven pounds, most included cigarettes, a can of powdered Klim (milk spelled backward), a one-pound can of oleo margarine, half a pound of sugar cubes, half a pound of Kraft cheese, K ration biscuits, a four-ounce can of coffee, plus jam or peanut butter, Spam or corned beef, vitamin tablets, soap, and chocolate bars. This was the only soap the Rangers had. They sometimes bribed the Germans in the camp kitchen to provide hot water for washing. Otherwise, they had to use the cold water from the one outdoor spigot. Most POWs became barterers, trading food for cigarettes or vice versa.[58]

Stalag IIB was particularly infamous among the POW camps for its wretched conditions and the punishments meted out for trivial infractions.[59] In January 1945, the roster showed 7,087 Americans held at Stalag IIB,[60] among whom were 237 Rangers from the 1st Battalion and 256 from the 3rd Battalion.[61] There was supposed to be some organized entertainment at prison camps, but at Stalag IIB it mostly went unnoticed by the prisoners. The camp supposedly had a library of around five thousand books, but none of the Rangers ever mentioned going there. A few inmates formed a band with instruments provided by the Red Cross. Pfc. Steve Ketzer, 1/C, got to star in a play. Ketzer had been captured in January 1943 in North Africa and had been an inmate for over a year before the arrival of fellow Rangers from Cisterna, one of whom was a good friend and a talented artist. Ketzer:

> One day in early 1944, I had the surprise of my life as friends from the Rangers came straggling into camp. Most were in bad shape after being stuffed into small boxcars for the trip from Italy to Poland. I knew what it was like to be cold and to be deprived of food, water, and rest for so many weeks. It was devastating to learn of their losses at Cisterna, and many were still in some form of shock from being captured. One of the arrivals was Staff Sergeant Dennis Bergstrom, 1/Hq., captured at Cisterna, known as the "Ranger artist." He could draw or paint anything, including a pencil drawing made while a POW and dated 9 March 1944, depicting battles of the 1st Ranger Battalion from North Africa, through Sicily and Italy, until their capture at Anzio and ultimate imprisonment at Stalag IIB. I was able to sneak that into my jacket, and it survived the death march back to freedom in 1945.[62]

Enlisted men often volunteered to work on *kommandos,* potato or dairy farms that were operated with prison labor, where food was more plentiful and men had a better chance of escaping. At some, men cut trees and hauled them to a sawmill. Even at the *kommandos* there was never enough food, no replacement of clothing, and it was always wet and cold.[63] NCOs were not supposed to have to work, but the Germans were short of labor. Capt. Springer, the German officer in charge of assembling crews, always included NCOs and medical corpsmen in the work parties. Those who objected were sometimes forced into a job at the point of a bayonet. Many sergeants had lost the identification that proved they were NCOs, sometimes on purpose, and most Jewish soldiers had also "lost" their dog tags, because they knew what Germans did to Jews.[64]

Pvt. Arthur Wilson, 1/D, was picked to work outside the camp cutting down trees for a sawmill, or sometimes planting or picking potatoes. When he showed some other men an easier way to unload a wagon of potatoes, the Germans beat him.[65] Cpl. William Zartman, 1/F, worked on a farm digging potatoes. A daily food ration consisted of a bowl of potato soup plus about a fifth of a loaf of bread, which had the year the loaf was made stamped on the bottom. The Germans had experimented with preserving food, and many loaves dated from the 1920s. The "bread" was dark brown with a crust that could hardly be cut. It took a good set of teeth to eat it, and men dunked it in the soup to try to soften it. At the same farm the Rangers also harvested and threshed wheat. Zartman:

> When no one was looking, someone dropped a pitchfork into the in-feed, and the loud grinding sound attracted the attention of the guards who came on a run. They threatened to shoot all of [us] POWs but did not.
>
> We were all returned to Stalag IIB where the guards were cruel, often beating POWs. A guard named Hortman Springer was investigated as a war criminal after the war. He was known as a butcher and was accused of executing at least nine POWs.[66]

Pfc. Zelly Dineen, 1/E, was friendly with one other Ranger after the war, but, like so many Rangers who would not speak of the horrors they endured, he never told his daughter, Joyce, more than that he was a Ranger and was captured. In 2004, trying to find information about her father's war experience, Joyce wrote on an online Ranger guestbook site that her father was a World War II Ranger and asked for any information that anyone had on him. I contacted her, and eventually we spoke by phone. Joyce told me that her father had finally begun talking about his Ranger experience, but what he said did not make sense. He said that Gen. Roosevelt was with the Rangers in Italy, but she knew that Roosevelt was the president. She said he talked about a sergeant whose name sounded like "Hehaw" and a Capt. Miller. I asked to speak with Mr. Dineen and asked him what he did before the war. He said that he had worked in a sawmill near Sacramento. Bingo! I was in the lumber business, and that became the topic of our first call—nothing about his military service. After more telephone calls I was able to write his story.

The level of detail that Dineen recounted without hesitation confirmed my belief that the Rangers never got their war experiences out of their minds, even if they tried to forget. Dineen was a member of the 1st Ranger Battalion, E Company. His first sergeant was SGM Robert Ehalt (not Hehaw), who Dineen, a brand new volunteer, quite possibly never spoke with, and he may not have known Ehalt's correct name. His company commander was Capt. Beverly Miller. Gen. Theodore Roosevelt, the son of President Theodore Roosevelt, was deputy commander of the U.S. 45th Infantry Division, fighting in close proximity to the Rangers. That explained the names. Dineen joined the Rangers just prior to the Anzio invasion, only a few weeks before the Cisterna battle, where he was captured. I have written the following account as if Dineen were speaking. The exact words are mine, but they are an edited version of the story as he told it to me.

> Capt. Beverly Miller, 1/E, always picked me to go out on recon patrols. I never knew why except that maybe I was older. The picture of me shows creases in my pants, new pants I got right before the Anzio campaign. That's how I remember when the picture was taken.
>
> After our capture, we had to stand up in the boxcars; they were so packed, but some guy managed to have a shelter half and he made a hammock in the car. As we went through the Alps, we were all about to die of thirst while freezing to death. The only water came from defrost inside the cars. Finally, we came to Stalag VIIA, which mainly housed British Commandos who were in bad shape. After one to two days there, with little to eat, we were put back on a train and taken north to Stalag IIB.
>
> After I had been there about a week, some Red Cross parcels arrived, which we split up. They contained powered milk, Spam, margarine, cigarettes, and dominos of all things. It was enough to keep me from starving—but that was about it. Once a day we were fed from a tub which had something that looked like grits. It wasn't much. I had a tin can to eat out of but no spoon. After a while, I was assigned to work on a farm, planting potatoes. But because I had had experience working in the woods the Germans put me to work in their forest.[67]

Dineen did not know about Ranger reunions. After the war he worked two jobs to get along in life. He went to the Veterans Administration to get medical assistance from time to time, and he had a hip replacement as a result of some injuries. Before Cisterna, Capt. Miller had promoted him to corporal, the rank he held when he was captured. However, the U.S. Army had no record of it. He never got any medals, and he never got a Purple Heart, even though the VA knew about his injuries.[68]

Sgt. Carl Harrison Lehmann Jr., 3/C, hated Germans like vermin:

> After being insulted with the march around the Colosseum in Rome, we eventually found our way to Stalag IIB, crammed into boxcars with barely enough room to sit down. At the POW camp we were told to strip naked so they could delouse our clothes in a "gas chamber" while we went through communal showers. This stuck in my mind years later when I watched movies of Jews being put through a similar routine of fumigating clothes and bodies, except for the Jews, their showerheads spewed Zyklon-B.[69]

Pvt. George Richardson, 1/C, noted that one of the most serious things the POWs had to deal with was protecting Jewish comrades from the Germans, even if they were not Rangers: "A guard came running toward us with his pistol drawn, screaming Altschuler's name. . . . We huddled around Altschuler so that the guard couldn't get to him. Finally, we just buried him on the ground under us to prevent . . . him getting shot. Other guards came a few minutes later and dragged him off. We never saw him again."[70]

Today there is nothing left of Stalag IIB. It was in Germany then, but the site is now part of Poland. The Russians and Germans fought a battle on that very spot after the Allied POWs were evacuated. The site is now a desolate pine forest that has grown up after the war. Around the former prison site are scattered gravestones, many presumably Russians, because they have the hammer and sickle emblem. There are no German grave markers, nor are there any names of persons who might be buried there except for an occasional personal marker set out by family members. A little-used trail going through the pine forest ends at an abandoned rail line, probably the same railroad used to haul Rangers and other prisoners to Stalag IIB. On the main road leading into the site is a granite slab with a Polish inscription: "In memory of 65,000 prisoners of war who were starved, tortured and murdered by the Nazis in the Stalag IIB Hammerstein POW camp in Czarnem."

POW memorial monument at Stalag IIB in Poland. The plaque reads (translated): "In memory of 65,000 prisoners of war who were starved, tortured and murdered by the Nazis at Stalag 2B Hammerstein POW camp in Czarnem." Photograph by Mikola Kepinski.

STALAG IIIA: LUCKENWALDE, NEAR BERLIN, GERMANY

Tech/5 Mickey Romine, 3/Hq., a medic, was one of the few Rangers held at Stalag IIIA:

> They put eighty of us in one of those little boxcars and locked the doors and then wrapped barbed wire around the entire car. We were dive-bombed every day. They would stop the train and run for the ditches, but left us in the

box-cars. We expected any minute to have a bomb hit the boxcar we were in. We were all screaming for them to let us out. This happened every day for three days. They gave us no food while we were in the boxcars. After we got to Austria, I came down with diphtheria. I had so little meat on my arms and legs, that they could not stick a needle in me, so they shot me in the butt and hit the bone. I was in the hospital for ten days, then I was put in the camp with my buddies; they had been told that I died.

When I got out of the hospital, I was . . . interrogated on four different times. . . . One time they made me strip stark naked and put me on a balcony facing a north wind for four hours. The times that I was beaten, the officer would call in a guard and he would kick me on the back of my legs and hit me with a board on my back and shoulders. I would have welts an inch high. When the [Russians] started getting closer to our camp, the Germans marched us out of camp in groups of 100. . . . When some of the weaker men would collapse alongside the road, I would try to help them, and I would get a rifle butt in my back. . . . In April 1945 the Russians set us free. However, they would not let us cross the Elbe River to the side held by the Americans. . . . Sometime in late May, we managed to bluff our way across. After I was discharged from the army, I found it very difficult to hold a job. . . . I had trouble sleeping at night and when I did sleep, I would wake up with nightmares. I was very embarrassed and said nothing to anybody. When I would hear a car backfire, I would hit the dirt and my friends would make fun of me. So, I would grit my teeth and keep my problem to myself.[71]

STALAG IIIB: CAMP FOR NCOS, IN FURSTENBERG, GERMANY

Cpl. Paul Hermsen, 1/C, captured in Tunisia, was one of the few Rangers held at Stalag IIIB, home to about three thousand POWs:

I was elected the barracks chief, probably because I was the only Ranger there at the time. My duties were to keep order. Germans counted heads morning and evening, and sometimes in the middle of the night. All the men were lined up outside to be counted no matter what the weather was. At times the Gestapo would search the barracks, in which case we would have to stand outside in the cold for hours. The camp was surrounded by two rows of very high barbed wire fencing with rolls of barbed wire in between. There were several guard towers, each with machine guns and spotlights. Anyone out at night would be shot. I still wore the clothes I was captured in.

We had showers about once a month, with three men to a showerhead for only one minute. We were very hungry and weak, making it easier for the Germans to control us, and many lost their will to survive. Two of the POW's had made a deal with the guards to accumulate radio parts, and they were able to assemble a radio, keeping it hidden under a bottom bunk against the wall. From that we learned how the war was progressing.

I attempted to escape on three occasions. The first time I went over to the French compound and went out with a French working party to collect firewood. I slipped away and walked to the town of Guben, located on the Neisse River on the border between Germany and Poland. There were some railroad cars going west loaded with pigs, and I hid myself among the pigs. I was on the train for three days when it came to a stop, and I was found by some German soldiers. They washed me off with a hose, and in a few days, I was back at Stalag IIIB where I was put into solitary confinement for three weeks.[72]

OFLAG 64: SZUBIN, IN NORTHWESTERN POLAND

Ranger officers met with somewhat better conditions than enlisted men. Oflag 64, in Szubin, Poland, was a former girls' school. It possessed good facilities and a reasonable German commandant and staff. The camp was well run and had some substantial structures, including a stone chapel and an administrative building known as the "White House."[73] Prisoners were allowed to have a garden and supplement their diet with a few vegetables. Flowers were planted around the site so that when inspectors came from the International Red Cross they would be impressed with the quality of life.[74] Inspectors never got to see what the POWs really endured. First Lt. Lynn Olesen, 1/E:

The Germans began to contraband Lifebouy soap after someone figured out a way to make an explosive from it. They blew the lock off of the potato cellar. The floor of the barracks was brick like the streets used to be and we would loosen the bricks, dig a hole, place a box in the hole, then put the bricks back

> in place. We used to store contraband there and the potatoes we got from the cellar. One of the main things that was contraband was radios. The Germans didn't want us to listen to the BBC Radio. They always told us that Germany was winning the war. We didn't find out any different until one day the Russians came and liberated us. However, we weren't sure the war was completed because they held us for one month before turning us over to the Americans.[75]

Second Lt. Donald Frederick, 4/E, captured near Venafro, arrived at Oflag 64 on 16 December 1943. He was taken to the "White House" to meet Lt. Col. John Waters, Gen. Patton's son-in-law, who had been captured in North Africa. When asked his name, Lt. Frederick said, "Bill Darby." Walters replied, "Well, Don, Bill Darby was my classmate at West Point." The mind games ended there and Frederick answered the colonel's questions truthfully. Several months later, Frederick was moved to the third floor of the "White House" and assigned the task of constructing escape maps.[76] The escape committee approved only three escapes, and none was successful. POWs figured the war was about to end. Why risk death if they only had to endure this for a few more months? Housing at Oflag 64 was in old wooden barracks with fifty-plus guys in bunk beds. Straw mattresses and thin blankets were little help without adequate heating. Each morning, Frederick and the other POWs stood for *appel.* Breakfast consisted of whatever was left from Red Cross parcels and ersatz coffee. Noon lunch was watery soup, sometimes supplemented with a small piece of black bread.[77]

ESCAPE FROM THE POW CAMPS

Many Rangers attempted to escape, but most were caught and returned to their camp. The normal punishment for failed escape was two to four weeks in the *kooler,* a tiny, solitary cell where bread and water were intermittently provided. After a successful getaway, guards would ransack the POWs' huts and enact some sort of collective punishment on the rest of the POWs.[78]

Pfc. Steve Ketzer, 1/C, described his third failed escape attempt from Stalag IIB: "I was making a run for it across a field when they turned the dogs loose on me. There was a tree in the field, and I made it to the tree, climbing out of the dogs' reach. The Germans told me that if I made another attempt to escape, they would shoot me, and I believed them."[79]

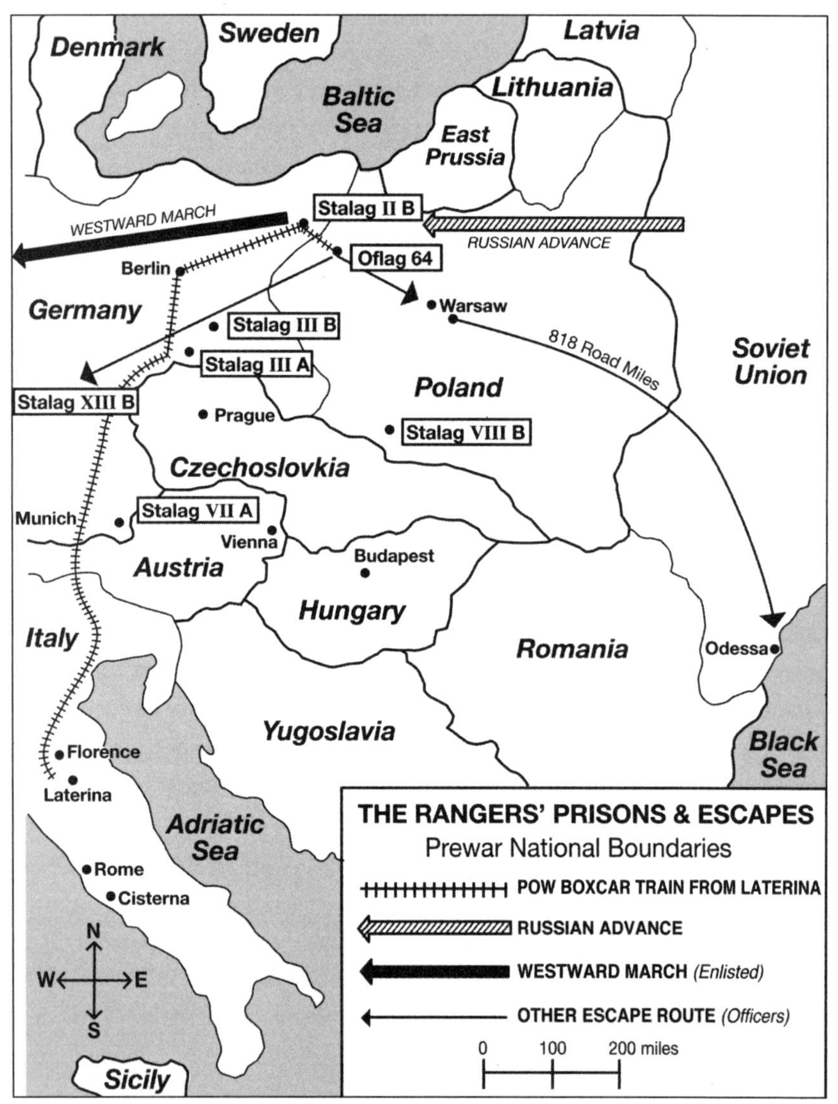

The Route of Ranger Escapes

First Sgt. Frank Mattivi, 1/F, was a member of the escape committee who actually knew about escape plans:

> We were shipped by train to Stalag IIB in Hammerstein. . . . After interrogation, we went to our barracks. During my stay I worked in the post office, knowing that our M/Sgt. Robert Ehalt was supplied a code before leaving New York. I kept watching for packages with that code letter. One finally came. In it we received a radio and escape equipment. We didn't know where to put the radio, so we decided to take up a brick at the bottom bunk and dig a hole large enough for two people . . . We received news from the BBC. We knew when F.D.R. died and about the invasion on June 6th.[80]

First Sgt. George Kopanda, 3/F, was trucked to a farm that made bricks out of peat. The bricks were dried and used for fuel. The prisoners fed peat into a mixer, then forced it through an opening that compacted it into 8-inch-long bricks, then stacked them to dry. On more than one occasion the Rangers "accidentally" dropped tools into the hopper, bringing production to a halt. When caught, they had their rations cut or were forced to work overtime.[81] Two weeks after arriving at the farm, Kopanda teamed up with Cpl. Louis Wojcik, 1/Hq., to plan their first escape:

> On this particular night we noticed that there was no guard on duty for a long period of time. At that moment, we decided to make our move. We unscrewed the nuts on one bar, and with two men tugging we finally jerked it loose. . . . We tried to keep the noise to a minimum and were successful. . . . The next move was to squeeze through the opening in order to see if it was big enough. . . . [Guided by a compass one quarter inch in diameter, we] took a course to the north towards the Baltic coast. Our plan was to walk along the coast until we saw an opportunity to either board a ship or a boat, or to steal one . . . and make our way to Sweden. After seven days of traveling by night and looking for a wooded area to sleep in at dawn, we covered a distance of about 60 kilometers.[82]

On the seventh day of the adventure both men became ill with chills and fever, possibly a relapse of the malaria they caught in Sicily. Stopping at a farmhouse to ask for help, they were turned in to a local constable, who notified the guards at Stalag IIB. After twelve days in the camp hospital, it was ten days in solitary confinement subsisting on two slices of bread, a two-inch piece of bologna, and a cup of water a day.[83]

THE MARCH TO THE WEST FROM STALAG IIB

As the Americans and British invaded at Normandy and began advancing eastward toward Germany, the Russians were moving toward Germany from the east. Hoping to use the Allied POWs as bargaining chips for negotiations at the end of the war, the Germans wanted to be sure that their prisoners did not fall into Russian hands. Consequently, the Germans forced the POWs to march west, away from the Russians.[84] The winter of 1944–1945 was the coldest on record in Europe, and the POWs had to slog through ice and snow. Walking through blizzards with little or no food, many fell by the wayside. Nevertheless, there were better opportunities for escape than in the camps.[85]

Pvt. Arthur Wilson, 1/D, walking for three months in ice and snow, encountered people worse off than he was:

> We walked hundreds of miles in the dead of one of the worst winters that area had experienced. We walked for nearly three months in the snow. We slept in groups to keep warm and ate whatever was dead lying along the road. . . . The German army was moving so fast that a lot of people—soldiers, POWs, men, women and children just died and were left frozen on the roads. . . . We were again put into boxcars and taken to Berlin. There we were left to be bombed and strafed by the Air Force. Some of the POWs were killed. From there we were sent to a camp close to Bremen. As we were being marched into the camp the guards were forcing the other prisoners out. These people wore black and white striped uniforms and some were helped by others, dragged, carried or piggybacked. We could not tell the difference between men and women because the women had their heads shaved. . . . These were political prisoners and Jewish people.[86]

One night there was heavy firing close to the camp. The British army discovered the camp and rescued the POWs. Wilson aged during these war years:

"I learned to hate the enemy. I entered the army as a young, innocent, and naïve man, but I came home much older."[87]

Hunger was always an issue, yet hunger was sometimes worse than some of the food, as Tech/5 Larry Kushner, 3/Hq., discovered:

> Eight of us slipped away from the forced march. It was in January 1945, the coldest winter on record in Poland. We had been living on burnt bread. We burned it to make charcoal which helped our constant diarrhea. On the run, we stumbled into a farm where the man took pity on us, feeding us hot soup and sawdust bread with a thick layer of lard and honey. We all threw up and were in worse shape than when we were hungry. The bread had a date stamp of 1924 on the crust.[88]

POWs tried hard not to be "liberated" by the Russians. Pfc. Clarence Goad, 3/B, tells why:

> After breaking away from the march . . . I was taken prisoner by the Polish army and later that day turned over to the Russians. They put me on a train that was headed to Moscow and was full of Russian soldiers that had been prisoners of the Germans. . . . The train stopped in the middle of nowhere, and armed Russian guards took the soldiers off the train, formed them up, and marched them off. We watched them disappear from sight and waited for an hour or so. No one was allowed off the train. Suddenly we heard machine gun fire, lots of it, and then the guards returned. The train started up, and I put two and two together. I had heard that Stalin had ordered the execution of any returning Russian POW, and now I had seen it, or at least that had to be what I had witnessed.
>
> At the next stop they put me in a boxcar with twenty-five other people headed to Kiev in the Ukraine, along with a Russian girl who spoke some English. I had met her along the way, and she wanted to get home. We stayed at her brother's house. He worked at a railroad repair station, and to get food, I worked there too. On my third day at work, I was about twenty feet from the track when a train rolled in. Russian soldiers got off with machine guns. Then I heard voices, and they were speaking English. The high windows of the train had steel bars on them, and one GI was wearing the little brown cap with the

wool lip that we wore under our helmets. I asked where they were going? The girl with me said, "They go to Siberia, and never come back. Very bad place." I said, "But they are Americans." She told me not to ever speak of this again, the same thing she had said after the Russian POWs were shot.[89]

Cpl. Paul Hermsen, 1/C, described his forced march to the West and escape:

Some of the men fell off to the side of the road and were shot and killed by the German guards. During the march, we passed a group of prisoners in striped uniforms. The guard said they were political prisoners. They may have been Jewish people or gypsies.

Upon reaching Stalag IIIA, we found there were six large tents and about 400 POWs were put in each tent. . . . The ground was very damp and cold. I was with two other Rangers, [S/Sgt. Gene] Castle, 1/C, and [1st Sgt. Victor] Morasti, 1/C. There was one water spigot for 2,400 men. There were no showers during this period and most of us had lice. . . . This time was the worst part of the war for me. The latter part of April, a group of seven of the Rangers and myself managed to escape from the compound. Our plan was to get to Odessa in Russia and hopefully get on ships going to the United States.

[After a bad experience with the Russians], we decided against trying to get to Odessa and would instead attempt to find the American lines. We finally got to a town called Torgau, which is located on the Elbe river . . . Some French D.P.s [displaced persons] were holding a kangaroo court in a nearby wooden area. . . . Several of the D.P. had capitulated to the Germans [and] were hanging from the trees. There were both men and women. We crossed the river . . . we had found the American lines.[90]

Pfc. Zelly Dineen, 1/E, talked about being on a forced march all the way across Germany in January 1945:

Sometime in early 1945, the Germans began a forced march of POWs to keep us from being rescued by the Russians. Heading towards the Elbe River, one day when we stopped to rest, I lay down in some grass and when the whistle blew, I just didn't get up. After the rest of the men marched off, I moved into some woods and stayed for one or two days. There were four of us in the group

> that escaped. One of the guys had a bad cough, and I was afraid he would give us away at night and we would be caught and killed. So, I and another guy, I can't remember his name, took off by ourselves, but I did see the guy with the cough back at Lucky Strike, so I know he made it home.[91]

Dineen and his companion slept in the woods at night. Using a trick learned in training, he would tie a trip wire near their hiding place and hang tin cans on it, so that anybody approaching them would make noise. Dineen stumbled onto a German civilian with whom he exchanged his cigarette lighter for some flour to make bread. Dineen made a borscht and ate on it for thirteen days.[92] Dineen: "One night, when we had walked about as far as we could and bedded down. After a bit, we woke up when we heard tanks cranking up. We had almost walked into a German armored unit. We laid there very still, smelling the gas and listening to the Germans talk. When there was plenty of noise coming from the other side, we eased off through the woods to get away."[93]

One night he could hear ack-ack guns close by, which made him think that Allied forces were nearby. The next day Dineen ran into a German woman, and in exchange for directions he gave her the rest of his flour.[94]

> On the way I ran into a German enlisted man who spoke pretty good English. He was armed and extremely nervous, patting his side like he was fixing to reach into his pocket for a grenade. I figured he was probably a runaway and I ran away from him, looking back for a while, and finally I saw him taking off in the opposite direction. I passed some Russians POWs working on a farm, and they gave me some chunks of horse meat to chew on.
>
> However, I didn't get a chance to eat because a jeep came by at that moment and a British Major said, "Halt, put up your hands and drop what you have." The major and an enlisted man with him both had British sten guns pointed at me. I put my hands up. I remember I was clean shaved that morning because I had always carried a German razor, and I always shaved when possible. I told the major I was from the 1st Ranger Battalion, and that I had POW tags in my pocket to prove it. The major told me to put my hand in my pocket and pull it out very slowly. When he saw the dog tags, he told me to get into the jeep. I sat in the front and the major sat behind me, holding the gun on me.[95]

Dineen was fed bread and butter sandwiches, deloused, and that night put on an American C-47 to be flown out. The plane was almost shot down by American ack-ack guns.

> I could hear shrapnel hitting the plane and pinging all over the place. I was sure that this was going to be the end of it. The plane dropped down real low almost to ground level, dropping orange flares, and the ack-ack stopped. We landed in Brussels, where I was given a British outfit to wear, and then flown to France, spending only twenty-four hours there, just long enough to get a haircut. I was finally on the way home.[96]

Cpl. William Zartman, 1/F, was one of eighty, all in bad physical shape, who were forced marched out of Stalag IIB just ahead of the Russian advance. On a bitter cold day in January 1945 with three or four inches of snow on the ground, they were told by the guards that escapees would be shot. But one night he and four other Rangers attempted to escape from a barn.[97] Zartman: "Problem #1 . . . was to exit the barn . . . well before sunrise. The boarded windows and locked doors would make this a difficult task. . . . Fortunately, the night was dark . . . the guards did not have dogs. . . . If we could make it outside the barn undetected, we were fairly confident . . . that we would be unchallenged for the remainder of the night."[98] Sometime later in the morning, after slipping out of the barn, three members of the group split off to take a road west, while Zartman and one other man continued south and east toward the Russians. "We decided that traveling together made us too visible and might lead to our recapture . . . [therefore], we parted. I decided to travel only at night, and before daybreak I came across an abandoned farmhouse. . . . I entered the barn to sleep for a few hours. . . . As I pulled myself up into the straw . . . my right hand came down . . . on a human shoulder."[99] The shoulder belonged to a British soldier named Jock, captured at Dunkirk in 1940, who had survived over four years in German POW camps. Shortly after daylight Zartman and Jock were jolted from sleep by the sound of artillery fire. Venturing outside, they entered the farmhouse and checked out the basement, where they found candles, food, water, and blankets. They covered the windows so the candlelight would not be visible outside. The artillery fire became greater the next morning, and in the afternoon several trucks and Sherman tanks roared by the farmhouse.[100]

Zartman:

Jock and I were glued to the window. . . . We considered that these Russian troops might be our Allies, but we remained wary . . . because we might be mistaken for Germans, in which case we would certainly be shot before we had a chance to prove our nationality. . . . I remembered what I had learned from the Russian POWs. Front line troops will probably shoot anyone they see, thinking them to be German. Lay low until follow-on units come through and try to surrender to them. Don't give any indication you are German, or you'll not be given a chance to explain. The first moments will determine whether you live or die.

Sometime after dark . . . the thunder of horses' hooves shook our fragile senses and we found ourselves in the path of a cavalry charge. Dozens of horsemen were galloping at a good pace toward us and we knew instinctively that they would not pass without pausing. . . . I knew that if I uttered a single German word, or even a sound that sounded German, it would likely be my last. . . . We heard a lot of noise from the Russian soldiers ransacking and glass breaking. I imagine that they were searching for food and . . . alcohol. Minutes later, we heard boots pounding down the basement stairs. . . . When two Russians entered, Jock and I found ourselves staring into their flashlights. . . . Each had a machine gun aimed at the two of us. . . . One of the Russians yelled "Germania!" He thought we were Germans, confirming my worst fears, and I immediately said, in my best Russian "One American comrade, one English comrade." I repeated these words several times. . . . And I shouted "Nyet, No Germania." One of the soldiers . . . motioned for us to put our hands on top of our heads and we complied immediately. The other soldier frisked us, no doubt looking for weapons. We had none. . . . But he pulled the wallet from my back pocket and began examining its contents. . . . It may have saved our lives. The Germans had taken my money and watch, but they had left the wallet, which still held various personal cards. When they came to my driver's license I uttered the words "Americanski, Chevrolet," while gesturing with my hands as though I were turning a steering wheel.[101]

The next thing Zartman knew he was listening to boisterous singing with a glass of vodka in his hand, the Russians toasting Roosevelt, Stalin, then Roosevelt again. The next morning, an officer gave Jock and Zartman each a pistol because there were still Germans in the area. After many more weeks of traveling by foot and by boxcar, moving though the Polish countryside, devastated first by the Germans then by the Russians, Zartman and Jock walked through what was left of Warsaw and on to Odessa, a distance of 818 miles. They caught a ship there for Naples and eventually to American custody.[102]

THE MARCH WEST FROM OFLAG 64

On Saturday, 20 January 1945, almost a year after the Rangers were captured at Cisterna, the POWs of Oflag 64, all officers, were given less than one day's warning that the Russians were approaching and that they would be marched deep into Germany. Three thousand Red Cross parcels "arrived" that day and were distributed to the POWs. German doctors allowed about seventy-five POWs who were in poor health to remain at Szubin, which was soon overrun by the Russians. In the morning the Rangers saw roads jammed with German families and their belongings headed west. During the war the Nazis had allowed them to take over and operate confiscated Polish farms. Now these German families faced death either from the Russians or the Polish resistance, which was hunting them down.[103]

The POWs of Oflag 64 trudged at gunpoint or at the point of a German bayonet, sometimes sleeping on pews in churches, but more often in barns alongside animals. The men packed themselves in hay for warmth even though it was infested with lice. One morning at about 0500 hours, Maj. John Dobson, the commanding officer of the 1st Ranger Battalion, seriously wounded at Cisterna, and two other Ranger officers, whose names are lost to time, climbed into a hay loft to escape the march. They heard German guards opening the barn door and pulled hay over themselves, hoping that the Germans would not look for them by thrusting bayonets into the hay. This fortunately did not happen. A few hours later a young boy appeared, telling them the marchers had gone. Later that morning the boy's father brought them coffee—a great risk, as it was a capital crime to assist a POW in war-torn Germany.[104]

The barn was on the grounds of a castle where the Germans left about eighty POWs behind because they were too sick to march. Among them were a medic and two American colonels, whom the Germans put in charge. Maj. Dobson negotiated with the colonels, who agreed to let the Rangers stay under cover in the barn for the rest of the day, but they had to leave after dark to not endanger the others if they were discovered by the Germans.[105] Suddenly the men heard the clanking of approaching tanks. Russian soldiers hanging onto the tanks were singing the "Star Spangled Banner." Dobson: "After walking over a hundred miles in knee-deep snow, we had finally met the Russians on the outskirts of Warsaw."[106] The group finally got a ride on an open railroad flatcar. Despite the freezing weather, they eventually made it to Odessa in the Ukraine, where they got a ship to Naples.[107]

Lt. Don Frederick kept a diary during a 440-mile trek to Stalag XIIIB near Hammelburg, in west-central Germany. A few American officers were present, but discipline was lacking and morale was poor. Lt. Frederick: "Food supplies were almost non-existent. If Red Cross parcels had not been available, some POWs would not have survived." On the 26th of March 1945, Task Force Baum of the 4th Armored Division, U.S. Third Army, crashed through the front gate of the camp to rescue Lt. Col. John Waters. But seeing the huge number of POWs, Capt. Abraham Baum, having already lost a lot of men and vehicles, and being low on fuel, realized that he would not be able to evacuate everyone.[108]

As Baum's men were eliminating the camp guards, Frederick jumped on a tank. Unfortunately, a round from a German panzerfaust hit the tank. The wounded Frederick was recaptured and returned to the camp. Only a handful of American POWs were rescued, at a high cost in American casualties. The Germans transported the remaining American POWs to Stalag VIIA at Moosburg, in Bavaria. This proved to be the last stop for these Americans. Tanks of the 14th Armored Division came blasting through the gates with Gen. Patton standing up in his vehicle, shouting, "By God, I'll have you guys out of here in forty-eight hours." Patton kept his word, and Frederick and his fellow soldiers were trucked to Landshut Airport, where C-47s delivered them to Reims, France, and then to Camp Lucky Strike, where everyone was out-processed.[109]

Capt. Warren "Bing" Evans, commanding officer of 3/F, narrowly escaped execution by the Germans for escape and theft:

> I was on the forced march with other Rangers from Oflag 64, heading away from the advancing Russians. One night I got away, and when looking for a hiding place that offered protection from the extremely cold winter, I came

> upon a potato cellar. Deep inside were potatoes that I could eat raw. After a couple of days, a boy from the farm came down to get some potatoes for dinner. When he saw me, he went back to the farmhouse, and his father sent him back with a warm coat.[110]

The next day or so, the door to the cellar opened and an SS officer descended the steps with his pistol drawn. Bing was forced to stand alongside the Polish family while the solders severely beat the man and his wife in front of their three children. Evans:

> The SS officer shot the children and then the farmer, and lastly the wife. The parents were stark-raving mad before they were killed. I thought I would be next, but instead I was taken to a holding cell to stand trial. A court-martial convened, and I was found guilty of being a spy. Because I ate a few German potatoes I was also found guilty of stealing food, a capital crime in itself, and finally, guilty of escaping again. I was sentenced to be shot. I was stripped naked and put into solitary confinement in a room so small you could not stand up. The heat was turned so high I thought I would suffocate, and then turned off so that the air was again freezing. This was repeated numerous times, all the while I was getting almost nothing to eat or drink.[111]

Evans was next thrown into the Russian compound, where thousands of Russian POWs starved to death because the Germans, who hated the Russians, would not feed them. With Evans at the breaking point, a German soldier threw some horse bones, with a little meat on them, over the fence into the Russian compound. Evans fought Russian soldiers for one of the bones, which he broke open and sucked out the marrow. "I was at the lowest point of my captivity; to think that I had fallen to the level of a starving animal to survive. I made up my mind that if given another chance to escape, I would try, come life or death."[112]

Evans's chance came one day on the forced march, making it to the Elbe River, where the Russians were halted. The American army was just across the river, but the Germans had blown the bridge. Bing was a good swimmer and figured this was his only chance. Taking on the current in that swift river, he made it three-fourths of the way across and grabbed onto a girder for support.

He saw an American soldier and yelled for help, telling the soldier he was an escaped Ranger. The American, suspicious of the swimmer, wouldn't budge.[113] Evans made a last desperate effort and his feet hit bottom. It took some explaining to convince the officer in charge that he was a Ranger.

Finding himself in Leipzig, Bing had never forgotten the German named Hans whom his men had killed back near San Pietro. He asked around until he found an older couple there who had a hotel and a son named Hans. Bing told the parents how their son had died and corresponded with the German family for several years after the war until one day a letter was returned, marked "undeliverable."[114]

EPILOGUE

RANGERS COME HOME

A RANGER'S LIFE AFTER THE WAR

The war was over for those heroes who lost their lives on the field of battle. For the rest, the fight was just beginning. PTSD, called "combat fatigue" during World War II, was something many of Darby's Rangers brought home. Many carried survivor guilt, thinking they had not done all they could. Most had been wounded, and almost all had been captured. When the POWs came home, they found a job and went to work, trying to forget about the war.[1] Many used the GI Bill to get a college education, and most led respectable lives raising families and holding jobs. Some had successful careers in the army. Some were killed in Korea and Vietnam.[2]

PTSD has probably been around as long as wars have been fought. Some returning soldiers dealt with it every day, while others escaped it for months or years until a sound, a smell, a word, or a dream suddenly brought horrifying experiences back to their minds as fresh as if they were happening for the first time. Some handled it well, while others were crippled by it. But for all of them, it was a constant presence in the back of their minds from which they were never free.[3]

Most chose to avoid speaking of the war because of the excruciating memories it brought back. They were either too embarrassed to talk to their family or they feared that they would not be believed. Most would sooner talk to a stranger than to a loved one. Almost all felt alone by this hidden, inner burden.[4]

Many Rangers had nightmares, some for the rest of their lives. Some of the nightmares did not begin until years later, which bewildered their family and friends. Former Rangers seldom spoke of Cisterna, nor of their time as POWs. Were they embarrassed about being POWs? Did the remembrance of the day and the subsequent imprisonment so traumatize these Rangers that some blocked any memory of it? Many of these thoughts were taken to the grave by brave men who fought hard, either unwilling or unable to express themselves.[5]

The stories of individual Rangers that follow are only a small sample of the experiences of the Rangers who were either killed or who survived the war and returned to the United States. I have included accounts of some of the most prominent Rangers who have appeared in these pages along with others whose stories have become known to me. This is, therefore, a sampling, necessarily omitting hundreds of other stories that are equally worth telling.

BRIG. GEN. WILLIAM ORLANDO DARBY

Col. William O. Darby, a graduate of the U.S. Military Academy at West Point, led the 1st, 3rd, and 4th Ranger Battalions through every campaign, battle, and raid, to their demise at Cisterna. Col. Darby was not blamed for the Cisterna fiasco and was appointed commander of the 179th Infantry Regiment of the 45th Infantry Division, and continued to fight in Italy.[6]

When his Rangers were returned to the United States, Darby was assigned to the Pentagon and placed in charge of troop movements. Working with him were Maj. Herman Dammer, Maj. Howard Karbel, and Capt. Alex Anderson. On a few nights during June and July 1944, Darby dictated the book *We Led the Way: Darby's Rangers,* which was not published until thirty-five years after his death by his classmate, then Maj. Gen. William H. Baumer.[7]

Sgt. Schunemann: "When I visited Darby at the Pentagon he shut and locked the door, asking for details about our capture and time as POWs."[8] Capt. Anderson: "All Darby wanted was to get back to the war, and he corresponded with all the general officers he knew, asking if anyone needed him."[9]

Darby went on a tour of military forts, one being Fort Benning, Georgia, where he visited with five of his former officers who were instructors at the Infantry School. A picture taken at that time shows Maj. Stephen Meade, Col. William O. Darby, Capt. Earl Carran, Capt. Dean Knudson, Capt. George Sunshine, and Capt. James B. Lyle, who at that time was teaching a course on how to capture a walled city.[10]

Learning that an old mentor, Maj. Gen. George Hays, commander of the 10th Mountain Division fighting in northern Italy, needed a deputy com-

Never-before-published photograph from James B. Lyle's files of Col. William O. Darby meeting with five former officers of the 1st Ranger Battalion at Fort Benning, Georgia, circa May 1944. *Left to right:* Maj. Stephen Meade, Capt. Earl Carran, Col. William O. Darby, Capt. Dean Knudson, Capt. George Sunshine, and Capt. James B. Lyle. Courtesy U.S. Army Infantry School, Fort Benning, Georgia, 1944.

mander, Darby asked for the job and was hired.[11] On 30 April 1945, after a meeting of senior officers at a hotel in Torbole, Italy, Darby and other officers were standing in front of the hotel talking. Lt. Kenneth Templeton, 10th Mountain Division, was an eyewitness to what happened:

> The regimental jeep came around . . . and pulled up near Darby, ready to take him on his next mission. I felt anxious to be on the move when an [enemy] barrage struck, the explosion of 88 mm shells coming apparently at the very moment we heard the whine. Only two or three of the initial shells landed along the waterfront [near the hotel], but just one of those produced [a] small fragment that [pierced Darby's heart]. Carried into the hotel and laid down, Darby did not regain consciousness and died within two minutes of being hit.[12]

Col. Darby was buried at the National Cemetery in his hometown of Fort Smith, Arkansas, with full military honors. At the time of his death, Darby's name was on the list to be promoted to brigadier general, and President Truman signed off on the promotion posthumously, making Darby the only American solder ever promoted to flag rank after his death.[13]

MEMBERS OF THE RANGER BATTALIONS ASSOCIATION OF WORLD WAR II, INC. (RBA)

LT. JAMES ALTIERI, 1/F AND CO OF 4/F

Altieri was an Original Ranger who rose to the rank of platoon sergeant in the 1st Battalion, and near the end of the Italian campaign was awarded a battlefield commission in the 4th Battalion. After the war he authored *The Spearheaders,* the first book to be published about Darby's Rangers in World War II. Later he wrote *Darby's Rangers,* incorporating photographs of many of the Originals who returned home after the Ranger battalions were destroyed at Cisterna.

CPL. ANDERS KJAR ARNBAL, 1/B

In 1993, Arnbal authored *The Barrel-Land Dance Hall Rangers.* At the 1997 RBA reunion in Kissimmee, Florida, Arnbal introduced me to almost everyone there, including dozens of Rangers who knew my uncle. Arnbal was honored with induction into the Ranger Hall of Fame.

BRIG. GEN. JOHN DOBSON, CO OF 1ST BATTALION

After being wounded at Cisterna, Maj. Dobson was operated on at a German mobile surgical unit and eventually got corrective surgery in a Vienna hospital. Months later he wound up at Oflag 64 with the other Ranger officers and had a successful career in the army.[14]

CAPT. WARREN "BING" EVANS, SERGEANT MAJOR OF THE 1ST RANGER BATTALION AND CO OF 3/F

Evans returned to Italy for the fiftieth anniversary of the Italian invasion. As he got off the bus at Nettuno, near Anzio, he found himself facing a statue of a little orphan girl named "Angelica" who had wandered into the Rangers' camp. Evans fell to his knees. Evans's men had taken care of her at Anzio until nuns arrived to take her to a nearby convent. Unbeknownst to the Rangers, after the jeep left the front line it was hit by an enemy shell, killing everyone. Evans knew without a doubt that she was the angel who had watched over him those many months when he was in German captivity.[15] Evans described the PTSD that almost ruined his life:

> My father-in-law asked me to attend a civic club lunch and speak about my experiences in the war. Afterward one of the members approached my father-in-law and said: "There is no way Bing was telling the truth. No one man could have endured or done so much." After that I just kept it inside.
>
> After a few years the nightmares came more often, and I couldn't shake off the terrible memories of those battles and of being forced at gunpoint to watch the Germans execute an entire family whose sole crime was feeding me and letting me hide in their potato cellar.
>
> I turned to the bottle. I would be late for work. Some days I'd ask my wife to call in sick for me, and I would not get out of bed. I eventually lost my job.[16]

Then Evans learned about the RBA. He attended one of their reunions and met men he had served with, men he could relate to. The U.S. 75th Ranger Regiment recognized Evans for being the first sergeant major in the original 1st Ranger Battalion. Warren Evans was named "Honorary Sergeant Major," an official position he held for sixteen years, during which time he was inducted into the U.S. Army Ranger Hall of Fame. Evans was instrumental in the formation of the Sons & Daughters of World War II Rangers, Inc, which in 2011 consolidated with the RBA to become the Descendants of World War II Rangers, Inc.[17]

1ST LT. L. LEW HENRY, 1/F AND 4/A

Henry, who became an attorney, summed up the essence of combat in a letter to his parents written during the war:

> War cannot be described; only those who have experienced combat can have any conception of the term. . . . To the combat soldier who lives in holes like

> animals, whose existence is characterized only by the barest minimum of the necessities of life, and who has for almost a year and a half suffered day after day from heat or cold, in desert or in icy, muddy mountains, going without sleep, or bathing, or changing clothes for days, weeks and months, life has been crystallized into the expression of one desire—to return home.[18]

BRIG. GEN. EDWARD KITCHENS, CO OF 3/C

Edward Kitchens was captured at Cisterna and later served in Korea and Vietnam. His alma mater, Louisiana State University, inducted him into its Hall of Honor, inscribing his name on its granite wall.

CAPT. LESTER KNESS, 1/E AND 4/A

Lester Kness, an Original, served as Lyle's platoon sergeant in North Africa. Awarded a battlefield commission and later inducted into the U.S. Army Ranger Hall of Fame, Kness was one of the 4th Battalion's most reliable company commanders.

SGT. CARL HARRISON LEHMANN JR., 1/B AND 3/C

Becoming an attorney in Baltimore after the war, Lehmann was a national president of the RBA. He indignantly rejected the allegations made by numerous writers that the Rangers were ambushed on their night assault into Cisterna. Lehmann:

> Revisionist historians, most in swaddling clothes when Rangers' ramps went down, and who, obviously plagiarizing one another, state that the Rangers were ambushed at Cisterna. . . . It is safe to conclude also that the hundreds of bivouaced Krauts just rolling out of their blankets at the first shots, as Rangers sprang shooting from the ditch, were ignorant of such an elaborate and clever plan. And if it were an ambush, how come it took all day for two divisions [of Germans] to cream about seven hundred Rangers? No, Carlo D'Este [the famous World War II historian] got it right; the two German divisions moving into the Cisterna area the night before, dictated the result without any divination by the Krauts of the intended Ranger infiltration.[19]

COL. JAMES B. LYLE, CO OF 1/C AND 1/A

Col. Lyle, a native of DeRidder, Louisiana, left home in 1935 to enlist in the army. As a staff sergeant, in 1941 he was selected to attend the U.S. Army Infantry Officer Candidate School (OCS) at Fort Benning, Georgia. When the Japanese attacked Pearl Harbor on 7 December 1941, the army commissioned the candidates early. Others in Lyle's OCS class who joined the 1st Ranger Battalion when it was formed in Ireland in 1942 were 2nd Lt. Charles Shunstrom, who became a platoon leader in Lyle's company in Tunisia, and 2nd Lt. Howard Karbel, who became the adjutant for the 1st Ranger Battalion.

At an RBA reunion in 1997, I met Col. Roy A. Murray, who asked, "Is Jim still alive?" He wanted to know the details of Lyle getting hurt in a combat jump in Korea. This meeting with Col. Murray, and many that followed with other Rangers, made such an indelible impression on me that I began a mission to make sure my uncle and the other Rangers were never forgotten.[20] Lyle was twenty-eight years old in 1942, one of the oldest officers in the 1st Ranger Battalion, and Darby relied on him because of his experience and judgment. Col. Lyle retired from the army in 1965. Like many of the Rangers, he was a modest man, and no one would ever guess the life he had lived as a warrior. In 1959, Lyle was inducted into the Infantry OCS Hall of Fame, and in 2003 he was inducted posthumously into the U.S. Army Ranger Hall of Fame, the only officer in Darby's Rangers to be honored by both organizations.

CPL. KENNETH MARKHAM, 1/F

One of Darby's toughest scouts, Markham was captured at Cisterna, escaped, and was recaptured, only to escape again. He was one of numerous Rangers who regularly attended Ranger Rendezvous at Fort Benning and were interviewed several times by me.[21]

COL. ROY A. MURRAY, CO OF 4TH BATTALION

After the losses at Cisterna, the remnants of Col. Murray's 4th Ranger Battalion continued to fight until May 1944, when the Originals of all three battalions who had not been captured were returned to the United States, receiving a hero's welcome at Camp Butner, North Carolina. Col. Murray completed a distinguished career in the army and played himself in the movie *Darby's Rangers*.[22]

TECH/5 THOMAS PRUDHOMME, 1/HQ.

Prudhomme was an Original Ranger and a revered medic in every campaign from 1942 to 1944:

> Before the war, near my home in Natchitoches, Louisiana, I had a favorite spot for hunting squirrels. . . . A neighbor's kid came over one day asking if he could hunt on the property, and I told him "Absolutely not." It was my private hunting reserve. After I returned from the war I saw the young man . . . he was home on leave prior to going to Korea for that war. Without any hesitation, I told that boy that the woods were his.[23]

OTHER RBA OFFICERS

Lt. Col. Herman Dammer, Capt. James Larkin, Capt. George Sunshine, Capt. Stephen Meade, and Capt. Leilyn Young all became full colonels.

OTHER RANGERS

BRIG. GEN. WILLIAM ROSS BOND, CO OF 1/A

Captured at Cisterna, Capt. Bond had followed Lyle in command of company 1/A in Italy. Bond later fought in Korea and Vietnam. When one of his battalions was being overrun by North Vietnamese, Bond flew by helicopter into the midst of battle. He was shot and killed by an enemy sniper, one of five flag officers to die in Vietnam. Bond was the only flag officer killed in ground combat.[24]

PFC. HAROLD RINARD, 1/B

Rinard, captured at Cisterna, escaped from the Germans twice. He lost a hundred pounds while a German POW. In Korea, after leading an attack on a key hill position with the 1st Ranger Company, Rinard was killed by enemy artillery.[25]

COL. MAX SCHNEIDER, CO OF 1/E AND 4/HQ.

Max Schneider, an Original, commanded 1/E in North Africa and was promoted in Sicily to executive officer of the 4th Ranger Battalion. After fighting through Sicily and Italy with four night invasions of defended enemy beaches, Schneider was ordered to England to assume the role of executive officer to Col. James Earl Rudder, who was training the 2nd and 5th Ranger Battalions for the invasion of Normandy. Schneider, then a lieutenant colonel, commanded the 5th Ranger Battalion and was credited with saving the battalion from destruction on its landing at Omaha Beach on D-Day, 6 June 1944. Despite suffering from severe PTSD for the rest of his life, Schneider had a distinguished career. He was inducted posthumously into the U.S. Army Ranger Hall of Fame.[26]

CAPT. CHARLES MERTON SHUNSTROM, CO OF 1/C AND RANGER CANNON COMPANY

Shunstrom, called "Chuck" by most of his fellow officers, was perhaps the most complicated man—and no doubt one of the toughest—in Darby's Rangers. He was afraid of no one, and several Rangers said that they were more afraid of him than they were of the Germans.[27] Shunstrom asked for and got some of the most dangerous assignments.[28] Like many, Shunstrom returned home suffering from severe PTSD, from which he never recovered. Upon his death, Ranger Allen Merrill wrote to Shunstrom's sister, saying, "We can best remember him as the brother that went off to war and died a hero's death on a hillside in Italy, the way he might have really wanted it." Merrill went on, "Those of us who made it back, live out our lives in quiet desperation."[29] Col. Jim Lyle said of Shunstrom, "He was a fine officer."[30]

2ND LT. EDWARD LOUSTALOT, 1/F

Lt. Loustalot, an LSU graduate, was killed on the Dieppe raid. The Rangers and Commandos accompanying him were all either killed or taken prisoner, so his body was left behind, leaving him characterized as Missing in Action until his body was found in 1948 and identified by U.S. Army forensic specialists. His skeletal remains, still wrapped in U.S. Army wool clothing with an Engineer insignia on the collar, matched his height and tooth chart. A hand grenade was attached to his belt, and in his pocket was an envelope labeled, "In the event of my death please return the contents of this envelope to my mother, Mrs. Emma Loustalot, Franklin, Louisiana."[31] On 4 November 2000, Lt. Loustalot was inducted posthumously into LSU's Hall of Honor.

Capt. Charles Merton Shunstrom, 1st Ranger Battalion, Company C, heavily decorated for bravery and considered by many to be Darby's right-hand man. He was the first Ranger to escape from the Germans after capture at Cisterna. Courtesy Ranger Phil Stern, 1945.

CPL. GEORGE W. "JACK" HALL, 3/D

Cpl. Hall, who preferred to be called "Jack," joined the Rangers at Nemours to avoid jail time for killing a prostitute. Jack, captured at Cisterna and brutally beaten, killed a guard on his final successful escape. After the war, a drug dealer got Jack's twelve-year-old son hooked. When his son committed suicide, Jack found the drug dealer and killed him. Sentenced to life in prison at the Iowa State Penitentiary, Jack was never sorry that he had killed the drug dealer. In the final weeks of Jack's life, his family asked for a compassionate commutation from the governor. A prison board offered to release Jack Hall to hospice care if he would admit he was wrong to have killed the drug dealer. In a wheelchair, in front of a microphone and a camera, Hall stated, "If I had a gun in my hand I would shoot the drug dealer again." Jack Hall died in prison, defiant to the end.[32]

PFC. JOE C. RENFRO, 3/C

Initially, Renfro was buried in the military cemetery at Nettuno, Italy. After the war, in August 1948, his body was brought home, escorted by Pfc. Nelson Rice, the friend he had saved, and reinterred in the family's hillside church cemetery.[33]

1ST LT. CARL R. "BOB" HOOD, 4/E

First Lt. Hood joined the Rangers at Nemours but was killed in the Anzio landing. Two letters he wrote to his family, one from Sicily and one from Venafro, are the only ones I have ever seen that were written by a Ranger who was later killed in action. His letter from Sicily gave me the story of his daring and heroic account of a scouting mission on the road to Butera found in chapter 8. The Venafro letter gave his account of evading a German patrol by climbing a tree, which I told in chapter 10. How many priceless stories like these, which until now were never known outside Lt. Hood's family, have been lost to history? I am grateful to Bob Hood's Gold Star family for sharing them. More than eighty years later, his family still misses him.

Every Ranger had a story, all worth telling, and together they could fill several more volumes.

AFTERWORD AND ACKNOWLEDGMENTS

In the fall of 1967, I was a 2nd lieutenant in the U.S. Army being trained to lead an armored unit. After training, I was assigned to the Mobility Equipment Research and Development Center at Fort Belvoir, Virginia. In my first year I assisted in the design, building, and operation of a war room for command and control of projects at the center, and in the second year I helped develop new sandbags for Vietnam.

Although told that my job was more important than commanding a platoon of tanks, I had a gnawing feeling of guilt in not going to Vietnam. One weekend my wife and I went to visit my uncle, a World War II Ranger, Col. James B. Lyle (now deceased), who appears frequently in the preceding chapters. I always called him "Jim." His wife, Maj. Shirley McCorquodale (deceased), nicknamed "Corky," was a registered nurse who served twenty years on active duty in the Army Nurse Corps, three and a half of which were in the Pacific Theater, from 1942 to 1945.

Lyle became an officer in 1942 and fought with Darby's Rangers. In the Korean War, then a major, he volunteered as a paratrooper, serving as the executive officer in the 2nd Battalion, 187th Regimental Combat Team. On a combat airborne operation in October 1950, his parachute fouled, and he hit the ground hard, fracturing his legs and hips.

I'll never forget the morning I answered the telephone call from Western Union telling my mother that Jim was missing in action in Korea. I was seven years old. Weeks passed before she heard again. Jim was in an army hospital in Japan. After being shipped back to the United States, he would undergo several surgeries over a two-year period before going back on active duty. Jim could have taken a disability retirement because of his severe injuries, but he was a Darby Ranger. Because of his amazing combat record, he was allowed to return to active status so long as he could pass the army's annual physical fitness test, which he did. Not a day went by that he didn't suffer pain from his injuries, but only his wife was aware of this. I already knew these things about my uncle, but until that weekend visit with him, I really knew little of what made him the man he was.

Jim had seven siblings, but I was the only one in the family that he confided in. As I later learned, most Ranger veterans consider their combat service too sacred to be discussed with anyone other than a brother-in-arms. But Jim chose me. He was a modest man who never mentioned any honors, medals, or other recognition. He didn't have to. His nineteen framed medals hung on the wall.

On the fireplace mantle was his Fairbairn-Sykes knife, given to him by the British Commandos in 1942, which no one was allowed to touch. He had killed with it, but when returning to the United States from Italy as a patient on a hospital ship, he was ordered to turn it in. He refused. Warned that he could be court-martialed for disobeying hospital ship rules, Lyle answered, "fire away," and taped the knife to his body.

I very hesitantly asked if he had killed with the knife. Jim paused: "A man thinks about things like that every day of his life. Blood gets all over you, and I can still smell it. The only way I could deal with cutting a man's throat was to never look him in the eye. Chuck Shunstrom told me that we were killing uniforms, not men."

Over the next years, until his death in 1992, Jim and I spoke regularly. Through my conversations with Jim, I had unknowingly opened up a part of his life that he had not even shared with his wife. After his funeral, Corky gave me his briefcase, medals, Sykes Commando knife, and two boxes of files and records. Jim belonged to the RBA but did not enjoy going to reunions because all his close friends were dead, including the two men he had served under, Col. Darby and Col. Max Schneider. Three of his platoon leaders, Capt. Charles Shunstrom, Lt. Walter Wojcik, and Brig. Gen. William Bond, were also dead. Every Christmas he talked by telephone with Lester Kness, his former platoon sergeant in 1/E, and Edwin Dean, his scout in 1/E, both of whom had served under him in North Africa.

After Jim Lyle's death in 1992, I used the Internet to try to locate some of Darby's officers who might have known him. Not knowing that he had been killed at Dieppe, I first searched for Edward Loustalot, thinking he might be close by in Louisiana. I reached Edward's brother, Albert, who teared up on the phone, saying that no one had asked about Edward in twenty-five years.

I attended the 1997 RBA reunion and met Warren "Bing" Evans, who introduced me to numerous Rangers who remembered my uncle. Kenneth Markham, first scout in Company F of the 1st Battalion, said, "I probably won't remember your name, so I'll just call you Jim because you look like him." Ken and I became friends, and I was "Jim" to several of these men.

Anders "Andy" Arnbal remembered Jim and sold me a copy of his book, *The Barrel-Land Dance Hall Rangers.* Mrs. Padrucco, whose husband, Sgt. Francis Padrucco (deceased), had served in my uncle's company in North Africa, told me that she and her husband had visited Jim monthly when he was hospitalized after his parachute injury in Korea. I wanted to learn more.

At the 1999 Columbus, Georgia, reunion, I set up a display of some of Jim's records in a hallway. Bing Evans came out of the RBA business meeting: "David, the men want to elect me president, whose job it is to put on the national reunions. No one else is willing to take the job, but if you'll help me, I'll accept the job." "What do you want me to do?" I asked. That's how it began. I was the first non-Ranger ever to be inducted as a member of the RBA, and I still carry the RBA membership card.

Bing invited me to join six other Rangers at his home in Huntingburg, Indiana, to plan the 2001 reunion. We chose New Orleans for the location. After dinner on Saturday evening, Bing said, "I have something to show you." We drove ten miles to Jasper, Indiana, to the very old St. Joseph Catholic Church. Walking down the center aisle at 9:30 p.m., I wondered what we were doing there. Standing there in total silence for what seemed longer than it was, Bing turned to me, put his hand on my shoulder, and said simply, "Never let this die." I took these words to be my marching orders—to make certain that the sacrifices and accomplishments of World War II Rangers would always be remembered. Bing's orders continue to guide me.

The first day of the reunion, which I chaired, was Tuesday, September 11, 2001. A handful of other Ranger family members were on hand to assist at this reunion. As the towers in New York fell and airplanes were grounded, Rangers and family members were stranded across the United States. They rented cars, took buses, and on Friday some flew. I learned how important it was to these men to get together, and the reunion that was almost cancelled instead succeeded because of the determination of those Rangers. It became known as the 9/11 Reunion.

At Bing's request, I created the "Ranger Wall," a movable light-weight replica of the World War II Ranger monument at Fort Benning, inscribed with the names of all the World War II Rangers killed in action. This was unveiled during the reunion at the memorial service at the D-Day Museum in New Orleans and is still used at reunions.

At that reunion, the Sons & Daughters of World War II Rangers, Inc. (S&D) was born, and I was elected the first president. The S&D continued to arrange the RBA reunions until 2011, when the Rangers decided they were too old to continue their separate organization. The RBA and the S&D were legally consolidated to form the Descendants of World War II Rangers, Inc. (the Descendants). The few surviving Rangers became members of the Descendants, and in 2017 I was elected president of the Descendants.

For twenty-six years I interviewed and emailed Rangers and acquired manuscripts, notes, correspondence, and books. I now have an extensive library of World War II Ranger information. I was fortunate to have personal conversations with many Rangers who shared their stories, most of which have never been published or recorded. I am deeply thankful for and indebted to the Rangers and their family members who trusted me with their memories.

As far as we know, every World War II Ranger from Darby's Rangers is now deceased. Ranger voices in this manuscript came from interviews, personal conversations, letters, manuscripts, and other personal memorabilia, as well as from official records and published sources. I was honored to be the one chosen by my uncle Col. James B. Lyle to hear his stories and to receive his records, which led me on the journey of a lifetime, and it is to his memory and that of the other World War II Rangers that I dedicate this book.

When I sold my business in 2020, my wife, Jane Ellen, who also was very close to Jim and Corky, said, "If you are going to write a book you better get busy." It is due to her continued encouragement and ideas, her editing over many months, and finally her entering the endnotes that this work was completed. Our entire family sacrificed and gave encouragement, knowing I was "working on the book."

The unsung hero of this work is my editor, Arthur White, Ph.D., a professor of history. I first met Dr. White when he taught two of my children at the Episcopal School of Acadiana in Cade, Louisiana. A published author, he then taught at the University of Louisiana until retirement. When I asked Dr. White to be my editor, he said, "Are you sure you want me?" I had no idea what he meant until he ripped through the first few chapters. Then I knew I had the right person, but I immediately realized that this would be a lot harder than I first thought. I learned not to mention a place without identifying where it was located, and I learned rules of grammar that I had long forgotten.

Dr. White drew up the original versions of the maps in this book, insisting that everything on a map had to be verified and to scale. Kimberly Morse, a professional graphic designer, took Dr. White's hand-drawn maps and converted them into polished form fit for publication.

Scanning and formatting large documents could not have been accomplished without the professional touch and experience of Richard Domas and Ben Hebert of Louisiana Digital Reproductions in Lafayette, Louisiana.

Two members of the Descendants of World War II Rangers, Inc., Julie Belanger from Maine, webmaster for the Descendants, and J. Ronald Hudnell, a Ranger himself from North Carolina, furnished valuable information and helped me confirm many facts. Both are tremendous Ranger historians who have spent years studying World War II Rangers and assisting family members and authors. I especially appreciate Cheylee Teitsch, the great-granddaughter of Maj. Alvah Miller, for giving me permission to publish the poem "The Men of My Command."

I could not have completed this manuscript without the detailed rosters of the 1st, 3rd, and 4th Ranger Battalions showing names and ranks published in *Darby's Rangers* by World War II Ranger James Altieri and in Col. Robert Black's *Ranger Force,* whose roster included company affiliation and serial numbers. These men were the first to publish the rosters that have become the "Bible" for researchers. I also appreciate Lt. Col. Clarence Meltesen (deceased), captured at Cisterna, for recording many Ranger escape stories.

Of no less importance was the encouragement of Brig. Gen. William J. Leszczynski Jr. (U.S. Army retired), commander of the 75th Ranger Regiment from 1995 to 1997. Gen. Leszczynski knew many of the Rangers featured in this book, and I asked that he preview the book to make certain I had correctly portrayed the Rangers' military operations. I am humbled by a letter he wrote recommending the book with a final comment, "*The Road to Cisterna* will be the definitive account of the 1st Ranger Battalion in World War II and will far eclipse anything previously written."

Finally, I hope and pray that Rangers Warren "Bing" Evans and my uncle, James B. Lyle, would be pleased with the results of my labors.

Rangers Lead the Way!

APPENDIX

THE CALENDAR AND THE CLOCK

The Cisterna Battle of 30–31 January 1944 lasted from before daylight on the 30th until the afternoon of the 31st and consisted of dozens of skirmishes from below Isola Bella to Cisterna. No one has ever attempted to tell the specific details of the entire battle, much less in its sequence and time frame. I established a methodology to estimate the timing of events using a combination of known recorded times and deductions made from these and from other information, as described below:

Clarence Meltesen recorded the astronomical times for Anzio on 30 July 1944. He noted that the U.S. Army was probably on "War Time" and in agreement with Italian local time.

In his book, *After the Battle: Ranger Evasion and Escape,* Meltesen provides the astronomical times of the day for the battle and his interpretation of the amount of light.

1. Astronomical Twilight—When the sun is 18 degrees below the horizon. It is still dark.
2. 0554 Hours: Nautical Twilight—The sun is 12 degrees below the horizon. One can see forms and shapes.
3. 0654 Hours: Civil Twilight—The sun is 6 degrees below the horizon. There is enough light to read a newspaper.
4. 0724 Hours: Sunrise.

continued

THE METHODOLOGY

1. For the approach to Cisterna, the order of march of the companies for the 1st and 3rd Battalions and the number of men in each company was known.

2. Knowing that the Rangers marched fifteen feet apart, I estimated the length of the marching columns and their rate of march, somewhat slowed by the wet conditions in the ditches.

3. Zartman said it was the "first light of dawn" when the 1st Battalion encountered the enemy. (I called that nautical twilight. This is one example of how I deduced clock times.)

4. Most Rangers had wristwatches, but they were not looking at them. In referring to time, they made such comments as first light, breaking day, dawn, the sun breaking through, and full daylight. They also made comments such as "about noon," early afternoon, and late evening.

5. Darby recorded the times he spoke by radio to the 1st Battalion.

6. The times of other radio transmissions are recorded.

7. The Rangers' own testimony was the basis for determining their positions on the battlefield.

8. An estimate was made for the time to move from one place to another in the ditches and on the battlefield.

9. With the knowledge of astronomical times for Cisterna, the comments of Rangers describing the amount of light, the known times of radio transmissions, and the sequence of events established, it was possible to estimate clock times.

10. Sources of time: Journal = Ranger Force Journal; Log of Action = coded radio messages on Darby's radio net; Darby = *We Led the Way;* Black = *Ranger Force;* Murray = Murray and Schneider; Davis = Arnold Davis; Estimate = author's estimate.

GLOSSARY

ack-ack. Antiaircraft fire.

After Action Report. Also called "Report of Action." A formal military after action report prepared by any level of command.

approach-march formation. The marching formation used when contact with the enemy is or may be imminent.

assembly area. An area protected by friendly forces where a unit can halt for a short period to plan, reorganize, and rest prior to continuing its mission.

BAR. Browning automatic rifle. Weight: 19.4 pounds; capacity: 20-round magazine; rate of fire: 650 rounds per minute. It can be fired in single or multiple bursts, from the shoulder, hip, or a tripod.

bazooka. The common name for an American shoulder-fired recoilless rocket gun, firing a 2.35-inch rocket, mainly against tanks and bunkers, first introduced in 1942.

booby trap. A device that is disguised as something innocent, intended to kill or injure a person, usually triggered by actions of its victim. It is sometimes designed to lure the victim toward it.

Bren gun. A British light machine gun first produced in the 1930s with a sustained rate of fire of 500 rounds per minute. It can be handheld or mounted on a tracked carrier, similar to a personnel carrier

bully beef. British rations, boiled corned beef packaged in gelatin, delivered in a tin container.

burp gun. The German submachine gun, shoulder fired at 450 to 550 rounds per minute.

cadre. The officers and NCOs of a military unit.

carbine. A lightweight semiautomatic rifle issued in the U.S. military during World War II.

C ration. Canned or packaged food rations prepared for US troops containing items that varied from time to time, including canned meat, canned spread, crackers, canned fruit, canned milk, cigarettes and matches, toilet paper, coffee, sugar, and salt.

concussion grenade. A round grenade, thrown by hand, that makes a loud explosion, temporarily disorienting the enemy while inflicting minimal wounds, used for close combat.

CO. Commanding Officer.

CP. Command Post.

Descendants. The Descendants of World War II Rangers, Inc., an organization for the family members of World War II Rangers.

D bars. A military-grade chocolate bar high in energy and easy to carry. Could be life sustaining.

DOW. Died of Wounds.

88s. A German 88 mm antiaircraft or antitank artillery round. Range was 9,900 meters, with a muzzle velocity of 2,690 feet per second (f/s). Because the speed of sound is 1,125 f/s, one could not hear the 88 coming because it traveled faster than the speed of sound. It was one of the most dangerous and feared German weapons in World War II.

E-boat. A fast attack craft of the German navy in World War II. Similar to a American PT boat but larger.

FSSF. First Special Service Force. An elite American-Canadian commando unit in World War II, under the command of the U.S. Fifth Army.

flak wagon. German guns mounted on a mobile platform, sometimes armored, for the purpose of shooting down Allied airplanes, but also used against infantry troops. Some of these were simply called "tanks" by Rangers at Cisterna because the men who were new to the Rangers often did not know the correct nomenclature for enemy vehicles. Caliber could be from 20 mm up to 88 mm.

FOD. Finding of Death.

Free French. Volunteer French forces that fought against the Axis forces in World War II.

half-track. An American armored personnel carrier that had tires in the front and tracks in the back, widely used by the Allies.

Higgins boat. Landing craft designed by Andrew Higgins and built by Higgins Industries in New Orleans during World War II. Usually made from plywood, they could carry vehicles or personnel and were used throughout the war in all theaters of operation.

Generaloberst. Colonel General, a German four-star general, one rank below field marshal.

Itye. American soldiers' nickname for an Italian soldier in World War II.

Jerry. American soldiers' nickname for a German soldier in World War II.

K ration. A nonperishable, ready-to-eat food ration designed to be carried in a soldier's pocket. A typical ration contained canned meat and eggs, fruit bars, instant coffee, and cigarettes. Variations included chewing gum, toilet paper, powdered milk, candy, and biscuits.

KIA. Killed in Action.

Kommando. German work camps for prisoners of war.

Kraut. American soldiers' nickname for a German soldier in World War II..

Limey. American soldiers' nickname for an English soldier in World War II.

LD. Line of departure; an imaginary line from which troops would begin a mission into hostile territory.

Luftwaffe. The aerial warfare branch of the German Wehrmacht.

Mae West. A life preserver developed for the military in World War II that, when inflated, gave the appearance of a buxom chest; named for the actress of that name, famous for her ample bust.

M1 Garand. The standard army rifle in World War II, .30 caliber, semiautomatic, gas operated, with a rate of fire of 40 to 50 rounds per minute.

machine pistol. A German pistol, with or without a stock, capable of firing fully automatic.

MIA. Missing in Action.

mortar. A smoothbore muzzle-loaded weapon (60 mm and 81mm) that fired a high-arching exploding warhead, with a portable base plate, a lightweight bipod mount, and a sight. The 4.2-inch mortar was rifled, high arching, and fired a larger high-explosive warhead similar to artillery.

Nebelwerfer. A German 150 mm multiple rocket launcher carrying high explosives, fired from a six-tube mobile launcher. The rockets gave a loud, piercing screaming noise prior to exploding, giving them the name "screaming memees."

Oflag. A German POW camp for officers.

OP. Observation Post; a place from which troops could observe the enemy or watch for possible enemy movements.

open city. A city that the occupying military has stated will not be destroyed when they withdraw or abandon the city.

Panther tank. A German tank copied from the Russian T-34, with a high-velocity 75 mm gun.

panzer. A generic term used by Allied troops in World War II to describe any of several different German tanks.

Panzerfaust. A German single-shot antitank weapon fired from the shoulder.

panzer grenadiers. German soldiers riding in an open-topped armored vehicle.

partisans. Italian citizens fighting the Fascists and Nazis in World War II.

phase line. An easily identifiable landmark or terrain used to control or coordinate the advance or withdrawal of troops.

port arms. A position for carrying a rifle in which the rifle is held diagonally across the chest with the muzzle pointing upward and to the left.

POW. Prisoner of War.

radio. SCR-610. A portable radio that could be jeep mounted or carried, with a five-mile range.

RBA. Ranger Battalions Association of World War II, Inc., the veterans organization of World War II Rangers. The RBA was consolidated into the Descendants in 2011.

Repple Depple. Replacement depots for American troops in World War II. Troops arriving from the United States would be assigned to a replacement depot until permanently assigned to a regular unit.

Report of Action. (See **After Action Report.**)

RFHQ. Ranger Force Headquarters.

R&R. Rest and Relaxation; a term used for troops getting a temporary break from combat.

rocket gun. (See **bazooka.**)

Screaming Memees. (See **Nebelwerfer.**)

self-propelled gun. Artillery with its own propulsion system. Some German self-propelled guns had open crew areas in the rear, which made the crew vulnerable to attack.

shelter half. One half of a pup tent used by infantry troops. Each soldier carried one shelter half, and two soldiers buttoned their two halves together to form a weatherproof pup tent.

six-by-six truck. A heavy tactical truck built for the U.S. Army during World War II. It could carry six short tons and could travel in all types of weather and terrain.

skirmish line. A line of infantry troops forming for an attack, generally with bayonets fixed to scare the enemy into surrendering.

speed march. A fast walk, or a "slow run," developed by British Commandos and adopted by U.S. Army Rangers, designed to move troops far and fast.

Stalag. A German POW camp for enlisted men.

Sten gun. A 9 mm handheld machine gun used by the British in World War II.

sticky grenade. A British handheld grenade designed for use against tanks or fortified buildings consisting of an explosive charge inside a glass cover with a wooden handle. When thrown against a target, a sticky substance on the outside of the glass caused the grenade to stick to the target. At the same time, the glass broke and the device exploded.

tank destroyer. Similar to tanks, with a long-range artillery gun but with lighter armor on the sides and rear in order to be lighter, faster, and easier to manufacture. They were designed to destroy enemy tanks and other armored vehicles.

Tiger tank. The heaviest German tank that the Rangers encountered on the battlefield, equipped with an 88 mm gun.

time-fused air-burst shells. Shells that were produced for use at the Battle of El Guettar, designed to burst in the air above enemy troops.

TO&E. Table of Organization and Equipment, which specifies the organization, staffing, and equipment of military units.

tracer. A bullet, generally found in a belt of machine gun ammunition, with a pyrotechnic charge that ignites when the bullet is fired to let the shooter see where the bullets are landing.

trooper. The shortened name for paratrooper.

U-boats. German submarines.

wadi. An Arabic term for a stream or lake bed that is generally dry except during the rainy season.

Wehrmacht. The German army in World War II.

WIA. Wounded in Action.

NOTES

PREFACE

1. [Mountbatten], *Combined Operations,* 2–4.
2. Black, *Rangers in World War II,* 10.
3. Ibid., 36.

1. NEWS FILTERS BACK

1. King, *Leavenworth Papers,* 150.
2. Ibid.
3. Darby and Baumer, *We Led the Way,* 162.
4. Altieri, *Darby's Rangers,* 119.
5. Ibid., 46.

2. FORMATION AND TRAINING

1. Black, *Ranger Force,* 2–5.
2. Truscott, *Command Missions,* 37.
3. Ibid., 38.
4. [Mountbatten], *Combined Operations,* v.
5. Ibid., 79.
6. Ibid., 87.
7. Truscott, *Command Missions,* 40.
8. Ibid., 39.
9. Hutchinson to Baumer, 4 October 1979.
10. Black, *Ranger Force,* 10.
11. Ibid., 11.
12. Warren "Bing" Evans, conversations with David Lyle Williams.
13. Lyle, conversations with David Lyle Williams.
14. Altieri, *Spearheaders.* 22–23.
15. Black, *Ranger Force,* 13.
16. Altieri, *Spearheaders,* 22–23.
17. Hunt, personal notes and memorabilia.

18. Hermsen, "My Story," unpublished memoir.
19. Reed, "A Life, Mine Own," unpublished autobiography.
20. Altieri, *Spearheaders*, 36.
21. Hayes, excerpts from an interview by Dora Jane Hamblin.
22. Black, *Ranger Force*, 23.
23. Altieri, *Spearheaders*, 28.
24. Ibid., 29.
25. Kazura, "Charles H. Kazura."
26. Kelly, *Home Away from Home*, 78–79.
27. Flanagan, "The Ranger Is a Tough Fighting Man," 192.
28. Black, *Ranger Force*, 22.
29. Thompson, conversation with David Lyle Williams.
30. Altieri, *Spearheaders*, 41.
31. Black, *Ranger Force*, 21.
32. Mauritz, *The Secret of Anzio Bay*, 215.
33. Kelly, *Home Away from Home*, 79.
34. Black, *Ranger Force*, 30–31.
35. Reed, "A Life, Mine Own," unpublished autobiography, 43.
36. Ibid.
37. Carl Lehmann to Landreth, 31 March 1997.
38. Black, *Ranger Force*, 56.
39. Darby and Baumer, *We Led the Way*, 47.
40. King, *William O. Darby*, 40, 44.

3. DIEPPE

1. Atkinson, *Army at Dawn*, 11–13.
2. Darby and Baumer, *We Led the Way*, 40–41.
3. Ibid.
4. Ibid.
5. Black, *Ranger Force*, 37.
6. Black, *Rangers in World War II*, 29.
7. Darby and Baumer, *We Led the Way*, 41.
8. [Mountbatten], *Combined Operations*, 110–116.
9. Black, *Rangers in World War II*, 30–31.
10. Szima, open letter.
11. Ibid.
12. Darby and Baumer, *We Led the Way*, 42–43.
13. Ibid.
14. [Mountbatten], *Combined Operations*, 118–119.
15. Ibid., 118.
16. Furru, conversations with David Lyle Williams.
17. Ibid.

18. Black, *Rangers in World War II*, 37.

19. Furru to Swank, 14 September 1980.

20. Darby and Baumer, *We Led the Way*, 44.

21. Szima, "Report to Knickerbocker."

22. Ibid.

23. Ibid.

24. Ibid.

25. "Diary of the First Ranger Battalion, 8 June 1942–20 May 1943."

26. Swank, speech delivered at the dedication of the memorial to those killed in the Dieppe raid.

27. Szima, open letter.

28. Ibid.

4. NORTH AFRICA

1. Atkinson, *Army at Dawn*, 5–6.

2. Black, *Ranger Force*, 66–68.

3. Frederick, "Notes."

4. Atkinson, *Army at Dawn*, 79–80.

5. Kelly, *Home Away from Home*, 91.

6. Black, *Ranger Force*, 70.

7. James Larkin, After Action Report.

8. Hayes, excerpts from an interview by Dora Jane Hamblin.

9. Black, *Ranger Force*, 73.

10. James Larkin, After Action Report.

11. Arnbal, *The Barrel-Land Dance Hall Rangers*, 10–12. The weapon Cpl. Arnbal used was like an M1919 Browning machine gun.

12. Ibid., 12–13.

13. Cpt. Manning Jacob, 1/A, Report of Action, 1st Ranger Battalion, 1/A, Arzew, Algeria, 15 November 1942.

14. Black, *Ranger Force*, 76.

15. Hermsen, "My Story," unpublished memoir.

16. Atkinson, *Army at Dawn*, 80.

17. Black, *Ranger Force*, 76.

18. Atkinson, *Army at Dawn*, 80.

19. U.S. War Department, Signal Intelligence Service press release, 875, Mercuriali.

20. U.S. War Department, Signal Intelligence Service press release, 876, Bevan.

21. Rorex, "Silk Sheets." 36.

22. Black, *Ranger Force*, 79.

23. Ibid.

24. Ibid., 79–81.

25. U.S. War Department, Signal Intelligence Service press release, 921, Bacon.

26. Black, *Ranger Force*, 81.

27. U.S. War Department, Signal Intelligence Service press release, 901, Boudreau.
28. Warren "Bing" Evans, conversations with David Lyle Williams.
29. Szima, open letter.
30. Arnbal, *The Barrel-Land Dance Hall Rangers,* 20–21.
31. Ibid., 26.
32. Kness, conversations with David Lyle Williams.
33. Kelly, *Home Away from Home,* 84.
34. Ibid.
35. Warren "Bing" Evans, conversations with David Lyle Williams.
36. Pyle, *Here Is Your War,* 34.
37. Ibid., 35.
38. Ibid., 87.
39. Black, *Ranger Force,* 91.

5. TUNISIA

1. Gelb, *Desperate Venture,* 311.
2. Breuer, *Operation Torch,* 87.
3. Goerlitz, *History of the German General Staff,* 477.
4. Carter, "Operations of the First Battalion, 18th Infantry," 4.
5. Black, *Ranger Force,* 102.
6. Ibid., 103.
7. Ibid., 91.
8. "Diary of the First Ranger Battalion, 8 June 1942–20 May 1943."
9. J. Austin Miller, "J. Austin Miller," 40.
10. Flanagan, "The Ranger Is a Tough Fighting Man," 193.
11. Murray, conversation with David Lyle Williams.
12. Darby and Baumer, *We Led the Way,* 56.
13. Black, *Ranger Force,* 93.
14. Morriss, "Rangers Come Home."
15. Black, *Ranger Force,* 93.
16. Altieri, *Spearheaders,* 201–202.
17. Young, "Rangers in a Night Operation."
18. Frederick, "Notes."
19. Altieri, *Spearheaders,* 206.
20. Ibid., 207.
21. Black, *Ranger Force,* 96.
22. Ibid.
23. Warren "Bing" Evans, conversations with David Lyle Williams.
24. Ibid.
25. Ibid.
26. Ibid.
27. Altieri, *Spearheaders,* 209.

28. Darby and Baumer, *We Led the Way,* 58.
29. Darby, Headquarters, First Ranger Battalion, Report of Action, Sened Station, Tunisia.
30. Ibid.
31. O'Donnell, *Beyond Valor,* 35.
32. Gelb, *Desperate Venture,* 303–307.
33. Darby and Baumer, *We Led the Way,* 58.
34. Arnbal, *The Barrel-Land Dance Hall Rangers,* 46–50.
35. VanArtsdalen, "The Great Colonel Darby Speech."
36. Arnbal, *The Barrel-Land Dance Hall Rangers,* 45.
37. Ibid., 46.
38. Ibid., 47.
39. Lyle, conversations with David Lyle Williams.
40. Darby and Baumer, *We Led the Way,* 61.
41. Arnbal, *The Barrel-Land Dance Hall Rangers,* 48–49.
42. Ibid., 49.
43. Ibid.
44. Ibid.
45. Ibid., 53.
46. Hermsen, "My Story," unpublished memoir.
47. Blumenson, *Kasserine Pass,* 235.
48. Gelb, *Desperate Venture,* 304.
49. Lyle, conversations with David Lyle Williams.
50. Gelb, *Desperate Venture,* 308.
51. Arnbal, *The Barrel-Land Dance Hall Rangers,* 54.
52. Allen to Darby, 22 February 1943.
53. Black, *Ranger Force,* 106.
54. Gelb, *Desperate Venture,* 307.

6. THE BATTLE OF DJEBEL EL ANK

1. Atkinson, *Army at Dawn,* 389.
2. Davis, "American Light Infantry Battles," 210.
3. Darby and Baumer, *We Led the Way,* 68–71.
4. Ibid., 69.
5. Ketzer, "Steve Ketzer," 26–27.
6. Gelb, *Desperate Venture,* 296–298.
7. Ibid., 297.
8. Ibid., 309.
9. Frederick, "Notes."
10. Lyle, conversations with David Lyle Williams.
11. Blumenson, *The Patton Papers,* 184.
12. Atkinson, *Army at Dawn,* 441.
13. Lyle, "Graduation Address."

14. Ibid.
15. Black, *Ranger Force,* 109.
16. Street, "Inf. Operations of the First Ranger Battalion," 8.
17. Lyle, "Graduation Address."
18. Black, *Ranger Force,* 111.
19. Ibid.
20. Ingersoll, *The Battle Is the Payoff,* 125.
21. Ibid., 126.
22. Lyle, "Graduation Address."
23. Ingersoll, *The Battle Is the Payoff,* 142.
24. Ibid., 142–144.
25. Ibid.
26. Lyle, "Graduation Address."
27. Lyle, conversations with David Lyle Williams.
28. Ingersoll, *The Battle Is the Payoff,* 143.
29. Lyle, "Graduation Address."
30. Ingersoll, *The Battle Is the Payoff,* 155–157.
31. Ibid.
32. Ibid., 155.
33. Ibid., 156.
34. Ibid., 151.
35. Ibid., 161
36. Ibid., 161–162.
37. Darby and Baumer, *We Led the Way,* 73.
38. U.S. War Department, Signal Intelligence Service press release, 866, Wells.
39. Lyle, "Graduation Address."
40. Street, "Inf. Operations of the First Ranger Battalion," 15.

7. THE BATTLE OF EL GUETTAR

1. Street, "Inf. Operations of the First Ranger Battalion," 8.
2. Astor, *Terrible Terry Allen,* 164.
3. Bradley, *A Soldier's Story,* 54.
4. Arnbal, *The Barrel-Land Dance Hall Rangers,* 65.
5. Darby and Baumer, *We Led the Way,* 75.
6. Stern and Bradner, *Snapdragon,* 206.
7. Arnbal, *The Barrel-Land Dance Hall Rangers,* 65–66.
8. Shead, email to David Lyle Williams.
9. Slade, "Natchitoches Man Remembers Fallen Friends Every Day."
10. Ibid.
11. U.S. War Department, Signal Intelligence Service press release, 890, Costello.
12. Arnbal, *The Barrel-Land Dance Hall Rangers,* 67.
13. Darby, Headquarters, First Ranger Battalion, Report of Action, Djebel el Ank, Tunisia.

14. Arnbal, *The Barrel-Land Dance Hall Rangers,* 70–71.

15. Ibid., 70.

16. Ibid., 72.

17. Warren "Bing" Evans, conversations with David Lyle Williams.

18. Darby and Baumer, *We Led the Way,* 76.

19. Ibid.

20. Ibid.

21. Arnbal, *The Barrel-Land Dance Hall Rangers,* 74.

22. Darby and Baumer, *We Led the Way,* 76–77.

23. Darby, Headquarters, First Ranger Battalion, Report of Action, Djebel el Ank, Tunisia.

24. Darby and Baumer, *We Led the Way,* 77.

25. Arnbal, *The Barrel-Land Dance Hall Rangers,* 78–80.

26. Ibid., 81–82.

27. Ibid., 81–82.

28. Ibid., 82.

29. Lyle, conversations with David Lyle Williams.

30. Darby and Baumer, *We Led the Way,* 78.

31. First Ranger Battalion, Report of Action, casualties, 11 January 1943, 5 March 1943, 6 March 1943, and 9 April 1943.

32. Atkinson, *Army at Dawn,* 523–529.

8. SICILY

1. Black, *Ranger Force,* 116–117.

2. Hummer, *An Infantryman's Journal,* 12.

3. Altieri, *Spearheaders,* 247.

4. Skinner, conversation with David Lyle Williams.

5. Hall, "Ranger Scout," 5.

6. Hummer, *An Infantryman's Journal,* 12.

7. Black, *Ranger Force,* 117.

8. Lyle, conversations with David Lyle Williams.

9. Markham, conversations with David Lyle Williams.

10. Ibid.

11. Hummer, *An Infantryman's Journal,* 13.

12. Ibid.

13. Lawrence Gilbert, conversations with David Lyle Williams.

14. Hummer, *An Infantryman's Journal,* 15–17.

15. Earnest, "Notes."

16. Hummer, *An Infantryman's Journal,* 15.

17. Kegley, conversations with David Lyle Williams.

18. Hayes, excerpts from an interview by Dora Jane Hamblin.

19. Altieri, *Spearheaders,* 248.

20. Earnest, "Notes."

21. Darby and Baumer, *We Led the Way,* 81.
22. Bradley, *A Soldier's Story,* 103–105.
23. Garland and Smyth, *Sicily and the Surrender of Italy,* 64–65.
24. Darby and Baumer, *We Led the Way,* 81.
25. Blumenson, *The Patton Papers,* 306.
26. Black, *Ranger Force,* 128.
27. Ibid., 129–131.
28. Truscott, *Command Missions,* 198.
29. Hummer, *An Infantryman's Journal,* 20.
30. Hood to his parents, from Sicily, n.d.
31. Earnest, "Notes."
32. Ibid.
33. Morison, *Sicily—Salerno—Anzio,* 69–70.
34. Haggerty, "A History of the Ranger Battalions in World War II," 144.
35. Morison, *Sicily—Salerno—Anzio,* 92.
36. Astor, *Terrible Terry Allen,* 194.
37. Bradley, *A Soldier's Story,* 126.
38. Black, *Ranger Force,* 129.
39. Mitcham and von Stauffenberg, *The Battle of Sicily,* 78, 82.
40. Morison, *Sicily—Salerno—Anzio,* 100.
41. Mitcham and von Stauffenberg, *The Battle of Sicily,* 102–103.
42. Morison, *Sicily—Salerno—Anzio,* 105–107.
43. Hood to his parents, from Sicily, n.d.
44. Lyle, conversations with David Lyle Williams.
45. Lyle, "Operations of Companies A and B, First Ranger Battalion," 8.
46. Darby, "The United States Rangers," 21.
47. Lyle, "Operations of Companies A and B, First Ranger Battalion," 9.
48. Hood to his parents, from Sicily, n.d.
49. Lyle, "Operations of Companies A and B, First Ranger Battalion," 10.
50. Black, *Ranger Force,* 130.
51. Ibid., 131.
52. Darby, "The United States Rangers," 22–23.
53. Fleser, conversations with David Lyle Williams.
54. Lyle, conversations with David Lyle Williams.
55. Darby and Baumer, *We Led the Way,* 87.
56. U.S. War Department, Signal Intelligence Service press release, 877, Kissman.
57. Lyle, conversations with David Lyle Williams.
58. Murray and Schneider, "The Fourth Ranger Battalion."
59. Hood to his parents, from Sicily, n.d.
60. U.S. War Department, Signal Intelligence Service press release, 898, Folsom.
61. Lyle, "Operations of Companies A and B, First Ranger Battalion," 11.
62. Darby, "The United States Rangers," 23.
63. Lyle, "Operations of Companies A and B, First Ranger Battalion," 11.

64. Lyle, conversations with David Lyle Williams.
65. Lyle, "Operations of Companies A and B, First Ranger Battalion," 12.
66. Ibid.
67. O'Donnell, *Beyond Valor*, 42.
68. Ibid.
69. Black, *Ranger Force*, 132–133.
70. Randall Harris, "The Harris Family in World War II, Letters and Memories," 319.
71. Hood to his parents, from Sicily, n.d.
72. Lyle, "Operations of Companies A and B, First Ranger Battalion," 12.
73. Ibid.
74. Ibid., 13–14.
75. Lyle, conversations with David Lyle Williams.
76. Lyle, "Operations of Companies A and B, First Ranger Battalion," 16.
77. Ibid.
78. Ibid., 17–18.
79. Lyle, conversations with David Lyle Williams.
80. Hood to his parents, from Sicily, n.d.
81. Ibid.
82. Altieri, *Spearheaders*, 267.
83. Ibid., 269.
84. Ibid., 270.
85. Earnest, "Notes."
86. Ibid.
87. Mitcham and von Stauffenberg, *The Battle of Sicily*, 129.
88. Ibid.
89. U.S. War Department, Signal Intelligence Service press release, 916, Jacobs.
90. Morison, *Sicily—Salerno—Anzio*, 95.
91. Mitcham and von Stauffenberg, *The Battle of Sicily*, 122–123.
92. Black, *Ranger Force*, 140–144.
93. Atkinson, *The Day of Battle*, 80.
94. Darby and Baumer, *We Led the Way*, 90.
95. Lyle, "Operations of Companies A and B, First Ranger Battalion," 15.
96. Morriss, "Rangers Come Home," 4.
97. Hood to his parents, from Sicily, n.d.
98. Morriss, "Rangers Come Home," 4.
99. Lyle, "Operations of Companies A and B, First Ranger Battalion," 17.
100. Ibid., 18.
101. Black, *Ranger Force*, 143.
102. Lyle, "Operations of Companies A and B, First Ranger Battalion," 16.
103. Ibid., 18.
104. Ibid., 19.
105. Ibid.
106. Ibid.

107. Blumenson, *The Patton Papers,* 280.
108. Darby and Baumer, *We Led the Way,* 91.
109. Hood to his parents, from Sicily, n.d.
110. Ibid.
111. Worth, "Duty/Love/War, Memories of a Swoose at War," 14.
112. Darby and Baumer, *We Led the Way,* 91–92.
113. Darby, "The United States Rangers," 25.
114. Ibid., 26.
115. Lyle, "Divide and Conquer," 21.
116. Darby and Baumer, *We Led the Way,* 96.
117. Lyle, "Divide and Conquer," 21
118. Darby and Baumer, *We Led the Way,* 93.
119. Ibid.
120. Lyle, "Divide and Conquer," 22.
121. Earnest, "Notes."
122. Morriss, "Rangers Come Home," 4.
123. Earnest, "Notes."
124. Black, *Ranger Force,* 150.
125. Worth, conversations with David Lyle Williams.
126. Ibid.
127. Lyle, "Divide and Conquer," 22.
128. Ibid.
129. Ibid.
130. Ibid.
131. Morriss, "Rangers Come Home," 4.
132. Lyle, "Divide and Conquer," 24.
133. Lyle, conversations with David Lyle Williams.
134. Kitchens, "Operations of the Third Ranger Battalion in the Landing at Licata," 10.
135. Arnbal, *The Barrel-Land Dance Hall Rangers,* 102.
136. Ibid., 103.
137. James Larkin, "Onetime Soldier," part 2, 42–43.
138. Kitchens, "Operations of the Third Ranger Battalion in the Landing at Licata," 12.
139. Darby, "The United States Rangers," 28.
140. Arnbal, *The Barrel-Land Dance Hall Rangers,* 104–105.
141. Ibid., 106–107.
142. Ibid., 108.
143. Ibid.
144. Kitchens, "Operations of the Third Ranger Battalion in the Landing at Licata," 17.
145. Black, *Ranger Force,* 156.
146. Darby and Baumer, *We Led the Way,* 112.
147. Ibid., 157.
148. Hayes, excerpts from an interview by Dora Jane Hamblin.
149. Black, *Ranger Force,* 158.
150. Warren "Bing" Evans, conversations with David Lyle Williams.

151. Arnbal, *The Barrel-Land Dance Hall Rangers,* 118.
152. Ibid., 112–113.
153. Arnbal, conversations with David Lyle Williams.
154. Arnbal, *The Barrel-Land Dance Hall Rangers,* 113–114.
155. Truscott, *Command Missions,* 218.
156. Kitchens, "Operations of the Third Ranger Battalion in the Landing at Licata," 22–23.
157. Darby and Baumer, *We Led the Way,* 98–99.
158. Arnbal, *The Barrel-Land Dance Hall Rangers,* 116.
159. Darby, "The United States Rangers," 30.
160. Ibid.
161. Ibid., 31.
162. Ibid.
163. Black, *Ranger Force,* 165
164. Hayes, excerpts from an interview by Dora Jane Hamblin.
165. Arnbal, *The Barrel-Land Dance Hall Rangers,* 119.
166. Black, *Ranger Force,* 169.
167. Arnbal, *The Barrel-Land Dance Hall Rangers,* 138.
168. Ibid., 140.
169. Truscott, *Command Missions,* 243.
170. Arnbal, *The Barrel-Land Dance Hall Rangers,* 142–143.
171. Eineichner, "Assault on Messina," 70.
172. Mitcham and von Stauffenberg, *The Battle of Sicily,* 297.
173. Hayes, excerpts from an interview by Dora Jane Hamblin.
174. Darby, "The United States Rangers," 33.

9. ITALY

1. Black, *Ranger Force,* 177.
2. Darby and Baumer, *We Led the Way,* 112.
3. Starr, *From Salerno to the Alps,* 10–12.
4. Black, *Ranger Force,* 177.
5. Morris, *Salerno,* 41.
6. Ibid., 43.
7. Morris, *Salerno,* 63–64.
8. Darby and Baumer, *We Led the Way,* 114.
9. Earnest, "Notes."
10. Darby and Baumer, *We Led the Way,* 114–115.
11. Murray and Schneider, "The Fourth Ranger Battalion."
12. Frederick, "Notes."
13. Ibid.
14. Murray and Schneider, "The Fourth Ranger Battalion."
15. Ibid.
16. Earnest, "Notes."
17. Black, *Rangers in World War II,* 117.

18. Carl Lehmann, "3rd Ranger Battalion History."
19. Ibid.
20. Earnest, "Notes."
21. Carl Lehmann, "3rd Ranger Battalion History."
22. Darby and Baumer, *We Led the Way*, 114.
23. Carl Lehmann, "3rd Ranger Battalion History."
24. Anderson, conversations with David Lyle Williams.
25. U.S. War Department, Signal Intelligence Service press release, 888, Fitzhugh.
26. Black, *Ranger Force*, 189.
27. Murray and Schneider, "The Fourth Ranger Battalion."
28. U.S. War Department, Signal Intelligence Service press release, Westrum.
29. Reed, "A Life, Mine Own," unpublished autobiography, 18.
30. U.S. War Department, Signal Intelligence Service press release, 888, Yarboro.
31. U.S. War Department, Signal Intelligence Service press release, 896, Szcesniak.
32. Kness, "Iowa," 98.
33. Yandell, "Bravery Was Automatic to U.S. Rangers."
34. Pond, *Salerno*, 161.
35. Earnest, "Notes."
36. Lawrence Gilbert, conversations with David Lyle Williams.
37. Reed, "A Life, Mine Own," unpublished autobiography, 19.
38. U.S. War Department, Signal Intelligence Service press release, 879, Hoffines.
39. Carl Lehmann to Landreth, 31 March 1997.
40. Anderson, conversations with David Lyle Williams.
41. James Larkin, "Onetime Soldier," part 2, 54.
42. Ibid.
43. Carl Lehmann, "3rd Ranger Battalion History."
44. Reed, "A Life, Mine Own," unpublished autobiography, 19.
45. Jim Harris, email to David Lyle Williams.
46. Ibid.
47. Steen, conversation with David Lyle Williams.
48. Jim Harris, email to David Lyle Williams.
49. Lawrence Gilbert, conversations with David Lyle Williams.
50. Atkinson, *The Day of Battle*. 241–242.
51. Arnbal, *The Barrel-Land Dance Hall Rangers*, 161.
52. Ibid., 162.
53. James Larkin, "Onetime Soldier," part 2, 56.
54. Arnbal, *The Barrel-Land Dance Hall Rangers*, 164.
55. Ibid., 168.
56. Harlow, unpublished notes.
57. Ibid.
58. Arnbal, *The Barrel-Land Dance Hall Rangers*, 165–168.
59. Ibid., 172–173.

10. VENAFRO

1. Darby and Baumer, *We Led the Way,* 128.
2. Atkinson, *The Day of Battle,* 279.
3. Darby and Baumer, *We Led the Way,* 125.
4. Ibid., 127.
5. King, *William O. Darby,* 127.
6. Ibid., 128–129.
7. Murray and Schneider, "The Fourth Ranger Battalion."
8. Ibid.
9. Altieri, *Darby's Rangers,* 63.
10. Ibid.
11. Harlow, unpublished notes.
12. Boron, conversations with David Lyle Williams.
13. Murray and Schneider, "The Fourth Ranger Battalion."
14. Altieri, *Darby's Rangers,* 63.
15. Murray and Schneider, "The Fourth Ranger Battalion."
16. Altieri, *Darby's Rangers,* 65.
17. Cook, "Pill Box," 98.
18. Ibid.
19. Hood to his parents, from Venafro, n.d.
20. Haywood, unpublished memoir.
21. Auger, unpublished notes.
22. Kness, "Fourth Ranger Battalion-Venafro," 84.
23. Ibid.
24. Ibid.
25. Kness, conversations with David Lyle Williams.
26. Kness, "Fourth Ranger Battalion-Venafro," 85–86.
27. Ibid., 87–88.
28. Ibid., 88–91.
29. Ibid., 91.
30. Murray and Schneider, "The Fourth Ranger Battalion."
31. Darby and Baumer, *We Led the Way,* 131.
32. U.S. War Department, Signal Intelligence Service press release, 866, Wells.
33. U.S. War Department, Signal Intelligence Service press release, 868, Arnold.
34. Fleser, conversations with David Lyle Williams.
35. Scharf, "Remembrances of My Service in World War II."
36. Emmons, email to Joyce Dineen.
37. U.S. War Department, Signal Intelligence Service press release, 872, Tremblay.
38. Zartmann, *East to the Russkies,* 117–118.
39. Ibid., 115, 120.
40. Darby and Baumer, *We Led the Way,* 131.

11. SAN PIETRO

1. Darby and Baumer, *We Led the Way,* 140.
2. Strand, "Alpha Officer," 50.
3. Ibid.
4. Ibid.
5. Ibid.
6. Ibid., 50–51.
7. Ibid., 51.
8. Ibid.
9. Ibid.
10. U.S. War Department, Signal Intelligence Service press release, 892, McMahon.
11. Arnbal, *The Barrel-Land Dance Hall Rangers,* 190–192.
12. Hall, "Ranger Scout."
13. Arnbal, *The Barrel-Land Dance Hall Rangers,* 193.
14. Kazura, "Charles H. Kazura."
15. Lehman, "Rangers Fought Ahead of Everybody," 48.
16. Gray, "End of the Line," 212–214.
17. U.S. War Department, Signal Intelligence Service press release, 872, Musegades.
18. Cavazos, email to David Lyle Williams.
19. Morriss, "Rangers Come Home."
20. Warren "Bing" Evans, conversations with David Lyle Williams.
21. Ibid.
22. Golde, "Donald Golde."
23. Romine, "My Life in Combat and as a POW."
24. Milton Lehman, "Rangers Fought Ahead of Everybody," 49.
25. Earnest, "Notes."
26. Black, *Ranger Force,* 224.
27. First Ranger Battalion, Report of Action, casualties, 15 November 1943 and 15 December 1943; Third Ranger Battalion, Report of Action, casualties, 31 July 1943, 31 August 1943, 25 November 1943, and 5 January 1943; Fourth Ranger Battalion, Report of Action, casualties, 9 August 1943, 5 October 1943, 10 November 1943, and 14 December 1943; Hudnell, "World War II Rangers Who Died Overseas During World War II."
28. Darby and Baumer, *We Led the Way,* 141.
29. King, *William O. Darby,* 135–136.

12. ANZIO INVASION

1. Darby and Baumer, *We Led the Way,* 145.
2. Ranger Battalions Association, *Rangers Lead the Way,* 19.
3. Altieri, *Darby's Rangers,* 68–69.
4. Truscott, *Command Missions,* 301–305.
5. Darby and Baumer, *We Led the Way,* 144.

6. Starr, *From Salerno to the Alps*, 83–85.
7. Truscott, *Command Missions*, 288–290.
8. Black, *Ranger Force*, 228.
9. Atkinson, *The Day of Battle*, 377.
10. Darby and Baumer, *We Led the Way*, 229.
11. Atkinson, *The Day of Battle*, 353–354.
12. Morris, *Circles of Hell*, 260.
13. Black, *Ranger Force*, 229.
14. Atkinson, *The Day of Battle*, 354–357.
15. King, *William O. Darby*, 144–145.
16. Haywood, unpublished memoir.
17. Zartman, *East to the Russkies*, 123.
18. Haywood, unpublished memoir.
19. King, *William O. Darby*, 140–141.
20. Krzysztofiak, emails to David Lyle Williams.
21. Haywood, unpublished memoir.
22. Altieri, *Spearheaders*, 307.
23. King, *William O. Darby*, 147–148.
24. Markham, "My Version of the Landing at Anzio," 69.
25. Stabler and Smith, *No One Ever Asked Me*, 77.
26. Altieri, *Darby's Rangers*, 69.
27. Haywood, unpublished memoir.
28. Markham, "My Version of the Landing at Anzio," 52.
29. Haywood, unpublished memoir.
30. Ibid.
31. Altieri, *Darby's Rangers*, 71–72.
32. U.S. War Department, Signal Intelligence Service press release, 916, Jacobs.
33. Stabler and Smith, *No One Ever Asked Me*, 85–86.
34. Rice to the mother of Joe Renfro, 18 January 1948.
35. Martin, "Veterans History Project: 'G.W. Guynes.'"
36. Kolisch, Special Report, Headquarters, Fifth Army, G-2 Section, IPW.
37. Tipton, "Surgery under Stress."
38. Ibid., 46.
39. Romine, "My Life in Combat and as a POW," 88.
40. Truscott, Field Order.
41. Warren "Bing" Evans, conversations with David Lyle Williams.
42. Ibid.
43. Arnbal, *The Barrel-Land Dance Hall Rangers*, 227–228.

13. THE BATTLE FOR CISTERNA DI LITTORIA

1. Truscott, Estimate of the Situation.
2. D'Este, *Fatal Decision*, 129–132.

3. Stewart, "The Ranger Force at the Battle of Cisterna," 28–29.
4. Black, *Ranger Force,* 255.
5. Truscott, *Command Missions,* 312.
6. Truscott, Field Order.
7. Black, *Ranger Force,* 243.
8. Truscott, Annex to Field Order 3.
9. Ibid.
10. Darby and Baumer, *We Led the Way,* 159.
11. Ibid.
12. Markham, "My Version of the Landing at Anzio," 52.
13. Schunemann, "Memoirs of a Ranger," 7.
14. Darby and Baumer, *We Led the Way,* 161.
15. James Miller, conversation with David Lyle Williams.
16. Warren "Bing" Evans, conversations with David Lyle Williams.
17. Ranger Force Journal, From 1200 Hours 28 January 1944 through 31 January 1944, 3.
18. Stewart, "The Ranger Force at the Battle of Cisterna," 31–33.
19. Meltesen, *After the Battle,* 19.
20. Darby and Baumer, *We Led the Way,* 161.
21. Darby, Field Order 2.
22. Black, *Ranger Force,* 254.
23. Ibid., 251.
24. Darby and Baumer, *We Led the Way,* 161.
25. Black, *Ranger Force,* 243.
26. Zartman, *East to the Russkies,* 127.
27. Warren "Bing" Evans, conversations with David Lyle Williams.
28. Meltesen, *After the Battle,* 10.
29. Markham, conversations with David Lyle Williams.
30. Black, *Ranger Force,* 261.
31. Markham, "My Version of the Landing at Anzio," 53.
32. Zartman, *East to the Russkies,* 127.
33. Markham, conversations with David Lyle Williams.
34. Ibid.
35. Williams, unpublished biography of Zelly Dineen.
36. Altieri, *Darby's Rangers,* 83.
37. Meltesen, *After the Battle,* 19.
38. Stewart, "The Ranger Force at the Battle of Cisterna," 32.
39. Black, *Ranger Force,* 256.
40. Stewart, "The Ranger Force at the Battle of Cisterna," 32.
41. Ranger Force Journal, From 1200 Hours 28 January 1944 through 31 January 1944, 3.
42. King, *William O. Darby,* 152.
43. Ibid.
44. Murray and Schneider, "The Fourth Ranger Battalion."
45. Ibid.

46. Ranger Force Journal, From 1200 Hours 28 January 1944 through 31 January 1944, 4.

47. Ibid.

48. Kopanda, "Behind German Lines," 2.

49. Shunstrom, "Capture of the First and Third Ranger Battalions," 1.

50. Stewart, "The Ranger Force at the Battle of Cisterna," 33.

51. Davis, "Pat's Notes."

52. Darby and Baumer, *We Led the Way*, 161.

53. Altieri, *Darby's Rangers*, 83.

54. Ibid.

55. Dobson to Altieri, 21 April 1984.

56. Davis, "Pat's Notes."

57. Black, *Rangers in World War II*, 163.

58. Markham, conversations with David Lyle Williams.

59. Zartman, *East to the Russkies*, 127–128.

60. Schunemann, "Memoirs of a Ranger," 7–8.

61. Dobson to Altieri, 21 April 1984.

62. Markham, "My Version of the Landing at Anzio," 53.

63. Ranger Force Journal, From 1200 Hours 28 January 1944 through 31 January 1944, 4.

64. Zartman, *East to the Russkies*, 128.

65. Ibid.

66. Altieri, *Darby's Rangers*, 83.

67. Sadoski, Library of Congress, Veterans History Project, 18.

68. Altieri, *Darby's Rangers*, 83.

69. Meltesen, *After the Battle*, 23.

70. American Battle Monuments Commission, Sicily-Rome American Cemetery, Nettuno, Italy, "Wall of the Missing."

71. Meltesen, *After the Battle*, 23.

72. Zartman, *East to the Russkies*, 128–129.

73. Ibid., 129.

74. Meltesen, *After the Battle*, 23.

75. Ibid., 24–25.

76. Carl Lehmann, "3rd Ranger Battalion History."

77. Meltesen, *After the Battle*, 26.

78. Ibid.

79. Ibid.

80. Ibid.

81. Ibid.

82. Eineichner, Remembrances, 3.

83. Meltesen, *After the Battle*, 27.

84. James Larkin, "Onetime Soldier," part 2.

85. Warren "Bing" Evans, conversations with David Lyle Williams.

86. James Larkin, "Onetime Soldier," part 2, 69.

87. Eineichner, Remembrances, 3.

88. Krise, conversations with David Lyle Williams.
89. Eineichner, Remembrances, 3.
90. Ranger Force Journal, From 1200 Hours 28 January 1944 through 31 January 1944, 4.
91. Ibid.
92. Black, *Ranger Force,* 258.
93. Altieri, "Ranger Battalions of World War II," 12.
94. James Larkin, "Onetime Soldier," part 2, 70.
95. Meltesen, *After the Battle,* 29.
96. Ibid., 31.
97. Romine, "My Life in Combat and as a POW," 89.
98. Eineichner, Remembrances, 3.
99. Markham, conversations with David Lyle Williams.
100. Markham, "My Version of the Landing at Anzio," 53.
101. Markham, conversations with David Lyle Williams.
102. Ibid.
103. Shunstrom, "Capture of the First and Third Ranger Battalions," 1.
104. Darby and Baumer, *We Led the Way,* 162–164.
105. Ranger Force Journal, From 1200 Hours 28 January 1944 through 31 January 1944, 5.
106. Darby, "Account of Ranger Force, 28 to 31 January 1944."
107. Altieri, *Spearheaders,* 311.
108. Harlow, unpublished notes.
109. Cashen, email to David Lyle Williams.
110. Fordham, email to David Lyle Williams, re. Max Fordham.
111. Boron, conversations with David Lyle Williams.
112. Dobson to Altieri, 2 April 1984.
113. Alloway, "Condensed Story, Life of Norman L. Alloway."
114. Darby, "The First Rangers in Mediterranean Combat."
115. Shunstrom, "Capture of the First and Third Ranger Battalions," 2.
116. Ibid.
117. Altieri, *Darby's Rangers,* 83.
118. Meltesen, *After the Battle,* 25.
119. Dobson to Altieri, 2 April 1984.
120. Williams, unpublished biography of Zelly Dineen.
121. Kitchens to Lehmann, 15 January 1998.
122. Sadoski, Library of Congress, Veterans History Project, 18.
123. Ibid., 19.
124. Darby and Baumer, *We Led the Way,* 164.
125. Wilson to Adams, 13 February 2005.
126. Altieri, *Darby's Rangers,* 83.
127. Sadoski, Library of Congress, Veterans History Project, 19.
128. Milton Lehman, "Rangers Fought Ahead of Everybody," 49.
129. Alloway, conversations with David Lyle Williams.
130. Williams, unpublished biography of Zelly Dineen.

131. Meltesen, *After the Battle*, 29.

132. Ibid.

133. Ibid.

134. Ibid., 27–29.

135. Ibid., 29.

136. Hall, "Ranger Scout."

137. Meltesen, *After the Battle*, 31.

138. Ibid.

139. Davis, "Anzio, First Ranger Battalion, E Company."

140. Meltesen, *After the Battle*, 36.

141. Altieri, *Darby's Rangers*, 83.

142. Davis, "Pat's Notes."

143. Ranger Force Radio Log, 1200 hours on 29 January 1944 to 1200 hours on 30 January 1944.

144. Meltesen, *After the Battle*, 31.

145. Ibid.

146. Lawrence Gilbert, conversations with David Lyle Williams.

147. Altieri, *Darby's Rangers*, 81.

148. Warren "Bing" Evans, conversations with David Lyle Williams.

149. Meltesen, *After the Battle*, 32.

150. Dobson to Altieri, 21 April 1984.

151. Black, *Ranger Force*, 267.

152. Darby and Baumer, *We Led the Way*, 165.

153. Kopanda, "Behind German Lines," 3.

154. Stewart, "The Ranger Force at the Battle of Cisterna," 36–37.

155. Williams, unpublished biography of Zelly Dineen.

156. Meltesen, *After the Battle*, 23.

157. Ranger Force Radio Log, 1200 hours on 29 January 1944 to 1200 hours on 30 January 1944.

158. Meltesen, *After the Battle*, 13.

159. Romine, "My Life in Combat and as a POW."

160. Krise, conversations with David Lyle Williams.

161. Key and Kimbler, scrapbook of notes, clippings, and memorabilia.

162. Warren "Bing" Evans, conversations with David Lyle Williams.

163. Meltesen, *After the Battle*, 13.

164. Ranger Force Radio Log, 1200 hours on 29 January 1944 to 1200 hours on 30 January 1944.

165. Meltesen, *After the Battle*, 13.

166. Shunstrom, "Capture of the First and Third Ranger Battalions," 3.

167. Alloway, conversations with David Lyle Williams.

168. Stewart, "The Ranger Force at the Battle of Cisterna," 37.

169. O'Reilly and Syroid, "A Tough Decision," in *Darby's Rangers*.

170. Warren "Bing" Evans, conversations with David Lyle Williams.

171. Ibid.

172. Ibid.

173. Kopanda, "Behind German Lines," 4.

174. Sadoski, Library of Congress, Veterans History Project, 19.

175. Cooney, "Notes."

176. Zartman, *East to the Russkies,* 130–131.

177. Meltesen, *After the Battle,* 35.

178. Darby and Baumer, *We Led the Way,* 169.

179. Ibid.

180. O'Reilly and Syroid, "A Tough Decision," in *Darby's Rangers.*

181. Newnan to the father of Pfc. John J. Burke, 31 August 1944.

182. Meltesen, *After the Battle,* 34.

183. Markham, conversations with David Lyle Williams.

184. Ranger Force Radio Log, 1200 hours on 29 January 1944 to 1200 hours on 30 January 1944.

185. Schunemann, "Memoirs of a Ranger," 8.

186. Markham, conversations with David Lyle Williams.

187. Ranger Force Radio Log, 1200 hours on 29 January 1944 to 1200 hours on 30 January 1944.

188. Ibid.

189. Darby, "Account of Ranger Force, 28 to 31 January 1944."

190. Ibid.

191. Darby and Baumer, *We Led the Way,* 167.

192. Krise, conversations with David Lyle Williams.

193. Sadoski, Library of Congress, Veterans History Project, 20.

194. Ibid.

195. Meltesen, *After the Battle,* 36.

196. Ibid.

197. Ibid., 37–38.

198. Ibid., 38.

199. Ibid.

200. Ruona, conversation with David Lyle Williams and Kelly Gangnath.

201. Ibid.

202. Ibid.

203. O'Reilly and Syroid, "A Tough Decision," in *Darby's Rangers.*

204. Shunstrom, "Capture of the First and Third Ranger Battalions," 3.

205. Warren "Bing" Evans, conversations with David Lyle Williams.

206. Meltesen, *After the Battle,* 35.

207. Warren "Bing" Evans, conversations with David Lyle Williams.

208. Altieri, *Darby's Rangers,* 83.

209. Warren "Bing" Evans, conversations with David Lyle Williams.

210. Shunstrom, "Capture of the First and Third Ranger Battalions," 3.

211. Kushner, note sent to David Lyle Williams.

212. Ibid.

213. Altieri, *Darby's Rangers,* 83.

214. Hall, "Ranger Scout."
215. Black, *Ranger Force*, 271.
216. Shunstrom, "Capture of the First and Third Ranger Battalions," 3.
217. Ibid.
218. Williams, unpublished biography of Zelly Dineen.
219. Markham, "My Version of the Landing at Anzio," 53.
220. Markham, conversations with David Lyle Williams.
221. Eineichner, Remembrances, 4.
222. Romine, "My Life in Combat and as a POW."
223. Meltesen, "My Version of the Landing at Anzio," 53.
224. Alloway, conversations with David Lyle Williams.
225. Mauritz, *The Secret of Anzio Bay*, 212.
226. Ibid., 212–213.
227. Ibid., 213.
228. Schunemann, "Memoirs of a Ranger," 8.
229. Annechino, *More Than a Soldier*, 115.
230. Skoch, "Escape Hatch Found," 36.
231. Meltesen, *After the Battle*, 39.
232. Ibid.
233. Krise, conversations with David Lyle Williams.
234. Meltesen, *After the Battle*, 12.
235. Ibid., 37.
236. Eineichner, Remembrances, 4.
237. Farrar, *William O. Darby*, 48.
238. Krise, conversations with David Lyle Williams.
239. Altieri, "Ranger Battalions of World War II," 12.
240. Murray and Schneider, "The Fourth Ranger Battalion."
241. Anderson, conversations with David Lyle Williams.
242. Murray and Schneider, "The Fourth Ranger Battalion."
243. Altieri, "Ranger Battalions of World War II," 12.
244. Ibid.
245. Boron, conversations with David Lyle Williams.
246. Davis, "Ranger Force, Section 1/B."
247. Ranger Force Journal, From 1200 Hours 28 January 1944 through 31 January 1944, 6.
248. Anderson, conversations with David Lyle Williams.
249. Ranger Force Journal, From 1200 Hours 28 January 1944 through 31 January 1944, 7.
250. Ibid., 8.
251. Fourth Ranger Battalion, Report of Action, casualties, 15 February 1944.
252. Ranger Force Journal, From 1200 Hours 28 January 1944 through 31 January 1944, 8.
253. Ibid.
254. Ibid.
255. Davis, "Ranger Force, Section 1/B."
256. Black, *Ranger Force*, 285.

257. Darby and Baumer, *We Led the Way,* 175.
258. Black, *Ranger Force,* 288.
259. Ibid.
260. Darby and Baumer, *We Led the Way,* 176.
261. Altieri, *Darby's Rangers,* 122, 120, 121, 123.
262. Ibid., 104.
263. Starr, *From Salerno to the Alps,* 133.
264. Stewart, "The Ranger Force at the Battle of Cisterna."
265. King, *William O. Darby,* 158–159.
266. Arnbal, *The Barrel-Land Dance Hall Rangers,* 227.
267. Altieri, "Ranger Battalions of World War II."
268. Darby and Baumer, *We Led the Way,* 162.
269. Ibid., 160.
270. Ibid., 166.
271. Shunstrom, "Capture of the First and Third Ranger Battalions."
272. Markham, conversations with David Lyle Williams.
273. Joan Larkin, conversation with David Lyle Williams.
274. Dobson to Altieri, 21 April 1984.
275. Ibid.
276. Ibid.
277. United States Fifth Army Headquarters to Lucas, "Violations of Radio Security."
278. Truscott, *Command Missions,* 314.
279. Ibid.

14. AFTER THE BATTLE

1. Adjutant General, United States Army, to Breuers, n.d..
2. Warren "Bing" Evans, conversations with David Lyle Williams.
3. Altieri, *Spearheaders,* 313.
4. U.S. War Department, Signal Intelligence Service press release, 912, Ryan.
5. Davis, "Ranger Force, Section 1/B."
6. Ibid.
7. Ibid.
8. Meltesen, *After the Battle,* 6.
9. Ibid., 7.
10. Ibid., 8.
11. Ibid., 8–9.
12. Ibid., 9.
13. Palmer, "I Survived the Battle of Cisterna."
14. Milton Lehman, "Rangers Died Fighting at Dawn."
15. Ranger Battalions Association, "Newsletter."
16. Golde, "Donald Golde."
17. Ward, conversation with David Lyle Williams.

18. Goad, conversations with David Lyle Williams.

19. Meltesen, conversations with David Lyle Williams.

20. Zartman, *East to the Russkies,* 135.

21. Ibid.

22. Ibid.

23. Romine, "My Life in Combat and as a POW," 89.

24. Meltesen, conversations with David Lyle Williams.

25. James Larkin, "Onetime Soldier," part 2, 2.

26. Krise, conversations with David Lyle Williams.

27. Eineichner, Remembrances, 4–5.

28. Ibid., 5.

29. Mauritz, *The Secret of Anzio Bay,* 74.

30. Tremblay, Casualty List for the Period 22 January 1944 to 5 February 1944, 1st Ranger Battalion.

31. Mitchell, Report of Action.

32. Nye, Report of Casualties, 4th Ranger Infantry Battalion.

33. Murray and Schneider, "The Fourth Ranger Battalion."

34. Belanger, "Report on Ranger Force Casualties during Anzio and Cisterna."

35. Belanger, "Third Ranger Battalion Casualties, Anzio/Cisterna."

36. Ibid.

37. Belanger, "Report on Ranger Force Casualties during Anzio and Cisterna."

38. Belanger, "Summary of Casualties. Fourth Ranger Battalion at the Battle of Cisterna."

39. Altieri, *Darby's Rangers,* 102–105.

40. Walker to Commanding General, Sixth Army Group, U.S. Army, 15 November 1944.

41. Mitchell, Memorandum to Col. Edwin A. Walker, Commanding Officer, Headquarters, 1st Special Service Force.

42. Ibid.

43. American Battle Monuments Commission, Sicily-Rome American Cemetery, Nettuno, Italy, "Wall of the Missing."

15. THE MARCH IN ROME

1. Meltesen, *After the Battle,* 45.

2. Eineichner, Remembrances, 5.

3. Wilson to Adams, 13 February 2005.

4. Schunemann, "Memoirs of a Ranger," 9.

5. Lee, General Order 212.

6. Carl Lehmann, "Life as a German P. O. W."

7. *United States v. General Kurt Maelzer,* testimony of Frank.

8. *United States v. General Kurt Maelzer,* testimony of Bond.

9. *United States v. General Kurt Maelzer,* testimony of McCall.

10. *United States v. General Kurt Maelzer,* testimony of Palumbo.

11. *United States v. General Kurt Maelzer,* testimony of Wood.

12. Ibid.
13. *United States v. General Kurt Maelzer,* defense summary.
14. *United States v. General Kurt Maelzer,* prosecutor's summary.
15. Lee, General Order 212.

16. AFTER THE MARCH

1. Newnan, *Escape in Italy,* 3–4.
2. Meltesen, *After the Battle,* 57.
3. Williams, unpublished biography of Zelly Dineen.
4. Ruona, conversation with David Lyle Williams and Kelly Gangnath.
5. Porter, "Lord Love You Captain," 59–62.
6. Mauritz, *The Secret of Anzio Bay,* 61.
7. Ibid., 217.
8. Evans, conversations with David Lyle Williams.
9. Mauritz, *The Secret of Anzio Bay,* 80–81.
10. Ibid.
11. Ibid., 94.
12. Ibid., 97–98.
13. Ibid., 166.
14. Ibid., 190.
15. Meltesen, *After the Battle,* 60.
16. Black, *Ranger Force,* 278.
17. Newnan, *Escape in Italy,* 1.
18. Ibid., 3.
19. Ibid., 8.
20. Ibid., 9.
21. Ibid., 17.
22. Ibid., 25.
23. Ibid., 25–26.
24. Ibid., 31.
25. Ibid., 35.
26. Ibid., 45.
27. Ibid., 46–47.
28. Meltesen, *After the Battle,* 125.
29. D'Amato, "God Was on Our Side."
30. Meltesen, *After the Battle,* 83.
31. Wilson to Adams, 13 February 2005.
32. Kopanda, "Behind German Lines."
33. Markham, "My Version of the Landing at Anzio," 54.
34. Schunemann, "Memoirs of a Ranger," 10.
35. Markham, "My Version of the Landing at Anzio," 54.
36. Ibid., 54–55.

37. Ibid., 55.
38. Ibid., 55–56.
39. Schunemann, "Memoirs of a Ranger," 11–13.
40. Ibid., 13.
41. Ibid., 14–15.
42. Ibid., 15.
43. Annechino, *More Than a Soldier,* 138–235.
44. Ibid.
45. Ibid.
46. Mascari, "A Group of Four, Captured and Escaped."
47. Ibid.
48. Meltesen, *After the Battle,* 106–129.
49. Adjutant General, U.S. Army, to Breuers, 6 June 1944.
50. Adrian Gilbert, *POW: Allied Prisoners of War in Europe,* 65–66.
51. Ibid., 66.
52. Hall, "Ranger Scout."
53. Carl Lehmann, "Life as a German P. O. W."
54. Suominen, *Twice to Freedom,* 84.
55. Ruona, conversation with David Lyle Williams and Kelly Gangnath.
56. Carl Lehmann, conversations with David Lyle Williams.
57. Ibid.
58. Zartman, *East to the Russkies,* 152–154.
59. Suominen, *Twice to Freedom,* 66.
60. Sanders, Sauter, and Kirkwood, *Soldiers of Misfortune,* 52.
61. Belanger, "Report on Ranger Force Casualties during Anzio and Cisterna."
62. Ketzer, "Steve Ketzer," 26–27.
63. Carl Lehmann, conversations with David Lyle Williams.
64. Ibid.
65. Wilson, conversations with David Lyle Williams.
66. Zartman, *East to the Russkies,* 157–158.
67. Williams, unpublished biography of Zelly Dineen.
68. Ibid.
69. Carl Lehmann, "Life as a German P. O. W."
70. Richardson, notes, 3.
71. Romine, "My Life in Combat and as a POW," 89–90.
72. Hermsen, "My Story," unpublished memoir.
73. Adrian Gilbert, *POW: Allied Prisoners of War in Europe,* 82.
74. Warren "Bing" Evans, conversations with David Lyle Williams.
75. Farrar, *William O. Darby.*
76. Frederick, "Notes."
77. Ibid.
78. Warren "Bing" Evans, conversations with David Lyle Williams.
79. Ketzer, "Steve Ketzer," 26–27.

80. Mattivi, "Frank Joey Mattivi," 117–118.
81. Kopanda, "Behind German Lines," 6
82. Ibid., 8.
83. Ibid., 9–10.
84. Carl Lehmann, conversations with David Lyle Williams.
85. Adrian Gilbert, *POW: Allied Prisoners of War in Europe*, 300–304.
86. Wilson to Adams, 13 February 2005.
87. Ibid.
88. Kushner, note sent to David Lyle Williams.
89. Goad, email to David Lyle Williams.
90. Hermsen, "My Story," unpublished memoir.
91. Williams, unpublished biography of Zelly Dineen.
92. Ibid.
93. Ibid.
94. Ibid.
95. Ibid.
96. Ibid.
97. Zartman, *East to the Russkies*, 179–182.
98. Ibid., 183–188.
99. Ibid., 189–193.
100. Ibid.
101. Ibid., 194–222.
102. Ibid.
103. Ellsworth, *Yank*, 270–274.
104. Ibid., 275.
105. Ibid., 276.
106. Ibid., 309.
107. Ibid., 314.
108. Frederick, "Notes."
109. Ibid.
110. Warren "Bing" Evans, conversations with David Lyle Williams.
111. Ibid.
112. Ibid.
113. Ibid.
114. Ibid.

EPILOGUE

1. Warren "Bing" Evans, conversations with David Lyle Williams.
2. Lyle, conversations with David Lyle Williams.
3. Warren "Bing" Evans, conversations with David Lyle Williams.
4. Lyle, conversations with David Lyle Williams.
5. Warren "Bing" Evans, conversations with David Lyle Williams.

6. King, *William O. Darby,* 160.
7. Darby, "The First Rangers in Mediterranean Combat."
8. Schunemann, "Memoirs of a Ranger," 16.
9. Anderson, conversations with David Lyle Williams.
10. King, *William O. Darby,* 167.
11. Darby and Baumer, *We Led the Way,* 178.
12. Templeton to Darby Foundation, 12 April 1998.
13. King, *William O. Darby,* 175.
14. Lyle, conversations with David Lyle Williams.
15. Warren "Bing" Evans, conversations with David Lyle Williams.
16. Ibid.
17. Ibid.
18. Henry to his parents, 9 April 1944.
19. Carl Lehmann, conversations with David Lyle Williams.
20. Murray, conversation with David Lyle Williams.
21. Markham, conversations with David Lyle Williams.
22. Murray, conversation with David Lyle Williams.
23. Prudhomme, conversation with David Lyle Williams.
24. Brown, *Fallen in Battle.*
25. Seventy-Fifth Ranger Regiment, U.S. Army. "Citation, Ranger Hall of Fame."
26. Schneider, *My Father's War.*
27. Markham, conversations with David Lyle Williams.
28. Porter, "Lord Love You Captain."
29. Merrill to Elaine Hawes, n.d.
30. Lyle, conversations with David Lyle Williams.
31. U.S. Army Graves Registration Service. Report of Burial, Corrected Copy, 27 July 1949.
32. Skinner, conversation with David Lyle Williams.
33. Rice to the mother of Joe Renfro, 18 January 1948.

BIBLIOGRAPHY

PRIMARY SOURCES

Adjutant General, U.S. Army, to Henry Breuers. Western Union telegram, n.d. Author's collection.

——— to Henry Breuers. Western Union telegram, 6 June 1944. Author's collection.

Allen, Maj. Gen. Terry de la Mesa, Sr., Commander, First Infantry Division, to Lt. Col. William Orlando Darby, 22 February 1943. Author's collection.

Alloway, 2nd Lt. Norman L., 1/A. "Condensed Story, Life of Norman L. Alloway." Unpublished memoir, n.d. Author's collection.

Altieri, 2nd Lt. James, 4/F. "Affidavit on behalf of Raymond Noel Dye presented to the Veteran's Administration, 2 February 1992." Author's collection.

———. *Darby's Rangers.* Fort Smith, Ark.: The Ranger Book Committee, 1977. National Archives.

———. "Ranger Battalions of World War II." Dallas, Tex.: *Northwind, Newsletter of the Town North Lions Club,* 1984. Author's collection.

———. *The Spearheaders.* New York: Bobbs-Merrill, 1960.

American Battle Monuments Commission. Sicily-Rome American Cemetery, Nettuno, Italy. "Wall of the Missing."

Arnbal, Cpl. Anders Kjar, 1/B. *The Barrel-Land Dance Hall Rangers.* New York: Vantage Press, 1993.

Blumenson, Martin. *The Patton Papers, 1940–1945.* New York: Da Capo Press, 1996.

Bolte, Brig. Gen. Charles L. Special Orders, Number 2. Headquarters European Theater of Operations, U.S. Army. Author's collection.

Bradley, Gen. Omar N. *A Soldier's Story.* New York: Holt, 1951.

Bresnahan, Pfc. Walter A., 1/B, to Marcel Swank, 5 August 1980. Author's collection.

Butler, Maj. Allen S. "Operations of the First Battalion, 18th Infantry, at El Guettar, Tunisia, 20–30 March 1943." Report for Advance Infantry Officer's Course. Fort Benning, Ga., 1943. Fort Moore Library.

Carter, Maj. Sam. "Operations of the First Battalion, 18th Infantry, at El Guettar, Tunisia, 20–30 March, 1943." Report for Advance Infantry Officer's Class. Fort Benning, Ga., 1947–1948. Fort Moore Library.

Clark, Gen. Mark W. *Calculated Risk.* New York: Harper Brothers, 1950.

Cook, Sgt. Lester, 4/A. "Pill Box." Ranger Battalions Association, World War II, National Reunion. Fort Wayne, Ind., 25–30 August 2004. Author's collection.

Cooney, 2nd Lt. James D. 1/C. "Notes." Unpublished, n.d. Author's collection.

D'Amato, Cpl. Pasquale J., 3/E. "God Was on Our Side." Unpublished memoir, n.d. Author's collection.

Darby, Col. William Orlando. "Account of Ranger Force, 28 to 31 January 1944." 2 February 1944. Author's collection.

———. Efficiency Report, re: Cpt.. James B. Lyle, 29 July 1944. Author's collection.

———. "The First Rangers in Mediterranean Combat." Original draft of *We Led the Way* by Darby and Baumer, dictated June/July 1944, unpublished. Author's collection.

———. Headquarters, First Ranger Battalion. Report of Action Against the Enemy. Arzew, Algeria, 1 January 1943. Fort Moore Library.

———. Headquarters, First Ranger Battalion. Report of Action. Sened Station, Tunisia, 5 March 1943. Fort Moore Library.

———. Headquarters, First Ranger Battalion. Report of Action. Djebel el Ank, Tunisia, 9 April 1943. Fort Moore Library.

———. Headquarters Ranger Force (Prov). Field Order Number 2, 29 January 1944. Fort Moore Library.

———. "The United States Rangers." Speech to the Army and Navy Staff College. Washington, D.C., 27 October 1944. Author's collection.

Darby, Col. William Orlando, and William H. Baumer. *We Led the Way: Darby's Rangers.* San Rafael, Calif.: Presidio Press, 1980.

Davis, Pfc. Arnold "Pat", 1/E. "American Light Infantry Battles." Unpublished, n.d. Author's collection.

———. "Anzio, First Ranger Battalion, E Company." Unpublished, 1 August 1986. Author's collection.

———. "Pat's Notes." Unpublished, n.d. Author's collection.

———. "Ranger Force, Section 1/B." Unpublished, n.d. Author's collection.

"Diary of the First Ranger Battalion, 8 June 1942–20 May 1943." Unpublished, n.d. Author's collection.

Dobson, Brig. Gen. John W., Commanding Officer, 1st Ranger Battalion, to James Altieri, 2 April 1984. Author's collection.

——— to James Altieri, 21 April 1984. Author's collection.

Earnest, Pfc. Roy Wade, 1/C. "Notes." Unpublished, n.d. Author's collection.

Eineichner, Tech/5 Clarence, 3/Hq. "Assault on Messina." Ranger Battalions Association, World War II, National Reunion. Fort Wayne, Ind., 2004. Author's collection.

———. Remembrances. Unpublished, n.d. Author's collection.

Ellsworth, Ted [Theodore]. *Yank: Memoirs of a World War II Soldier (1941–1945): From the Desert War of North Africa to the Allied Invasion of Europe.* New York: Thunder's Mouth Press, 2006.

Emmons, Ora, Jr., email to Joyce Dineen, 16 April 2000. Author's collection.

Farrar, Jackie Marie. ed. *William O. Darby, "A Man to Remember."* Claremore, Okla.: Country Lane Press, 1987.

First Ranger Battalion. Report of Action, 11 January 1943. Fort Moore Library.

———. Report of Action, 5 March 1943. Fort Moore Library.

———. Report of Action, 6 March 1943. Fort Moore Library.

———. Report of Action, 9 April 1943. Fort Moore Library.

———. Report of Action, 15 November 1943. Fort Moore Library.

———. Report of Action, 15 December 1943. Fort Moore Library.

———. Report of Action, 31 March 1944. Fort Moore Library.

Flanagan, Cpt. Robert, 1/E. "The Ranger Is a Tough Fighting Man." *The Ordinance Sergeant* 6, no. 4 (October 1943). Author's collection.

Fourth Infantry Division. Estimate of the Situation, 29 January 1944. Fort Moore Library.

Fourth Ranger Battalion, Report of Action, 9 August 1943. Fort Moore Library.

———. Report of Action, 5 October 1943. Fort Moore Library.

———. Ranger Battalion, Report of Action, 10 November 1943. Fort Moore Library.

———. Report of Action, 14 December 1943. Fort Moore Library.

———. Battle Casualties for the period 22 Jan 44 to 31 Jan 44. Fort Moore Library.

———. Report of Action, 17 March 1944. Fort Moore Library.

Furru, Pfc. Edwin R., 1/Hq., to Marcel Swank, 14 September 1980. Author's collection.

Golde, Donald G. "Donald Golde." Ranger Battalions Association, World War II, National Reunion. Fort Wayne, Ind., 2004. Author's collection.

Gray, Pvt. Justin, 3/C. "The End of the Line." *Yank, the Army Weekly*, 24 January 1944, repr. New York: St. Martin's Press, n.d.

Hall, Cpl. George W. "Ranger Scout." Unpublished memoir, n.d. Author's collection.

Harlow, Pvt. Robert, 1/C. Unpublished notes, 12 August 2000. Author's collection.

Harris, Randall. "The Harris Family in World War II, Letters and Memories." Los Angeles, unpublished, 1996. Author's collection.

Hayes, Tech/5 Donald, 1/B and 3/C. Excerpts from an interview by Dora Jane Hamblin, 11 March 1944. Author's collection.

Haywood, Pvt. Edward, Jr., 1/C. Unpublished memoir, n.d. Author's collection.

Henry, Lt. L. Lew, 4/A, to his parents, Mr. and Mrs. A. M. Henry, 9 April 1944. Author's collection.

Hermsen, Cpl. Paul, 1/C. "My Story." Unpublished memoir, n.d. Author's collection.

Hood, 1st Lt. Carl R. "Bob" to his parents, Carl and Marbye Hood, from Sicily, n.d. Author's collection.

——— to his parents, Carl and Marbye Hood, from Venafro, n.d. Author's collection.

Hudnell, J. Ronald. "World War II Rangers Who Died Overseas During World War II, A Study." Unpublished, n.d. Author's collection.

Hummer, Maj. John F., 1/C. *An Infantryman's Journal.* Manassas, Va.: Ranger Associates, 1981.

Hunt, S/Sgt. Russell, 1/D. Personal notes and memorabilia. Unpublished, n.d. Author's collection.

Hutchinson, William S., Jr., to Maj. Gen. William H. Baumer, 4 October 1979. Author's collection.

Ingersoll, Cpt. Ralph. *The Battle Is the Payoff.* New York: Harcourt Brace, 1943.

Jackson, Gen. Sir William G. F. *The Battle for North Africa, 1940–1943.* New York: Mason/Charter, 1975.

Jacob, Cpt. Manning, 1/A. Report of Action. 1st Ranger Battalion, 1/A. Arzew, Algeria, 15 November 1942. Fort Moore Library.

Kazura, Mrs. Charles H. "Charles H. Kazura." *Rangers Lead the Way: Ranger Battalions Association World War II, Biennial Reunion.* New Orleans, 2001. Author's collection.

Ketzer, Steve, Jr. "Steve Ketzer." *Rangers Lead the Way: Ranger Battalions Association World War II, Biennial Reunion.* New Orleans, 2001, 26–27.

Key, Carl, 3/Hq., and Pvt. Clifford Kimbler, 3/Hq. Scrapbook of notes, clippings, and memorabilia, n.d. Author's collection.

Kimbler, Pvt. Clifford, 3/Hq. "Back at Ranger Force Headquarters." Unpublished memoir, n.d. Author's collection.

Kitchens, Brig. Gen. Edward, to Carl Lehmann, 15 January 1998. Author's collection.

Kitchens, Capt. Edward, 3/C. "Operations of the Third Ranger Battalion in the Landing at Licata." Report for Advanced Infantry Officer's Class no. 2. Fort Benning, Ga., 1950. Fort Moore Library.

Kness, Capt. Lester, 4/A. "Fourth Ranger Battalion-Venafro." Ranger Battalions Association, World War II, National Reunion. Phoenix, Ariz., 2005. Author's collection.

———. "Iowa Farm Boy." Ranger Battalions Association, World War II, National Reunion. Fort Wayne, Ind., 2004. Author's collection.

Kolisch, 1st. Lt. Joseph M. Special Report, Headquarters, Fifth Army, G-2 Section, IPW, 9 March 1944. Author's collection.

Kopanda, Rob. "Behind German Lines: The WW II Prison Escapes of Sgt. George Kopanda." Unpublished, 23 December 1995. Author's collection.

Lamandre, S/Sgt. Dominick, 4/F. "A Ranger Who Put His Premonition of Death into Poetry." *Rangers Lead the Way: Ranger Battalions Association World War II, Biennial Reunion.* New Orleans, 2001. Author's collection.

Larkin, 2nd Lt. James J., 1/B and 3/E. After Action Report, 1st Ranger Battalion, B Company. Arzew, Algeria, 16 November 1942. Author's collection.

———. "Onetime Soldier, 1st and 3rd Ranger Battalions—1942–1943." 2 vols. Unpublished, 1988. Author's collection.

Lee, Lt. Gen. John C. H. General Order 212. War Trials Commission. Headquarters, Mediterranean Theater of Operations. Trial of General Kurt Maelzer. 10 December 1946. Author's collection.

Lehmann, Sgt. Carl H., Jr., 3/C. "An Interesting Recollection." *Ranger Battalions Association Newsletter,* fall 2008. Author's collection.

———. "Life as a German P. O. W." Unpublished, n.d. Author's collection.

———. "3rd Ranger Battalion History." Unpublished, n.d. Author's collection.

——— to Mary Landreth, 31 March 1997. Author's collection.

Lyle, Col. James B., 1/ C, B, and A. "Divide and Conquer: The Capture of Butera." *Infantry Journal,* February 1945. Author's collection.

———. "Graduation Address to Ranger OCS Class Number One." 16 September 1959. Author's collection.

———. "Operations of Companies A and B, First Ranger Battalion, at Gela, Sicily, 10–11 July 1943." Report for Advanced Infantry Officer's Course, Fort Benning, Ga., 1949. Author's collection.

Markham, Cpl. Kenneth, 1/F. "My Version of the Landing at Anzio." Ranger Battalions Association, World War II, National Reunion. Fort Wayne, Ind., 2004. Author's collection.

Martin, Jennifer. "Veterans History Project: 'G.W. Guynes.'" Television interview, WLBT 3, Jackson, Miss., 10 April 2011.

Mascari, Pfc. Thomas, 1/A. "A Group of Four, Captured and Escaped." Unpublished, n.d. Author's collection.

Mattivi, 1st Sgt. Frank, 1/F. "Frank Mattivi." *Rangers Lead the Way: Ranger Battalions Association, Twenty-Seventh Biennial Reunion.* New Orleans, La., 11–16 September 2001.

———. "Frank Joey Mattivi," *Ranger 75th Anniversary WW II Rangers 1942–2017.* Columbus, Ga., 27—30 June 2017. Author's collection.

Mauritz, Lt. Michael, Army Air Corps. *The Secret of Anzio Bay.* Tarentum, Pa.: Word Association Publishers, 2002.

Meltesen, 1st Lt. Clarence, 3/C. *After the Battle: Ranger Evasion and Escape.* San Francisco: Self-published as Oflag 64 Press, 1997.

Merrill, Allen E., to Elaine Hawes, n.d. Author's collection.

Miller, J. Austin. "J. Austin Miller." Ranger Battalions Association, World War II, National Reunion. Fort Wayne, Ind., 25–30 August 2004. Author's collection.

Miller, Maj. Alvah M., 3/Hq. "The Men of My Command." Anzio Beachhead, 29 January 1944. Author's collection.

Mitchell, Capt. Peronneau. Memorandum to Col. Edwin A. Walker, Commanding Officer, Headquarters, 1st Special Service Force, 13 November 1944. Author's collection.

Mitchell, 1st Lt. Peronneau. Report of Action, 3rd Ranger Infantry Battalion, 3 April 1944. Fort Moore Library.

Morriss, Sgt. Mack. "Rangers Come Home." *Yank, the Army Weekly*, 4 August 1944.

[Mountbatten, Vice Admiral Lord Louis]. *Combined Operations: The Official Story of the Commandos with a Foreword by Vice-Admiral Lord Louis Mountbatten.* New York: McMillan, 1943.

Murray, Col. Roy A. Report of Action, 22 to 31 January 1944, Fourth Ranger Battalion, 17 March 1944. Fort Moore Library.

Murray, Col. Roy A., 4/Hq., and Maj. Max Schneider, 4/Hq. "The Fourth Ranger Battalion." Unpublished paper, n.d. Author's collection.

National Ranger Association. 1992 Inductees. http//www.nationalrgrassociation.com.

Newnan, 2nd Lt. William Loring, 3/B. *Escape in Italy: The Narrative of Lt. William L, Newnan.* Ann Arbor: Univ. of Michigan Press, 1945.

——— to the father of Pfc. John J. Burke, 31 August 1944. Author's collection.

Nye, Maj. Walter. Report of Casualties, 4th Ranger Infantry Battalion. 1944. Fort Moore Library.

O'Reilly, Tech/5 James, 3/B, and Sgt. Mike Syroid, 3/B. "A Tough Decision," in *Darby's Rangers.* Fort Smith, Ark.: The Ranger Book Committee, 1977.

Palmer, Pfc. James M., 1/E. "I Survived the Battle of Cisterna." Unpublished memoir, 2015. Author's collection.

Porter, (first name unknown). "Lord Love You Captain." *Colliers,* 7 October 1944, 59–62. Author's collection.

Pyle, Earnest Taylor. *Brave Men.* New York: Holt. 1943.

———. *Here Is Your War: America's Favorite Correspondent Tells the Story of Our Soldiers' First Big Campaign.* New York: Holt, 1943.

Ranger Battalions Association WW II. "Newsletter." March 2010. Author's collection.

Ranger Force Journal, From 1200 Hours 28 January 1944 through 31 January 1944. Author's collection.

Ranger Force Radio Log, 1200 hours on 29 January 1944 to 1200 hours on 30 January 1944. Author's collection.

RBA National Reunion. Ranger Battalions Association News. March 2010. Author's collection.

Reed, S/Sgt. Robert J., 3/Hq. "A Life, Mine Own." Unpublished autobiography. Author's collection.

Rice, Pfc. Nelson E., to the mother of Joe Renfro, 18 January 1948. Author's collection.

Richardson, Gordon J. Personal notes, May 1997. Author's collection.

Romine, Sgt. Mickey T., 3/Hq. "My Life in Combat and as a POW." Ranger Battalions Association, World War II, National Reunion. Fort Wayne, Ind., 2004. Author's collection.

Rorex, Tech/Sgt. James, 1/Hq. and 3/Hq. "An Elite Original from the United States." Ranger Battalions Association, World War II, National Reunion. Fort Wayne, Ind., 2004. Author's collection.

———. "Silk Sheets." Ranger Battalions Association, World War II, National Reunion. Fort Wayne, Ind., 2004. Author's collection.

Sadoski, Raymond C., 1/F. Library of Congress, Veterans History Project, 22 July 2007.

Scharf, Pvt. Erich, 1/B. "Remembrances of My Service in World War II." Unpublished, n.d. Author's collection.

Schunemann, SGM Gustav, 1/F. "Memoirs of a Ranger." Unpublished, n.d. Author's collection.

Seventy-Fifth Ranger Regiment, U.S. Army. "Citation, Ranger Hall of Fame."

Shunstrom, Cpt. Charles M., 1/Hq., to Col. William O. Darby, 10 July 1944. Author's collection.

———. "Capture of the First and Third Ranger Battalions, Cisterna Di Littoria, Italy on the day of 30 January 1944," 10 July 1944.

Staab, William E. *Not for Glory: The Memoirs of Sgts. Evan J. "Tommy" Thompson, Ronald "Rip" Peterson, and Roger Twigg, First Ranger Battalion.* New York: Vantage Press, 2009.

Stabler, Pvt. Hollis, 4/Hq., and Victoria Smith. *No One Ever Asked Me: The World War II Memoirs of an Omaha Indian Soldier.* American Indian Lives. Lincoln: Univ. of Nebraska Press, 2005.

Street, Maj. Jack B., "Inf. Operations of the First Ranger Battalion, El Guettar, Tunisia, 21–26 March, 1943." Report for Advanced Infantry Officer's Course, Fort Benning, Ga., 1948. Fort Moore Library.

Szima, Sgt. Alex, 1/Hq.. Open letter to Rangers, 30 November 1978. Author's collection.

———. "Report to Knickerbocker," 20 August 1942. Author's collection.

Templeton, 2nd Lt. Kenneth S., to Darby Foundation, April 12, 1998. Author's collection.

Third Infantry Division. "G-2 Estimate of the Situation." 29 January 1944. Author's collection.

Third Ranger Battalion. Report of Action, 31 July 1943. Fort Moore Library.

———. Report of Action, 31 August 1943. Fort Moore Library.

———. Report of Action, 25 November 1943. Fort Moore Library.

———. Report of Action, 5 January 1944. Fort Moore Library.

———. Report of Action, 3 April 1944. Fort Moore Library.

Tremblay, 1st Lt. Russell R. Casualty List for the Period 22 January 1944 to 5 February 1944, 1st Ranger Battalion. Author's collection.

Truscott, Lt. Gen. Lucian K. Annex to Field Order 3, 29 January 1944. Fort Moore Library.

———. *Command Missions.* Novato, Calif.: Presidio Press, 1954.

———. Estimate of the Situation, 29 January 1944. Fort Moore Library.

———. Field Order, 28 January 1944. Fort Moore Library.

Tryon, Pfc. William 1/B. "Cisterna Story." Unpublished, n.d. Author's collection.

U.S. Army Graves Registration Service. Report of Burial, Corrected Copy, 27 July 1949. National Archives.

U.S. Fifth Army Headquarters to Commanding General VI Corps. "Violations of Radio Security." AG 371.2-S. n.d. [between 31 January and 27 March 1944]. Author's collection.

United States v. General Kurt Maelzer. War Trial Commission. Headquarters, Mediterranean Theater of Operations. General Order No. 212. Testimony of Capt. William Ross Bond, 1/Hq., 10 May 1945. Author's collection.

———. War Trial Commission. Headquarters, Mediterranean Theater of Operations. General Order No. 212. Testimony of S/Sgt. Martin John Frank. 1/F, 25 July 1945. Author's collection.

———. War Trial Commission. Headquarters, Mediterranean Theater of Operations. General Order No. 212. Testimony of Pfc. Daniel W. McCall, 3/E, 24 August 1945. Author's collection.

———. War Trial Commission. Headquarters, Mediterranean Theater of Operations. General Order No. 212. Testimony of 1st. Lt. Charles L. Palumbo, 3/A, 22 June 1945. Author's collection.

———. War Trial Commission. Headquarters, Mediterranean Theater of Operations. General Order No. 212. Testimony of Cpl. William Albert Wood, 3 July 1945. Author's collection.

United States War Department. Bureau of Public Relations, Signal Intelligence Service press releases, May 1944. National Archives.

Williams, David L. Unpublished biography of Zelly Dineen compiled from interviews by Williams with Dineen, 2002. Author's collection.

Wilson, Pvt. Arthur, 1/D, to Devin Adams, 13 February 2005.

———. Letter to unknown. Author's collection.

Worth, Capt. Alexander McAlister, Jr. "Duty/Love/War, Memories of a Swoose at War." Unpublished autobiography, n.d. Author's collection.

Yandell, Sgt. Ray, 3/E. "Bravery Was Automatic to U.S. Rangers." Unpublished, n.d. Author's collection.

Young, Cpt. Leilyn M., 1/Hq. "Rangers in a Night Operation." *Military Review,* July 1944, 64–69. Author's collection.

———. Unpublished notes, 1 January 1943—29 November 1943. Author's collection.

Zartmann, Cpl. William D., 1/F. *East to the Russkies.* Morgan Hill, Calif.: Bookstand Publishers, 2012.

SECONDARY SOURCES

Annechino, Daniel M. *More Than a Soldier: One Ranger's Daring Escape from the Nazis.* Self-published, 2016.

Astor, Gerald. *The Greatest War: Americans in Combat, 1941–1945.* Novato, Calif.: Presidio Press, 1991.

———. *Terrible Terry Allen.* New York: Ballantine Books, 2003.

Atkinson, Rick. *An Army at Dawn: The War in North Africa, 1942–1943.* New York: Holt, 2002.

———. *The Day of Battle: The War in Sicily and Italy, 1943–1944.* New York: Holt , 2007.

Belanger, Julie Anne Foley. "Report on Ranger Force Casualties during Anzio and Cisterna." Unpublished research database. Albion, Maine: 12 January 2022. Author's collection.

———. "Summary of Casualties. Fourth Ranger Battalion at the Battle of Cisterna." Unpublished. Albion, Maine: 7 December 2023. Author's collection.

———. "Third Ranger Battalion Casualties, Anzio/Cisterna." Unpublished research database. Albion, Maine: 12 January 2022. Author's collection.

Belden, Jack. *Still Time to Die.* Philadelphia: The Blakiston Company, 1943.

Black, Robert. *Ranger Force.* Mechanicsburg, Pa.: Stackpole Books, 2009.

———. *Rangers in World War II.* New York: Ivy Books, 1992.

Blumenson, Martin. *Anzio: The Gamble That Failed.* New York: J. B. Lippincott, 1963.

———. *Kasserine Pass: Where America Lost Her Military Innocence.* Boston: Houghton Mifflin, 1967.

Breuer, William B. *Agony at Anzio: The Allies' Most Controversial and Bizarre Operation of World War II.* St. Louis: Zeus Publishers, 1985.

———. *Drop Zone Sicily: Allied Airborne Strike, July 1943.* Novato, Calif.: Presidio Press. 1983.

———. *Operation Torch: The Allied Gamble to Invade North Africa.* New York: St. Martin's Press. 1985.

Brown, Russell K. *Fallen in Battle: American General Officer Combat Fatalities from 1775*. New York: Greenwood Press, 1988.

Carnes, Cecil. "The 101 Days of Private Perlmutter." *Saturday Evening Post,* 21 April 1944.

D'Este, Carlo. *Fatal Decision: Anzio and the Battle for Rome*. New York: Harper Collins, 1991.

DeFelice, Jim. *Rangers at Dieppe: The First Combat Action of U.S. Army Rangers in World War II*. New York: Berkley Caliber, 2008.

Duncan, William H. "Gordon Keppel, Ranger Surgeon." The Historical Society of Delaware. *Delaware History* (fall–winter 1999–2000): 281–284.

Durshimer, A. H., III. *Leading the Way: Darby's Ranger Noel Dye*. Bennington, Vt.: Merriam Press, 2014.

Eisenhower, John S. D. *They Fought at Anzio,* vol 1. Columbia: Univ. of Missouri Press, 2007.

Federazione Autotrasportatori Italiani. *Italia Centro, 1:200.000, Atlante Stradale*. Milano: Touring Editore, 2011.

Garland, Lt. Col. Albert N., and Howard McGaw Smyth. *Sicily and the Surrender of Italy: U.S. Army in World War II, Mediterranean Theater of Operations*. Washington, D.C.: Office of the Chief of Military History, Department of the Army, 1965.

Gelb, Norman. *Desperate Venture: The Story of Operation Torch*. New York: William Morrow, 1992.

Gilbert, Adrian. *POW: Allied Prisoners of War in Europe, 1939–1945*. London: John Murray Publishers, 2006.

Goerlitz, Walter. *History of the German General Staff*. New York: Praeger, 1953.

Haggerty, Jerome Joseph. "A History of the Ranger Battalions in World War II." Ph.D. diss., Fordham University, 1982.

Jeffers, Harry Paul. *Command of Honor: General Lucian Truscott's Path to Victory in World War II*. New York: NAL Caliber, Penguin Group, 2008.

Kelly, Mary Pat. *Home Away from Home: The Yanks in Ireland*. Belfast: Appletree Press, 1994.

King, Michael. *Leavenworth Papers: Selected Combat Operations in World War II*. Fort Leavenworth, Kans.: Combat Studies Institute, 1985.

———. *William O. Darby, a Military Biography*. Hamden, Conn.: Archon Books, 1981.

Ladd, James. *Commandos and Rangers of World War II*. New York. St. Martin's Press, 1978.

Lehman, Sgt. Milton. "Rangers Died Fighting at Dawn." *Stars and Stripes Weekly*. Republished in *Saturday Evening Post,* 18 March 1944.

———. "Rangers Fought Ahead of Everybody." *Stars and Stripes Weekly*. Republished in *Saturday Evening Post,* 15 June 1946.

Mitcham, Samuel W., Jr. and Friedrich von Stauffenberg. *The Battle of Sicily: How the Allies Lost Their Chance for Total Victory.* New York: Orion Books, 1991.

Morison, Rear Admiral Samuel Eliot, USN. *Sicily—Salerno—Anzio.* Vol. 9 of *History of United States Naval Operations in World War II.* Boston: Little, Brown, 1984.

Morris, Eric. *Circles of Hell: The War in Italy 1943–1945.* New York: Crown Publishers, 1993.

———. *Salerno: A Military Fiasco.* New York: Stein and Day, 1983.

O'Donnell, Patrick K. *Beyond Valor: World War II's Ranger and Airborne Veterans Reveal the Heart of Combat.* New York: The Free Press, 2001.

Pond, Hugh. *Salerno.* London: Kimber, 1961.

———. *Sicily.* London: Kimber, 1962.

Reynolds, Quentin James. *Dress Rehearsal: The Story of Dieppe.* New York: Blue Ribbon Books, 1943.

Sanders, Pfc. James D., Mark A. Sauter, and R. Cort Kirkwood. *Soldiers of Misfortune: Washington's Secret Betrayal of POWs in the Soviet Union.* Washington, D.C.: National Press Books, 1992.

Schneider, James F. *My Father's War: The Story of Max Ferguson Schneider.* Boise, Idaho: Self-published by Lulu Press, 2012.

Shapiro, Milton J. *Ranger Battalion: American Rangers in World War II.* New York: Julian Messner, 1979.

Skoch, George F. "Escape Hatch Found: Escaping from a POW Camp in Italy Was One Thing. The Next Was Living off a War-Torn Land among Partisans, Spies, Fascists and German Patrols." *Military History* (October 1988), 35–41. Author's collection.

Slade, Jeff. "Natchitoches Man Remembers Fallen Friends Every Day." *Alexandria Town Talk.* Alexandria, La., 29 May 1989. Author's collection.

Starr, Lt. Col. Chester G. *From Salerno to the Alps: A History of the Fifth Army, 1943–1945.* Washington, D.C.: Infantry Journal Press, 1948.

Stern, Phil, and Liesl Bradner. *Snapdragon: The World War II Exploits of Darby's Ranger and Combat Photographer Phil Stern.* Oxford, UK: Bloomsbury Publishing, 2018.

Stewart, Lt. Col. Jeff. "The Ranger Force at the Battle of Cisterna." Paper presented to the U.S. Army Command and General Staff College, Fort Leavenworth, Kansas, 2004. Fort Leavenworth Library.

Strand, William. "Alpha Officer: One of the Yanks Lost Behind Nazi Fighting Line." Ranger Battalions Association, World War II, 2004 National Reunion, Fort Wayne, Ind., 25–30 August 2004. Author's collection.

Sunshine, Col. Michael. "Military History of Ltc. George P. Sunshine, 1/Hq." Unpublished, n.d. Author's collection.

Suominen, Mary M. *Twice to Freedom.* Kearney, Nebr.: Morris Publishing. 1999.

Swank, Lt. Col. Marcel. Speech delivered at the dedication of the memorial to those killed in the Dieppe raid, Dieppe, France, 19 August 1942. Author's collection.

Tipton, Dr. George W. "Surgery under Stress." *Bulletin of the American College of Surgeons,* June 2006, 44–48.

Tracy, Rick. "*Tribute to Virgil H. Wood, Co. D. 1st Ranger Battalion.*" unpublished, n.d. Author's collection.

VanArtsdalen, Pfc. Donald, 1/E. "The Great Colonel Darby Speech." Ranger Battalions Association, World War II, 2004 National Reunion, Fort Wayne, Ind., 25–30 August 2004. Author's collection.

Van Lunteren, Frank. *Birth of a Regiment: The 504th Parachute Infantry Regiment in Sicily and Salerno.* New York: Permuted Press, 2022.

Villareal, Cpl. Ray, 3/Hq. "Killing the First Nazi Is the Toughest." Ranger Battalions Association, World War II, 2004 National Reunion, Fort Wayne, Ind., 25–30 August 2004. Author's collection.

Walker, Col. Edwin A., Headquarters, 1st Special Service Force, to Commanding General, Sixth Army Group, U.S. Army, 15 November 1944. Fort Moore Library.

"War Hero Vindicated After Death." *The Spotlight,* Buffalo, N.Y., 29 September 1976.

RANGERS' COMMUNICATIONS WITH DAVID LYLE WILLIAMS

Alloway, 2nd Lt. Norman L., 1/A. Conversations with David Lyle Williams, Columbus, Ga., 14 October 1999.

Anderson, 1st Lt. Axel. Conversations with David Lyle Williams, 1999, 2000, and 2001.

Arnbal, Cpl. Anders Kjar, 1/B. Conversations with David Lyle Williams, 1997—2000.

Auger, Pvt. Ulysses, 4/Hq. Unpublished notes, n.d.

Boron, Pfc. Raymond, 4/Hq. Conversations with David Lyle Williams, Fort Benning, Ga., October 2000.

Cashen, Pvt. Louis. Email to David Lyle Williams, 5 May 1999.

Cavazos, Pfc. Julian, 1/B. Email to David Lyle Williams, 22 December 2000.

Cook, Sgt. Lester, 4/A. Conversations with David Lyle Williams, 2002–2004.

D'Amato, James. Email to David Lyle Williams, 8 June 2016.

Dean, 2nd Lt. Edwin, 1/E and 4/A. Conversations with David Lyle Williams, New Orleans, La., 14 September 2001.

Evans, Honorary Sergeant Major Warren "Bing," 75th Ranger Regiment. Telephone conversations with David Lyle Williams, 1997–2010.

Fleser, Sgt. Theodore, 1/D. Conversations with David Lyle Williams, New Orleans, La., 2002.

Fordham, Matt. Email to David Lyle Williams, re. Max Fordham, 11 April 2000.

Frederick, 2nd Lt. Donald, 4/E. "Notes," unpublished, n.d.

Furru, Pfc. Edwin R., 1/Hq. Conversations with David Lyle Williams, October 1997.

Gilbert, Tech/5 Lawrence, 1/F. Conversations with David Lyle Williams, Columbus, Ga., 1999–2000.

Goad, Pfc. Clarence, 3/B. Conversations with David Lyle Williams, January 2000.

———. Email to David Lyle Williams, 20 January 2001.

Harris, Pfc. Jim, 1/B. Email to David Lyle Williams, 1 May 2001.

Jech, Cpl. Randolph, 4/F. Email to David Lyle Williams, 5 June 1999.

Kegley, Pvt. Green, 1/E. Conversations with David Lyle Williams, 2001–2004.

Kness, Capt. Lester, 4/A. Conversations with David Lyle Williams, 2001–2003.

Krise, Lt. Col. Edward, 3/F. Conversations with David Lyle Williams, Columbus, Ga., October 2000.

Krzysztofiak, Elinor Y. Emails to David Lyle Williams, 23 July and 11 August 2002.

Kushner. Tech/5 Larry, 3/A. Note sent to David Lyle Williams, n.d.

Larkin, Joan. Telephone conversation with David Lyle Williams, 2001.

Larsh, Helen Pickett. Conversations with David Lyle Williams, Lafayette, La., 2 October 2023.

Lehmann, Sgt. Carl H., Jr., 3/C. Conversations with David Lyle Williams, 1999—2002.

———. Email to David Lyle Williams, 7 March 2010.

Lyle, Col. James B., 1/C, B, and A. Conversations with David Lyle Williams, 1968–1986.

Markham, Cpl. Kenneth, 1/F. Conversations with David Lyle Williams, Columbus, Ga., 1997–2002

Mascari, Pfc. Thomas, 1/A. Conversations with David Lyle Williams, 1997–2001.

Meltesen, 1st Lt. Clarence, 3/C. Conversations with David Lyle Williams, 2001–2002.

Miller, James. Telephone conversation with David Lyle Williams, 2001.

Murray, Col. Roy A. Conversation with David Lyle Williams, Ranger Battalions Association, World War II, 25th Biennial Reunion, Orlando, Fla., 5 October 1997.

Prudhomme, Tech/5 Thomas, 1/Hq. Conversation with David Lyle Williams, Ranger Battalions Association, World War II, 25th Biennial Reunion, Orlando, Fla., 4 October 1997.

Ruona, S/Sgt. Wayne, 3/C. Telephone conversation with David Lyle Williams and Kelly Gangnath, 17 September 2001.

Shead, Barry. Email to David Lyle Williams, 3 May 2018.

Skinner, Donald. Conversation with David Lyle Williams, 23 July 2011.

Steen, Orville. Telephone conversation with David Lyle Williams, September 2002.

Sunshine, Lt. Col. George, 1/Hq. Conversations with David Lyle Williams, September 2000.

Thompson, Tech/5 Clyde, 1/F. Telephone conversation, New Orleans, La., 2001.

Ward, Clay. Conversations with David Lyle Williams, January 2023.

———. Email to David Lyle Williams, 19 December 1999.

Williams, David L. "Eulogy for Arthur Wilson." Shelby Township, Mich., 21 August 2020.

Wilson, Pvt. Arthur, 1/D. Conversations with David Lyle Williams, 2002–2004.

Worth, Capt. Alexander McAlister, Jr. Conversations with David Lyle Williams, 27 June 2010.

INDEX